SEXUAL OFFENDER TREATMENT

WILEY SERIES IN
FORENSIC CLINICAL PSYCHOLOGY

Edited by

Clive R. Hollin
Clinical Division of Psychiatry, University of Leicester, UK

and

Mary McMurran
School of Psychology, Cardiff University, UK

SEXUAL OFFENDER TREATMENT
Controversial Issues

Edited by

William L. Marshall
Queen's University, Canada and Rockwood Psychological Services,
Kingston, Ontario, Canada

Yolanda M. Fernandez
Millhaven Assessment Unit, Canada

Liam E. Marshall
Millhaven Institution, Canada and Rockwood Psychological Services, Canada

Geris A. Serran
Bath Institution, Canada and Rockwood Psychological Services, Canada

John Wiley & Sons, Ltd

Other Wiley Editorial Offices

John Wiley & Sons Inc., 111 River Street, Hoboken, NJ 07030, USA

Jossey-Bass, 989 Market Street, San Francisco, CA 94103-1741, USA

Wiley-VCH Verlag GmbH, Boschstr. 12, D-69469 Weinheim, Germany

John Wiley & Sons Australia Ltd, 42 McDougall Street, Milton, Queensland 4064, Australia

John Wiley & Sons (Asia) Pte Ltd, 2 Clementi Loop #02-01, Jin Xing Distripark, Singapore 129809

John Wiley & Sons Canada Ltd, 22 Worcester Road, Etobicoke, Ontario, Canada M9W 1L1

Wiley also publishes its books in a variety of electronic formats. Some content that appears
in print may not be available in electronic books.

Library of Congress Cataloging-in-Publication Data

Sexual offender treatment : controversial issues / edited by W. L. Marshall ... [et al.].
    p. cm.—(Wiley series in forensic clinical psychology)
  Includes bibliographical references and index.
  ISBN 0-470-86773-6 (cloth : alk. paper)—ISBN 0-470-86774-4 (pbk. : alk. paper)
  1. Sex offenders.   2. Sex offenders—Rehabilitation.   I. Marshall, William L.   II. series.
  HV6556.S44   2005
  616.85'83—dc22

                                                                              2005007861

British Library Cataloguing in Publication Data

A catalogue record for this book is available from the British Library

ISBN-13   978-0-470-86773-0 (hbk)   978-0-470-86774-7 (pbk)
ISBN-10   0-470-86773-6 (hbk)   0-470-86774-4 (pbk)

Typeset in 10/12 pt Palatino by TechBooks, New Delhi, India
Printed and bound in Great Britain by Antony Rowe Ltd, Chippenham, Wiltshire
This book is printed on acid-free paper responsibly manufactured from sustainable forestry
in which at least two trees are planted for each one used for paper production.

CONTENTS

ABOUT THE EDITORS

William L. Marshall, PhD, FRSC. Bill is Professor Emeritus of Psychology and Psychiatry at Queen's University, Canada and Director of Rockwood Psychological Services, Kingston, Ontario, which provides sexual offender treatment in two Canadian federal penitentiaries. Bill has 35 years experience in assessment, treatment and research with sexual offenders. He has over 300 publications including 16 books. In 1999 Bill received the Santiago Grisolia Prize from the Queen Sophia Centre in Spain for his worldwide contributions to the reduction of violence and in 2000 he was elected a Fellow of the Royal Society of Canada. In 2003, Bill was one of six invited experts to advise the Vatican on how best to deal with sexual abuse within the Church.

Yolanda M. Fernandez, PhD. Yolanda graduated with a PhD in Clinical/Forensic Psychology in 2001 from Queen's University in Kingston, Ontario. As a registered psychologist she currently holds the position of Regional Coordinator of Sexual Offender Treatment Programs within Correctional Services of Canada at the Millhaven Assessment Unit. Previously, she spent a year working as a psychologist in the maximum-security unit at Millhaven Institution. Yolanda has also worked as the Clinical Director of Rockwood Psychological Services, and the Clinical Director of the Sexual Offender Treatment Program located at Bath Institution (a medium-security federal penitentiary). In 1999 Yolanda designed a training package to teach effective therapist skills to clinicians working with sexual offenders. She has provided this training within Canada, the United States and several European countries. In addition to her clinical work Yolanda is an active researcher who currently has several presentations at international conferences and over 20 publications. Her publications include an edited book, two co-authored books and three co-edited books. Yolanda's research interests include therapeutic process in sexual offender treatment, empathy deficits in sexual offenders, and phallometric testing with sexual offenders. She has been an active member of the Association for the Treatment of Sexual Abusers since 1996, including spending two years as the Student Representative to the Board of Directors.

Liam E. Marshall, MA. Liam received his Master's degree in Psychology in 2002 from Queen's University in Kingston, Canada. He is currently enrolled in the doctoral program in the Department of Psychology at Queen's University. Liam has been the graduate student representative on the Queen's University Psychology

Department ethics, headship, and departmental committees. He has worked directly with sexual offenders in correctional settings for over eight years. Liam is the lead therapist for the Millhaven Institution Sexual Offenders' Preparatory Program and is also a therapist for the Bath Institution Sexual Offenders' Moderate-Intensity, Deniers, and Maintenance Programs. Liam has trained therapists in the delivery of sexual offender programming for the British, Scottish, Australian, New Zealand and Canadian Prison Services. He is also on the editorial board of the *Journal of Sexual Addiction and Compulsivity*.

Geris A. Serran, PhD.   Geris graduated with a doctoral degree in Clinical Psychology from the University of Ottawa in 2003. She is currently employed at Rockwood Psychological Services where she works as the senior therapist of the Bath Institution Sexual Offenders' Program. In addition to her clinical work, Geris' research interests include therapeutic process, coping strategies, and treatment of sexual offenders. She has authored several book chapters, journal articles and presentations at international conferences in these domains.

LIST OF CONTRIBUTORS

Howard Barbaree

Professor and Head, Law and Mental Health Program, Centre for Addiction and Mental Health, 1001 Queen Street West, Toronto, Ontario M6J 1H4, Canada

Éric Beauregard

Clinical Criminologist and PhD candidate, University of Montreal, CP 6128, Succ. Centre-ville, Montreal, Quebec H3C 3J7, Canada

Etienne Blais

Criminologist and PhD candidate, University of Montreal, CP 6128, Succ. Centre-ville, Montreal, Quebec H3C 3J7, Canada

Al Cooper (deceased 11 May 2004)

Sometime Director, San Jose Marital and Sexuality Center, Suite 275, 100N, Winchester Boulevard, Santa Clara, California 95050, USA

Dennis M. Doren

Director, Sand Ridge Secure Treatment Centre Evaluation Unit, 301 Troy Drive, Madison, Wisconsin 53704-1521, USA

Yolanda Fernandez

Coordinator, Regional Sexual Offenders Programs, Millhaven Institution, PO Box 280, Bath, Ontario K0H 1G0, Canada

Dawn Fisher

Head, Psychological Services, Llanarth Court Hospital, Llanarth, Raglan, Usk, Gwent, South Wales NP15 2YD, UK

Gale Golden

Private practice, University of Vermont Medical College, 70 South Winooski Avenue, Burlington, Vermont 050401, USA

R. Karl Hanson

Senior Researcher, Corrections Research, Department of the Solicitor General of Canada, 340 Laurier Avenue West, Ottawa, Ontario K1A 0P8, Canada

Kevin Howells

Professor and Academic Chair, Peaks Unit, Rampton Hospital, Retford, Nottinghamshire DN22 0PD, UK

Calvin Langton

Assistant Professor, University of Toronto and Research Associate at the Law and Mental Health Program of the Centre for Addiction and Mental Health, 250 College Street, Toronto, Ontario M5T 1R8, Canada

D. Richard Laws

Director, Pacific Psychological Assessment Corporation, PO Box 23036, 4–313 Cook Street, Victoria, British Columbia V8V 4Z8, Canada

Ruth E. Mann

Director, Sex Offender Treatment Programmes, HM Prison Service, Room 725, Abell House, John Islip Street, London SW14 4LH, UK

Liam E. Marshall

Therapist, Rockwood Psychological Services, Suite 403, 303 Bagot Street, Kingston, Ontario K7K 5W7, Canada

William L. Marshall

Director, Rockwood Psychological Services, Suite 403, 303 Bagot Street, Kingston, Ontario K7K 5W7, Canada

Heather M. Moulden

Therapist, School of Psychology, University of Ottawa, 145 Jean-Jacques-Lussier Street, Ottawa, Ontario K1N 6N5, Canada

Edward Peacock

Warkworth Institution, PO Box 760, Campbellford, Ontario K0L 1L0, Canada

M. Proeve

Lecturer, School of Psychology, University of South Australia, GPO Box 2471, South Australia 5001, Australia

Jean Proulx

Professor, Department of Criminology, University of Montreal, CP 6128, Succ. Centre-ville, Montreal, Quebec H3C 3J7, Canada

Anita Schlank

Forensic Psychologist, The Human Development Center, 1401 East First Street, Duluth, Minnesota 55805, USA

Geris A. Serran

Senior Therapist, Rockwood Psychological Services, Suite 403, 303 Bagot Street, Kingston K7K 5W7, Canada

Jo Shingler

Forensic Psychologist, Hampshire Probation Service, 3rd Floor Barclays House, 20–24 Upper Market Street, Eastleigh, Hampshire SO50 9FD, UK

Stephen W. Smallbone

Senior Lecturer, School of Criminology and Criminal Justice, Mt Gravatt Campus, Griffith University, Brisbane, Queensland 4111, Australia

Tony Ward

Professor, School of Psychology, Victoria University, PO Box 600, Wellington, New Zealand

SERIES EDITORS' PREFACE

ABOUT THE SERIES

At the time of writing it is clear that we live in a time, certainly in the UK and other parts of Europe, if perhaps less so in other areas of the world, when there is renewed enthusiasm for constructive approaches to working with offenders to prevent crime. What do we mean by this statement and what basis do we have for making it?

First, by "constructive approaches to working with offenders", we mean bringing the use of effective methods and techniques of behaviour change into work with offenders. Indeed, this view might pass as a definition of forensic clinical psychology. Thus, our focus is the application of theory and research in order to develop practice aimed at bringing about a change in the offender's functioning. The word *constructive* is important and can be set against approaches to behaviour change that seek to operate by destructive means. Such destructive approaches are typically based on the principles of deterrence and punishment, seeking to suppress the offender's actions through fear and intimidation. A constructive approach, on the other hand, seeks to bring about changes in an offender's functioning that will produce, say, enhanced possibilities of employment, greater levels of self-control, better family functioning, or increased awareness of the pain of victims.

A constructive approach faces the criticism of being a "soft" response to the damage caused by offenders, neither inflicting pain and punishment nor delivering retribution. This point raises a serious question for those involved in working with offenders. Should advocates of constructive approaches oppose retribution as a goal of the criminal justice system as a process that is incompatible with treatment and rehabilitation? Alternatively, should constructive work with offenders take place within a system given to retribution? We believe that this issue merits serious debate.

However, to return to our starting point, history shows that criminal justice systems are littered with many attempts at constructive work with offenders, not all of which have been successful. In raising the spectre of success, the second part of our opening sentence now merits attention: that is, "constructive approaches to working with offenders *to prevent crime*". In order to achieve the goal of preventing crime, interventions must focus on the right targets for behaviour change. In addressing this crucial point, Andrews and Bonta (1994) have formulated the *need principle*:

> Many offenders, especially high-risk offenders, have a variety of needs. They need places to live and work and/or they need to stop taking drugs. Some have poor self-esteem, chronic headaches or cavities in their teeth. These are all "needs". The need principle draws our attention to the distinction between *criminogenic* and *noncriminogenic* needs. Criminogenic needs are a subset of an offender's risk level. They are dynamic attributes of an offender that, when changed, are associated with changes in the probability of recidivism. Non-criminogenic needs are also dynamic and changeable, but these changes are not necessarily associated with the probability of recidivism. (p. 176)

Thus, successful work with offenders can be judged in terms of bringing about change in noncriminogenic need *or* in terms of bringing about change in criminogenic need. While the former is important and, indeed, may be a necessary precursor to offence-focused work, it is changing criminogenic need that we argue should be the touchstone in working with offenders.

While, as noted above, the history of work with offenders is not replete with success, the research base developed since the early 1990s, particularly the meta-analyses (e.g. Lösel, 1995), now strongly supports the position that effective work with offenders to prevent further offending is possible. The parameters of such evidence-based practice have become well established and widely disseminated under the banner of "What Works" (McGuire, 1995).

It is important to state that we are not advocating that there is only one approach to preventing crime. Clearly there are many approaches, with different theoretical underpinnings, that can be applied. Nonetheless, a tangible momentum has grown in the wake of the "What Works" movement as academics, practitioners, and policy makers seek to capitalise on the possibilities that this research raises for preventing crime. The task now facing many service agencies lies in turning the research into effective practice.

Our aim in developing this Series in Forensic Clinical Psychology is to produce texts that review research and draw on clinical expertise to advance effective work with offenders. We are both committed to the ideal of evidence-based practice and we will encourage contributors to the Series to follow this approach. Thus, the books published in the Series will not be practice manuals or "cook books", they will offer readers authoritative and critical information through which forensic clinical practice can develop. We are both enthusiastic about the contribution to effective practice that this Series can make and look forward to continuing to develop it in the years to come.

ABOUT THIS BOOK

In the history of forensic therapeutic endeavour, the development of effective interventions with sex offenders will undoubtedly be seen as a major contribution. There are two particular areas in which work with sex offenders has led the field of forensic clinical psychology.

The first contribution flows from the integration of mainstream therapeutic theories and techniques into the forensic field. This is partly explicable by the fact that sexual problems, disorders and dysfunctions, are of longstanding interest within mainstream psychology. Thus, those working with sex offenders had a strong therapeutic base from which to take on the challenge posed by sexual offending. As is seen in this text, clinical approaches to working with sex offenders have now become highly sophisticated, with advances in assessment and treatment methods that have grown from work with sex offenders. In particular, the difficulties of working with people who refuse to recognise that there is a need for them to change have been highlighted by this area of practice. The application and refinement of techniques such as motivational interviewing and working with denial have been notable contributions.

Of course, the problem of sexual offending extends well beyond the bounds of the individual distress of the client, as might be the case in mainstream clinical work. It was clear from a very early stage that work with sex offenders would take forensic practice into an area in which there are very strong feelings and opinions. While the treatment of sex offenders gives rise to spirited discussion among its proponents, this pales to insignificance when set against the vehemence of the disagreement voiced by opponents of this approach. There are professional opponents who offer a different analysis of the causes of sex offending and see no room for treatment. There are political opponents who see punishment, not treatment, as the only way to deal with offenders. There are, perhaps most significantly, ferocious opponents among the general population who see little reason in treating those who commit terrible crimes. In all, there is little doubt that the treatment versus punishment debate is at its sharpest when the treatment of sex offenders is on the agenda. It follows that the reality of the public face of their work was not one that could be avoided by those seriously engaged in this work. Some of those working in the field, including Professor Marshall, took on the difficult task of communicating with other professions, with politicians, and with the public to state their point of view. It would be wrong to say that the argument is over—perhaps there is strength in acknowledging that debate is healthy and should always be with us—but the growth of treatment for sex offenders across different criminal justice systems suggests that the arguments in favour of a treatment approach have had some success.

Alongside developing clinical practice, the second contribution made by those working with sex offenders lies in their research output. One of the core values of this Series in that research is paramount in sustaining and advancing clinical practice. As is highlighted by research into the effectiveness of sex offender treatment, empirical evidence is fundamentally important for two reasons. First, as is so evident in this book, empirical research provides the stimulus for refining existing clinical techniques and developing new methods. It is also true that new research findings stimulate advances in theory, as seen both here and in other books in this Series. The continual interplay between research, practice and theory is, we argue, absolutely essential from a professional perspective.

However, the production of research evidence has another function, equally if not more important than professional considerations. In a system in which the treatment of offenders is viewed with caution at best and hostility at worst, evidence that interventions work is critically important. It is a harsh reality that political and public interest lies not in whether treatments work in the sense that offenders change at a clinical level, but the over-riding concern is with reduction in offending. The question is simple: does the treatment of sex offenders reduce the crimes they commit? Of course, a reduction in crime has many benefits, both in terms of reducing victimisation and the financial and societal costs of crime. Finding an answer to the question of whether treatment works on a scale that is worth sustaining in terms of reductions in offending has been at the forefront of outcome research with sex offenders. The low baseline rate of reconviction in sex offender populations has led researchers to develop their skills to attempt to produce evidence that is professionally acceptable and which can be used in political and public arenas.

Overall, it is clear that the treatment of sex offenders raises a host of issues. In bringing together and editing the chapters for this book Professor Marshall has made another significant contribution to the field. We hope it will reach a wide readership both within and outside the forensic clinical community.

REFERENCES

Andrews, D.A. & Bonta, J. (1994). *The psychology of criminal conduct*. Cincinnati, OH: Anderson Publishing.

Lösel, F. (1995). Increasing consensus in the evaluation of offender rehabilitation? *Psychology, Crime, & Law*, **2**, 19–39.

McGuire, J. (ed). (1995). *What works: Reducing reoffending*. Chichester: John Wiley & Sons.

PREFACE

Although the sexual offender literature has a long early history (Laws & Marshall, 2003) it is really only since the 1970s that publications on various issues related to our understanding assessment and treatment of these offenders began to proliferate (Marshall & Laws, 2003). Particularly from the early 1980s onwards the growth in the number of published reports has been accelerating (Prentky, 2003). The knowledge base has become so extensive that it is now time to reflect on where we are, what is it that we understand, what are the limitations of our knowledge, and how stable are the foundations of our knowledge.

It occurred to us that the time was ripe to ask questions. It seems always to be true in any area of research or clinical practice that certain things become accepted as facts simply because they appear to work. A prime example of this in the treatment of sexual offenders was the uncritical acceptance of the relapse prevention model originally introduced by Marques and Pithers (1981) and subsequently elaborated by Pithers, Marques, Gibat and Marlatt (1983). There is no doubt about the significant impact of this model on the treatment of sexual offenders. Within a short time after its introduction, almost all programs in North America (Knopp, 1984, 1986) and subsequently in Britain (Grubin & Thornton, 1994), Australia (Nisbet, Wilson & Smallbone, 2004), the Netherlands (Van Beek & Mulder, 1998) and Spain (Marshall & Redondo, 2002) adopted the RP approach to treatment. It was not until Ward and his colleagues (Ward & Hudson, 1996; Ward, Hudson & Siegert, 1995) began to publish a series of critical analyses of what had by then become the traditional RP approach, that treatment providers began to modify, or at least question, their approach. We believe the same thing is true in various other areas.

With these thoughts in mind we began to consider which areas of research and practice might profit from more detailed examination. Some areas, for example the potential for psychopaths to profit from treatment, are inherently controversial although fraught with hardly questioned assumptions. The same is true for the so-called "Sexually Violent Predator laws", Internet access to child pornography, and sexual murderers. In other areas, for example the appropriate methods of evaluating treatment outcome, consistent disagreement has prevailed for many years. Some areas, for example diagnostic practices concerning the paraphilias, have not generated much discussion but seem to need it. Risk assessment has become more sophisticated and comprehensive in recent years, so an update and suggestions for current practice seems needed. There are also, of course, possibilities concerning emerging issues such as the role of schemas in directing sexual offending, or the influence of therapeutic processes on the changes aimed for in treatment, or the value of pre-treatment preparatory programs. We could also ask what role attachments, mood, coping abilities, and shame or guilt, might play in the enactment of offending and treatment of the offender.

As a result of these considerations we identified authors who were either acknowledged experts on a topic, or who had novel ideas, to write the chapters of the present book. We asked our authors to feel free to speculate and to make controversial comments relatively unrestrained by available data. However we did require them to offer supportive data (not necessarily from the sexual offender field alone) where possible. We believe our authors successfully met this challenge and we are delighted to have the honour to edit this collection. We hope our readers will be equally pleased.

William L. Marshall
Yolanda M. Fernandez
Liam E. Marshall
Geris A. Serran

REFERENCES

Grubin, D. & Thornton, D. (1994). A national program for the assessment and treatment of sex offenders in the English Prison System. *Criminal Justice and Behavior*, **21**, 55–71.

Knopp, F.H. (1984). *Retraining Adult Sex Offenders: Methods and Models*. Syracuse, NY: Safer Society Press.

Knopp, F.H. (1986). *National Survey of Juvenile and Adult Sex Offender Treatment Programs*. Orwell, VT: Safer Society Press.

Laws, D.R. & Marshall, W.L. (2003). A brief history of behavioral and cognitive behavioral approaches to sexual offender treatment: Part 1. Early developments. *Sexual Abuse: A Journal of Research and Treatment*, **15**, 75–92.

Marques, J.K. & Pithers, W.K. (1981, November). Relapse prevention with sex offenders. Paper presented at the International Conference on the Treatment of Addictive Behaviors, Grand Canyon, Arizona.

Marshall, W.L. & Laws, D.R. (2003). A brief history of behavioral and cognitive behavioral approaches to sexual offender treatment: Part 2. The modern era. *Sexual Abuse: A Journal of Research and Treatment*, **15**, 93–120.

Marshall, W.L. & Redondo, S. (2002). Control y tratamiento de la agresion sexual. In S. Redondo (ed.), *Delincuencia sexual y sociedad* (pp. 301–28). Valencia: Ariel.

Nisbet, I.A., Wilson, P.H. & Smallbone, S.W. (2004). A prospective longitudinal study of sexual recidivism among adolescent sex offenders. *Sexual Abuse: A Journal of Research and Treatment*, **16**, 223–34.

Pithers, W.D., Marques, J.K., Gibat, C.C. & Marlatt, G.A. (1983). Relapse prevention: A self-control model of treatment and maintenance of change for sexual aggressives. In J. Greer & I.R. Stuart (eds), *Sexual Aggression: Current Perspectives on Treatment* (pp. 214–19). New York: Van Nostrand Reinhold.

Prentky, R.A. (2003). A 15-year retrospective on sexual coercion: advances and projections. *New York Academy of Sciences*, **989**, 13–32.

Van Beek, D. & Mulder, J. (1998). The treatment of sexually aggressive offenders in the Dr. Henri van der Hoeven Kliniek: a forensic psychiatric institute in the Netherlands. In W.L. Marshall, Y.M. Fernandez, S.M. Hudson & T. Ward (eds), *Sourcebook of Treatment Programs for Sexual Offenders* (pp. 203–19). New York: Plenum Press.

Ward, T. & Hudson, S.M. (1996). Relapse prevention: A critical analysis. *Sexual Abuse: A Journal of Research and Treatment*, **8**, 177–200.

Ward, T., Hudson, S.M. & Siegert, R. (1995). A critical comment on Pithers' relapse prevention model. *Sexual Abuse: A Journal of Research and Treatment*, **7**, 167–75.

ACKNOWLEDGEMENTS

We wish to acknowledge the excellent effort of our authors. Most particularly we wish to thank Jean Webber for her patience and persistence in typing this manuscript and providing helpful feedback. We would like to dedicate this book to our dear colleague, Al Cooper, whose recent untimely death left all who knew him deeply saddened.

PART I

GENERAL ISSUES

Chapter 1

RECIDIVISM RISK ASSESSMENTS: MAKING SENSE OF CONTROVERSIES

DENNIS M. DOREN, PH.D.

Sand Ridge Secure Treatment Center—Evaluation Unit, Madison, Wisconsin, USA

A risk assessment involving a sexual offender usually means there is a potential real-life high cost to be paid by someone. Depending on the evaluation's recommendation, an offender's freedom to be in the community may be at stake, such as in parole board decisions and civil commitment determinations (in the United States). If the offender gains freedom as a result of the evaluation, the placement of the offender in the community increases the risk for new victimization of law-abiding members of society. The protection of one right (for individual freedom versus community safety) necessarily cuts into the protection of the other.

Given the context of such high-stakes assessments, the reader may not be surprised that various areas of contention have arisen in the professional practice of conducting evaluations of recidivism risk. This chapter describes some of the areas of contention within the current practice of sexual offender risk assessment, bringing these arguments together in one place. Hopefully more important is the real purpose in writing this chapter; that is, to offer resolutions based on current research results and statistical realities.

Topics to be covered in this chapter include: the relative accuracy of "actuarial versus clinical" assessments; whether or not "adjustments" to actuarial results are appropriate; risk assessment versus recidivism prediction; and instrument construction versus meaningfulness. In my attempt to address each of the above listed "controversies", I will first overtly state the bias to my analyses herein. They concentrate on two considerations: (1) existing empirical evidence, and (2) where applicable, an analysis of the logic/illogic of a position, and the potential statistical viability within a given debate. By the first factor, I mean to suggest that any opposition to my conclusion based on empirical results cannot be made without discounting existing research findings, indicating problems in the comprehensiveness of my literature review, and/or describing problems in my interpretation of empirical results. Likewise, by including the second type of analysis (i.e. the process simply

Sexual Offender Treatment: Controversial Issues. Edited by W.L. Marshall, Y.M. Fernandez, L.E. Marshall and G.A. Serran. © 2006 John Wiley & Sons, Ltd.

of showing an inherent inconsistency or statistical flaw in the argument), I will be able to address some areas that are beyond existing research results.

My goal with the following analyses is not to "settle" arguments for one side or the other. I am most interested instead in showing that the supposed "debate" of certain topics misses a larger point, and when that larger point is addressed directly, the original issue often becomes minimal or even moot.

ACTUARIAL VERSUS CLINICAL RISK ASSESSMENTS

The debate about what is "the" proper model for conducting a risk assessment began about 50 years ago (Meehl, 1954). That this issue (i.e. actuarial vs. clinical assessments) is still argued can be demonstrated by recent publications (e.g. Grove, Zald, Lebow, Snitz & Nelson, 2000, as compared to Litwack, 2001). While Dvoskin and Heilbrun (2001) offered a potential resolution to the "great debate", others seem to have ignored this by continuing to argue their own one-sided perspective (e.g. Berlin, Galbreath, Geary & McGlone, 2003; Quinsey, Harris, Rice & Cormier, 1998), the "sides" representing one versus another assessment methodology as listed in Table 1.1.

After 50 years, one might have thought this issue would have been resolved. For the first 30 of those years, the debate was largely academic, as practitioners did not have actuarial instruments available that were specifically designed to assess risk. During the past 20 years, however, such instruments have been developed for various risk assessment purposes (see Table 1.2), including risk for general criminal recidivism (e.g. Level of Service Inventory—Revised, LSI-R; Andrews & Bonta, 1995), violent recidivism (e.g. Violence Risk Appraisal Guide, VRAG; Webster, Harris, Rice, Cormier & Quinsey, 1994), and sexual recidivism both of a general criminal nature (e.g. Rapid Risk Assessment for Sexual Offender Recidivism, RRA-SOR; Hanson, 1997) and specifically involving physical contact (e.g. Minnesota Sex Offender Screening Test—Revised, MnSOST-R; Epperson, Kaul, Huot, Hesselton, Alexander & Goldman, 1999). The existence and easy availability of these instruments, and their growing popularity (Doren, 2002) are probably what has given this debate new life, as practitioners now have a real choice about what to use when conducting a sexual offender risk assessment.

Or do they? I think that much of the recent argument has ignored certain facts that become obvious upon consideration.

Issues within the Debate: The Best Tool for the Job

There are two issues that stand out when we look at how risk assessments are conducted. The first issue, often ignored in these debates, is that the choice of an evaluation procedure (actuarial or clinical) is currently connected to the type of risk assessment needed. For instance, a first question that always needs to be asked before starting a risk assessment is "Risk for what?" Risk is by no means a unitary concept. There are differences in the type of relevant behavior (e.g. general criminal, violent, sexual, suicide, domestic abuse, probation failure, failure to complete

Table 1.1 Risk assessment methodologies

Method	Description of assessment procedure	Relative degree of structure imposed by method in the risk assessment
(Pure) actuarial	Solely uses actuarial instrument result(s)	Highest
Adjusted actuarial	Use of actuarial instrument(s) for grounding the assessment; then adjustments to overall assessment based on other considerations not in the instrument(s)	If possible adjustments determined on a priori basis, then second highest structure (especially if solely determined by empirical results versus clinician conjecture); if not, then degree of structure to method is lower
Structured clinical	Factors considered of relevance determined on a priori basis; clinician determines how to weigh each factor in making overall risk assessment	Lower than pure actuarial, lower than "a priori" adjusted actuarial, higher than unguided clinical
Unguided clinical	Factors considered of relevance in assessing risk determined on case-by-case basis	Lowest

Table 1.2 Currently commonly used risk assessment instruments

Instrument name	Abbreviation	Measurement design	Primary (secondary) type of risk assessed
Estimate of Risk of Adolescent Sexual Offense Recidivism	ERASOR	Structured Clinical	Sexual
Historical Clinical Risk Management—20	HCR-20	Structured Clinical	Violent
Juvenile Sex Offender Assessment Protocol—II	J-SOAP-II	Actuarial	Sexual
Level of Service Inventory—Revised	LSI-R	Actuarial	General (violent)
Minnesota Sex Offender Screening Tool—Revised	MnSOST-R	Actuarial	Sexual
Rapid Risk Assessment for Sex Offender Recidivism	RRASOR	Actuarial	Sexual
Sex Offender Risk Appraisal Guide	SORAG	Actuarial	Violent (sexual)
Sexual Violence Risk—20	SVR-20	Structured clinical	Sexual
Static-99	(Static-99)	Actuarial	Sexual (violent)
Vermont Assessment of Sexual Offender Risk	VASOR	Actuarial	Violent
Violence Risk Appraisal Guide	VRAG	Actuarial	Violent (sexual)
Youth Assessment and Screening Instrument	YASI	Actuarial	General

treatment) and in the time frame within which risk is assessed (imminent, weeks, months, years, remaining lifetime). Similarly, there can be concerns with the likely frequency of the behavior, its severity (sometimes called degree of harm), and with the overall probability of the behavior.

The point is that virtually all existing empirically validated actuarial risk assessment instruments concentrate on the probability of the unwanted outcome and little else (e.g. Static-99 [Hanson & Thornton, 2000] assesses the likelihood for being reconvicted for a new sexual offense over certain time frames measured in years). These instruments typically do not tell us about the imminence, frequency or severity of the offender's sexual recidivism risk. There are exceptions. The LSI-R has been found to be related to frequency as well as probability, and the Vermont Assessment of Sexual Offender Risk (VASOR; McGrath & Hoke, 2002) also takes severity into consideration. For the most part, however, assessments of the risk considerations beyond simple probability require the practitioner to look beyond actuarial instruments. At the moment, this means a greater reliance on clinical judgment.

A similar limitation to the current actuarial instruments, often ignored in the debates, stems from the question: "As applied to whom?" At the time of writing this chapter, there appears to be no empirically based actuarial instrument to assess the recidivism risk (of any type) for female sexual offenders. In addition, only one empirically validated actuarial instrument exists for younger adolescent offenders (Youth Assessment and Screening Instrument, YASI; Barnoski, 2003), and that one simply tells us about general criminal recidivism risk over a relatively short time period. If a practitioner needs to assess any type of recidivism risk for a female sexual offender, or the risk of violent or sexual recidivism for a younger adolescent, the practitioner needs to look for a method beyond using current actuarial instruments. An actuarial instrument showing promise in assessing juvenile sexual recidivism risk is the Juvenile Sex Offender Assessment Protocol [J-SOAP; Prentky, Harris, Frizzell & Righthand, 2000] and its successor, the J-SOAP-II. The developers of these instruments have cautioned against their use beyond research purposes until further empirical validity testing has been completed. One example of a structured clinical instrument designed for assessing the sexual recidivism risk of juveniles is the Estimate of Risk of Adolescent Sexual Offense Recidivism (ERASOR; Worling, 2001).

The context in which the offender resides can also matter in the debate between actuarial versus clinical risk assessments. Risk for violent recidivism in the outside community can be assessed using the VRAG, the Sex Offender Risk Appraisal Guide (SORAG; Quinsey et al., 1998), or the VASOR. On the other hand, those instruments were not designed, and to date have not been tested, for applicability to the assessment of violent behavior within a civil psychiatric inpatient setting. In contrast, the Historical, Clinical, Risk Management—20 (HCR-20; Webster, Douglas, Eaves & Hart, 1997), a list of risk considerations to be used as a structure for clinical risk assessments and not as an actuarial instrument, has been shown to be useful within such an inpatient and shorter-term context.

Some of the above risk considerations beyond simple probability, such as severity and imminence, apparently can be assessed with accuracy using such a structured, guided approach to clinical judgments (Douglas & Weir, 2003). Clinicians wishing to make accurate risk assessments involving considerations beyond probability, female or younger adolescent offenders, or inpatient contexts, have no real choice at the current time but to use some form of clinical approach. On the other hand, current actuarial instruments provide a choice when it comes to a very specific type of risk probability assessment such as of a certain type of recidivism over a certain period of time (measured in years) for a certain type of offender (e.g. male who was convicted as an adult for a sexual offense).

Within the specialized context for which an actuarial instrument exists, logic would seem to dictate that the instrument should be used. Nothing has been demonstrated to be better than existing actuarial devices within their specific context. Research to date has quite regularly found the empirically validated actuarial instruments to be of at least equal, if not superior accuracy, to more general clinical methods (Doren, 2002; Grove *et al.*, 2000; Hanson & Bussière, 1998; Hanson, Morton & Harris, 2003), and with a large number of studies to back up those findings (e.g. the LSI-R has been cross-validated in approximately 50 studies [Andrews & Bonta, 2001]).

At the same time, using an actuarial instrument to assess risk beyond the instrument's known effective range seems questionable. If a structured list of risk considerations has been shown to be useful in assessing a certain type of risk, and no actuarial instrument exists to do the work even as well, then there is no basis for using an actuarial instrument.

Issues within the Debate: The Degree of Clinical Judgment

There is a notion within the actuarial versus clinical judgment debate that these methods for risk assessments are mutually exclusive categories. In reality, they represent differing degrees of independent clinical judgment on a continuum. Very few clinicians actually espouse or utilize a purely actuarial risk assessment procedure in any real-life evaluation. Clinical considerations about a subject's age (e.g. elderly or not), treatment progress (e.g. program completion or not), and the combination of psychopathy with sexual deviance are commonly included when making risk assessments of various types, although these risk assessments are often grounded in the use of actuarial instruments. The real clinical issues in any assessment involving an actuarial instrument are which additional factors to consider, and what weight to give each of those factors concomitant to the actuarial results (a topic discussed below).

On the flip side, the risk factors used by people employing the structured clinical approach typically include those on a relevant actuarial instrument and the same additional considerations that "adjusted actuarialists" use to determine overall risk assessment results. The main difference between the two methodologies is the application of a numerical scheme for interpretation of probability (in actuarial instruments) compared to the lack of an a priori numerical interpretive scheme for the structured clinical method. Both approaches involve some degree of clinical judgment—it is just a matter of degree. Even the rarely found pure actuarialists, people who truly do not stray from current actuarial results, need to use judgment to determine which, if any, actuarial instrument (and, hence, which set of risk factors) is appropriate for a specific risk assessment.

Arguments with Questionable Logic

A specific combination of two arguments has been made in some training presentations and some court testimony that together involve questionable logic. The first argument is that, given the current state of the science, the use of actuarial instruments is premature even where the probability of recidivism is the main concern. The second argument is that clinicians should use certain structured lists of risk factors instead of an actuarial instrument even when a relevant actuarial instrument exists (e.g. clinicians should use the Sexual Violence Risk—20, [SVR-20; Boer, Hart, Kropp & Webster, 1997] instead of the RRASOR or Static-99). The illogic here is that instruments such as the SVR-20 have been studied far fewer times, with more questionable inter-rater reliability for at least some items, and with no better predictive validity than the commonly used actuarial instruments such as the RRASOR and Static-99 (Doren, 2003). Likewise, while the HCR-20 (another instrument for structuring clinical judgment) has been studied rather frequently relative to violent recidivism, the VRAG (an actuarial instrument also designed to assess violent recidivism risk) has been studied about the same amount relative to the same type of outcome. Direct empirical comparisons of the effectiveness of the HCR-20 and the VRAG are still few (Doren, 2002), but those that exist show the VRAG to be of at least equal accuracy compared to the HCR-20.

Based on these findings, it is faulty to conclude that instruments for use in the structured clinical risk assessment method are ready for prime time (for probability risk assessments) when one also concludes the best actuarial instruments are not. An argument may be made that the actuarial instruments are not good enough for a specific task (depending on how high the bar is set in defining "good enough"), and one can argue that certain instruments for structuring clinical judgment are good enough for the same task, but one cannot argue both ways either logically or with empirical support.

Suggested Resolution

My suggestion for resolving the "actuarial versus clinical" debate is for practitioners to concentrate on taking advantage of the best we have for the task at hand: employ validated actuarial risk assessment instrumentation when these are available for the specific type of person and risk being evaluated, while using a more clinically oriented approach (ideally utilizing a structured list of risk considerations) at other times. When we first think in terms of a "specialized instrument", if one exists for the specific purpose at hand, and a more "general" approach as the reasonable backup approach, the actuarial/clinical debate seems to fade in importance. Both approaches are needed at this time and likely for years into the future, to cover the vastly different risk assessment contexts that exist.

ARE "ADJUSTMENTS" TO ACTUARIAL RESULTS APPROPRIATE?

This controversy involves two issues, one of which is a simple misunderstanding. That misunderstanding involves the idea that an adjustment to an actuarial result involves an alteration of the actuarial score or to its typical interpretation as a stand-alone finding. In making whatever "adjustments" to actuarial findings that are considered appropriate, actuarial scores are not lowered or raised; nor are the associated risk percentages "fudged" in some way. Any procedure of these types is simply wrong and destroys any utility derived from the instrument's underlying empirical support.

The procedure of true relevance to the debate concerns the process where a practitioner takes the actuarial results as they are, and then looks at other variables in addition to those included in the actuarial instrument(s) and potentially adjusts the overall risk estimate for the subject either up or down (compared to the actuarial results alone) based on one or more of those other considerations. The controversy concerns whether or not this process of altering an overall risk assessment using clinical considerations beyond actuarial results is appropriate.

The argument has been made that adjustments to actuarial findings make no sense—if one believes in actuarial assessment procedures over clinical, then any use of clinical procedures should be seen as dampening the effectiveness of the empirically based actuarial results (Otto & Petrila, 2002). Quinsey *et al.* (1998) argue that clinical risk assessment procedures should be abandoned altogether in favor of pure actuarial procedures without any clinical adjustments except under the most rare of circumstances.

At the same time, it appears that most people who use actuarial instruments for applied purposes also rely on some degree of clinical consideration in determining final risk assessments (see Doren, 2002). A discrepancy in perspective clearly exists. This debate can also be resolved.

Issues to be Addressed

There are a lot of unscientific reasons for making clinical adjustments to actuarial findings (e.g. "gut reactions" to the offender or the offender's history, beliefs about the importance of a salient variable without an empirical basis for that belief). There are also some scientifically supported reasons for making *certain* adjustments. Doren (2002) reviewed a set of research findings indicating that certain types of variables were of relevance either in increasing or decreasing overall sexual recidivism risk beyond what current actuarial results indicated.

For instance, McGrath, Cumming, Livingston and Hoke (2003) found that the completion of treatment programming lowered sexual recidivism rates compared to non-starters (inclusive or not of treatment dropouts) when the subjects' scores on either the RRASOR or Static-99 were matched and controlled. In other words, the completion of treatment programming showed relevance in the risk assessment (in potentially lowering risk) beyond what some current actuarial instruments indicated. Similarly, due to the consistently high degree of violent and sexual recidivism risk associated with the combination of psychopathy and sexual deviance, Harris *et al.* (2003) concluded "because of the robustness of this interaction and its prognostic significance, its inclusion in the next generation of actuarial instruments for sex offenders should increase predictive accuracy further" (p. 421). Notably, this quote essentially comes from the same people who argued in Quinsey *et al.* (1998) for the avoidance of clinical adjustments to pure actuarial assessments.

Overall, there appear to be some empirical findings indicating that considerations of *certain* variables beyond those in current actuarial instruments can increase the overall predictive validity of risk assessments. By no means, however, does this circumstance stand as reason for clinicians to "adjust" ("discount") actuarial findings based on anything the clinician thinks to be of importance.

Arguments with Questionable Logic

The argument has been made that it makes no sense to use an actuarial instrument and then make adjustments to that actuarial finding; but instead it makes more sense to use either a structured list of risk considerations or unguided clinical judgment. The logic here is faulty.

To whatever extent an instrument for structuring clinical judgment (such as the HCR-20 or SVR-20) is used to conduct a risk assessment, the user needs to impose some degree of clinically determined weights to each factor and combination of factors considered. At worst, this is what occurs with clinically determined "adjustments" to actuarial results. The only difference is that the person using an actuarial instrument has a scientific grounding or framework available upon which those adjustments are made, as opposed to a lesser degree of that characteristic when using a structured risk factor list. This statement assumes the risk assessment concerns "probability", something for which current actuarial instruments are designed. That assumption is made to ensure that the use of an actuarial instrument was appropriate in the first place. In other words, the process of *any* current risk assessment, except the most purely actuarial, involves this same "adjustment" process, with the only difference being the degree of empirical support for the foundation upon which the "adjustment" is made. Arguments that the adjusted-actuarial approach is fundamentally different from or inherently less credible than the structured clinical approach seem to miss the above point and potentially mislead naïve listeners.

Suggested Resolution

As with the suggested resolution to the actuarial-clinical procedural debate, the resolution to the controversy about "clinical adjustments" to actuarial findings seems to reside within existing empirical results. We should concentrate on what research has demonstrated to be true, rather than what "makes sense" to people through argument. If there is research indicating that a variable is of significant sequential importance in a risk assessment when added to an actuarial result, then we should use that variable along with the relevant actuarial instrument. If there is no empirical basis for using a variable to "adjust" an actuarial estimate of risk, then we need to acknowledge that fact and forego using that variable in our risk assessment. In effect, these statements for attempted resolution stem from the fact that our current actuarial instruments are known not to be fully inclusive of every variable thought to be of independent relevance in determining someone's recidivism risk. Until our instruments are that good, clinical "adjustments" would seem necessary, though never a license for discounting actuarial results based on non-empirical guesses or gut reactions.

RISK ASSESSMENT VERSUS RECIDIVISM PREDICTION

Differences in the terminology we use can represent far more than interchangeable representations of the same thing, but instead can demonstrate there exists a fundamental misunderstanding of important concepts. Such is the case when people refer to the process of making "predictions" when they are really describing "risk assessments". This kind of confusion can be found even in titles of professional journal articles (e.g. Berlin et al., 2003).

Making a prediction is an either-or, future-oriented process. A statement is made that something will (or will not) happen in the future, and that statement is either fully correct or fully incorrect. It is like calling for a coin to land "heads" upon being flipped—after the flip you are either correct or not, and you could not know ahead of time which it would be. Doing a risk assessment, however, means the evaluator focuses on a degree of possibility (versus either-or outcomes) within the current here-and-now (versus future-oriented) circumstance. Metaphorically, the result of a risk assessment for the coin flipping heads in the previous example is 50%, something we can know now, without any flipping of the coin. Likewise, the result of a flip of the coin, no matter which way it turns out, does not negate or even affect the accuracy of the earlier "risk assessment".

Issue to be Addressed

The term "risk prediction" is a non sequitur, whereas the phrases "risk assessment" and "recidivism prediction" have meaning. Evaluators of risk (using any assessment methodology) do not make behavioral predictions, but instead assess a person's risk of falling into some type of category of relevance. All too often, this difference between a risk assessment and the prediction of recidivism is forgotten or confused.

This conceptual difference is of consequence, yet this confusion shows up in important ways in the professional literature. For example, Campbell (2000) described the idea that there are four possible outcomes to "risk assessments made for sexual predator hearings" (p. 114), these four being descriptive of true positives, false positives, true negatives and false negatives (where a "positive" is a prediction for recidivism and a "negative" is a prediction for no recidivism). Campbell goes on to talk about issues such as sensitivity and specificity (apparently to determine if any current procedure is good enough to be used in forensic testimony). This step represents the true problem. Statistics such as those discussed by Campbell are useful when describing the accuracy of a prediction, but they are simply the wrong statistics to evaluate the accuracy of a risk assessment. To be fair to Campbell, serious errors in confusing risk assessment with behavioral prediction can be found in other professional publications as well. Berlin *et al.* (2003), for instance, used the phrases "predict the likelihood", "risk prediction", "risk of recidivism" and "predicting dangerousness" interchangeably while also invoking arguments about "false positives"; all within an evaluative context in which predictions are never made. Risk assessment specifically involves the concept of probability. As such, the proper statistical method for evaluating the accuracy of a risk assessment should include a determination of confidence intervals (or probability intervals).

Arguments with Questionable Logic

Statistics based on true/false positives/negatives require that yes-no predictions be made. The fact is that no current actuarial instrument offers yes-no results, and any such interpretation of an existing actuarial instrument in that way necessarily involves an arbitrary cut-score. This is why it is improper to talk about the sensitivity, specificity or similar statistic of an actuarial instrument as a whole. Likewise, formal evaluations of risk quite regularly do not state the person will recidivate or will not recidivate (i.e. they avoid predictive conclusions, quite contrary to Campbell's assertion), such that statistical concepts such as sensitivity and specificity (or true/false positives/negatives) to assess the accuracy of risk assessments cannot be applied without contortion.

Suggested Resolution

The described issues can be resolved only through the proper application of statistical concepts and the avoidance of obfuscation. People need to stop talking about risk assessments as if they result in predictive statements. They simply are not the same, and risk assessments rarely result in any kind of predictive statement. If there truly is an issue about the predictive accuracy of an instrument, the relevant statistics can be computed using any chosen (though arbitrary) cut-score(s). If people wish to discuss the accuracy of a risk assessment using an instrument, however, they need to avoid talking about predictions as if these are the same concepts or are statistically assessed in the same manner.

INSTRUMENT CONSTRUCTION VERSUS MEANINGFULNESS

There have been criticisms concerning how at least certain risk assessment instruments have been developed. Lloyd and Grove (2003) and Wollert (2002), for example, describe perceived faults with the development of the MnSOST-R. The enumerated faults range from the sampling technique to the type of statistical analyses conducted in formulating the instrument. Similarly, the SVR-20 (a structured list of risk considerations, rather than an actuarial instrument) has been criticized based on the fact that nine of its 20 items are described in its own manual as having unknown statistical relationships with sexual recidivism (Doren, 2003). These criticisms have been used to suggest that the instruments in question are therefore not of sufficient quality to be used. Despite these criticisms, the developmental process of an instrument is simply not so damning.

Issue to be Addressed

The ultimate issues in the use of any assessment tool are whether or not it works in the way it is supposed to, and does so consistently with different users. The real utility of an instrument is therefore determined by empirical tests concerning whether or not the instrument consistently cross-validates, no matter how it was developed. Statistical procedures typically used in the development of measurement tools are designed to maximize the likelihood that the final product will do this, given the inputting data.

The arguments made against certain assessment instruments based on their developmental process emphasize that things could have been better. That issue in instrument development really misses the ultimate points about whether the instrument works and does so consistently. It really does not matter how an instrument was developed if it consistently works with a variety of samples and users. The meaningfulness of an instrument stems from accumulated evidence from a number of validity studies using various methodologies (Campbell & Fiske, 1959), not simply an assessment of developmental procedures. The use of proper statistical procedures for instrument development helps ensure that potential users of the instrument have trust in the meaningfulness of what the instrument gives them even before several validation studies have been conducted. Likewise, enumerations of risk considerations will generate the greatest degree of user confidence if there exists a well-documented research basis for the inclusion of each item.

These issues of user confidence notwithstanding, however, the determination of the potential utility of an instrument does not stem from how it was developed, but to what degree it shows consistent success in inter-rater reliability and cross-validation studies. Even if someone simply made up an instrument without consulting the research literature and without using any statistical analysis, a significantly consistent and large number of successful cross-validation studies would indicate that the instrument was worthy of use (under tested conditions).

Suggested Resolution

The resolution to the controversy in this area seems to be to divide the critiques of any assessment instrument into two types: those that explore the development of the instrument, and those that investigate the tested validity of the instrument. Critiques of the former type have meaning, and can show us where improvements in the instrument may be made. The results from this set of critiques notwithstanding, however, consistent results from cross-validation studies tell us a great deal about the validity of the instrument as it currently exists. Of course, faults in the development of an instrument may suggest that further improvements might be made even after cross-validation studies are found supportive to the original instrument, but that is an argument for a different day.

FINAL COMMENT

The field of sexual offender risk assessment has expanded greatly both in practice and research in recent years. Some professional controversies can be expected in such situations. On the other hand, some controversies represent misunderstandings or poorly applied principles instead of accurate representations of the cutting edges of the field where reasoned professional differences can be expected. My hope is that the above exploration of some debated areas helps to move us on from misunderstandings to more productive explorations of our science.

AUTHOR'S NOTE

The opinions expressed in this chapter do not necessarily reflect those of the Wisconsin Department of Health and Family Services.

REFERENCES

Andrews, D.A. & Bonta, J.L. (1995). *The Level of Service Inventory—Revised: User's Manual.* North Tonawanda, NY: Multi-Health Systems, Inc.

Andrews, D.A. & Bonta, J.L. (2001). *The Level of Service Inventory—Revised: User's Manual.* North Tonawanda, NY: Multi-Health Systems, Inc.

Barnoski, R. (2003). *Washington State Juvenile Court Assessment Manual, Version 2.1* (Olympia: Washington State Institute for Public Policy, 2003). Available at http://www.wsipp.wa.gov. The Youth Assessment and Screening Instrument is available at www.orbispartners.com.

Berlin, F.S., Galbreath, N.W., Geary, B. & McGlone, G. (2003). The use of actuarials at civil commitment hearings to predict the likelihood of future sexual violence. *Sexual Abuse: A Journal of Research and Treatment*, **15**, 377–82.

Boer, D.P., Hart, S.D., Kropp, P.R. & Webster, C.D. (1997). *Manual for the Sexual Violence Risk—20: Professional Guidelines for Assessing Risk of Sexual Violence.* Vancouver: Simon Fraser University and British Columbia Forensic Psychiatric Services Commission.

Campbell, D. & Fiske, D. (1959). Convergent and discriminant validation by the multitrait-multimethod matrix. *Psychological Bulletin*, **56**, 81–105.

Campbell, T.W. (2000). Sexual predator evaluations and phrenology: considering issues of evidentiary reliability. *Behavioral Sciences and the Law*, **18**, 111–30.

Doren, D.M. (2002). *Evaluating Sex Offenders: A Manual for Civil Commitments and Beyond.* Thousand Oaks, CA: Sage Publications.

Doren, D.M. (2003, November). Conducting risk assessments: the details of what we know from research. Workshop presented at the 22nd Annual Research and Treatment Conference of the Association for the Treatment of Sexual Abusers, St. Louis.

Douglas, K.S. & Weir, J. (2003). HCR-20 violence risk assessment scheme: Overview and annotated bibliography. Available at www.cvp.se/publications/downloadables/hcr% 2020%20annotated%20bibliography.pdf.

Dvoskin, J.A. & Heilbrun, K. (2001). Risk assessment and release decision-making: toward resolving the great debate. *Journal of the American Academy of Psychiatry and Law*, **29**, 6–10.

Epperson, D.L., Kaul, J.D., Huot, S.J., Hesselton, D., Alexander, W. & Goldman, R. (1999). Minnesota Sex Offender Screening Tool—Revised (MnSOST-R): development, performance, and recommended risk level cut scores. Available at www.psychology.iastate.edu/faculty/epperson/mnsost_download.htm.

Grove, W.M., Zald, D.H., Lebow, B.S., Snitz, B.E. & Nelson, C. (2000). Clinical versus mechanical prediction: a meta-analysis. *Psychological Assessment*, **12**, 19–30.

Hanson, R.K. (1997). The development of a brief actuarial risk scale for sexual offense recidivism. Department of the Solicitor General of Canada, Ottawa, Ontario. Available at www.sgc.gc.ca/publications/corrections/199704e.pdf.

Hanson, R.K. & Bussière, M.T. (1998). Predicting relapse: a meta-analysis of sexual offender recidivism studies. *Journal of Consulting and Clinical Psychology*, **66**, 348–62.

Hanson, R.K., Morton, K.E. & Harris, A.J.R. (2003). Sexual offender recidivism risk: what we know and what we need to know. *Annals of the New York Academy of Sciences*, **989**, 154–66.

Hanson, R.K. & Thornton, D. (2000). Improving risk assessments for sex offenders: a comparison of three actuarial scales. *Law and Human Behavior*, **24**, 119–36.

Harris, G.T., Rice, M.E., Quinsey, V.L., Lalumière, M.L., Boer, D. & Lang, C. (2003). A multisite comparison of actuarial risk instruments for sex offenders. *Psychological Assessment*, **15**, 413–25.

Litwack, T.R. (2001). Actuarial versus clinical assessments of dangerousness. *Psychology, Public Policy, and the Law*, **7**, 409–43.

Lloyd, M.D. & Grove, W.M. (2003). *The Uselessness of the Minnesota Sex Offender Screening Tool-Revised (MnSOST-R) in Commitment Decisions*. Submitted for publication.

McGrath, R.J. & Hoke, S.E. (2002). *Vermont Assessment of Sex-Offender Risk Manual*. Middlebury, VT: Author (available at http://www.csom.org/pubs/VASOR.pdf).

McGrath, R.J., Cumming, G., Livingston, J.A. & Hoke, S.E. (2003). Outcome of a treatment program for adult sex offenders: from prison to community. *Journal of Interpersonal Violence*, **18**, 3–17.

Meehl, P.E. (1954). *Clinical vs. Statistical Prediction: A Theoretical Analysis and a Review of the Evidence*. Minneapolis: University of Minnesota Press.

Otto, R.K. & Petrila, J. (2002). Admissibility of testimony based on actuarial scales in sex offender commitments: a reply to Doren. *Sex Offender Law Report*, **3**, 14–15.

Prentky, R., Harris, B., Frizzell, K. & Righthand, S. (2000). An actuarial procedure for assessing risk for juvenile sex offenders. *Sexual Abuse: A Journal of Research and Treatment*, **12**, 71–93.

Quinsey, V.L., Harris, G.T., Rice, M.E. & Cormier, C.A. (1998). *Violent Offenders: Appraising and Managing Risk*. Washington, DC: American Psychological Association.

Webster, C.D., Douglas, K.S., Eaves, D. & Hart, S.D. (1997). *HCR-20: Assessing the Risk for Violence (Version 2)*. Vancouver: Mental Health, Law, and Policy Institute, Simon Fraser University.

Webster, C.D., Harris, G.T., Rice, M.E., Cormier, C. & Quinsey, V.L. (1994). *The Violence Prediction Scheme: Assessing Dangerousness in High Risk Men*. Toronto: University of Toronto, Centre of Criminology.

Wollert, R.W. (2002). The importance of cross-validation in actuarial test construction: shrinkage in the risk estimates for the Minnesota sex offender screening tool—revised. *Journal of Threat Assessment*, **2**, 87–102.

Worling, J.R. (2001, November). Comprehensive assessment of adolescent sex offenders: focus on risk assessment and the development of holistic treatment plans. Paper presented at the 20th Annual Research and Treatment Conference of the Association for the Treatment of Sexual Abusers, San Antonio, Texas.

Chapter 2

STABILITY AND CHANGE: DYNAMIC RISK FACTORS FOR SEXUAL OFFENDERS

R. Karl Hanson

Corrections Research, Public Safety and Emergency Preparedness Canada, Ottawa, Canada

Sexual offences are among the most disturbing of crimes, and the public has considerable concern about the risk posed by sexual offenders in the community. Approximately 1% to 2% of the male population will eventually be convicted of a sexual offence (Marshall, 1997). Follow-up studies, however, have found that once detected, most sexual offenders are never reconvicted for a new sexual offence (Langan, Schmitt & Durose, 2003), even when the follow-up period extends to 20 years (Hanson, Scott & Steffy, 1995). Some offenders, however, are much higher risk to sexually reoffend than others, with the observed recidivism rates varying between 10% and 50% (Hanson & Thornton, 2000).

There are different methods for distinguishing between the risk levels of offenders. One of my early supervisors recommended an offender assessment system based on two categories: (1) workable, and (2) "no good". Most current risk assessments are more complicated. Sexual offender risk assessments typically consider a range of risk and protective factors, with the higher risk offenders having more of the risk factors (and fewer protective factors) than the low risk offenders (Beech, Fisher & Thornton, 2003).

Risk factors can be classified as "static" or "dynamic". Static risk factors are unchangeable, historical characteristics, such as prior offences, early childhood problems and age. Dynamic risk factors are those that are potentially changeable and, when reduced, are associated with reductions in the recidivism risk. Dynamic risk factors can be further divided into "stable" and "acute" risk factors (Hanson & Harris, 2000). Stable risk factors, also called "criminogenic needs" (Andrews & Bonta, 2003) or "causal psychological risk factors" (Beech & Ward, 2004), are relatively enduring attributes associated with chronic recidivism risk. Stable dynamic risk factors (e.g. intimacy deficits, sexual self-regulation) are the most appropriate treatment targets, for changes in these traits should be related to enduring changes in recidivism potential. In contrast, the acute risk factors, also called "triggering

Sexual Offender Treatment: Controversial Issues. Edited by W.L. Marshall, Y.M. Fernandez, L.E. Marshall and G.A. Serran.   © 2006 John Wiley & Sons, Ltd.

events" or "contextual risk factors" (Beech & Ward, 2004) are short-term states that signal the timing of reoffending (e.g. subjective distress, intoxication).

The majority of research on sexual offender recidivism has focused on static, historical factors (Hanson & Bussière, 1998). Static factors are useful for long-term recidivism prediction, but have limited utility in many applied contexts. Static factors cannot be changed and, consequently, cannot be used to evaluate whether an offender is getting better or getting worse.

WHY SHOULD WE CARE ABOUT DYNAMIC RISK FACTORS?

There are several reasons why dynamic factors are worthy of attention by clinicians and researchers: to make a difference, to improve prediction, and to advance scientific understanding.

To Make a Difference

It is useful to know that an offender is at high risk to reoffend, but it is even more useful to know how to reduce that risk. Knowledge of acute dynamic risk factors is required to determine what needs to be restricted and monitored on community supervision (i.e. acute risk factors). Knowledge of stable risk factors is required for offenders to know what they need to change, and for therapists to know what should be addressed in treatment.

To Improve Prediction

Even for assessments that are only concerned about the probability of reoffending, the consideration of current characteristics (stable dynamic risk factors) improves predictive accuracy over that provided by static risk factors alone. Not infrequently, experts within the criminal justice system are asked whether an offender has made sufficient changes to justify release from some form of sanction (e.g. parole). Such assessments can be meaningful only when they are based on stable dynamic risk factors. A long history of bad behaviour may be sufficient to identify an offender as potentially high risk, but evaluators need to consider dynamic risk factors when evaluating changes in risk levels (e.g. has he benefited from treatment or community supervision?).

The existing actuarial risk scales are moderate to strong predictors of sexual recidivism (Hanson & Morton-Bourgon, 2004), but none of them include all relevant risk factors. Thornton (2002), for example, found that sexual recidivism in his sample was strongly predicted by Static-99 (ROC area of 0.92), an actuarial risk scale containing items such as prior sexual offences, victim characteristics and age (Hanson & Thornton, 2000). Despite the strong predictive accuracy of static factors, overall prediction was significantly improved by considering stable dynamic factors such as pro-offending attitudes, hostility and problems in self-regulation. Similarly, Hanson and Harris (2000) found that dynamic (stable and acute) risk factors significantly differentiated sexual recidivists and non-recidivists after considering the static, historical factors contained in the Violence Risk Appraisal Guide (VRAG; Quinsey, Harris, Rice & Cormier, 1998), the Rapid Risk Assessment for Sex Offence Recidivism (RRASOR; Hanson, 1997) and the Static-99. Evaluators who rely only on static, historical factors are neglecting potentially important information.

For Scientific Understanding

Even if it was possible to predict future behaviour using purely static factors, the advancement of scientific understanding requires the identification of dynamic risk factors. Static factors make unsatisfying scientific explanations. Even the worst offenders are not offending all the time; consequently, explanations of sexual offending must rely on latent potentials that are activated by proximal triggers (or intentions).

Consider the well established relationship between prior sex offences and future sex offences: in what sense do prior sex offences "cause" future offending? Most scientific explanations require that causal factors are contiguous with their effects (either directly or through intermediaries). Scientific theories typically do not accept that events that ended years ago cause future events. It would be unacceptable for a fire investigator to conclude that the current fire was caused by a similar fire on the same location ten years ago. An explanation of the association between prior and future sex offences requires an appeal to enduring characteristics or propensities of the individual, such as "habit strength", "insensitivity to sanctions", or "deviant sexual interests". An observed relationship does not specify which combination of conditions is linked to sexual offending, only that these conditions have re-occurred. A prediction based only on static risk factors is an admission of ignorance.

If you ask most people what makes a plant grow, they will talk about sunshine, "good soil" and water. Botanists can provide much more detailed explanations, referring to genes, photosynthesis and phosphorus. Although no explanation is ever complete, good explanations provide answers to common problems (e.g. why is this plant dying?) and suggest new possibilities (e.g. hydroponics). The most satisfying explanations not only solve specific problems, but do so using concepts that are compatible with other domains of knowledge. Just as good explanations for plant growth should conform to the laws of physics, good explanations for sexual recidivism should be consistent with what we know about human nature.

WHAT ARE PEOPLE LIKE?

The prediction of human behaviour is difficult because we are not entirely predictable. Most conceptions of human nature (and all modern legal systems) include a concept of free will or choice. Our choices, however, are not entirely "free": they are constrained by our environments and our individual characteristics. Humans live in societies, and many of our most meaningful choices concern how we relate to other people.

One useful way of describing individual differences is through the concept of "schema", defined à la Piaget, as perceptual-motor sequences (Piaget & Inhelder, 1969). Schemata can be thought of as latent cognitive structures that embody our past experiences and serve to guide ongoing perceptions and behaviours. Our simplest schemata involve physical actions (e.g. grasp objects), but we soon develop schemata for all forms of complex social interactions (e.g. dating, work, playing basketball). Most of our perceptions are fused with values and implied actions: "A postal box is where you mail a letter", "There is a great bar on Elgin Street with cheap drinks and great music." Thinking is a form of doing, and each time we enact a schema, it becomes increasingly believable and real. We share common schemata based on similar biology (e.g. sight) and culture (e.g. language). We develop different schemata based on our efforts to understand our own unique experiences, and as a result of the limitation that attention can only be focused on some of the available options.

WHAT ARE SEXUAL OFFENDERS LIKE?

Sexual offenders, like everybody else, choose their conduct based on their perception of the options available. Sexual offenders differ from many other people, however, by perceiving certain situations as ones in which a sexual crime is a legitimate option (i.e. they have a "sex offence schema"). Later, sexual offenders may wonder why they did it but, at the time, the sexual offence was perceived as something they could (should?) do. Sexual offenders who are at high risk for recidivism would be those whose sex offence schemata are readily accessible. Many situations would invoke their urge to offend, such as the sight of potential victims, or common internal states, such as frustration and loneliness. By practising their deviant sexual crimes in fantasy, they increase the probability of eventually enacting them. When they are able to question their habitual patterns of thought, the probability of recidivism decreases. An outline of this model is presented in Figure 2.1.

At the centre of the model are the deviant plans / scripts / schemata, surrounded by the major triggers. When the schema is activated, offenders will be focusing or ruminating on sexually deviant fantasies or behaviour. They may be aware of little else, and it would be difficult for them to perceive other alternatives: perhaps they are rehearsing a specific sexual crime scenario; perhaps they have an intense urge for sexual release (and the object of their lust is inconsequential); perhaps they are scanning the environment for potential victims. The enactment of the schema will last for a period of time and then stop (whether or not they act on it). The schemata are likely enacted many, many times, and only rarely will the enactment result in an actual sexual offence. Each time it is enacted, however, it becomes stronger and more accessible. Each time it is interrupted or questioned, it becomes weaker. It is unlikely to ever go away completely.

The specific factors that trigger deviant schemata will vary across offenders. Nevertheless, there are some common risk factors, the most obvious of which is the presence of potential victims. Other potential triggers include subjective distress, conflicts in intimate relationships and sexual arousal. In this model, schemata are distinguished from the offenders' explicit attitudes and values.

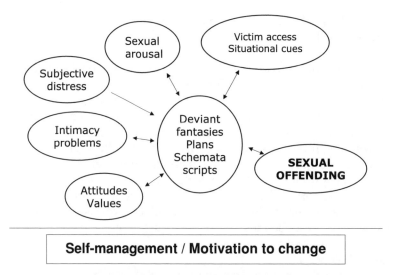

Figure 2.1   A model of recidivism risk among sexual offenders.

Attitudes are considered relatively conscious beliefs about what is and what ought to be. For example, some child molesters state that children want to have sex with adults, and that there is nothing really wrong with adult–child sexual contact (except that it is illegal). For the evaluation of sexual offender recidivism risk, the most important attitudes are permission-giving beliefs that are tolerant of sexual crimes.

Schemata exist within networks such that reciprocal activation is common. Thinking that it is OK to have sex with children may trigger images of sexually provocative children, which may trigger the urge to have sex with a particular child, which may trigger the thought that it is OK to have sex with children. As a reminder of these reciprocal relationships, most of the arrows in Figure 2.1 are bi-directional. There is one important exception: the arrow going from subjective distress to deviant fantasies is drawn in only one direction. Distress tends to invoke deviant schemata (Cortoni & Marshall, 2001) more often than deviant schemata invoke distress. Relapse prevention theory posits that minor lapses, such as deviant fantasies, should invoke subjective distress, but there appears to be little evidence for a classic abstinence violation effect among sexual offenders (Ward, Hudson & Marshall, 1994).

Another important facet to this model is the offenders' capacity for self-regulation and their motivation to change. Habit change is difficult, and offenders vary on the extent to which they are able to self-regulate. Offenders wishing to change need to become familiar with their deviant schemata, the urges that pull them, the situations in which they are invoked, and what they do to disengage them. Much of cognitive-behavioural therapy involves methods for identifying and disengaging deviant schemata (e.g. offence chains, avoid high risk situations). Although self-regulation deficits can directly lead to sexual crimes, self-regulation is particularly important for offenders wishing to change established patterns.

HOW CAN YOU TELL THAT SOMETHING IS A DYNAMIC RISK FACTOR?

There are two broad approaches to identifying risk factors: idiographic and nomothetic. The idiographic approach looks for patterns within individuals whereas the nomothetic approach looks for patterns among groups. The idiographic approach typically tries to identify the factors present at the time of offending and absent at the time of non-offending. For example, a rapist may start cruising for victims after having conflicts with his intimate partner. Identifying the significant idiographic factors is difficult because offenders often have many life problems and there are often few known offences from which to infer patterns.

If the schema theory is correct, then the idiographic approach could also productively focus on what offenders do to make themselves "feel like" offending. Although offenders often describe their offences as "just happening", it is possible to become aware of, and take responsibility for, the thoughts, intentions and emotions that direct behaviour.

The simplest approach to assessing schemata is to ask the offenders. Many are able to clearly articulate what "turns them on" and gives them the urge to offend. Valuable information can also be gained by examining the circumstances of previous offences and the accounts of victims. Specialized testing can also help offenders develop insight into what "hooks" them. Phallometric assessment has long been used to assess sexual arousal to deviant stimuli; more recently, Gene Abel has been working to create a standardized test based on the natural propensity of attractive models to capture our attention (Abel, Jordon, Hand, Holland & Phipps, 2001). In general, it would be possible to craft a range of scenarios (e.g. illustrated stories, role plays) to probe for the unique circumstances that engage deviant schemata.

Recent research has suggested that standard cognitive psychology paradigms can be used to assess the deviant schemata of sexual offenders. The Implicit Attitude Test was used to assess child molesters' latent association between sex and children (Gray, MacCulloch, Smith & Snowdon, 2002), a procedure that involves training specific responses to categories of stimuli. For example, subjects practise pushing a button with their right hand when presented with words related to children, and with the left hand when presented with words related to adults. In the next stage, they push the right hand button when they see words related to sex and the left hand button when they see neutral words. After the responses are trained, the instructions are reversed: now they push the left hand button when they see sex words and the right hand button for neutral words. The basis of the test is that reaction times are quicker when there is an implicit association between the concepts. As expected, Gray *et al.* (2002) found that child molesters' reaction times were quickest when they pressed the right hand button for both sex and children. For the comparison group, the reaction times were quickest when sex was paired with the concept of "adult".

A related cognitive paradigm is the Stroop task (Stroop, 1935). Subjects are presented with a list of words printed in different colours, with the instruction to say out loud the *colour* of each word (e.g. "red"). By changing the content of the words, it is possible to increase or decrease the time it takes individuals to say the colour names. The changes in naming speed are explained by interference created when subjects have to inhibit highly accessible schemata in order to respond to the requested task of naming the colours. Research has found, for example, that violent offenders are slow at naming the colour of words related to violence (Smith & Waterman, 2003), that smokers are slow at naming the colour of words related to smoking (Wertz & Sayette, 2001), and that sexual offenders are slow at naming the colour of words related to sexual crimes (Smith & Waterman, 2004).

The research on the cognitive paradigms is preliminary, and may never lead to practical applications. This research is important, however, because it demonstrates the types of enduring propensities associated with recidivism risk. Most of the time deviant schemata are latent, but they can rapidly structure perception given even minimal cues (e.g. single words). They are sufficiently fast and automatic that they attract little awareness. With training, however, it is possible for offenders to identify the times when they have "lost it" and succumbed to habitual patterns. With continued training, they can spend less time being hooked, and can increasingly take responsibility for their behaviours, thoughts and feelings.

GROUP DIFFERENCES BETWEEN RECIDIVISTS AND NON-RECIDIVISTS

Idiographic approaches to identifying risk factors have considerable clinical utility but are poorly suited to some assessment questions. For example, evaluators are often tasked with identifying whether an offender is "high" risk to reoffend, with high risk defined relative to other offenders, or as a recidivism probability (e.g. more likely than not). Answers to such questions require group data: specifically, they require follow-up studies that compare the recidivism rates of sexual offenders with or without particular characteristics.

We recently summarized the findings of 95 recidivism follow-up studies using meta-analysis (Hanson & Morton-Bourgon, 2004). Table 2.1 displays the dynamic risk factors that have received the strongest research in these follow-up studies. The results are reported in terms of d, the standardized mean difference. The d statistic is a measure of how much the recidivists are different from the non-recidivists, and compares that difference to how much recidivists and non-recidivists differ among themselves. According to Cohen (1988), d values of 0.20 are "small", 0.50 are "moderate" and 0.80 are "large".

Stable Risk Factors

Compared to non-recidivists, sexual recidivists are more likely to show signs of deviant sexual interests, particularly sexual interest in children and paraphilias (voyeurism, exhibitionism, fetishism, etc.). Although sexual interests tend to be rather stable, it is not unusual to find individuals whose sexual orientation has changed throughout their lifespan. The effectiveness of psychological interventions for changing sexual preferences remains controversial.

Sexual offenders often report high levels of diverse sexual activity (Kafka, 2003), and sexual preoccupations increase the risk of sexual recidivism (average d = 0.39).

Table 2.1   Potential dynamic predictors of sexual recidivism

	Average effect size (d)	Sample size (studies)
Sexual deviancy		
Any deviant sexual interest	0.31	2,769 (16)
Sexual interest in children (phallometric)	0.32	1,140 (7)
Paraphilic interests	0.21	477 (4)
Sexual preoccupations	0.39	1,119 (6)
Antisocial orientation		
General self-regulation problems	0.37	2,411 (15)
Antisocial personality disorder	0.21	3,267 (12)
Impulsivity, recklessness	0.25	775 (6)
Employment instability	0.22	5,357 (15)
Hostility	0.17	1,960 (9)
Attitudes		
Attitudes tolerant of sexual crime	0.22	1,617 (9)
Intimacy deficits		
Conflicts in intimate relationship	0.36	298 (4)
Emotional identification with children	0.42	419 (3)

Source: From Hanson & Morton-Bourgon (2004). *Predictors of sexual recidivism: An updated meta-analysis*. Corrections Policy User Report No. 2004–02. Ottawa: Corrections Policy, Public Safety and Emergency Preparedness Canada.

Such findings suggest that problems with sexual self-regulation form a core deficit associated with sexual offending. We all need to develop strategies for managing our sexual impulses, and sexual offenders would represent individuals whose sexual self-management skills are at the low end of the continuum. It is not unusual for "normal" adult men to have some sexual interest in deviant sexual behaviour, such as voyeurism, young girls or frottage. For non-offenders, however, the attractions are weak and fleeting. In contrast, many sexual offenders developed their deviant urges through rumination and masturbation fantasies, and by creating opportunities to enact their deviant desires.

Problems with sexual self-regulation can be understood within the larger context of general self-regulation problems and antisocial orientation. The association between low self-control and crime is so strong that Gottfredson and Hirschi (1990) considered it to be *the* cause of crime. Individuals who commit crimes tend to change jobs and residences, have unrealistic plans for the future, and engage in a variety of high risk behaviours (e.g. drinking, driving fast, unsafe work practises). In addition to low self-control, the other major indicator of antisocial orientation is hostility—often expressed as a chronic grievance against the world and those in it (Caspi *et al.*, 1994).

Antisocial orientation may directly result in sexual offences, but it is particularly important for those who have deviant sexual interests. An individual may find young boys sexually attractive, but never act on this attraction given sufficient self-control and good judgement. In contrast, individuals with an antisocial orientation may feel that they cannot control their impulses, and, besides, why should they? The world owes them something.

Attitudes tolerant of sexual crime showed a small, but significant, relationship to sexual recidivism. It is important to distinguish between believing that sexual offending is OK (which predicts recidivism) and efforts to minimize culpability (which are unrelated to recidivism). When we are caught doing something wrong, we typically struggle to find accounts that mitigate the negative social consequences of our transgressions. The most common strategies for diverting culpability are to deny that we did the act, or to minimize the consequences; sexual offenders are no different. Evaluators wishing to differentiate between pro-offending attitudes and defensiveness may benefit from considering the offenders' opinions about sexual offences committed by others. Attempting to justify one's own transgressions is quite different from believing that it is acceptable for others to do the same thing. Offenders who deny their offences are at least admitting that sexual offending is wrong.

Some of the most promising dynamic risk factors involve intimacy deficits. The lack of an intimate partner increases the risk of recidivism (Hanson & Bussière, 1998) as do conflicts within an existing intimate relationship (Hanson & Morton-Bourgon, 2004). Such findings are not surprising considering the strong natural links between sex and intimacy. Most people want their sexual partners to be likeable and attractive, and for their sexual partners to find them likeable and attractive. Sex deepens pair bonding, whether or not increased intimacy is even desired (consider sexual jealousy, attachment and loss in casual sexual relationships). Sexual offences, by definition, involve a disruption in the normal process of mutual sexual attraction.

Given that most sexual offenders have had difficult childhood environments, it is likely that their relationship problems started early and shaped the development of their sexual interests and activities. For rapists, adversarial or impersonal sexual relationships can be an extension of adversarial and impersonal relationships with family and peers. Child molesters, in contrast, may be attracted to immature, childish relationships, and may feel very much like children themselves (Wilson, 1999). Marshall (1989) has made an important contribution by focusing attention on the need to address intimacy deficits in the treatment of sexual offenders; further research is required, however, to determine the extent to which improved intimacy is associated with medium- or long-term reductions in recidivism risk.

Acute Risk Factors

The research on acute risk factors is much less developed than the research on static or stable factors. Acute risk factors are harder to assess than stable factors because measurements must be obtained just before the recidivism event. Pithers and colleagues used retrospective interviews with the offenders to identify precursors of sexual offending (Pithers, Kashima, Cumming, Beal & Buell, 1988). In their research, the risk factor most frequently mentioned by the offenders was negative mood (anger, loneliness). Researchers at Institut Philippe Pinel asked inmates to keep daily records of interpersonal conflicts, negative mood and deviant sexual fantasies (Proulx, McKibben & Lusignan, 1996; McKibben, Proulx & Lusignan, 1994). They, too, found that negative mood increased the likelihood of deviant sexual fantasies and masturbation.

Hanson and Harris (2000) used records from community supervision officers to identify the precursors of sexual recidivism. By comparing the factors present in the month prior to recidivism with the factors present six months previously, it was possible to identify the changes associated with recidivism risk. The acute factors suggested by this research including negative mood, hostility, substance use, victim access, sexual preoccupations, problematic social relationships and lack of cooperation with supervision. One weakness of the study was that most of the information was based on interviews with the supervising officers, which raises the possibility of retrospective recall biases. Subsequently, we have initiated a large ($n > 1,000$) prospective study of stable and acute predictors of recidivism during community supervision (Harris & Hanson, 2003), with results expected in 2006.

USING DYNAMIC FACTORS TO PREDICT RECIDIVISM

Although there is sufficient research evidence to indicate that dynamic risk factors contribute information not captured by static risk variables, we have much to learn about how to integrate dynamic risk factors into an overall evaluation. How is it possible to predict future events using characteristics that are inherently changing?

Consider, for example, three offenders with repeated assessment on "defiant hostility", rated from 1 to 10, with 10 indicating "extremely defiant, hostile" (see Table 2.2). Tom was very hostile at Time 1, Time 2 and Time 3, but displayed only mild hostility at Time 4; Dick was never very hostile; and Harry was usually agreeable, but showed moderate levels of hostility at Time 4. Which of the three offenders is at highest risk to recidivate at Time 5? Considering only the information at Time 4 suggests that Harry is higher risk than the other two. Considering prior assessments suggests that Tom is the highest risk. How then should evaluators appropriately integrate present and past evaluations?

The short answer is we don't know. Although a number of potentially change-able factors have been reliably associated with recidivism (e.g. intimacy deficits), we know very little about how changes in such variables should be considered to change estimations of risk. I will, however, provide concepts that are worth considering when broaching this question.

Stability of the Characteristic

Characteristics vary in their stability across time, and in the stability of their relationships with recidivism. Some degree of stability is required in order for there to be an association between the characteristic and subsequent recidivism. If the characteristic is of short duration and risk is only increased when the factor is

Table 2.2   Three hypothetical patterns of change

	Time 1	Time 2	Time 3	Time 4	Time 5
Tom	8	9	8	2	?
Dick	2	3	2	3	?
Harry	2	2	1	5	?

Note: Hypothetical scores on "defiant hostility", rated from 1 to 10, with 10 indicating "extremely defiant, hostile".

present at the time of the offence (e.g. intoxication), then the most recent assessment should provide the most information. If the link with recidivism is indirect (e.g. history of conflicts in intimate relationships) or the characteristic is highly stable, then predictions are most likely to be accurate when they consider the offenders' baseline functioning.

Baseline Level of Functioning

Offenders will vary as to their "typical" level of functioning. One of the important questions concerns the length of time required in order to establish a baseline, a question that is open to empirical investigation. Consider a study that conducted monthly assessments of "hostility" over a period of ten years. All things being equal, it is likely that the most recent assessment would be the most informative, followed by the previous, then the one before that. Eventually, consideration of the nth prior assessment would provide no new information. For rapidly changing risk factors (acute dynamic predictors), the current month's evaluation would be the most informative. For highly stable factors, the most recent assessment may be less informative than an average of the offender's functioning in preceding months or years. It is even possible that the first few assessments may provide the most valid information, with all subsequent assessments contaminated by response bias or other artefacts. For highly stable factors, any current deviation from baseline level of functioning is likely due to measurement error or temporary transient factors. If the attribute is highly stable, then an unusual reading is likely to revert back to baseline levels prior to the opportunity to recidivate.

From studies of habit change (e.g. smoking), we know that relapse is most likely in the first few months following cessation, and that there are relatively few new cases of relapse after two years of abstinence (Krall, Garvey & Garcia 2002). It is likely that many other behaviours follow a similar pattern in that several years are required to generate a new baseline.

Reversibility of Change

Once an individual has changed, how easy is it for the individual to revert back to previous modes of functioning? The reversibility of change is highly related to the stability of the characteristic, but the concepts are not identical. It is possible for a highly stable feature to change quickly to a new level (e.g. consider the effects of serious injury on physical performance). For most criminogenic features, however, there are few barriers to reverting back to prior ways of functioning. Consequently, offenders' recent changes are typically viewed with suspicion.

Deviant versus Non-deviant Levels of Functioning

Most problematic behaviour exists along a continuum. For some criminogenic needs, it is possible to specify a non-arbitrary distinction between problematic and acceptable functioning. Change within deviant or within non-deviant levels of functioning may have less significance than changes between levels. For example, consider deviant sexual interests indexed by a ratio of deviant to non-deviant arousal (measured in mm change in penis circumference; Howes, 2003). If the non-deviant arousal remains constant at 30 mm, a reduction in arousal to children from 40 mm to 20 mm would be more meaningful than a reduction from 60 mm to 40 mm.

IMPLICATIONS FOR RESEARCH

One important line of research would be to examine the stability of dynamic risk factors (with or without intervention). For evaluators, definitions of change (e.g. improvement during treatment) need to include some criteria for establishing the stability of the observed changes. If the observed changes are highly stable, then it would be possible for the recent assessments to completely "write over" previous assessments. Most people, however, are unlikely to completely escape from their past actions, although relapses into deviant levels of functioning can become increasingly rare over time.

One common paradigm for identifying dynamic risk factors is to examine whether post-treatment evaluations predict better than pre-treatment evaluations (e.g. Hanson, Steffy & Gauthier, 1992; Quinsey, Khanna & Malcolm, 1998). Although interesting, such designs are poorly matched to the clinical task. The basic task of prediction is to determine the probability that the characteristics necessary for sexual offending will be present at some point in the future when the opportunities for offending are also present. Clinicians need to consider past and present functioning, but the fundamental task of predicting future sexual crimes requires judgements concerning the offender's typical or baseline level of functioning in the months and years after treatment has been completed. Estimating the re-emergence or persistence of criminogenic needs is quite different from knowing how the offender is doing in the last treatment session.

In principle, evaluations made post-treatment should be more accurate than pre-treatment evaluations because more information is available. In practice, however, post-treatment evaluations have poor predictive accuracy (Hanson & Morton-Bourgon, 2004). It may be that the evaluators conducting the post-treatment assessments would be equally poor at assessing recidivism risk pre-treatment, but it is also possible that evaluators give undue importance to recent within-treatment behaviour. Although most post-treatment risk assessments have little relationship with recidivism, there are examples in which post-treatment evaluations provided moderate levels of predictive accuracy (Beech, Erikson, Friendship & Ditchfield, 2001, d = 0.50; Marques, Day, Wiederanders & Nelson, 2002, d = 0.55). These studies examined highly structured approaches to risk assessment in which the criteria for improvement were empirically based and objectively recorded. Given that structured, empirically based risk assessments are frequently superior to unguided clinical judgement, it is likely that increasing structure could improve the validity of post-treatment evaluations.

CONCLUSIONS

Dynamic factors provide the direction for advancing both the science and practice of risk assessment. A number of promising dynamic factors have been identified, and more will be discovered. Although we know that changeable factors, such as victim access and sexual preoccupations, contribute information not captured by purely static factors, little is known about how to combine static, stable and acute factors into an overall evaluation. Static and stable factors are correlated, which means that the degree of risk suggested by static factors will typically agree with the degree of risk suggested by the stable factors. Questions arise, however, when static and stable risk factors disagree. Given the solid research base establishing the validity of static risk factors, prudent evaluators will still rely heavily on static risk factors (e.g. age, the number of prior offences) for assessing long-term recidivism potential. For many questions (e.g. conditional release), evaluators must use dynamic factors even if the research evidence is inadequate because only changeable factors can address questions concerning change.

With increased scientific understanding, static factors will become less and less important. When evaluators are able to accurately identify the causes of recidivism (i.e. criminogenic needs, triggers), the practise of purely mechanical prediction using static factors will become a historical footnote.

AUTHOR NOTES

I would like to thank Jim Bonta and Andrew Harris for shaping my ideas about dynamic risk factors. The views expressed are those of the author and are not necessarily those of Public Safety and Emergency Preparedness Canada.

REFERENCES

Abel, G.G., Jordon, A., Hand, C.G., Holland, L.A. & Phipps, A. (2001). Classification models of child molesters utilizing the Abel Assessment for sexual interest. *Child Abuse and Neglect*, **25**, 703–18.

Andrews, D.A. & Bonta, J. (2003). *The Psychology of Criminal Conduct*, 3rd edn. Cincinnati: Anderson.

Beech, A., Erikson, M., Friendship, C. & Ditchfield, J. (2001). *A Six-year Follow-up of Men going through Probation-based Sex Offender Treatment Programmes* (Findings #144). London, UK: Home Office.

Beech, A.R., Fisher, D.D. & Thornton, D. (2003). Risk assessment of sex offenders. *Professional Psychology: Research and Practice*, **34**, 339–52.

Beech, A. & Ward, T. (2004). The integration of etiology and risk in sexual offenders: a theoretical framework. *Aggression and Violent Behavior*, **10**, 31–63.

Caspi, A., Moffit, T.E., Silva, P.A., Stouthamer-Loeber, M., Krueger, R.F. & Schmutte, P.S. (1994). Are some people crime-prone? Replications of the personality-crime relationship across countries, genders, races, and methods. *Criminology*, **32**, 163–95.

Cohen, J. (1988). *Statistical Power Analysis for the Behavioral Sciences*, 2nd edn. Hillsdale, NJ: Lawrence Erlbaum.

Cortoni, F. & Marshall, W.L. (2001). Sex as a coping strategy and its relationship to juvenile sexual history and intimacy in sexual offenders. *Sexual Abuse: A Journal of Research and Treatment*, **13**, 27–43.

Gottfredson, M.R. & Hirschi, T. (1990). *A General Theory of Crime*. Stanford, CA: Stanford University Press.

Gray, N.S., MacCulloch, M., Smith, J. & Snowdon, R.J. (2002, September). Abnormal associations between children and sex in paedophiles as measured by the covert association task (CAT). Presentation at the 7th Biennial Conference of the International Association for the Treatment of Sexual Offenders, Vienna.

Hanson, R.K. (1997). *The Development of a Brief Actuarial Risk Scale for Sexual Offense Recidivism.* (User Report 97–04). Ottawa: Department of the Solicitor General of Canada.

Hanson, R.K. & Bussière, M.T. (1998). Predicting relapse: a meta-analysis of sexual offender recidivism studies. *Journal of Consulting and Clinical Psychology*, **66**, 348–62.

Hanson, R.K. & Harris, A.J.R. (2000). Where should we intervene? Dynamic predictors of sex offense recidivism. *Criminal Justice and Behavior*, **27**, 6–35.

Hanson, R.K. & Morton-Bourgon, K. (2004). Predictors of sexual recidivism: an updated meta-analysis. Corrections Policy User Report No. 2004-02. Ottawa: Corrections Policy, Public Safety and Emergency Preparedness Canada.

Hanson, R.K., Scott, H. & Steffy, R.A. (1995). A comparison of child molesters and non-sexual criminals: risk predictors and long-term recidivism. *Journal of Research in Crime and Delinquency*, **32**, 325–37.

Hanson, R.K., Steffy, R.A. & Gauthier, R. (1992). *Long-term Follow-up of Child Molesters: Risk Prediction and Treatment Outcome.* (User Report No. 1992-02.) Ottawa: Corrections Branch, Ministry of the Solicitor General of Canada.

Hanson, R.K. & Thornton, D. (2000). Improving risk assessments for sex offenders: a comparison of three actuarial scales. *Law and Human Behavior*, **24**, 119–36.

Harris, A.J.R. & Hanson, R.K. (2003). The Dynamic Supervision Project: improving the community supervision of sex offenders. *Corrections Today*, **65**, 60–2, 64.

Howes, R.J. (2003). Circumferential change scores in phallometric assessment: normative data. *Sexual Abuse: A Journal of Research and Treatment*, **15**, 365–75.

Kafka, M.P. (2003). Sex offending and sexual appetite: the clinical and theoretical relevance of hypersexual desire. *International Journal of Offender Therapy and Comparative Criminology*, **47**, 439–51.

Krall, E.A., Garvey, A.J. & Garcia, R.I. (2002). Smoking relapse after 2 years of abstinence: findings from the VA Normative Aging Study. *Nicotine and Tobacco Research*, **4**, 95–100.

Langan, P.A., Schmitt, E.L. & Durose, M.R. (2003). Recidivism of sex offenders released from prison in 1984. Bureau of Justice Statistics NCJ 198281. Washington, DC: US Department of Justice.

Marques, J.K., Day, D.M., Wiederanders, M. & Nelson, C. (2002, October). Main effects and beyond: new findings from California's Sex Offender Treatment and Evaluation Project (SOTEP). Paper presented at the 21st annual conference of the Association for the Treatment of Sexual Abusers, Montreal.

Marshall, P. (1997). The prevalence of convictions for sexual offending. Research Finding No. 55. Research and Statistics Directorate. London: Home Office.

Marshall, W.L. (1989). Invited essay: Intimacy, loneliness and sexual offenders. *Behaviour Research and Therapy*, **27**, 491–503.

McKibben, A., Proulx, J. & Lusignan, R. (1994). Relationship between conflict, affect and deviant sexual behaviors in rapists and child molesters. *Behaviour Research and Therapy*, **32**, 571–5.

Piaget, J. & Inhelder, B. (1969). *The Psychology of the Child*. New York: Basic Books.

Pithers, W.D., Kashima, K., Cumming, G.F., Beal, L.S. & Buell, M. (1988). Relapse prevention of sexual aggression. In R. Prentky & V. Quinsey (eds), *Human Sexual Aggression: Current Perspectives* (pp. 244–60). New York: New York Academy of Sciences.

Proulx, J., McKibben, A. & Lusignan, R. (1996). Relationship between affective components and sexual behaviors in sexual aggressors. *Sexual Abuse: A Journal of Research and Treatment*, **8**, 279–89.

Quinsey, V.L., Harris, G.T., Rice, M.E. & Cormier, C.A. (1998). *Violent Offenders: Appraising and Managing Risk.* Washington, DC: American Psychological Association.

Quinsey, V.L., Khanna, A. & Malcolm, P.B. (1998). A retrospective evaluation of the Regional Treatment Centre Sex Offender Treatment Program. *Journal of Interpersonal Violence,* **13**, 621–44.

Smith, P. & Waterman, M. (2003). Processing bias for aggression words in forensic and nonforensic samples. *Cognition and Emotion,* **17**, 681–701.

Smith, P. & Waterman, M. (2004). Processing bias for sexual material: the emotional Stroop and sexual offenders. *Sexual Abuse: A Journal of Research and Treatment,* **16**, 163–71.

Stroop, J.R. (1935). Studies of interference in serial verbal reactions. *Journal of Experimental Psychology,* **18**, 643–62.

Thornton, D. (2002). Constructing and testing a framework for dynamic risk assessment. *Sexual Abuse: A Journal of Research and Treatment,* **14**, 139–53.

Ward, T., Hudson, S.M. & Marshall, W.L. (1994). The abstinence violation effect in child molesters. *Behaviour Research and Therapy,* **32**, 431–7.

Wertz, J.M. & Sayette, M.A. (2001). Effects of smoking opportunity on attentional bias in smokers. *Psychology of Addictive Behaviors,* **15**, 268–71.

Wilson, R.J. (1999). Emotional congruence in sexual offenders against children. *Sexual Abuse: A Journal of Research and Treatment,* **11**, 33–47.

Chapter 3

DIAGNOSTIC PROBLEMS WITH SEXUAL OFFENDERS

WILLIAM L. MARSHALL

Rockwood Psychological Services, Kingston, Ontario, Canada

Diagnostic issues are thought to be relevant to the conceptualization of the problems presented by sexual offenders. Some clinicians and researchers consider it necessary (or they are required) to apply a diagnosis to their sexual offending clients. Such diagnoses typically derive from the application of criteria outlined in one or another version of the *Diagnostic and Statistical Manual (DSM)* of the American Psychiatric Association. In the research literature, however, things are even more complicated with many reports using the label "pedophile" to describe *all* child molesters even in the absence of the application of diagnostic criteria, while others use "child molesters" without bothering to evaluate how many meet *DSM* criteria for pedophilia. Furthermore, some distinguish "pedophiles" (those who molest prepubescent children) from "hebephiles" (those who molest post-pubescent children). Obviously it would be preferable if all clinicians and researchers used the same terminology and *DSM* categories are certainly one option. The question this chapter raises is, does the diagnostic manual provide a sound basis for a universally agreed upon nomenclature, particularly one that might guide treatment?

PROBLEM-SPECIFIC DIAGNOSES

The current versions of *DSM* (i.e. *DSM-IV* and *DSM-IV-TR*, American Psychiatric Association, 1994; 2000) list diagnoses that are directly relevant to persons who sexually offend. In this section, specific diagnoses relevant to two categories of sexual offending behaviors will be examined. The application of *DSM* criteria to child molesters and sadists will be the focus, although similar problems beset other types of sexual offending behaviors (e.g. exhibitionism, frottage, voyeurism, bestiality, telephone scatologia, necrophilia). In particular the *DSM* has no category for men who sexually assault adults (i.e. rapists). The authors of the *Diagnostic and*

Sexual Offender Treatment: Controversial Issues. Edited by W.L. Marshall, Y.M. Fernandez, L.E. Marshall and G.A. Serran. © 2006 John Wiley & Sons, Ltd.

Statistical Manual have resisted pleas to have rape included (Abel & Rouleau, 1990), which appears to have forced clinicians into categorizing persistent rapists as "paraphilia NOS" (Doren, 2002; Levenson, 2003). This is definitely not a satisfactory solution to the problem as the *DSM* offers no criteria under paraphilia NOS for diagnosing rape.

On all aspects of functioning that have been examined, sexual offenders of any particular type have been shown to vary quite considerably. As a result various efforts have been made to reduce variability by grouping sexual offenders into categories of offenders having similar features. Knight and Prentky's (1990) work exemplifies an empirical approach to classification, which, although elegant, has not received broad application. The *DSM*, on the other hand, enjoys almost universal use, and in many clinics its application to all clients is required.

For any classification system to be useful it must be shown that the categories (or diagnoses) can be applied reliably (Nelson-Gray, 1991). The primary reliability of concern here is across diagnosticians; that is, different diagnosticians examining the same client, and having the same information available to them, should come to the same diagnostic conclusion. The authors of *DSM* conduct field trials to determine interdiagnostician reliability of the various diagnoses (see e.g. American Psychiatric Association, 1997). Unfortunately the conditions under which these field trials are conducted are likely to artificially inflate estimates of reliability. What is of most concern is the reliability with which diagnoses are applied in actual clinical practice. In attempting to determine acceptable levels of reliability for decisions having an important impact on people's lives, psychometricians state that levels of interrater agreement should be at least at the level indicated by a kappa coefficient of 0.90 (i.e. above 90% interrater agreement), while more trivial decisions still need a kappa of at least 0.60 (Hair, Anderson, Tatham & Black, 1998; Murphy & Davidshofer, 1998).

In the case of the paraphilias that describe sexual offenders, specific interdiagnostician reliabilities were not reported for *DSM-III* (American Psychological Association, 1980). O'Donohue, Regev and Hagstrom (2000) note that *DSM-III* reports a kappa coefficient (an index of agreement that corrects for chance) of 0.92 for the psychosexual disorders. While this is quite high, it covers all such disorders, including sexual dysfunctions and paraphilias, and was based on only seven cases (O'Donohue & Geer, 1993). In a second part of the trial only five cases were employed and the kappa coefficient fell to just 0.75. These problems notwithstanding, the authors of *DSM-IV* (American Psychological Association, 1997) did not conduct further field trials to determine the reliability of the paraphilias apparently because they believed the diagnoses remained essentially the same (see comments, American Psychiatric Association, 1996, p. 1133). In fact the diagnostic criteria for all the relevant paraphilias were changed from *DSM-III* and *DSM-III-R* to *DSM-IV* and, in any case, reliabilities were unknown for the paraphilias in the earlier versions of the manual.

One of the most relevant studies of diagnostic reliability was conducted by Levenson (2004). She examined the interdiagnostician reliability of four specific paraphilias, as well as the presence of any paraphilia. Utilizing a sample of 295 cases drawn from the entire sample of cases referred between July 2000 and June 2001 to clinicians in Florida for sexually violent predator (SVP) civil commitment consideration, Levenson compared diagnoses assigned to each case by at least two different clinicians. Thus, Levenson's study is an examination of the reliability of actual diagnostic practices under conditions (potential for SVP commitment) where the diagnosis has extremely important real-life implications for both the subject being examined and the public at large. No doubt the diagnosticians also saw their task as very serious and one would hope they exercised great care in arriving at their conclusions. Unfortunately the resultant estimates of interdiagnostician reliability fell far short of acceptable standards. For pedophilia agreement was low (kappa = 0.65), while for sexual sadism (kappa = 0.30), exhibitionism (kappa = 0.47) and paraphilia NOS (kappa = 0.36) the levels of agreement were unacceptable by any standard. Even in the application of any paraphilic diagnosis agreement was unacceptably low (kappa = 0.47).

As can be seen, none of the reliability coefficients meets acceptable standards for important decisions. Levenson's (2004) findings are an indictment not only of *DSM-IV* diagnoses, as they are applied in practice, but also of the SVP civil commitment process in so far as these processes rely on the accuracy of diagnoses (Doren, 2002).

Pedophilia

First, it is important to note that the *DSM* diagnosis of pedophilia is not meant to apply to all persons who sexually molest children. Indeed, as early as *DSM-III* (American Psychiatric Association, 1980) it was noted that "Isolated sexual acts with children do not warrant the diagnosis of pedophilia" (p. 271). Until the publication of *DSM-IV* (American Psychiatric Association, 1994) it was quite clear that the diagnosis of pedophilia applied only to those child molesters who had "recurrent intense sexual urges and sexually arousing fantasies involving sexual activity with a prepubescent child or children" (American Psychiatric Association, 1987, p. 85). This has been consistently interpreted in publications as referring to a persistent sexual interest in (often seen as a sexual preference for) children (Freund, 1987).

DSM-IV, however, added to the earlier criteria of fantasies and urges, the specification "or behaviors involving sexual activity with a prepubescent child or children" (American Psychiatric Association, 1994; p. 528) and this is repeated in *DSM-IV-TR* (American Psychiatric Association, 2000). This significantly complicates matters. Previous criteria (i.e. simply recurrent fantasies or urges) presented serious enough problems of their own in that the only person who could know the client was experiencing such recurrent fantasies or urges was the client himself, yet it is clear that sexual offenders are typically reticent about sharing such information.

The characteristic solution to sexual offenders' reticence, or dissimulation, has been either to infer the presence of fantasies and urges, or to phallometrically assess the clients' sexual interests. In fact, Freund (Freund, 1987; Freund & Blanchard, 1989) specifically employs phallometric evaluations to diagnose pedophilia, where arousal to child stimuli greater than arousal to adult stimuli is the criterion for the diagnosis. Barbaree and Seto (1997) agree with this, saying that "The diagnosis of pedophilia can be made from (1) the individual's self-report ... (2) psychometric testing ... and (3) phallometric testing" (p. 177). Since not all child molesters display arousal to children at phallometric assessment, Freund and

Blanchard (1989) declare that these results indicate who is or who is not a pedophile. On the other hand, since we cannot know in advance who is or who is not a pedophile among a group of child molesters, there is no way to validate or disconfirm Freund and Blanchard's claim. Unfortunately for these claims, phallometry has not yet demonstrated that it meets reasonable psychometric standards (Marshall & Fernandez, 2003). Until it does phallometry can hardly provide the basis for diagnoses.

As noted, the changes with *DSM-IV* to include actual enactments of sexual activities with children in the criteria for pedophilia have not necessarily eased the diagnostic decision. Stating the criteria in terms of "sexually arousing fantasies, sexual urges, *or* behaviors ..." (italics added) means that all men who recurrently molest children are pedophiles whether or not they have recurrent fantasies or urges, or display arousal to children at phallometric testing. This would certainly reduce uncertainty about the diagnosis providing all diagnosticians adhere to this interpretation of the criteria. O'Donohue *et al.* (2000) raise interesting questions about just what is meant by "behavior" in *DSM-IV* criteria. They offer the example of a man who becomes a school bus driver to feed his sexual fantasies of children. Does this behavior, they ask, meet criteria for pedophilia? What if he never acts on his fuelled fantasies; is he nevertheless a pedophile? O'Donohue *et al.* also note the persistent use of child pornography for masturbatory purposes. If such a man never actually offends, is he a pedophile? Fortunately, *DSM-IV-TR* deals with this problem. In this latest version of *DSM*, Criterion B states: "The person has acted on these sexual urges, or the sexual urges or fantasies cause marked distress or interpersonal difficulties" (American Psychiatric Association, 2000, p. 572). Thus a person can have sexual fantasies of children without acting on them and still be a pedophile. Not surprisingly, very few such people appear at clinics. Adding the term "behavior" to the criteria, however, does not appear to have influenced the practice of all clinicians. In fact descriptions of pedophilia appearing in the literature since the publication of *DSM-IV* appear to retain the idea that the presence of fantasies and urges (and/or deviant sexual preferences) is critical to the diagnosis (see, for example, Barbaree & Seto, 1997). In these studies some men who have molested children are said not to be pedophiles.

The criterion in *DSM-IV-TR* that the fantasies, urges or behaviors must be "over a period of at least 6 months" seems arbitrary. If a man has molested several children (suppose eight to ten children) all within a two- to three-month period, is this insufficient for a diagnosis of pedophilia? In fact, how many victims are required for the diagnosis or is it simply repetitive behaviors? If it is the latter, then most incest offenders should be diagnosed as pedophiles since they repeatedly offend (often against the same child) over many years. Yet diagnosticians appear reluctant to identify incest offenders as pedophilic. These problems concern not only the six months criterion but also the requirement that the behaviors be recurrent. As for recurrent fantasies and urges, Marshall (1997) reports that after gaining the confidence of his child molesting clients, only 60% of the nonfamilial offenders and 75% of the incest offenders admitted having recurrent fantasies and urges. Many of these fantasies and urges only occurred immediately prior to an offence rather than being ongoing. It seems very unlikely that a man could commit a sexual offense against a child in the absence of at least transitory urges or thoughts about the act. This might essentially mean that if behaviors remain as criteria in the diagnostic manual, then the inclusion of fantasies and urges is redundant.

The criterion of "intense sexual urges and sexually arousing fantasies ... " also raises problems. O'Donohue *et al.* (2000) inquire: "On what dimension is intensity measured ... ?" (p. 100). They raise the issue of whether an intense fantasy is more vivid or more arousing than other fantasies. In addition, what are we to make of a man who has persistent fantasies that are of moderate or low intensity (however this is measured)?

DSM-IV criteria identify fantasies, urges and behaviors with prepubescent children only as diagnostic of pedophilia. One problem that faces diagnosticians then is determining how old the victim was at the time of the abuse. Official information is not always available to the clinician on this issue, in which case they must rely on the offender's report. Many offenders seem to think that if they claim the victim was post-pubescent then this will make them seem less deviant. Of course pubescence does not onset at the same age for all children so the diagnostic manual suggests "generally age 13 years or younger". Recent evidence on changes in the onset of puberty in girls suggests the average age of onset to be closer to age ten years (Bancroft, in press). Does this mean that if the victim is 11 years of age but has already passed puberty then the offender is not, by these criteria, a pedophile? Also what about the offenders who began abusing children when the victims were eight or nine years old but continued molesting them until the victims reported it when they were in their mid-teens? Is it the age when the child identifies the abuse or the age at which it started? In fact, an offender who began molesting an eight-year-old and continued molesting this child into adolescence would, according to the diagnostic manual's criteria, be a pedophile until the victim pubesced after which he would not meet criteria for any disorder. This, of course, is absurd.

The most important implication for clinical practice of this requirement that the victims be prepubescent, is that men who molest children in the age range 13 to 15 years do not meet diagnostic criteria for any paraphilia even when their offending is recurrent and involves fantasies and urges. Levenson (2004) reports that in the state of Florida clinicians diagnose such offenders as "paraphilia NOS". This does not seem appropriate in terms of diagnostic practice but it may be a clinical necessity for a treatment provider to receive funding. Levenson reports that this characteristically happens in assessments for SVP civil commitment evaluations. Such commitments in most, if not all, jurisdictions require a *DSM* diagnosis for commitment to be successfully applied (Doren, 2002). Such pressures disrupt the proper application of diagnostic procedures not only in these cases but also in the case of adult rapes where, as we have seen, the same diagnosis (paraphilia NOS) is frequently used.

As we have seen, the reliability of the diagnosis of pedophilia across diagnosticians is less than adequate. Levenson (2004) reports an interdiagnostician reliability (kappa = 0.65) that was slightly above the level considered by psychometricians to be minimal (kappa = 0.60) for relatively unimportant decisions. Levenson's diagnoses were done by clinicians who knew that at least one other clinician would be diagnosing the same client, and where their diagnosis would be examined and likely challenged in court. It seems likely that these conditions would cause clinicians to be very careful in arriving at a diagnosis and should, therefore, be optimal conditions for maximizing interdiagnostician agreement. Yet the observed agreement does not come close to acceptable standards (kappa = 0.90) required for a very important decision; namely, whether or not the client meets criteria for civil commitment as a sexually violent predator. Levenson's data, considered in the context of O'Donohue *et al.*'s (2000) appraisal of the reliability of the *DSM-IV* diagnosis of pedophilia, casts serious doubts on the value of this diagnosis and raises concerns about the wisdom of the *DSM-IV* authors in deciding not to examine the diagnostic reliability of the specific paraphilias.

Finally, in examining a sample of 138 child molesters, Wilson, Abracen, Picheca, Malcolm and Prinzo (2003) found that a *DSM-IV* diagnosis of pedophilia bore no relationship to long-term recidivism. Thus the diagnosis does not achieve one of the purposes that should be expected of such a system; namely, indicating likely prognosis.

Sexual Sadism

DSM-IV-TR defines sexual sadism as "recurrent, intense sexually arousing fantasies, sexual urges, or behaviors involving acts (real, not simulated) in which the psychological or physical suffering (including humiliation) of the victim is sexually exciting to the person" (American Psychiatric Association, 2000, p. 574). Various aspects of this definition (e.g. the meaning of "recurrent", "intense") have been discussed above in the context of the diagnosis of pedophilia. The primary problem with the interpretation of *DSM* criteria for sexual sadism concerns the identification of the fantasies, urges or acts with sexual excitement in the client. Such excitement is known only to the client and it seems unlikely that most of these offenders would admit to being aroused by sadistic acts.

In their review of the literature on sexual sadism, Marshall and Kennedy (2003) noted that the reliance of *DSM-IV* criteria for sexual sadism on the clinician making inferences (in this case about an offender's motivation for causing the victim of his assault to suffer or be humiliated) represents an oddity in the changes from *DSM-II* to *DSM-III* and its descendants. Beginning with *DSM-III*, the manual's authors moved away from reliance on subjective inferences by making criteria for diagnoses more explicitly observable. Just why the paraphilias generally, and sexual sadism specifically, continue to require diagnosticians to make inferential leaps is unclear when behavioral criteria could readily be specified. In fact, as Marshall and Kennedy (2003) showed, researchers examining sexual sadists typically set their own criteria, which for the most part involve observable features such as: degree and type of victim injury; degree of forcefulness; enslavement; abduction; bondage; trophy collections; evidence of control and humiliation, torture or cruelty; mutilation; and various other crime scene data as well as confessions by the client. Unfortunately, each researcher typically establishes criteria that have unique features or are a unique combination of some of the above mentioned features. This makes it well-nigh impossible to draw general inferences from the extant literature on sexual sadists but, most importantly, it points to a serious diagnostic problem.

Given this diversity of criteria, it is not surprising that the diagnostic reliability of sexual sadism is unsatisfactory. Note particularly that of all the paraphilias, sexual sadism is the one likely to carry the most serious implications for both the client and the public so that the highest standards of reliability should be required (i.e. kappa = 0.90). Levenson's (2004) observation that interdiagnostician reliability is unacceptably low for sexual sadism (kappa = 0.30) is in line with observations made by Marshall and his colleagues. In their first study, Marshall, Kennedy and Yates (2002) examined the actual clinical application of the diagnosis. They reviewed the files of all sexual offenders incarcerated in Ontario federal penitentiaries for whom a psychiatric evaluation had been conducted within a ten-year period. Marshall *et al.* compared the offense features, self-reports and phallometric data of those who were diagnosed as sexual sadists with those who were evaluated as having another diagnosis or who were judged not to have any diagnosable disorder. On almost all features the nonsadists appeared more problem-ridden than the sadists. Table 3.1 lists the features that either differentiated the two groups or did not differentiate them.

As can be seen, six features significantly differentiated the two groups with all six indicating that the nonsadists were more problematic than the sadists. The non-sadists were far more likely to have beaten or tortured their victims, their offenses had more sadistic features, and they were more sexually aroused by nonsexual violence toward a victim. Oddly enough more of the so-called sadists displayed far greater sexual arousal to normative consenting sex than did the nonsadists. Marshall, Kennedy and Yates (2002) concluded that "the nonsadists actually displayed more of the putatively sadistic features than did those diagnosed as sadists" (p. 310). They note that these results reflect badly on the diagnostic practice of labelling sexual offenders as sadists or not within Correctional Service of Canada prisons. Since the diagnosis of sexual sadism decreases the likelihood of the release of the offender, whereas its absence may increase the offender's chance of release, these results have very important implications for both the rights of the offenders and the protection of the public.

As this study was a retrospective analysis of actual diagnostic practices under conditions that might have underestimated reliability, Marshall, Kennedy, Yates and Serran (2002) designed a study similar to *DSM's* field trials. Detailed information (offense features, life history, self-reports, psychological and phallometric test data) was extracted on 12 clients who were among those evaluated in the earlier study. Six clients were randomly chosen from each of the sadists and nonsadists (so diagnosed by the clinicians in the prior study). Detailed vignettes on these 12 subjects were provided to 15 psychiatrists, each of whom was considered to be a forensic expert with extensive experience. Experts were asked to complete several tasks, the most important of which was to determine which of the subjects in the vignettes were, or were not, sexual sadists. Agreement across these diagnosticians was extremely poor (kappa = 0.14) casting further serious doubt on the reliability of the diagnosis.

Marshall, Kennedy, Yates and Serran (2002) also asked the experts to rate (on a scale of 1 to 4) the importance of various features in making their diagnosis of sexual sadism. Only four features were consistently rated as either important (rating of 3) or crucial (rating of 4): (1) exerts control, domination, or power over victims; (2) humiliates or degrades victims; (3) is cruel or tortures victims; and (4) evidence from phallometry or self-reports of deviant sexual interests. While these features essentially reflect what most reports in the literature include in their criteria for

Table 3.1 Characteristics of sexual sadists and nonsadists

Features that failed to differentiate			*Features that did differentiate*		
	Sadists	Nonsadists		Sadists	Nonsadists
Offense features			***Offense features***		
Abduction/confinement	22.0*	27.8	Beating	24.4*	61.1 (p = 0.008)
Humiliation	12.2	5.6	Torture	9.8	38.9 (p = 0.013)
Bondage	29.3	22.2			
Strangle/suffocate	36.6	38.9	***Phallometric results***		
Mutilation	7.3	5.6	Nonsexual violence	0	16.7 (p = 0.03)
Murder	29.3	27.8	Consenting adults	24.4	0 (p = 0.02)
Post mortem damage	4.9	5.6			
Bizarre sexual acts	9.8	5.6	***Composite scores***		
			Sadism in offense	80.5	100 (p = 0.04)
Client admits			Sadism in phallometrics	17.1	44.4 (p = 0.03)
Sadistic fantasies	12.2	11.1			
Sadistic acts	9.8	11.1			
Violent sexual fantasies	12.2	27.8			
Phallometric results					
Rape	24.4	44.4			
Sexual violence	31.7	33.3			
Composite scores					
Sadism in self-reports	51.2	38.9			

Note: * Percentage of each group where feature was present.
Source: Adapted from Marshall, Kennedy & Yates (2002) Issues concerning the reliability and validity of the diagnosis of sexual sadism applied in prison settings. *Sexual Abuse: A Journal of Research and Treatment,* **14**, 310–11.

sexual sadism, Marshall *et al.* note that except for cruelty and torture, these features are common in all sexual assaults. For example, numerous authors report that the exercise of power and control by the offender characterizes most if not all rapes (Amir, 1971; Brownmiller, 1975; Groth, 1979). Child molesters are similarly in control of their young victims (Frosh, 1993; Groth, Hobson & Gray, 1982), and this exercise of control appears to be important for child molesters (Howells, 1979). Similarly, Darke (1990) demonstrated that one of the primary aims of rape, as described by the rapists themselves, is to humiliate and degrade their victims. Also among those sexual offenders who do display deviant sexual arousal at phallometric testing (Marshall & Fernandez, 2003) the sadistic rapists appear no more deviant than do nonsadistic rapists (Seto & Kuban, 1996).

CONCLUSIONS

Although only two sexual offender related diagnoses (pedophilia and sexual sadism) have been examined here, the inadequacy of the criteria and the associated poor reliability of these two diagnoses suggest likely diagnostic problems with the other paraphilias relevant to sexual offending. In fact, in terms of diagnostic considerations (adequacy and clarity of criteria, reliability issues) limited research is available on any of the paraphilias, with pedophilia and sexual sadism being the two diagnoses receiving the greatest (albeit limited) attention. Levenson's (2004) data shows that none of the paraphilias were reliably diagnosed, and the data provided by Marshall and his colleagues (Marshall, Kennedy & Yates, 2002; Marshall, Kennedy, Yates & Serran, 2002) further calls into question the reliability of the paraphilias. Unless diagnostic criteria are reliable, then questions about their validity and utility are moot.

Many authors have called for a replacement of the categorical nature of *DSM* diagnoses with a dimensional system (Livesley, Schroeder, Jackson & Jang, 1994; Widiger & Costa, 1994). Specifically, Marshall and Kennedy (2003) suggest "that a description of the acts of sexual offenders, along various dimensions, would be more useful than an attempt to categorize these offenders" (p. 15). They propose that, for rapists, clinicians should rate the offenders on dimensions of, for example, power, forcefulness, inflicted injury and humiliating acts. Similarly, child molesters could be rated on these same dimensions as well as the degree of planning, impulsivity and sexual intrusiveness. No doubt other features of sexual offenders would be revealed as relevant by a detailed survey of the research literature. Such dimensional ratings should provide a better guide to assessors, treatment providers, researchers, theoreticians and the courts. They should also be more relevant to the prediction of long-term outcome. It should also be far easier to generate reliable dimensional ratings since all the dimensions involve observable behaviors. Phallometric responses, where available, should also be included.

Given the evidence and concerns presented in this chapter, either the *DSM* authors need to radically change their approach with respect to the paraphilias, or clinicians dealing with sexual offenders need to persuade their sources of funding that *DSM* diagnoses are not helpful in designing appropriate treatment or in making prognoses.

REFERENCES

Abel, G.G. & Rouleau, J.L. (1990). The nature and extent of sexual assault. In W.L. Marshall, D.R. Laws & H.E. Barbaree (eds), *Handbook of Sexual Assault: Issues, Theories, and Treatment of the Offender* (pp. 9–21). New York: Plenum Press.

American Psychiatric Association (1980). *Diagnostic and Statistical Manual of Mental Disorders*, 3rd edn. Washington, DC: American Psychiatric Association.

American Psychiatric Association (1987). *Diagnostic and Statistical Manual of Mental Disorders*, 3rd edn rev. Washington, DC: American Psychiatric Association.

American Psychiatric Association (1994). *Diagnostic and Statistical Manual of Mental Disorders*, 4th edn. Washington, DC: American Psychiatric Association.

American Psychiatric Association (1996). *Diagnostic and Statistical Manual of Mental Disorders*, 4th edn, Sourcebook (Vol. 2). Washington, DC: American Psychiatric Association.

American Psychiatric Association (1997). *Diagnostic and Statistical Manual of Mental Disorders*, 4th edn, Sourcebook (Vol. 3). Washington, DC: American Psychiatric Association.

American Psychiatric Association (2000). *Diagnostic and Statistical Manual of Mental Disorders*, 4th edn text rev. Washington, DC: American Psychiatric Association.

Amir, M. (1971). *Patterns of Forcible Rape*. Chicago: University of Chicago Press.

Bancroft, J. (in press). The development of human sexuality. In H.E. Barbaree & W.L. Marshall (eds), *The Juvenile Sex Offender*, 2nd edn. New York: Guilford Press.

Barbaree, H.E. & Seto, M.C. (1997). Pedophilia: assessment and treatment. In D.R. Laws & W. O'Donohue (eds), *Sexual Deviance: Theory, Assessment, and Treatment* (pp. 175–93). New York: Guilford Press.

Brownmiller, S. (1975). *Against Our Will: Men, Women, and Rape*. New York: Bantam Books.

Darke, J.L. (1990). Sexual aggression: achieving power through humiliation. In W.L. Marshall, D.R. Laws & H.E. Barbaree (eds), *Handbook of Sexual Assault: Issues, Theories, and Treatment of the Offender* (pp. 55–72). New York: Plenum Press.

Doren, D.M. (2002). *Evaluating Sex Offenders: A Manual for Civil Commitments and Beyond*. Thousand Oaks, CA: Sage Publications.

Freund, K. (1987). Erotic preference in paedophilia. *Behaviour Research and Therapy*, **25**, 339–48.

Freund, K. & Blanchard, R. (1989). Phallometric diagnoses of pedophilia. *Journal of Consulting and Clinical Psychology*, **57**, 100–5.

Frosh, S. (1993). The seeds of masculine sexuality. In J.A. Ussher & C.D. Baker (eds), *Psychological Perspectives on Sexual Problems: New Directions in Theory and Practice* (pp. 41–55). Boston: Routledge Kegan Paul.

Groth, A.N. (1979). *Men who Rape: The Psychology of the Offender*. New York: Plenum Press.

Groth, A.N., Hobson, W.F. & Gray, T.S. (1982). The child molester: clinical observations. In J. Conte & D. Shore (eds), *Social Work and Child Sexual Abuse* (pp. 129–42). New York: Haworth Press.

Hair, J.H., Anderson, R.E., Tatham, R.L. & Black, W.C. (1998). *Multivariate Data Analysis*, 5th edn. Hillside, NJ: Prentice Hall.

Howells, K. (1979). Some meanings of children for pedophiles. In M. Cook & G. Wilson (eds), *Love and Attraction: An International Conference* (pp. 519–26). Oxford: Pergamon Press.

Knight, R.A. & Prentky, R.A. (1990). Classifying sex offenders: the development and corroboration of taxonomic models. In W.L. Marshall, D.R. Laws & H.E. Barbaree (eds), *Handbook of Sexual Assault: Issues, Theories, and Treatment of the Offender* (pp. 23–52). New York: Plenum Press.

Levenson, J.S. (2004). Reliability of sexually violent predator civil commitment criteria. *Law and Human Behavior*, **28**, 357–68.

Livesley, W.J., Schroeder, M.L., Jackson, D.N. & Jang, K.L. (1994). Categorical distinctions in the study of personality disorder: implications for classification. *Journal of Abnormal Psychology*, **103**, 6–17.

Marshall, W.L. (1997). Pedophilia: psychopathology and theory. In D.R. Laws & W. O'Donohue (eds), *Handbook of Sexual Deviance: Theory and Application* (pp. 152–74). New York: Guilford Press.

Marshall, W.L. & Fernandez, Y.M. (2003). *Phallometric Testing with Sexual Offenders*. Brandon, VT: Safer Society Press.

Marshall, W.L. & Kennedy, P. (2003). Sexual sadism in sexual offenders: an elusive diagnosis. *Aggression and Violent Behavior: A Review Journal*, **8**, 1–22.

Marshall, W.L., Kennedy, P. & Yates, P. (2002). Issues concerning the reliability and validity of the diagnosis of sexual sadism applied in prison settings. *Sexual Abuse: A Journal of Research and Treatment*, **14**, 310–11.

Marshall, W.L., Kennedy, P., Yates, P. & Serran, G.A. (2002). Diagnosing sexual sadism in sexual offenders: reliability across diagnosticians. *International Journal of Offender Therapy and Comparative Criminology*, **46**, 668–76.

Murphy, K.R. & Davidshofer, C.O. (1998). *Psychological Testing: Principles and Applications*, 4th edn. Hillside, NJ: Prentice Hall.

Nelson-Gray, R.O. (1991). DSM-IV: Empirical guidelines from psychometrics. *Journal of Abnormal Psychology*, **100**, 308–15.

O'Donohue, W.T. & Geer, J.H. (1993). Research issues in sexual dysfunctions. In W. O'Donohue & J.H. Geer (eds), *Handbook of Sexual Dysfunctions* (pp. 1–14). Boston: Allyn & Bacon.

O'Donohue, W.T., Regev, L.G. & Hagstrom, A. (2000). Problems with the DSM-IV diagnosis of pedophilia. *Sexual Abuse: A Journal of Research and Treatment*, **12**, 95–105.

Seto, M.C. & Kuban, M. (1996). Criterion-related validity of a phallometric test for paraphilic rape and sadism. *Behaviour Research and Therapy*, **34**, 175–83.

Widiger, T.A. & Costa, P.T. (1994). Personality and personality disorders. *Journal of Abnormal Psychology*, **103**, 78–91.

Wilson, R.J., Abracen, J., Picheca, J.E., Malcolm, P.B. & Prinzo, M. (2003, October). Pedophilia: An evaluation of diagnostic and risk management methods. Paper presented at the 23rd Annual Research and Treatment Conference of the Association for the Treatment of Sexual Offenders, St. Louis.

Chapter 4

THE CIVIL COMMITMENT OF SEXUAL OFFENDERS: LESSONS LEARNED

ANITA SCHLANK

The Human Development Center, Duluth, MN, USA

It seemed like a good idea at the time. With high profile cases in the news reporting sexual offenders who re-offended shortly after being released from prison, it seemed sensible to devise a way to continue to incapacitate the most dangerous sexual offenders, especially those who were telling clinicians that they knew they were likely to re-offend. As noted by Shaw and Funderburk (1999), treatment providers in the United States had long been frustrated by their inability to insist that sexual offenders receive treatment prior to their release from prison, and also unable to insist that they remain in treatment long enough to successfully complete it. In addition, while ideally treatment would always be made available in prisons, in fact many states lack comprehensive treatment programs for sexual offenders in their prisons, leading to the problem of untreated sexual offenders returning to the community. For these reasons, the possibility of indeterminately committing the most dangerous untreated offenders to a treatment center seemed like a good idea. It was assumed that the only drawbacks would be the legal challenges that would be faced regarding constitutional issues. However, nobody was quite prepared for the difficulty in accurately identifying the highest risk sexual offenders, the high cost of such treatment centers, or the impediments to treatment that are present once an offender has completed his prison sentence.

HISTORY OF CIVIL COMMITMENT STATUTES

State laws have long allowed the commitment of mentally ill people who pose an imminent danger to others. As early as the 1930s, states attempted to identify sexual offenders who also might be in need of specialized treatment. Statutes, often called Mentally Disordered Sexual Offender (MDSO) statutes were developed. These statutes were intended to identify the most mentally disturbed sexual offenders

Sexual Offender Treatment: Controversial Issues. Edited by W.L. Marshall, Y.M. Fernandez, L.E. Marshall and G.A. Serran. © 2006 John Wiley & Sons, Ltd.

and divert them from the prison system into a treatment program (Held, 1999). There they would be kept until they no longer presented a risk for committing future offenses. While popular, these statutes were the subject of numerous constitutional challenges (LaFond & Winick, 1998). For example, some questioned the appropriateness of detaining individuals for treatment when they had often been deemed non-amenable for such treatment, and others questioned the legality of confining them in a treatment center where often no sexual offender-specific treatment was offered. There were incidents in which offenders attempted to present themselves as more mentally disordered than they were, in hopes of getting more humane treatment than in prison, and in some cases offenders were released from the treatment center far sooner than they would have been if ordered to serve their sentences (LaFond, 1998). Eventually, given both the concern about the possible infringement of civil liberties and also concerns about the quality of treatment offered, these statutes were repealed. By the late 1980s, most states no longer had MDSO statutes, and in the few states that retained them, they were infrequently used.

In the 1990s, after several highly publicized crimes committed by recently released offenders, many states began to reconsider the possibility of using civil commitment statutes for sexual offenders. This was somewhat surprising given the demise of the first generation of these statutes. Minnesota began by simply updating the Psychopathic Personality Statute, which had never been repealed, as well as adding a new one, called the "Sexually Dangerous Person" statute (1998). Other states also enacted laws, often called Sexually Violent Predator (SVP) statutes. These laws differed substantially from the earlier MDSO statutes. Instead of intending to divert sexual offenders in need of treatment from prison, they sought to incapacitate the highest risk offenders following the end of their prison sentence, until such time as they could be adequately treated to reduce their risk for re-offending. Across the states, these laws were similar, usually requiring previous convictions for sexual offenses (although some allowed for other types of confirmation of a sexually dangerous history) and a mental abnormality or personality disorder that made the individual likely to commit another crime. Almost immediately, there were numerous constitutional challenges; however, despite their controversial nature, hundreds of sexual offenders have been civilly committed in recent years (Barnickol, 2000).

CONSTITUTIONAL CHALLENGES

Perhaps the most well-known case challenging the constitutionality of the SVP statutes was the *Kansas v. Hendricks* (1997) case. Hendricks, who had admitted during the course of his SVP trial that he would get "stressed out" and become unable to "control the urge" to molest children, and had repeatedly abused children whenever he had not been confined, was found to meet the criteria for a sexually violent predator. Hendricks appealed to the State Supreme Court, noting three main issues: substantive due process (arguing that there was not sufficient basis for the government to restrict his rights), double jeopardy (arguing that he had already served time for his crime and civil commitment was equivalent to serving an additional sentence for the same crime), and *ex post facto* lawmaking (arguing that the court was retroactively increasing the punishment for crimes committed in the past). The State Supreme Court of Kansas agreed with the substantive due process argument and invalidated the Act on the grounds that the pre-commitment condition of a "mental abnormality" did not satisfy what it perceived to be the "substantive" due process requirement, and noted that there must be a finding of a "mental illness" before a person could be committed involuntarily (*In Re Hendricks*, 1996). The court did not address the double jeopardy or *ex post facto* lawmaking issues. That decision was reversed, however, upon appeal to the United States Supreme Court. The Supreme Court held that "mental illness" did not need to be the justification for commitment, and mental abnormality did satisfy the substantive due process requirement. The court also dismissed the double jeopardy and *ex post facto* arguments, stating that the statute was civil, rather than criminal in nature (*Kansas v. Hendricks*, 1997).

Since the time of the Supreme Court Decision, the focus of the constitutional challenges has shifted. Because the Supreme Court had alluded repeatedly to the offender's "inability to control" his behavior as narrowing the class of individuals eligible for confinement under the statutes, some opponents of the laws have focused on the difficulty in proving this element (Janus, 2001). Other attacks (see Petrila & Otto, 2001) were on the admissibility of expert testimony regarding dangerousness, stating that testimony based on actuarial assessment instruments failed to meet the requirements of the *Frye* test (whether the tests are generally accepted in the field) or the *Daubert* test (whether it is a technique of proven validity). Most recently, the focus of legal challenges relates to the conditions of confinement and adequacy of treatment provided. In Washington, residents of the civil commitment program filed lawsuits alleging that the conditions of their confinement at the facility violated their civil rights. In one case, *Turay v. Seling* (1997), a resident contended that his rights were violated due to the program's failure to provide him with adequate mental health treatment. US District Court Judge William L. Dwyer took steps to ensure that constitutionally adequate mental health treatment would be made available to the residents, including appointing a special master to provide expert assistance to the defendants in bringing the treatment program into compliance (Marques, Becker, Nelson & Schlank, 2001). This special master also set standards for such programs, noting that the programs needed to include such things as properly trained staff, adequate clinical supervision, individualized and comprehensive treatment plans, identifiable phases and conditional release, mechanisms for monitoring and feedback, a treatment-oriented environment with adequate space, consistently enforced policies with a mechanism for resident grievances, and the need to provide structure and activities for those residents who refuse sexual offender specific treatment (Marques, 2001). Appearing to follow the example of the Washington residents, residents of the California, Florida and Illinois programs have now focused on these standards, filing lawsuits claiming inadequacy of program conditions and treatment.

An additional concern is that in many states, treatment is not offered in prison or, if the prison programs do exist, they cannot provide services to all who need it. In those states, it is possible for an offender to have no method for attempting to lower the risk that he presents for re-offending while he is still in prison.

IDENTIFICATION OF "HIGH RISK" SEXUAL OFFENDERS

Given that this new revision of civil commitment laws provided for containment of sexual offenders after they had completed their prison time (instead of providing for a more therapeutic environment in lieu of, or as part of, their prison sentence), it became extremely important that accurate methods be used to determine which offenders were "high risk" enough to warrant commitment. This was a difficult task, however, given the lack of success mental health professionals had with predicting future dangerousness (Monahan, 1981). In the early 1990s it appeared that some offenders were being committed who appeared not to meet the standard for civil commitment. For example, in Minnesota, one man was committed who had a history of mental illness and had engaged in acts of exhibitionism, but had no known "hands-on" offenses (Marques et al., 2001). In that state, the Minnesota Sexual Offender Screening Tool—Revised (MnSOST-R) was being used to screen sexual offenders in prison (Epperson et al., 1995). Predictions were made that of those who score eight or higher on the MnSOST-R, 57% will re-offend. However, in a review of Minnesota inmates, among the 92 who scored well above eight on the MnSOST-R, 56 were not referred for civil commitment, while several who scored lower than eight were referred for consideration for civil commitment (Associated Press, 2004a). Other states also reported the presence of offenders in civil commitment programs who were committed prior to the widespread use of actuarial data and who would likely not meet the criteria if those tools had been used.

In addition to the difficulty with violence predictions, it has also been pointed out by opponents to the statutes that the disorders used in the commitment process were most often personality disorders, not diagnoses of "mental illness" or psychosexual disorders (Falk, 1999). One forensic psychologist claimed that a particular disorder often seen in the population of civilly committed sexual offenders, (i.e. Personality Disorder NOS) could apply to anyone who is "interesting" rather than someone who is dangerous (Massnerus, 2003).

With recent advances in the research on risk assessment and recidivism, and the increased use of actuarial tools (Hanson, 1999; Doren, 2002), it does appear that more appropriate referrals are being made for civil commitment. This may explain, in part, the decrease in the numbers being referred to some programs. For example, Minnesota has decreased from approximately 24 commitments per year in the early 1990s to approximately ten commitments per year in 2002 and 2003. And, in Missouri, a woman who was committed as a sexually violent predator was recently ordered to be released because the court determined there was insufficient research into the risk that female offenders presented for re-offending (Frankel, 2003).

In a recent Minnesota case, however, a man who was not referred for civil commitment is suspected of having committed a subsequent sex-related murder. This has led to a change in the referral process that could now result in a return to over-identification of those referred for civil commitment, at least in that state. The failure of the Minnesota Department of Corrections to refer this sexual offender for possible civil commitment led the state's Governor and Commissioner of Corrections to take away the input the Department of Corrections had regarding referrals to civil commitment, and place that burden instead entirely on the county attorneys.

While previously an assessment of all "Level Three" (highest risk) offenders would be conducted by Department of Corrections personnel to determine whether they should be referred for possible civil commitment, now all Level Three offenders are referred by the county attorneys. Also, in what some would describe as an over-reaction to this event, the state's Governor immediately began calling for a return of the death penalty in cases of serious sexual offenses (Lopez & Smith, 2003). When that failed, he then spoke of wanting released sexual offenders to be on GPS tracking and the public to be able to track offenders' movements on the Internet. When it was noted that current state law would not allow the public to access that information, he indicated that he believed it should be explored at the Legislature (Associated Press, 2004b).

There also continues to be confusion regarding how to determine when a decrease in risk is sufficient such that the commitment criteria are no longer met. Arizona's program noted that given the US and Arizona Supreme Court rulings, residents were being released through court order prior to obtaining the support of the treatment providers because it was believed the standard of "highly likely to offend" was no longer reached (D. Noggle, personal communication, 1 February 2003). Wisconsin also faced such a situation, with over 30 offenders being court-ordered for release due to evidence presented in court that their risk was below the "highly likely" standard, even though they had not completed treatment. A relatively high percentage of these offenders have already had their releases revoked. While most failed due to technical violations and no serious sexual offenses had been committed by them, some did return due to some form of sexual misconduct (L. Sinclair, personal communication, 1 December 2003).

SELF-INCRIMINATION

Critics of the SVP statutes believe that these laws may interfere with the treatment of sexual offenders in prison. Sexual offenders who do not seek treatment in prison are likely to be viewed as "treatment resistant" and referred for civil commitment; however, those who do participate in treatment must be told that statements made during therapy might be used against them in future civil commitment proceedings. While many offenders deal with that double-bind by attending treatment but failing to disclose their entire offense history, this is not in their best treatment interests as most treatment providers believe that rehabilitation begins with acceptance of responsibility. In addition, the utilization of the relapse prevention model is important in sexual offender treatment, and includes identifying common emotional states, thoughts and situations that occur prior to an offender's choice to commit past sexual offenses. The best relapse prevention plans can be made only if the full range of offenses in the offender's history is known. If any past offenses are left out of that analysis, particularly offenses that were exceedingly violent or targeted types of victims that seem uncharacteristic of the offender, the effectiveness of the relapse prevention plan is impaired. Noting this problem, the American Psychiatric Association has issued a statement against sexual predator statutes, and has included its opposition to the use of statements made in psychotherapy as evidence against patients (Massnerus, 2003).

LOCATION OF CIVIL COMMITMENT PROGRAMS

States adopting civil commitment statutes for sexual offenders have struggled with many obstacles including inadequate funding to begin the programs, a lack of trained staff available to run the programs, and complicated placement of the programs. For example, Washington attempted to locate its program within a prison setting while attempting to keep the patients separate from the prison inmates. This led to many difficulties including the assignment of inconvenient meal times to the civilly committed patients in order to keep them segregated from the inmates. In addition, treatment providers found they could not develop truly therapeutic environments for the civilly committed patients when they had to follow all of the personal item restrictions of a prison. Lawsuits also arose concerning the privacy of mail and phone calls and the clothing worn when on a transport. Several other states have attempted a joint placement within an existing prison, and have found similar difficulties.

Minnesota was the first state to build a stand-alone facility just for the civilly committed sexual offenders. Initially, it appeared that this program was ideal in that the patients could move freely within the secured environment, could wear their own clothing and have many of their own personal possessions, including TVs, VCRs and CD players. Each patient had his own room and, in an effort to provide a comfortable, non-prison like setting, each patient was allowed to decorate his room within some limits, and receive delivered orders from local restaurants and stores. Since residents had their civil rights restored, they also received minimum wage for all work completed in the facility. While it certainly appeared that this would be the optimal therapeutic environment, it was soon realized that this actually led to increased institutionalization among the patients. Many even noted that they feared their ability to obtain adequate work and health insurance once released, feared the stigma of public notification, and felt quite comfortable remaining in the civil commitment program (Schlank & Harry, 2003). Other states have followed suit by building separate facilities for the SVP population, but luckily many have learned from Minnesota's mistakes and have restricted the amount of personal possessions and comforts of the living situation.

Unfortunately, even those states that are willing to build separate treatment centers face difficulties from the residents in the surrounding communities. For example, in Petersburg, Virginia, residents sued the state to try to block the opening of a temporary facility for the SVP population. In their motion, they suggested sending the sexual offenders to a state that already had an existing program (Associated Press, 2003). It should be noted, however, that the states with existing programs were already struggling to find sufficient bed space and could not consider accepting out-of-state transfers. In order to avoid such protests, many states have built their facilities far from the most populated cities, which led to increased difficulty in recruiting and retaining experienced staff.

SLOW PROGRESS / RELEASE OF RESIDENTS

Many critics of the civil commitment process have pointed to the length of time required to complete the program, and the slow rate of release. Some fear it is merely a method to keep sexual offenders locked up for a lifetime (Associated Press, 2003; Massnerus, 2003). However, it should also be noted that in many states, only those offenders with the longest sexual offending histories and the most serious disorders will be referred for civil commitment, and these offenders often have been the most treatment resistant while in prison. For example, in Minnesota only approximately 4% of offenders who had been civilly committed had successfully completed a treatment program prior to their commitment. Most had either consistently refused treatment in prison or had been terminated early in the program due to their failure to comply with treatment expectations. An additional factor contributing to the slow rate of treatment progress in this population is the fact that the majority of offenders who are civilly committed suffer from personality disorders, most frequently Antisocial Personality Disorder. As noted in Price (2002), antisocial traits are a poor prognostic feature, due mainly to the offender's lack of motivation and lack of remorse. In addition, client openness (or non-defensiveness) and motivation for treatment are two factors that are often related to treatment outcome (Preston & Murphy, 2004) and are often lacking in these populations. Since civilly committed sexual offenders have already completed their prison sentence, treatment providers cannot use a decreased prison sentence as an incentive that can motivate participation. Not surprisingly, offenders referred for civil commitment sexual offender programs progress at a very slow pace. For example, in July 2002, among all the programs in the United States, only Arizona, Kansas and Minnesota had released any offenders after successful completion of treatment, and this number totaled only seven of the 2,145 residents housed in the facilities of all states which had civil commitment programs at that time.

In addition to the barriers to rapid progress presented by the motivational problems and presence of severe personality disorders, it is also difficult to determine when an offender's risk has been sufficiently reduced to allow a safe return to society. While extensive research has been recently conducted on variables that suggest an offender has a high risk for re-offending (Doren, 2002), far less research has been conducted on how to determine when a high risk sexual offender has made sufficient treatment progress to lower the risk to the community (Becker & Murphy, 1998). Currently, one of the few indicators of lowered risk appears to be the successful completion of comprehensive sexual offender treatment but, as mentioned above, successful completion rates are quite slow.

Additionally, given that civil commitment programs house only the highest risk sexual offenders, there appears to be a fair probability that even the most successful programs will have a high recidivism rate after release, simply because of the base rate of re-offending in this high risk subgroup of sexual offenders (Becker & Murphy, 1998). However, it is likely that even one incident of re-offending will make it more difficult for any future residents to be released. For example, one of the two residents who had been released from the Kansas program after successfully completing treatment re-offended within 18 months. It was noted that he committed a sexual crime that was even more violent than those he committed prior to entering the treatment program (Rizzo & Vendel, 2003). This, of course, raised fear in state officials about the efficacy of the program, and will certainly lead to increased caution in the already slow process of recommending release.

Many programs also lack a structured transition phase. Sexual offenders who have been civilly committed often have spent many years serving a prison sentence prior to their admission. After spending many more years completing civil commitment treatment, a gradual reintegration into the community should be mandatory. In addition, it appears clear that without careful monitoring and community support, releases into the community are quite risky, even if the offender has completed a residential treatment program (Matson, 2002; Schlank & Bidelman, 2001). Unfortunately, some states have no transition phase, while other states lack community-based treatment providers willing to accept an offender who has completed a civil commitment program.

ISSUES CONCERNING RESTORATION OF CIVIL RIGHTS

In prison-based treatment programs, participation may be required for parole, but is basically voluntary. Therefore, when an offender refuses to comply with rules and presents as a negative influence on others, he may be terminated from the program. In civil commitment programs, each offender is placed in the program for the purposes of obtaining treatment and there is no "general population" available in which to place the uncooperative offender. This can create an anti-therapeutic environment for those residents who are motivated to participate in treatment. Some believe that in *Hendricks*, the Supreme Court gave states some flexibility in continuing to hold, but reducing or eliminating treatment to civilly committed sexual offenders who are unamenable to the state's attempt at treatment (Burkhart, 2000). However, there is no clear way for determining amenability for treatment, and sometimes offenders who refuse treatment for many years actually demonstrate good progress in treatment once they finally decide to participate.

When an offender completes his prison term, he has his civil rights restored. It is difficult, however, to reconcile residents' civil liberties with the need for a secure, highly supervised setting. In addition, some of the rights that are restored actually appear to interfere with the provision of good sexual offender treatment. For example, once an offender leaves prison and is placed in a civil commitment program, he has the right to privacy while making telephone calls. While many would consider this a very important right, it can actually present risks for a sexual offender. Several sexual offenders who had been committed to the Minnesota program abused this right by contacting minors and engaging in sexually explicit conversations. These abuses were difficult for staff to detect without the ability to listen to the phone calls (Schlank & Harry, 2003). The right to privacy of communication through the mail also has presented problems for civil commitment programs. Many civilly committed offenders have continued their pattern of predation by abusing this right and preying on vulnerable adults or children. For example, one civilly committed offender in the Minnesota program created a false letterhead and convinced parents that he was running a modeling agency, soliciting pictures of their children (Schlank & Harry, 2003). As with the abuse of phone privileges, this type of offending behavior can be curtailed once it is detected, but without monitoring all residents' communication, there are many opportunities for the restricted offender to abuse the system.

In addition, the procedures used for isolating aggressive civilly committed patients are often inappropriate when applied to the sexual offender population because the procedures were written with the assumption that the aggression is a product of the mental illness. In mentally ill populations, isolation is necessary only until the symptoms of psychosis are stabilized. In a civilly committed population of sexual offenders, acts of aggression are more likely to be symptoms of a personality disorder and can be planned out months in advance. The resident can appear to be in behavioral control just seconds after completing an aggressive act. Treatment center "review boards" can be naïve about the difference in aggression between the mentally ill populations and the population of sexual offenders, and can insist that the same procedures are used for both populations. Without the ability to segregate the aggressive individuals for longer than is needed to obtain behavioral control, the sexual offender programs may be forced to return the individual back to the living unit shortly after the aggressive act. To add to the problem, law enforcement agencies are unfortunately often reluctant to move such residents into the available space in their crowded jails. They often fail to recognize that staff in the sexual offender program cannot use segregation in the way it can be used in prisons, and they assume that the offending individual is already in a secure setting, so there is no need to transfer him. This leads to not only an anti-therapeutic response to criminal aggression, but can lead to an unsafe environment for both staff and other residents.

Because of the problems encountered above, many of the states who most recently adopted civil commitment laws have recognized the need to curtail the liberties granted to civilly committed sexual offenders. Some states adopted policies that clearly limit these rights while others are seeking two separate Bill of Rights documents, one for mentally ill committed patients and one for the SVP population (C. Nelson, personal communication 3 March 2003; S. Wolf, personal communication 2 August 2003).

POLITICAL PRESSURES

Providing comprehensive treatment to the highest risk sexual offenders comes at a very high price to taxpayers. Costs for such programs typically range from $90,000 to approximately $120,000 per offender per year, which have led critics to wonder if such costs can be sustained (Lieb & Nelson, 2001). This high cost can cause anger in taxpayers, especially when it is realized that a fair number of the patients may be unwilling and unmotivated to take advantage of the treatment offered. Since the cost to house an offender in prison is only a fraction of the cost of a civil commitment program (Schlank & Harry, 2003), many taxpayers will prefer to focus on increasing the length of prison sentences rather than providing special treatment centers.

The Washington SVP program faced political pressure related to their efforts to transition patients into the community. Knowing that it is more effective to allow gradually increasing freedoms in the community rather than sudden outright release, the treatment providers attempted to arrange for periods of time when the offenders on their transition stage could engage in leisure activities in the community. However, the fear of public scrutiny of observing sexual offenders "having fun" while engaging in leisure activities (such as golfing), caused state administrators to prohibit such step-down activities (V. Gillogly, personal communication

21 June 2003). New Jersey, on the other hand, had to battle an attempted court order that a resident be placed in a specific phase of treatment when that phase would have been inappropriate based on his level of progress (G. Ferguson, personal communication, 25 August 2003).

Two examples of seemingly politically motivated pressures that were the most detrimental for the treatment of these offenders occurred in the States of Minnesota and Massachusetts. In Minnesota, treatment staff received pressure from a Central Office administrator to identify 40 residents for placement in the community under less than safe conditions, in an attempt to save the state money. The staff were also informed that the civilly committed sexual offenders were going to have to complete their transition process residing alongside transition patients who had been committed under the "Mental Retardation" and "Mentally Ill and Dangerous" statutes (and were thus quite vulnerable), again as an attempt to save money for the state. When challenges about these plans were raised by the treatment staff, their concerns were dismissed. These two issues led to the resignation of the program's clinical director and assistant clinical director. The resignation or retirement of many other experienced clinical staff members soon followed. Soon, the program once believed to be one of the best in the country (Cornwell, Jacobi & Witt, 1999; DesLauriers & Gardner, 1999) became a seriously understaffed program. It is noted that nine months after the clinical director's resignation, the program still had no doctoral level clinical staff, very few licensed therapists and a lack of on-site clinical direction. Luckily, however, the proposed plans never took place.

Bernstein (2003) reports that in Massachusetts, Dr Barbara Schwartz and Justice Resource Institute (JRI) had transformed the sexual offender treatment program in Bridgewater from what some believed was an embarrassment, to one that was deemed to be a national model. However, despite the praise for JRI's program, in July 2003, the treatment contract was re-bid and awarded to a different provider, Forensic Health Services (FHS). Reportedly, the Massachusetts Treatment Center's superintendent could not identify any problems with JRI's program and the seven-person team assessing competing bids gave high marks to the JRI program, while reportedly being unimpressed with the plan proposed by the agency that eventually received the contract (Bernstein, 2003). It was also noted that the financial difference between their bids was insignificant. Bernstein indicated that some suspect there were political pressures because JRI had actually been effective and was recommending some offenders be reintegrated into the community (Bernstein, 2003).

EFFECTS ON STAFF

While working in a comprehensive residential sexual offender treatment program can be rewarding, it can also have a negative impact on the therapists. Residents often displace their anger about their commitment onto the treatment providers, and the public's hatred for those who sexually abuse others can also be misdirected onto the people who are providing the treatment. Even the family members of offenders are not always supportive of the staff's efforts to treat their loved one, as they have frequently been given distorted versions of what occurs in these programs. Some, in fact, are anti-therapeutic in their communications with the resident.

It can also be very discouraging for staff to see offenders who appear to have no motivation to change their abusive ways. Some demonstrate this by continuing to attempt to obtain child pornography or other media that promotes sexual violence and some actually commit crimes from the treatment environment, such as making sexually abusive phone calls to minors in the community (Schlank & Harry, 2003). Other offenders continue their offending cycle through various methods of intimidation, such as employing threats in an attempt to control the behavior of others. They may try to keep staff members from documenting negative behaviors by continually filing lawsuits, grievances or license complaints each time their negative behavior is documented. This is similar to techniques they used in the past to dissuade victims from reporting their sexually abusive behaviors. While treatment providers recognize these offender tactics and are aware that they cannot allow themselves to be manipulated, it is often difficult for civil commitment programs to keep the energy level of all staff to the point where they are consistently challenging such efforts at intimidation. In addition, treatment staff can experience vicarious traumatization just from hearing the details of offense histories. The pressures of such a difficult population, combined with the political pressures and slow rate of progress of residents, can all contribute to problems with staff morale in civil commitment programs. In addition, the remote locations of some SVP programs can also erode morale.

INNOVATIONS IN TREATMENT PROGRAMS

Despite the numerous difficulties encountered, several states are attempting innovative methods for treating this difficult population. For example, Texas is utilizing an entirely outpatient method of treating these offenders. This is unique in that most states require that the offender be proven to be too high risk to be treated on an outpatient basis before being committed. Unfortunately, however, the numbers in Texas have also been so few that it is difficult to make judgments regarding the effectiveness of this model. Arizona's program was the first to have a "least restrictive alternative" (LRA) facility that was separate from the highly secure facility that housed most of the committed population. Residents could earn their way to the LRA or could be committed directly there by the courts (Marques *et al.*, 2001).

Minnesota's program was the first to train all staff, regardless of their position in the facility, on how to observe and chart progress toward treatment goals and on the relapse prevention model. Written minutes were also circulated twice a week that outlined all staff's observations about each resident throughout the facility. This method allowed for all staff members to be aware of how a resident was acting in his educational classes, at his work site, in every recreational activity, and for staff to be aware even of statements overheard in the smoking courtyard. Knowing what was observed in other areas led to increased communication among the various departments, resulting in true around-the-clock observation and assessment of the residents. Residents progressed only if their behavior outside of the treatment groups matched the impression they were giving to the treatment providers. This insured that residents did not just "talk the talk" in treatment groups, but actually incorporated changes into their daily activities (Marques *et al.*, 2001).

In addition, Minnesota was the first to open a prison-based site of their civil commitment program that was aimed at giving the high risk sexual offenders in prison a chance to obtain the same level of treatment they would receive if committed, but prior to their prison release. Since it is run by the same staff as the civil commitment program and provides the same comprehensiveness and level of intensity, it can avoid the need for offenders to continue to be detained. It can also provide a seamless transition for those prison inmates who do not quite complete the program prior to their release, but do get committed. These offenders can continue in their program in the SVP institution at the same phase they were in at the prison site. This new effort may be contributing to the decreasing number of offenders who are civilly committed each year in Minnesota. It also appears to be leading to increased motivation in those who are committed, since they enter at a higher phase of treatment and so are already working toward discharge.

Many programs have debated whether a different approach is necessary for those offenders who are assessed to be high on psychopathic traits. SVP programs have generally reported that approximately one-fifth of their residents score 30 or higher on the Psychopathy Checklist Revised (PCL-R) (Hare, 1991). These residents can be more difficult to treat and their attitudes sometimes have a detrimental effect on the progress of other residents. Most programs have made a decision to incorporate such residents with the rest of the participants, providing additional interventions to correct the increased cognitive-distortions and criminal attitudes that they tend to hold; however, one program has decided to provide an entirely separate track for such residents, including a separate living unit. Wisconsin's "Corrective Thinking" track is specifically for civilly committed residents who score 25 or higher on the PCL-R. The style of the therapists is also different in this track of the program. While questioning is more Socratic in the regular track, therapists in the Corrective Thinking track interrupt residents who are avoiding responsibility for their behavior. They are firmer and provide more challenging statements to the participants (L. Sinclair, personal communication, 1 December 2003). Sexual offender treatment providers are eagerly awaiting results to determine if this separation of residents and difference in approach will lead to increased success rates in treatment with these problematic clients.

An additional innovation in the Wisconsin program is that it is the first program to have a full-time therapist on staff for the care of the treatment providers. This psychotherapist's only task is to provide psychotherapy for the employee treatment providers and other staff, such as clerical staff, who have frequent contact with details of the resident's offense histories. There is strict confidentiality of therapy sessions, other than in cases of imminent risk of suicide, homicide, or serious threat of harm, or in cases of a severe security breach (L. Sinclair, personal communication, 1 December 2003). This appears to be a model other states' programs might follow.

SUMMARY AND DIRECTIONS FOR THE FUTURE

Are civil commitment statutes for sexual offenders a bad idea? While there may be no clear answer to that question, it does appear that in addition to constitutional challenges, there are many other difficulties faced when implementing these programs, including problems when political pressures cause central department administrators to dictate aspects of clinical treatment. There are also elements of the civil commitment process that actually interfere with the ability to provide the best sexual offender treatment; for example, the inability to remove unmotivated participants from the program. Also, the restoration of the offenders' civil rights and the expectation that they will be treated the same as other committed psychiatric patients can lead to environments that are actually anti-therapeutic in nature. Such an environment can provide continued opportunities for offenders to find ways to target victims in the community, and can lead to increased institutionalization. It is also clear that treatment of the highest risk, most disordered and most treatment resistant population is bound to be a slow high-cost process. Therefore, it appears that treatment can best be accomplished while the offender is still in prison but attention should be focused on improving the quality and comprehensiveness of prison programs.

If civil commitment is to be used for sexual offenders, it is important that this be only one aspect of a state's response. Some states already have the option for lengthier sentences for those determined to be "patterned sexual offenders'. For example, in Minnesota a court can sentence a sexual offender for double the presumptive sentence if it is proven that the offender is a danger to public safety and needs long-term treatment or supervision beyond the presumptive term of imprisonment. This decision is based on the offense history of the offender, the severity of the current offense, the social history of the offender, and an examination of the offender's mental status (Patterned Sex Offender Act, 2003). However, at times these options appear to be underused and, at times, are not pursued as part of plea bargain agreements. Some states also are considering the possibility of reintroducing open-ended sentences for dangerous sexual offenders. Such sentences could keep dangerous sexual offenders in prison until they complete treatment and a parole board has agreed they could be released safely. However, critics say these types of systems result in inconsistent sentences and the potential for biases based on race, gender or other social factors (Associated Press, 2004c).

Intensive parole is also a promising tool for the management of sexual offenders. In Massachusetts, a specialized unit of supervisors make twice per week in-person checks on sexual offenders. In addition, they impose curfews, use electronic monitoring, ban driving at night (along with other travel restrictions), require the use of daily logs, insist on regular drug testing, utilize polygraph examinations, and require treatment participation (Bernstein, 2003). Some states, such as Colorado and Utah, already allow for lifetime supervision of some sexual offenders (ACLU, 2000; Merz, 2003). Other states, such as New Jersey and Massachusetts, are proposing similar bills (Caywood, 2003; Sverapa, 2003).

It is also recommended that attention be focused on efforts, such as Minnesota's pilot project, to provide an additional site for the civil commitment program inside prison. This program could be offered to high risk sexual offenders who are interested in avoiding civil commitment at the end of their sentence. Plans such as this can decrease the number of admissions to civil commitment programs or at least decrease the length of stay in such programs. Attention is also needed on the issue of developing a distinct Bill of Rights for these patients, taking into consideration the risk they present. There is a need for stricter contraband rules and stricter supervision of communication than is usually required for civilly committed mentally ill populations. The potential for institutionalization should also be addressed in this Bill of Rights. Additionally, while recent research focusing on dynamic risk factors appears promising (Hanson & Harris, 2001; McGrath, Hoke, Livingston & Cumming, 2001), further work needs to be completed regarding methods for assessing when a high risk sexual offender has substantially lowered the risk presented to the community.

Finally, it is recommended that states planning to continue with civil commitment programs learn from the innovations of other states. For example, Wisconsin's foresight in providing a therapist for the treatment providers of the sexual offender program seems likely to result in decreased burnout and reduced turnover of staff as well as improved quality of services offered. In the future, it will also become clear whether Wisconsin's effort to separate the "high psychopathy" residents from other residents will lead to any added benefit to progress in treatment.

REFERENCES

American Civil Liberties Union (2000). Information about the department of corrections sexual offender registry. Press Release, 15 December.

Associated Press (2003). Residents seek to block sex-offender site. *Washington Times*. 14 June.

Associated Press (2004a). Many dangerous sexual offenders released. *Duluth News Tribune*. Monday 12 January.

Associated Press (2004b). GPS tracing of sexual offenders to begin this month. *Duluth News Tribune*. Sunday 18 January.

Associated Press (2004c). Alternative sentences considered. *Duluth News Tribune*. 4 January.

Barnickol, L. (2000). Missouri's sexually violent predator law: treatment or punishment. *Washington University Journal of Law and Policy*, **4**, 321–9.

Becker, J.V. & Murphy, W.D. (1998). What we know and do not know about assessing and treating sex offenders. *Psychology, Public Policy and Law*. March / June, 116–27.

Bernstein, D. (2003). A question of commitment. *Commonwealth*. Winter.

Burkhart, M. (2000, September). The Hendrick's Decision: Update. Presentation at the American Prosecutors Research Institute's Involuntary Commitment of Sexually Violent Predators conference, San Antonio.

Caywood, T. (2003). DA: Keep lifetime tab on offenders. *Boston Herald*. Tuesday 25 November.

Cornwell, J.K., Jacobi, J.V. & Witt, P.H. (1999). The New Jersey sexually violent predator act: analysis and recommendations for the treatment of sexual offenders in New Jersey. *Seton Hall Legislative Journal*, **24**, 1–20.

DesLauriers, A. & Gardner, J. (1999). The sexual predator treatment program of Kansas. In A. Schlank & F. Cohen (eds), *The Sexual Predator: Law, Policy, Evaluation and Treatment*, vol. I (pp. 11-2–11-24). Kingston, NJ: Civic Research Institute.

Doren, D. (2002). *Evaluating Sexual Offenders: A Manual for Civil Commitment and Beyond*. Thousand Oaks, CA: Sage Publications.

Epperson, D. L., Kaul, J. D., Huot, S. J., Hesselton, D., Alexander, W. & Goldman, R. (1995). *Minnesota Sexual Offender Screening Tool (MnSOST)*. St. Paul, MN: Minnesota Department of Corrections.

Falk, A.J. (1999). Sex offenders, mental illness and criminal responsibility: the constitutional boundaries of civil commitment after Kansas v. Hendricks. *American Journal of Law and Medicine*, **25**, 117–47.

Frankel, T.C. (2003). State's only woman sexual predator heads home. *St. Louis Post- Dispatch*. 5 November.

Hanson, R.K. (1999). What do we know about risk assessment? In A. Schlank & F. Cohen (eds), *The Sexual Predator: Law, Policy, Evaluation and Treatment*, vol. **I** (pp. 8-1–8-24). Kingston, NJ: Civic Research Institute.

Hanson, R. K. & Harris, A.J.R. (2001). A structured approach to evaluating change among sexual offenders. *Sexual Abuse: A Journal of Research and Treatment*, **13**, 105–22.

Hare, R. (1991). *Manual for the Psychopathy Checklist-Revised*. Toronto, CA: Multi-Health Systems, Inc.

Held, A. (1999). The civil commitment of sexual predators: experience under Minnesota law. In A. Schlank & F. Cohen (eds), *The Sexual Predator: Law, Policy, Evaluation and Treatment*, vol. **I** (pp. 2-4–2-22). Kingston: NJ: Civic Research Institute.

In re the Care and Treatment of Hendricks, 259 Kan. 246, 261, 912 P.2d 129 (1996).

Janus, E. (2001). Sexual offender commitments and the "inability to control": developing legal standards and a behavioral vocabulary for an elusive concept. In A. Schlank (ed.), *The Sexual Predator: Legal Issues, Clinical Issues, Special Populations*, vol. **II** (pp.1-1–1-30). Kingston, NJ: Civic Research Institute.

Kansas vs. Hendricks, 521 US 346 (1997).

LaFond, J. (1998). Sexually violent predator laws and registration and community notification laws: policy analysis: the costs of enacting a sexual predator law. *Psychology, Public Policy and the Law*, **4**, 468–72.

LaFond, J. & Winick, B. (1998). Sexual offenders and the law. *Psychology, Public Policy and the Law*, **4**, 11–16.

Lieb, R. & Nelson, C. (2001). Treatment programs for sexually violent predators: a review of states. In A. Schlank (ed.), *The Sexual Predator: Legal Issues, Clinical Issues, Special Populations*, vol. **II** (pp. 5-1–5-15). Kingston, NJ: Civic Research Institute.

Lopez, P. & Smith, D. (2003). Sjodin case spurs Pawlenty to push for death penalty. *Minneapolis Star Tribune*, 3 December.

Marques, J. (2001). Professional standards for civil commitment programs. In A. Schlank (ed.), *The Sexual Predator: Legal Issues, Clinical Issues, Special Populations*, vol. **II** (pp. 2-1–2-13). Kingston, NJ: Civic Research Institute.

Marques, J., Becker, J., Nelson, C. & Schlank, A. (2001, November). Best practices in civil commitment. Pre-conference workshop presented at the 20th Annual Research and Treatment Conference of the Association for the Treatment of Sexual Abusers, San Antonio.

Massnerus, L. (2003). Questions rise over imprisoning sexual offenders past their terms. *New York Times*. Monday 17 November.

Matson, S. (2002). Sexual offender treatment: A critical management tool. *Corrections Today*, **64**, 114–18.

McGrath, R. J., Hoke, S. E., Livingston, J. A. & Cumming, G. (2001, November). The Vermont Assessment of Sexual Offender Risk (VASOR): an initial reliability and validity study. Paper presented at the 20th Annual Research and Treatment Conference of the Association for the Treatment of Sexual Abusers, San Antonio.

Merz, M. (2003). Madigan proposes lifetime supervision of sexual offenders, seeks to implement evaluation and treatment standards. Press release: Office of the Illinois Attorney General, 5 March.

Monahan, J. (1981). *The Clinical Prediction of Violent Behavior*. Washington, DC: Government Printing Office (DHHS Publication Number ADM 81-921).

Patterned Sex Offender Act, MN Stat. 609.108 (2003).

Petrila, J. & Otto, R. (2001). Admissibility of expert testimony in SVP proceedings. In A. Schlank (ed.), *The Sexual Predator: Legal Issues, Clinical Issues, Special Populations*, vol. **II** (pp. 3-1–3-25). Kingston, NJ: Civic Research Institute.

Preston, D. & Murphy, S. (16 February 2004). *Motivating Treatment-resistant Clients in Therapy*, available at http://www.csc-scc.gc.ca/text/pblct/forum/e092/e092i.pdf

Price, K. (2002). Treating sexual offenders in a state hospital. *Psychiatric Times*, 1 June. available at http://www.psychiatrictimes.com/PO20671.html

Rizzo, T. & Vendel, C. (2003). As sexual predator returns to jail, Kansas reviews treatment regimen. *Kansas City Star*. Saturday 28 June.

Schlank, A. & Bidelman, P. (2001). Transition: challenges for the offender and the community. In A. Schlank (ed.), *The Sexual Predator: Legal Issues, Clinical Issues, Special Populations*, vol. **II** (pp. 10-1–10-13). Kingston, NJ: Civic Research Institute.

Schlank, A. & Harry, R. (2003). The treatment of the civilly committed sexual offender in Minnesota: a review of the past ten years. *William Mitchell Law Review*, **29**, 1221–39.

Sexually Dangerous Person Act, MN Stat., 253B.02, subd. 18b (1998).

Shaw, T. & Funderburk, J. (1999). Civil commitment of sexual offenders as therapeutic jurisprudence—a rational approach to community protection. In A. Schlank & F. Cohen (eds), *The Sexual Predator: Law, Policy, Evaluation and Treatment*, vol. **I** (pp. 5-1–5-8). Kingston, NJ: Civic Research Institute.

Sverapa, J. (2003). Sarlo-Girgenti bill modifies supervision laws for sexual offenders. *News from NJ Senate Democrats*. 25 November.

Turay vs. Seling. No. C91-664WD (unpub. Op., 1997), originally *Turay vs. Weston* N. C91-664WD (unpub. Op., W.D. Wash. 1994).

Chapter 5

SADISTIC SEXUAL AGGRESSORS

JEAN PROULX*, ETIENNE BLAIS[†] AND ÉRIC BEAUREGARD[‡]

* International Centre for Comparative Criminology University of Montreal, and
  Philippe Pinel Institute of Montreal, Canada
[†] University of Montreal, Canada
[‡] University of Montreal, Canada

The origin of the term "sadism" is found in the literary works of French writer Marquis de Sade (1740–1814). He describes scenes of torture, cruelty and murder that are committed in order to derive sexual pleasure. It was after the publication of *Psychopathia Sexualis* by Krafft-Ebing in 1886 that the term "sadism" was recognized as a diagnostic category. Krafft-Ebing defined sadism as "the experience of sexual, pleasurable sensations (including orgasm) produced by acts of cruelty... It may also consist of an innate desire to humiliate, hurt, wound or even destroy others thereby to create sexual pleasure in one's self" (p. 53).

In the *Diagnostic and Statistical Manual of Mental Disorders* (*DSM-IV*, American Psychiatric Association, 1994), the definition of sadism coincides largely with that offered by Krafft-Ebing over a century ago. The *DSM-IV* definition includes the following criteria: "Over a period of at least 6 months, recurrent, intense sexually arousing fantasies, sexual urges, or behaviors involving acts (real, not simulated) in which the psychological or physical suffering (including humiliation) of the victim is sexually exciting to the person" (p. 530).

This definition of sexual sadism indicates that the origins of sexual pleasure and sexual excitement are found in fantasies or acts in which physical or psychological torture causes the victim to suffer. However, for several authors, the essence of sadism is not the victim's suffering, but rather the absolute power exerted over them (Dietz, Hazelwood & Warren, 1990; Gratzer & Bradford, 1995; Johnson & Becker, 1997; MacCulloch, Snowden, Wood & Mills, 1983).

Even if the debate about the essence of sadism is not over, there is nonetheless a certain consensus as to its manifestations. After reviewing studies on sadism, Marshall and Kennedy (2003) have identified elements frequently associated with this sexual disorder. First, they noted the following characteristics of the crime scene: the use of a weapon, kidnapping, illegal confinement, torture, humiliation and mutilation of the victim, anal sex, penetration with an object, bizarre sexual acts, murder and postmortem mutilation. Second, fantasies reported by sadists included themes of control, sexual violence and sadism. Finally, during phallometric evaluation, sadists manifested a sexual preference for scenarios which involved sexual violence.

In order to clarify the scope of the manifestations of sadism, Hazelwood, Dietz and Warren (1992) stressed that the victim has to be conscious, otherwise she could not suffer or be enslaved. Moreover, they mentioned that postmortem mutilations are not necessarily manifestations of sexual sadism. In fact, these mutilations can have a purely instrumental purpose, such as eliminating elements that might allow the identification of the victim.

ETIOLOGICAL AND DEVELOPMENTAL FACTORS OF SADISM

Krafft-Ebing (1886) believed that sexual sadism constitutes an atavistic expression engraved in our genes. Contemporary authors such as Chessick (1997) defended a similar position: that "all humans are born with a primal biological archaic aggressive-destructive drive, the gratification of which gives satisfaction just like the sexual drive" (p. 612). However, the predominant point of view in recent studies stipulated that this innate capacity to destroy others expresses itself only if specific developmental factors favor its emergence (Marmor & Gorney, 1999).

As for the biological causes of sexual sadism, the study of neurologically impaired patients seems to be a promising avenue of research. In fact, physiopathologies of the right frontal lobe are frequent in sadistic sexual offenders (Hucker, 1997; Hucker et al., 1988; Langevin et al., 1985; Money, 1990). However, it has not been confirmed that cerebral damages cause sexual sadism. The role of these damages, whether they are genetic or the result of a trauma, is a question that requires further investigation.

In addition to the biological causes of sexual sadism, developmental factors appear to contribute to the emergence of this paraphilia in sexual offenders. Based on his clinical experience, Brittain (1970) concluded that the early childhood of sexual sadists was characterized by overprotective and controlling behaviors on the part of the mother, and by acts of violence by an authoritarian father. In response to these inadequate relationships with their parents, sexual sadists developed an insecure attachment style which expressed itself through attitudes of withdrawal. These conclusions, however, were not based on carefully collected evidence, but rather arose from Brittain's clinical contacts with sadists.

The results of a study by MacCulloch et al. (1983) indicated that all the subjects in their sample of sadistic sexual offenders (N = 13) said they had experienced difficulties in their interpersonal relationships and sociosexual interactions during adolescence. MacCulloch et al. interpreted these relational failures as responsible for the development of low self-esteem and also aggravated the social isolation of sexual sadists. In such conditions, sadistic sexual fantasies and paraphilic behaviors (voyeurism, exhibitionism, fetishism) were said by MacCulloch to have become established as a surrogate source of emotional and sexual gratification in these offenders. For a majority of MacCulloch *et al.*'s subjects (79%), deviant sexual fantasies became increasingly violent so as to maintain a high level of erotic stimulation. Finally, certain sadists (54%) conducted behavioral tryouts of their fantasies in order to further enhance them. For example, a sadistic sexual offender in the making might break into a woman's apartment and watch her while she sleeps.

PORTRAITS OF ADULT SADISTIC SEXUAL OFFENDERS' DAILY LIVES

Brittain's (1970) proposed profile of the sadistic sexual offender suggests that adulthood is a continuum of his childhood. Brittain describes the sadist as shy, anxious, introverted and socially isolated, but of superior intelligence. His view of the sadist is of someone who is studious, punctual, meticulous, prudish and does not consume alcohol. Brittain suggests that the sadist has little sexual experience and experiences difficulty achieving an erection with a partner. As a result Brittain says it is not surprising that the sadist considers himself inferior to other men where sex is concerned. The only aspect of the sadist's life in which he is triumphant is his secret world, which is dominated by sadistic sexual fantasies, paraphilic behaviors, the torture of animals and, ultimately, the commission of sexual aggression and sexual murder. Brittain's clinical view is that the sadist's world includes a particular interest in books or films with themes of enslavement and the suffering of others (e.g. nazism, witchcraft, sadomasochistic pornography). The sadist is seen as good mannered, as effeminate and pedantic, and as having problems openly expressing anger. Finally, Brittain claims sadists rarely have previous convictions, except for sexual nuisance offences (e.g. exhibitionism, voyeurism, obscene phone calls).

While some aspects of the clinical portrait of the sadistic sexual offender provided by Brittain (1970) have been confirmed by the empirical studies of Dietz and his colleagues (Dietz, Harry & Hazelwood, 1986; Dietz *et al.*, 1990; Hazelwood & Douglas, 1980; Warren, Hazelwood & Dietz, 1996), others have not. Dietz *et al.*'s studies were based on a small sample of 34 sexual sadists among whom sexual murderers were overrepresented (N = 20). In the two most recent studies, *DSM-III-R* (American Psychiatric Association, 1987), diagnostic criteria were used to identify sexually sadistic subjects. These subjects differed from Brittain's prototypical sadist by their abuse of alcohol and drugs (50%) and their criminal records (35%). These additional attributes identified in the sample used by Dietz and his collaborators are congruent with the severity of their sexual deviance (i.e. serial sexual murder).

The results of studies by Dietz and his colleagues showed that the majority of their subjects (80%) reported having sadistic sexual fantasies, whereas other paraphilias were infrequent (between 20% and 45%). These results differ from Brittain's sadistic prototype. Among the factors observed by Dietz *et al.* was an interest in police activities (30%), as well as car rides with no particular aim or purpose (40%). Dietz *et al.* also found that some of their subjects had a reputation for being good citizens as a result of their volunteer work and their involvement in charity events (30%). Finally, a majority of subjects were employed (75%) and married at the time of the offense (50%).

PHALLOMETRIC PROFILE

Some phallometric studies of sadists indicate that they have a preference for sexually coercive activities (Barbaree, Seto, Serin, Amos & Preston, 1994; Fedora *et al.*, 1992; Proulx, 2001). For example, the result of Proulx's (2001) study showed that sadistic sexual aggressors of women (N = 14), evaluated using the *MTC-R-3* sadism scale (Knight & Prentky, 1990), presented a mean Physical Rape Index (i.e. arousal to a physically abusive rape divided by arousal to consenting sex) of 1.6, whereas for nonsadists (N = 36) it was 0.7. For the Humiliation Rape Index (i.e. arousal to a humiliating rape divided by arousal to consenting sex), the mean was 1.6 for sadists and 0.6 for nonsadists. However, results of a study by Marshall, Kennedy and Yates (2002) indicated that sexual offenders identified by psychiatrists as nonsadistic had a more pronounced sexual preference for rape than did those identified as sadists. Finally, the results of studies by Seto and Kuban (1996) and Langevin *et al.* (1985) did not suggest any significant difference between sexual offenders identified as sadists and nonsadists. These differences in results may be due to discrepancies in the definitions of sadists or they may result from the different samples studied.

PSYCHOPATHOLOGICAL PROFILES

Some authors have concluded that sexual sadists are psychopathic and narcissistic (Dietz, 1986; Dietz *et al.*, 1990; Smith & Brown, 1977). However, these authors did not collect data to support their hypotheses on the personality disorders they attributed to sadistic sexual offenders. It appears personality disorders were assessed based on the characteristics of the offense and not on the basis of any careful evaluations of the sexual sadists.

Contrary to Dietz *et al.*'s opinion (1990), the results of a study by Holt, Meloy and Strack (1999) showed there was no significant link between psychopathy, evaluated using the *PCL-R* (Hare, 1991), and sexual sadism. This was the case both for sexual aggressors (N = 19) and for nonsexual offenders (N = 22).

The different opinions as to the personality disorders of sadistic sexual offenders presented above can be interpreted in several ways. First, Dietz *et al.*'s (1990) opinion is unfounded since they did not evaluate the personality disorders of their subjects. Second, it might be that in their everyday interpersonal relationships, sexual sadists present a functioning mode characterized by avoidant (introversion, low self-esteem) and schizoid (solitary) personality features, but adopt a psychopathic functioning mode (lack of empathy) in their sexual fantasies and sexual offenses. It is also possible that two types of sadistic sexual offenders exist, one having avoidant and schizoid personality disorders, the other psychopathic traits (Knight,

2002, personal communication). In fact, Siomopoulos and Goldsmith (1976) suggest the existence of five types of sadists. Finally, it is also possible, given the paucity of evidence, that sadists do not suffer from any type of personality disorder. Due to the lack of studies on the subject, it is not possible to decide in favor of one hypothesis over another. Nevertheless, the studies on personality disorders by Millon and Davis (1996) helped us weigh the respective value of these hypotheses.

In their theoretical model of psychological functioning, Millon and Davis (1996) stipulate that individuals with an avoidant personality disorder have several features in common with those presenting an antisocial-sadistic disorder. Both types are said to have suffered at the hands of violent parents and were exposed to models of violence during childhood. While avoidant personality types and sadists share the same mistrust and hostility as adults, their coping strategies differ.

> At first glance, one might be inclined to note that the polarity focus (in antisocial-sadist) is essentially the same as seen in the avoidant personality, where both pain and active polarities are preeminent as well. However, the avoidant actively anticipates and escapes from abuse, whereas the (antisocial) sadist actively assaults and degrades others. (Millon & Davis, 1996, p. 482)

Extrapolating from Millon and Davis' account, it might be expected that in sexual aggressors of women, both the avoidant and the antisocial sadist have the same propensity for violence. According to this view, the avoidant aggressor will only express this propensity in his fantasies and sexual offenses, whereas the antisocial aggressor expresses it daily in his interpersonal relationships, including his consenting sexual activities. Millon and Davis' (1996) model is compatible with both a psychopathic way of functioning as well as an avoidant personality disorder in sadistic sexual aggressors. Choosing what he sees as a weak victim (i.e. a woman), suits the avoidant because of his lack of self-confidence, whereas the antisocial sadist adopts a predatory mode with all people whom he considers inferior (Feister & Gay, 1991; Spitzer, Feister, Gay & Pfohl, 1991).

CRIME PHASES

As for the modus operandi of sadistic sexual offenders at the crime phase, the most complete study on this issue was conducted by Dietz et al. (1990). This study included 30 sadistic offenders, 17 of whom were serial murderers. The victims were of both sexes and of all ages. In most of the cases, the offenses were planned (93.3%), and the victim was usually unknown (83%). The victim was tortured (100%), tied up and gagged (87%), and the sexual acts were diverse including sodomy (73%), fellatio (71%) and vaginal intercourse (57%). If the victim was killed, it was often by asphyxia (58%). In cases where the victim was stabbed (10%), the blows were multiple and more abundant than what was necessary to kill the victim (overkill). Finally, in addition to recording the details of their crimes (53.3%), some sadists kept souvenirs (40%). These could be the victim's belongings (e.g., jewelry, clothes) (Hazelwood et al., 1992) or even body parts (Hazelwood & Douglas, 1980).

COMPARISONS OF SADISTIC AND NONSADISTIC SEXUAL OFFENDERS

Langevin *et al.* (1985)

Langevin *et al.* (1985) examined the sexological, psychological and developmental characteristics of 20 sexual aggressors of women (nine sadists and 11 nonsadists) and compared them to 20 nonsexual and nonviolent offenders. The criteria used to consider a sexual offender sadistic were the admission of sadistic sexual fantasies (N = 7) or an offense that included presumed elements of sadism (N = 2). The three groups did not differ in their phallometric responses (i.e. Rape Index) or in their scores on the Derogatis Sexual Functioning Inventory. However, sadists tended to have less sexual experience, knowledge and drive than did nonsadists. Scores on the Clarke Sex History scales confirmed that fewer sadists (75%) had nondeviant heterosexual experiences than did nonsadists (82%). Only sadists threatened and frightened their victims (25%). Sadists perceived themselves as sexually inadequate (63%) and reported a low sexual desire (38%), as well as a fear of being homosexual (38%). Finally, sadists found it difficult to speak to a woman (75%) and also felt anger towards women (38%).

With regard to the psychological characteristics, sadists were found to differ from nonsadists in some aspects. Many presented cerebral pathologies; that is, impairments to the right frontal lobe (56%) and nonspecific neurological impairments (33%) (see also Langevin, Ben-Aron, Wright, Marchese & Handy, 1988). Sadists rarely consumed other drugs, but they did consume alcohol (75%), although rarely prior to their offenses (25%). Finally, none of the sadistic sexual aggressors showed a psychopathic profile (4–9) on the *MMPI*.

During their childhood, Langevin *et al.* (1985) found that sadists suffered punishment for temper tantrums and enuresis more often than subjects in the two other groups. They were also more likely to collect weapons, but were less violent against others than the subjects in the other two groups.

Gratzer and Bradford (1995)

Gratzer and Bradford (1995), using *DMS-III-R* (American Psychiatric Association, 1987) criteria, conducted a study on the developmental, social and criminological characteristics of sexual offenders. Their study included 28 sadists (20 sexual murderers and eight sexual aggressors) and 29 nonsadists (14 sexual murderers and 15 sexual aggressors). Although this study included 34 sexual murderers, only four were serial murderers (three sadists and one nonsadist). The proportion of sadists (42.9%) who were physically abused during childhood was higher than for the nonsadists (12.9%). In adulthood, sadists reported sexually deviant activities (transvestism, voyeurism, exhibitionism) more frequently than did nonsadists.

In terms of the characteristics of their sexual offenses, Gratzer and Bradford (1995) found that sadists differed from nonsadists. The offenses of sadists were usually well planned (82.1%). They used a diversity of coercive acts such as torture (78.6%)

and blows resulting in injuries (64.3%). Their offenses also included a variety of sexual acts, such as intercourse (39.3%), sodomy (21.4%) and fellatio (17.9%). Sexual sadists reported having experienced emotional detachment during the crime (82.1%) and, in many cases, they suffered from a sexual dysfunction (50%). There was no significant difference between sadistic and nonsadistic murderers in the way they killed their victims. Finally, Gratzer and Bradford reported that 86% of sadists were diagnosed using *DSM-III-R* criteria (American Psychiatric Association, 1987) as having an antisocial personality disorder, and 55% had neurological anomalies.

Marshall, Kennedy and Yates (2002)

Marshall, Kennedy and Yates (2002) conducted a study on the psychological and criminological characteristics of incarcerated sexual offenders who had been diagnosed by psychiatrists as either sadistic (N = 41) or nonsadistic (N = 18) using either *DSM-III-R* or *DSM-IV* criteria. The proportion of sexual murderers was similar in both groups (sadists: 29.3%; nonsadists: 27.8%). All of the nonsadists' victims were women as were the majority of the sadists' victims. It is important to recognize that the subjects of this study were not representative of incarcerated sadistic and nonsadistic sexual offenders. In fact, this sample included only subjects for whom a psychiatric evaluation was conducted in order to assess their dangerousness.

The two groups of sexual aggressors had similar proportions of subjects diagnosed with antisocial personality disorder (sadists: 51.2%; nonsadists: 66.7%). However, more of the nonsadists (50%) were diagnosed with an additional personality disorder than were the sadists (17.1%). At phallometric evaluation, more of the nonsadists (44.4%) showed sexual arousal to violent rapes than did the sadists (17.1%), and in their crimes the nonsadists were more likely than the sadists to sexually mutilate and torture their victims. It is also important to note that the sadistic subjects in this study committed less coercive offenses than has been generally reported in studies on sexual sadism. Nevertheless, only the sadists reported a high frequency of murderous fantasies (41.5%).

Proulx, Blais and Beauregard (2003)

There have been relatively few empirical studies on sexual sadism and the existing ones suffered from certain limitations. Langevin *et al.*'s study (1985), as well as that by MacCulloch *et al.* (1983), both had a limited number of subjects. Moreover, samples of other studies were biased, with some being composed in large part of serial sexual murderers (Dietz *et al.*, 1990; Warren *et al.*, 1996). Finally, several samples were composed of mixed groups of sexual aggressors of women and those who assaulted children (Dietz *et al.*, 1990; Marshall, Kennedy & Yates, 2002). The aim of Proulx, Blais and Beauregard's (2003) study was to compare a large, unbiased sample of sadistic and nonsadistic sexual aggressors of women, with regard to their developmental, psychological, sexological and criminological characteristics.

Two sadism scales of the *MTC-R-3* (Knight & Prentky, 1990) were used to classify subjects as sexual sadists or not. Five items from the Sadism Scale A included: (1) presence of intense and recurring sexual and aggressive fantasies; (2) torture of the victim prior to death; (3) ritualized violence; (4) postmortem intercourse; and (5) postmortem mutilation. Three items from the Sadism Scale B identified: (1) marks of violence on erogenous zones (anus, vagina, breasts); (2) burns inflicted prior to or after the murder; and (3) insertion of objects into body cavities. To be classified in the sadist category, a subject had to present at least one of the five criteria of Scale A or at least two criteria of Scale B. In total, 43 subjects were classified as sadists (18 sexual murderers and 25 sexual aggressors of women) and 98 as nonsadists (22 sexual murderers and 76 sexual aggressors of women).

A French version of the *MCMI-I* (Millon Clinical Multiaxial Inventory) (Millon, 1983) was completed by 30 of the sadists and 70 of the nonsadists. The missing data were due to either a subject's refusal to complete the questionnaire, or his inability to do so because of a reading deficiency.

Phallometric assessments used French translations of the stimuli reported by Abel, Blanchard, Becker and Djenderedjian (1978). Satisfactory discriminant validity of the French translations was demonstrated in two studies (Earls & Proulx, 1986; Proulx, Aubut, McKibben & Côté, 1994). For each sexual aggressor whose phallometric data were valid, three deviance indexes were calculated: (1) a Physical Rape Index; (2) a Humiliation Rape Index; and (3) a Nonsexual Physical Violence Index (i.e. arousal to descriptions of nonsexual physical assault of a woman divided by arousal to consenting sex).

No statistically significant differences were found between the two groups in terms of their exposure during childhood to inadequate models. Nevertheless, a large proportion of both sadists and nonsadists were, as children, exposed to displays of physical (51.2% vs. 42.3% respectively) and psychological (51.2% vs. 47.4% respectively) violence. As children, more of the sadists (62.8%) were subjected to psychological violence (i.e. humiliation) than were the nonsadists (43.3%). Furthermore, both sadistic and nonsadistic offenders were often physically abused as children (55.8% vs. 44.3% respectively). Finally, a proportion of both sadists (51.2%) and nonsadists (39.2%) were abandoned by their parents.

Proulx *et al.* (2003) also reported the development of problematic behaviors in their subjects that were shown before age 18 years. Sadists were found to differ significantly from nonsadists with regard to the following: viewing pornographic videos (35.7% vs. 14.7% respectively), viewing pornographic magazines (35.7% vs. 18.1% respectively), visiting strip clubs (31.0% vs. 10.5% respectively), compulsive masturbation (25.0% vs. 11.7% respectively) and deviant sexual fantasies (48.8% vs. 18.6% respectively). Sadists reported lower self-esteem and nightmares more often than nonsadists (46.3% vs. 28.4% and 25.0% vs. 9.5% respectively). A number of both groups showed high levels of social isolation during childhood (sadists: 45.0%; nonsadists: 33.7%). Finally, during adolescence, sadists differed from nonsadists in terms of social isolation (52.5% vs. 34.7% respectively) and frequent temper tantrums (47.5% vs. 25.5% respectively).

Table 5.1 Mean scores and percentages of sadistic and nonsadistic sexual aggressors of women on the personality scales of the *MCMI*

Personality Disorders	Score (*MCMI*)		Percentage score > 84	
	Sadists (N = 30)	Nonsadists (N = 70)	Sadists (N = 30)	Nonsadist (N = 70)
Schizoid	*66.0	54.6	**44.0	14.3
Avoidant	*71.0	58.2	33.3	18.6
Dependent	69.9	70.2	46.7	38.6
Histrionic	*45.6	54.1	0.0	2.9
Narcissistic	55.8	61.9	10.0	11.4
Antisocial	56.9	58.8	6.7	7.1
Obsessive-compulsive	57.0	59.4	3.3	2.9
Passive-aggressive	57.5	48.0	26.7	17.1
Schizotypal	*62.0	56.5	6.7	0.0
Borderline	58.3	58.6	6.7	1.4
Paranoid	62.2	63.8	6.7	5.7

Note: * p < 0.05 ; ** p < 0.01.

There was no statistically significant difference between sadists and nonsadists with regard to criminal career parameters. The criminal activity of both groups was diversified and intense, resulting in several convictions. Neither sadists nor nonsadists specialized in sexual crime, as it accounted for only about 20% of their criminal activities.

The phallometric results reported by Proulx *et al.* (2003) showed the mean Humiliation Rape Index to be higher for the sadists (1.7) than for the nonsadists (0.6). Also, the mean Physical Rape Index was higher for the sadists (1.7) than for the nonsadists (0.7). However, the two groups did not differ in terms of their Nonsexual Physical Violence Index.

The mean scores and percentages of sadistic and nonsadistic subjects on the personality scales of the *MCMI* are shown in Table 5.1. Sadistic sexual aggressors of women scored significantly higher than nonsadists on the avoidant, schizoid and schizotypal scales. However, nonsadists had a higher score than did sadists on the histrionic personality scale. Finally, a larger proportion of sadists than nonsadists scored above 84 on the scale for schizoid personality disorder.

Proulx *et al.* (2003) carried out complementary analyses in order to clarify the relationship between the nature of personality disorders and sexual sadism. They determined whether the types of personality profiles, identified with a cluster analysis, were related to sexual sadism. The most frequent personality profile in sadistic sexual offenders (58.3%) was a combination of avoidant, schizoid, dependent and passive-aggressive elements, whereas the most representative personality profile of nonsadistic sexual aggressors (62.0%) included narcissistic and antisocial elements. This association (p = 0.08) between sexual sadism and personality disorder profiles, however, did not reach the usual level (p < 0.05) accepted for significance.

Table 5.2   Characteristics of the precrime phase of sadistic and nonsadistic sexual aggressors of women during the 48 hours prior to the offense

Characteristics	Percentage of sadists (N = 43)	Percentage of nonsadists (N = 98)
➢ Sexual dissatisfaction	12.2	6.3
➢ Perceived rejection	35.0	25.0
➢ Low self-esteem	39.0	32.6
➢ Specific conflicts with:		
• Partner	4.8	9.5
• Other woman	*11.9	2.1
• The victim	7.1	3.1
• A man	4.8	3.1
➢ Generalized conflicts with:		
• Women	***58.5	21.1
• Men	0.0	0.0
• The system (police, judge, laws)	31.7	20.0
➢ Emotional state		
• Anger	**65.8	39.0
• Sexual excitement	*13.5	32.5
➢ Alcohol	64.3	70.1
➢ Drugs	53.7	38.1
➢ Pornography	2.4	2.1
➢ Strip joint	20.0	15.4
➢ Deviant sexual fantasies	***46.5	17.3

Note: * p < 0.05 ; ** p < 0.01 ; *** p< 0.001.

Table 5.2 shows the proportion of precrime characteristics (48 hours prior to the offense) among the sadistic and nonsadistic sexual aggressors of women as reported by Proulx *et al.* (2003). As can be seen, a generalized conflict with women was observed more often in sadists than in nonsadists. Furthermore, anger was reported more often by sadists compared to nonsadists, as were deviant sexual fantasies. Even though there was no significant difference between the two groups, alcohol and drugs were frequently consumed in the hours leading up to the sexual offense.

Table 5.3 shows the proportion of offense characteristics in sadistic and non-sadistic sexual aggressors of women. The level of organization of the crime was higher for sadists than for nonsadists with the sadists being more likely to have planned their crimes than were the nonsadists. Moreover, compared to nonsadists, a higher proportion of sadists selected their victim according to specific criteria. The level of coercion during the offense was higher for sadists than for nonsadists with regard to the following elements: kidnapping and unlawful confinement; tying up the victim; enslavement of the victim (bondage); expressive violence; use of a weapon; psychological torture (humiliation); physical torture (mutilations); mutilation of erogenous zones; and insertion of objects into the vagina. Although

Table 5.3 Offenses characteristics of sadistic and nonsadistic sexual aggressors of women

Characteristics	Percentage of sadists (N = 43)	Percentage of nonsadists (N = 98)
➤ Planned offense	**86.0	60.8
➤ Selected victim	**52.5	28.7
➤ Unknown victim	83.8	80.6
➤ Accomplice	14.0	16.3
➤ Coercive strategies against the victim	15.0	18.5
➤ Kidnapping and unlawful confinement	*18.6	6.1
➤ Tied-up victim	*23.8	8.2
➤ Enslavement of the victim (bondage)	***16.3	0.0
➤ Use of a weapon	*55.8	37.8
➤ Expressive violence	***90.7	58.2
➤ Psychological torture (humiliation)	**53.7	26.7
➤ Physical torture (mutilations)	***30.2	1.1
➤ Mutilation of erogenous zones	***25.6	1.1
➤ Insertion of objects		
• Vagina	*9.3	1.1
• Anus	7.0	1.1
➤ Anal intercourse	14.3	6.5
➤ Fellatio	27.9	30.8
➤ Vaginal intercourse	67.4	62.8
➤ Insertion of fingers		
• Vagina	26.2	22.0
• Anus	7.1	5.4
➤ Cunnilingus	9.3	12.1
➤ Recording the offence	4.7	1.0
➤ Sexual murder	37.2	22.4
➤ Serial sexual murder	0.0	0.0

Note: * $p < 0.05$; ** $p < 0.01$; *** $p < 0.001$.

the difference was not statistically significant, the percentage of sexual murderers was higher in sadists than in nonsadists. Finally, the diversity of sexual acts (intercourse, fellatio, cunnilingus, sodomy) was considerable both for sadists and nonsadists.

Table 5.4 shows crime scene characteristics of 18 sadistic and 22 nonsadistic sexual murderers derived from Proulx et al.'s (2003) study. The most frequent cause of death in the victims of sadists was asphyxia by strangulation and this was far higher than among the murder victims of nonsadists. Nonsadists did not appear to have a preferred method of killing their victims. The victims of the sadists were found completely naked more often than were those of the nonsadists. Moreover, only the sadists engaged in postmortem intercourse and mutilation. Finally, we should note that a third of sexual murderers hid the body of their victims once they had committed their crimes.

Table 5.4   Crime scene characteristics of sadistic and nonsadistic sexual murderers

Characteristics	Percentage of sadists (N = 18)	Percentage of nonsadists (N = 22)
➢ Cause of death		
• Blows to the head	12.5	22.7
• Asphyxia		
– Strangulation	*50.0	27.3
– Suffocation	12.5	9.1
• Bullet wound	0.0	0.0
• Knife wound	25.0	22.7
• Drowning	0.0	9.1
• Other	0.0	9.1
➢ Hides body	33.3	36.3
➢ Body completely naked	***88.2	11.8
➢ Postmortem intercourse	**31.3	0.0
➢ Postmortem mutilation	***44.4	0.0
➢ Dismemberment of body	5.6	4.5
➢ Object in body cavity	16.7	0.0
➢ Inscriptions at the crime scene	5.6	0.0
➢ Symbolic artifact (e.g. crucifix, dead animals)	5.6	0.0

Note: * $p < 0.05$; ** $p < 0.01$; *** $p < 0.001$.

CONCLUSIONS

Proulx *et al*.'s (2003) study was based on a sample of 141 extrafamilial sexual aggressors of women. The sample included 95% of rapists evaluated at a Regional Reception Center of Correctional Service of Canada between 1995 and 2000 and 75% of the sexual murderers of women incarcerated in Quebec in 1999. The sample did not include offenders whose victims were male or children. Consequently, the emerging portrait of the sexual sadist, based on these results, is probably more clear than the portrait from previous studies.

On a developmental level, Proulx *et al*.'s (2003) results indicated that sadistic sexual offenders grew up in an inadequate environment. They were exposed to physical and psychological violence as well as alcohol abuse during childhood and adolescence. A large proportion were also victims of physical and sexual violence. These results are similar to those obtained in previous studies (Gratzer & Bradford, 1995; Langevin *et al*., 1985) and are compatible with the clinical portrait of the sexual sadist presented by Brittain (1970). Sadists were more likely than nonsadists to have suffered psychological violence (e.g. humiliation) during their developmental years. This form of victimization is compatible with the development of an avoidant personality disorder, which is characterized by a fear of being humiliated, criticized and rejected by others.

During childhood and adolescence, the sadistic sexual offenders in Proulx *et al*.'s sample differed from nonsadists in low self-esteem and pronounced social isolation. These results agree with those of MacCulloch *et al*. (1983), as well as the description of the sexual sadist outlined by Brittain (1970). It should be noted that these characteristics of the sexual sadist constitute crucial clinical manifestations of an avoidant personality disorder. However, the sexual sadist's temper tantrums in adolescence do not fit this personality disorder. One possible explanation for this inconsistency may lie in a typological approach of sexual sadism. The first type of sadist, socially isolated and devalued, presents an avoidant personality disorder, whereas the second type of sadist, short-tempered and violent with their next of kin, manifests an antisocial personality disorder.

The sadist's adolescence is dominated by sexual activities, setting them apart from nonsadists. They consume pornography and turn to violent sexual fantasies during their masturbatory activities. This overwhelming sexuality in the everyday lives of sexual sadists was also observed by MacCulloch and his colleagues (1983). They believe that, after a relationship failed, sexual sadists resorted to sexuality as a surrogate source of emotional gratification.

Results from Proulx et al.'s (2003) phallometric evaluations indicate that the sadistic aggressors had a sexual preference for rape (humiliation, physical violence). These sexual preferences reflected their pervasive sadistic sexual fantasies (35 out of 43 subjects reported such fantasies). These results match those observed in other phallometric studies (Barbaree et al., 1994; Fedora et al., 1992; Proulx, 2001). Thus, the violence exhibited by sadists during their sexual crimes seems to be an extension of their sadistic sexual fantasies and their preference for coercive sexual activities. Unfortunately, these results are not universally observed, since others have found that sadists do not have deviant sexual preferences (Langevin et al., 1985; Marshall, Kennedy & Yates, 2002; Seto & Kuban, 1996). It is possible that sample-related factors are relevant and the validity of some of the stimulus sets used to evaluate sexual preferences may be debatable. However, the most plausible explanation is a problem in the diagnosis of sexual sadism. For example, Seto and Kuban (1996) identified subjects as sadist if, during the commission of the offense, they used expressive violence and if the victim was physically injured. None of the sexual aggressors in the study by Seto and Kuban admitted having recurrent sadistic sexual fantasies. Thus, it is probable that their sample of sadists was composed of several types of sexual offenders: sadists, but also the angry type of rapist (Proulx, St-Yves, Guay & Ouimet, 1999). In fact, both types of sexual aggressors use expressive violence and injure their victims. However, the angry type does not exhibit a sexual preference for rape.

The psychopathological profile of sexual offenders in Proulx et al.'s (2003) study differed between sadists and nonsadists. The sadists were characterized by avoidant and schizoid personality disorders. Individuals with this personality profile have low self-esteem and isolate themselves in order to avoid being criticized and rejected. Their inner world is dominated by humiliation, suffering, anxiety and anger. This personality profile is compatible with the portrait of the sexual sadist who is dominated by low self-esteem and social isolation, and who withdraws into a world of sadistic fantasies. The likely function of both the fantasies and the sadistic sexual offenses is to compensate for the suffering, humiliation and anger that is felt and unexpressed by the sexual sadist in his everyday life. Thus, the physical and psychological (humiliation) suffering of the victim seems to serve a catharsis in the sexual sadist, temporarily releasing him from his own internal distress. However, due to the inflexible and inappropriate nature of his coping strategies, the sexual sadist remains devoted to sexual violence.

During the precrime phase, sadistic sexual offenders in Proulx *et al.*'s (2003) study displayed generalized conflict with women, as well as anger and coercive sexual fantasies. Results from other studies also highlight the presence of such fantasies in the hours leading up to the crime (MacCulloch *et al.*, 1983; Ressler, Burgess & Douglas, 1988). A possible explanation for the activation of sadistic fantasies is articulated around the personality profile of this type of sexual offender. Due to his avoidant and schizoid personality, the sadist feels inferior to others and believes that people he meets, especially women, reject and humiliate him. These distorted perceptions bring about feelings of rage, humiliation and suffering which remain unexpressed. The sadist thus retreats from relationships and flees into a world of sexually coercive fantasies. Due to the amount of time he dedicates to his sexual fantasies, they become elaborate and form an outlet for his unexpressed emotional states: rage, humiliation and suffering (Proulx, McKibben & Lusignan, 1996; Proulx *et al.*, 1999). However, the use of coercive sexual fantasies as a coping strategy may prove insufficient if the sadist experiences unusually intense, stressful events. The nature of this stress could be a generalized conflict with women, rejection or low self-esteem. Actualizing his fantasies through a sadistic sexual offense constitutes another coping strategy which the sadist resorts to in order to deal with his internal distress. Moreover, anger and an intoxicated state may act as disinhibiting factors that accentuate the intensity of the deviant sexual arousal, thereby providing the motivation to commit the offense.

As for the actual offense, it constitutes a continuation of the sexual sadist's coercive sexual fantasies. Consequently, it is not surprising to find that the offense is usually planned down to the smallest detail. The offenses of the sadists included elements of physical and psychological violence, which distinguished them from nonsadists. However, for the sadists in Proulx *et al.*'s (2003) study, humiliation of the victim occurred more frequently than did physical cruelty, whereas the opposite was true for the Gratzer and Bradford (1995) sample. This divergence is probably due to the higher percentage of sexual murderers in Gratzer and Bradford's study (71.4%) compared to Proulx *et al.*'s (28.3%). Indeed, a lethal sexual crime necessarily involves high levels of physical violence.

The crime scene elements of sexual murderers in Proulx *et al.*'s study are similar to those in the Gratzer and Bradford (1995) sample, but differ from those found by Dietz *et al.* (1990). A larger proportion of Dietz *et al.*'s subjects hid the bodies of their victims and inserted objects into body cavities. These characteristics highlight the high level of organization and ritualization of the offense, which might be considered an indicator of the severity of sexual deviance in the subjects of Dietz and his colleagues. This is in accordance with the high rate of serial sexual murderers in their study (56.7%), which was much higher than that in the Gratzer and Bradford study (10.7%) or Proulx *et al.*'s report (0%).

Overall, Proulx *et al.*'s (2003) results are in agreement with those of Gratzer and Bradford (1995), and show that sadistic sexual offenders differ from nonsadists on several levels. In both studies, the *DSM* diagnostic criteria (American Psychiatric Association, 1987, 1994) were used in order to distinguish sexual sadists from nonsadists. In spite of a high discriminant validity revealed in some studies that had used *DSM* diagnostic criteria, Marshall and Yates (in press) expressed reservations about this method of identifying sexual sadism. In addition, Marshall, Kennedy, Yates and Serran (2002) showed that internationally renowned forensic psychiatrists, all of whom were known for their work on sexual sadists, could not agree on who was and who was not a sadist. Consequently, the validity of studies on sexual sadism is limited by the absence of a consensus on the definition of sexual sadism. In order to better delimit the specificities of sexual sadists, a new sadism scale should be developed or a firm consensus should be established on the diagnostic criteria to be used.

REFERENCES

Abel, G.G., Blanchard, E.B., Becker, J.V. & Djenderedjian, A. (1978). Differentiating sexual aggressives with penile measures. *Criminal Justice and Behavior, 5*, 315–32.

American Psychiatric Association (1987). *Diagnostic and Statistical Manual of Mental Disorders*, 3rd edn rev. Washington, DC: American Psychiatric Association.

American Psychiatric Association (1994). *Diagnostic and Statistical Manual of Mental Disorders*, 4th edn. Washington, DC: American Psychiatric Association.

Barbaree, H.E., Seto, M.C., Serin, R.C., Amos, N.L. & Preston, D.L. (1994). Comparisons between sexual and nonsexual rapists subtypes: sexual arousal to rape, offense precursors and offense characteristics. *Criminal Justice and Behavior, 21*, 95–114.

Brittain, R.P. (1970). The sadistic murderer. *Medicine, Science and the Law, 10*, 198–207.

Chessick, R.D. (1997). Archaic sadism. *Journal of the American Academy of Psychoanalysis, 24*, 605–18.

Dietz, P.E. (1986). Mass, serial and sensational homicides. *Bulletin of the New York Academy of Medicine, 62*, 477–91.

Dietz, P.E., Harry, B. & Hazelwood, R.R. (1986). Detective magazines: pornography for the sexual sadists? *Journal of Forensic Sciences, 31*, 197–211.

Dietz, P.E., Hazelwood, R. & Warren, J. (1990). The sexually sadistic criminal and his offenses. *Bulletin of the American Academy of Psychiatry and the Law, 18*, 163–78.

Earls, C.M. & Proulx, J. (1986). The differentiation of francophone rapists and nonrapists using penile circumferential measures. *Criminal Justice and Behavior, 13*, 419–29.

Fedora, O., Reddon, J.R., Morrison, J.W., Fedora, S.K., Pascoe, H. & Yeudall, L. (1992). Sadism and other paraphilias in normal controls and aggressive and nonaggressive sex offenders. *Archives of Sexual Behavior, 21*, 1–15.

Feister, S.J. & Gay, M. (1991). Sadistic personality disorder: a review of data and recommendations for DSM-IV. *Journal of Personality Disorders, 5*, 376–85.

Gratzer, T. & Bradford, M.W. (1995). Offender and offense characteristics of sexual sadists: a comparative study. *Journal of Forensic Sciences, 40*, 450–5.

Hare, R.D. (1991). *The Hare Psychopathy Checklist-Revised*. Toronto: Multi-Health Systems.

Hazelwood, R.R., Dietz, P.E. & Warren, J.I. (1992). The criminal sexual sadist. *FBI Law Enforcement Bulletin, 61*, 12–20.

Hazelwood, R.R. & Douglas, J.E. (1980). The lust murderer. *FBI Law Enforcement Bulletin, 49*, 18–22.

Holt, S., Meloy, J.R. & Strack, S. (1999). Sadism and psychopathy in violent and sexually violent offenders. *Journal of American Academy of Psychiatry and the Law, 27*, 23–32.

Hucker, S.J. (1997). Sexual sadism: psychopathology and theory. In D.R. Laws & W. O'Donohue (eds), *Sexual Deviance: Theory, Assessment and Treatment* (pp. 194–209). New York: Guilford Press.

Hucker, S.J., Langevin, R., Dickey, R., Handy, L., Chambers, J. & Wright, P. (1988). Cerebral damage and dysfunction in sexually aggressive men. *Annals of Sex Research, 1*, 33–47.

Johnson, B.R. & Becker, J.V. (1997). Natural born killers?: the development of the sexually sadistic serial killer. *American Academy of Psychiatry and the Law*, **25**, 335–48.

Knight, R.A. & Prentky, R.A. (1990). Classifying sexual offenders: the development and corroboration of taxonomic models. In W.L. Marshall, D.R. Laws & H.E. Barbaree (eds), *Handbook of Sexual Assault: Issues, Theories and Treatment of the Offender* (pp. 23–52). New York: Plenum Press.

Krafft-Ebing, R. (1886). *Psychopathia Sexualis*. (F.S. Klaf-translation, 1965). New York: Arcade.

Langevin, R., Bain, J., Ben-Aron, M.K., Coulthard, R., Day, D., Handy, L., Heasman, G., Hucker, S.J., Purins, J.E., Roper, V., Russon, A.E., Webster, C.D. & Wortzman, G. (1985). Sexual aggression: constructing a predictive equation. In R. Langevin (ed.), *Erotic Preference, Gender Identity and Aggression in Men: New Research Studies* (pp. 39–76). Hillsdale NJ: Lawrence Erlbaum and Associates.

Langevin, R., Ben-Aron, M.H., Wright, P., Marchese, V. & Handy, L. (1988). The Sex Killer. *Annals of Sex Research*, **1**, 263–301.

MacCulloch, M.J., Snowden, P.R., Wood, P.J.W. & Mills, H.E. (1983). Sadistic fantasy, sadistic behaviour and offending. *British Journal of Psychiatry*, **143**, 20–9.

Marmor, J. & Gorney, R. (1999). Instinctual sadism: a recurrent myth about human nature. *Journal of the American Academy of Psychoanalysis*, **27**, 1–6.

Marshall, W.L. & Kennedy, P. (2003). Sexual sadism in sexual offenders: an elusive diagnosis. *Aggression and Violent Behavior: A Review Journal*, **8**, 1–22.

Marshall, W.L., Kennedy, P. & Yates, P. (2002). Issues concerning the reliability and validity of the diagnosis of sexual sadism applied in prison settings. *Sexual Abuse: A Journal of Research and Treatment*, **14**, 301–11.

Marshall, W.L. & Yates, P. (in press). Diagnostic issues in sexual sadism among sexual offenders. *Journal of Sexual Aggression*.

Marshall, W.L., Kennedy, P., Yates, P. & Serran, G. (2002). Diagnosing sexual sadism in sexual offenders: reliability across diagnosticians. *International Journal of Offender Therapy and Comparative Criminology*, **46**, 668–76.

Millon, T. (1983). *Millon Clinical Multiaxial Inventory Manual*. Minneapolis: Interpretive Scoring Systems.

Millon, T. & Davis, R.D. (1996). *Disorders of personality: DSM-IV and beyond*. New York: John Wiley & Sons.

Money, J. (1990). Forensic sexology: paraphilic serial rape (biastophilia) and lust murder (erotophonophilia). *American Journal of Psychotherapy*, **44**, 26–36.

Proulx, J. (2001, November). Sexual preferences and personality disorders of MTC-R3 rapists subtypes. Paper presented at the 20th Annual Research and Treatment Conference of the Association for the Treatment of Sexual Abusers. San Antonio, Texas.

Proulx, J., Aubut, J., McKibben, A. & Côté, M. (1994). Penile responses of rapists and non-rapists to rape stimuli involving physical violence or humiliation. *Archives of Sexual Behavior*, **23**, 295–310.

Proulx, J., Blais, E. & Beauregard, E. (2003). *Le sadisme sexuel*. Submitted for publication.

Proulx, J., McKibben, A. & Lusignan, R. (1996). Relationship between affective components and sexual behaviors in sexual aggressors. *Sexual Abuse: A Journal of Research and Treatment*, **8**, 279–89.

Proulx, J., St-Yves, M., Guay, J.P. & Ouimet, M. (1999). Les agresseurs sexuels de femmes: scénarios délictuels et troubles de la personnalité. In J. Proulx, M. Cusson & M. Ouimet (eds), *Les Violences Criminelles* (pp. 157–85). Saint-Nicolas, Québec: Presses de l'Université Laval.

Ressler, R.K., Burgess, A.W. & Douglas, J.E. (1988). *Sexual homicide: Patterns and Motives*. New York: Lexington.

Seto, M.C. & Kuban, M. (1996). Criterion-related validity of a phallometric test for rape and sadism. *Behaviour Research and Therapy*, **34**, 175–83.

Siomopoulos, V. & Goldsmith, J. (1976). Sadism revisited. *American Journal of Psychotherapy*, **30**, 631–40.

Smith, S. & Brown, C. (1977). Necrophilia and lust murder: report of a rare occurrence. *Bulletin of the American Academy of Psychiatry and the Law*, **6**, 259–68.

Spitzer, R.L., Feister, S., Gay, M. & Pfohl, B. (1991). Results of a survey of forensic psychiatrists on the validity of the sadistic personality disorder diagnosis. *American Journal of Psychiatry*, **148**, 875–9.

Warren, J., Hazelwood, R. & Dietz, P. (1996). The sexually sadistic serial killer. *Journal of Forensic Sciences*, **41**, 970–4.

Chapter 6

ONLINE SEXUALITY AND ONLINE SEXUAL PROBLEMS: SKATING ON THIN ICE

AL COOPER*, GALE GOLDEN[†] AND WILLIAM L. MARSHALL[‡]

* deceased
† private practice, University of Vermont Medical College, Burlington, Vermont, USA
‡ Rockwood Psychological Services, Kingston, Ontario, Canada

Observations about obsessional love and compulsive sexual behaviors are not new. Since human beings began to express themselves on granite walls and clay scrolls, there has been a fascination with sexuality. Secular and religious literature, oral history, art and music were all replete with both overt and oblique references to the power sex holds. About 4,000 years ago, the Sumarians wrote about the sexual conquests of the warrior Gilgamesh in *The Epic of Gilgamesh* which describes his behavior and reputation: "His lust leaves no virgin to her lover, neither the warrior's daughter nor the wife of the nobleman." Forty centuries later the Internet burst upon the world and has given us yet another outlet for the expression of sexuality. Its potential seems infinite, frightening and wondrous all at the same time.

In May 1997, the *Wall Street Journal* ran a story about a stripper, Danni Ashe, who was able to use her business skills to market sexually explicit images of herself and other models on the Internet. Lane (2001) reports how the journalist, Thomas E. Weber,

> described how Ashe's site, *Danni's Hard Drive*, was "bring [ing] in so much revenue that she has given up the stage and nude photo shoots . . . Now the pay site boasts 17,000 members, putting Ms. Ashe on pace for more than $2 million in revenue [in 1997] . . ." (Lane, 2001, p. XIII)

Furthermore Lane notes that in just over five years, "the number of World Wide Web users in the US alone has risen from zero to more than 100 million" (Lane 2001, p. 272). With this proliferation of web users, the number of people who use the Internet for online sexual activity has also increased dramatically. It is estimated that 25% of the 100 million users of the Internet engage in some form of online sexual activity (Egan, 2002). Thus approximately 25 million people are online seeking

Sexual Offender Treatment: Controversial Issues. Edited by W.L. Marshall, Y.M. Fernandez, L.E. Marshall and G.A. Serran. © 2006 John Wiley & Sons, Ltd.

some kind of sexual contact and this number grows every day. Furthermore, in a national survey of youth on the Internet, Finklehor, Mitchell and Wolak (2000) found that an alarming number of children are being exposed to the sexual content of the web and were being caught in it. Among a sample of 1,501 youth aged ten to 17 years, one in 33 received an unwelcome and aggressive sexual solicitation (e.g. a telephone call, letter, money or gifts) and one in four had unwanted exposure to pictures of people having sex or pictures of naked people. We are only beginning to understand the clinical, social and legal implications of such pervasive use of the Internet for sexual activity.

Why does the Internet have such power and popularity? Unlike the warrior Gilgamesh who had to leave home to pursue his prey and could not predict when and where he would find it, today's Internet user can pursue sexual contacts from their home and have an infinite variety of sexual experiences in the world of "virtual sex". Cooper (1997) claims that online sexual activities are turbocharged by a "Triple A Engine" which gives the user a sense of *accessibility, affordability* and *anonymity*. Ironically, it is just these qualities of the "Triple A Engine" that make sexual activities on the Internet intrinsically difficult to contain. Certainly the Internet makes the world of sexuality accessible in a way that no one could ever have imagined. Anyone, anytime can visit the Internet and access an infinite variety of sexual content. Affordability, on the other hand, can be an illusion. Some sites are expensive and an obsessed user can be online for many hours accumulating very large credit card charges. The costs in terms of quality of life, employment loss and wasted time are also great. Anonymity, or the implication of secrecy, is also a very powerful quality that may serve to heighten the attractiveness of the Internet. But, as technology improves, anonymity on line is becoming more and more an illusion than a fact. These days even a relatively unsophisticated but determined partner, spouse, family member, employer or police officer can track someone's Internet use and expose sexual pursuits. Exposed, the user may be found to have a more profound problem than was assumed. Galbreath, Berlin and Sawyer (2002, p. 189) characterize "cruising society's new red-light district" for sexual stimulation as being an expression of a powerful biological drive, and "like all basic biological drives . . . [the user] will recurrently crave satiation". The findings of Cooper, Boies, Mahieu and Greenfield (1999), on the other hand, assure us that the majority of people who visit sexual sites on the Internet do so for recreational purposes and do not suffer any negative consequences.

So one might ask why a chapter about online sexual activity would be included in a book focused on paraphilic behavior? What has cruising sexual sites anonymously and in private got to do with sexual offending? Our clinical work and emerging research informs us that for some who are online for sexual stimulation, it is simply not an occasional and innocent erotic event but instead, it is a result of an obsession that has the real potential for escalating into a criminal act. Indeed, this clearly happens (McCabe, 2000). Most men who are convicted of downloading child pornography from the Internet claim not to have actually offended against children. In fact, they often argue that masturbating to child pornography viewed on the Internet satisfies their urges, which might otherwise be expressed in actual sexual contact with a child. However, recent reports from Hernandez (2000, 2004) contradict these claims. He identified 29 men convicted of possession of child pornography downloaded from the Internet, who otherwise had no documented history of contact offenses and who denied ever committing an offense. After these men had completed an extensive sexual offender treatment program at a United States federal prison, 18 admitted to having molested an average of 12.3 child victims. Whether the remaining 11 were being truthful when they continued to deny contact offenses seems doubtful, but the fact remains that using Internet child pornography does not protect men from abusing children. Given evidence that some users of Internet pornography, with no previous history of deviant sexual interests, progress from original access to appropriate sexual images to progressively more deviant material (Cooper, Delmonico & Burg, 2000; Cooper, Putnam, Planchon & Boies, 1999; Greenfield, 1999; Schneider, 2000), it seems likely that at least some men who access child pornography sites on the Internet are led there by earlier access to more innocent sites.

It is also likely that for some, sexual activity on the Internet will fall just short of illegal behavior but will seriously interfere with the development or maintenance of a satisfying lifestyle. Increasingly we hear of children being pursued by adults in chat rooms for the purpose of arranging meetings for sexual contact. Research and clinical observations are beginning to confirm that online sexual activities can have both benign as well as problematic consequences (Cooper, Scherer, Boies & Gordon, 1999; Leiblum, 1997). Therefore, it is important for the benefit of all involved to better understand the variety of sexual activities online and how they are used if we are going to develop treatment strategies as well as public policy interventions.

DEFINING AND DESCRIBING ONLINE SEXUAL BEHAVIOR

Researchers and clinicians in the field of sexology are just beginning to describe the nuances and subtleties of sexual behaviors associated with the Internet. "These behaviors can be obsessive as well as compulsive, can appear to have many of the qualities we associate with addiction and may be either censored or tolerated by society" (Golden, 2001 p. 50). We think it is critical that leaders in the field work to develop a common language and taxonomy that will not only facilitate a dialogue about treatment methodologies but will aid in the development of research and public policy.

A useful way of categorizing and describing online sexual activity (OSA) and its subtypes has been developed by Cooper and Griffin-Shelley (2002).

> *Online Sexual Activity*: the use of the Internet for sexual activity of any type (e.g.: viewing live videos, participating in chat rooms, viewing sexual behavior of any kind, recreational or educational purposes).
>
> 1. cybersex: using the Internet to engage in sexually gratifying activities (e.g. similar to telephone sex and can be called cybersexing).
> 2. online sexual problems (OSP): the full range of problems people can have by engaging in OSA.
> 3. online sexual compulsivity (OSC): a type of OSP which refers to the full spectrum of problematic situations that result from excessive OSA including the loss of control over one's behavior and one's activities of daily living.

Personal expressions of sexuality are infinitely unique and evolve over time. OSA is no different. It also has the potential for mutating, escalating and becoming problematic as the behaviors continue. When OSAs become problematic, they may be categorized as hypersexuality. Kafka (2000) defines hypersexuality as "the disinhibited or exaggerated expressions of human sexual arousal and appetitive behavior" (p. 472). Hypersexuality can be either paraphilic or nonparaphilic, both of which are defined by "excesses of fantasies, urges and overt sexual behaviors" (Kafka, 2000, p. 472). The difference between these two types of hypersexual behaviors is that paraphilias are socially censored and may be illegal while nonparaphilic behaviors are not. Kafka (2000) unites nonparaphilic hypersexuality and sexual compulsivity/addiction disorders under a common label he calls *paraphilia-related disorders* (PRDs). There is evidence that paraphilias and paraphilia-related disorders have common clinical patterns and it has been suggested that PRDs may be common among paraphilic males (Kafka, 2000). Therefore, online sexual problems and online sexual compulsivity can be classified as paraphilia-related disorders and in some cases these may eventually develop into, or become an integral part of, a full-fledged paraphilia.

Not everyone who uses the Internet for OSA is, of course, out of control or has a paraphilia-related disorder but the potential for problems, or even for developing a paraphilia, are realistic concerns for those who pursue sexual stimulation on the Internet. Three common types of OSAs are: (1) cruising the Internet for sexually explicit stimuli such as pictures, stories or videos of a wide variety of sexual behaviors; (2) entering chat rooms for sexually explicit conversations; or (3) finding people to meet off-line for the purposes of romantic or sexual relationships. Cooper, Putnam *et al.* (1999) describe three types of users who engage in OSA: (1) recreational or nonpathological users; (2) users who have a pre-existing disposition for sexual compulsions; (3) users with no pre-existing disposition for compulsivity but whose exposure to the Internet challenges their inner resources and their impulse control so they cannot resist the Internet's powerful force.

There is a myth that only men develop paraphilias. However, research is beginning to reveal that significant numbers of women are not only involved in childhood sexual abuse but in paraphilias and paraphilia-related disorders as well (David, Hislop & Dunbar, 1999; Fedoroff, Fishell & Fedoroff, 1999; Leitenberg & Henning, 1995). More to the point, Finkelhor *et al.* (2000) report, in their study of online victimization of children, that the gender of the harasser was female in 24% of the reported incidents. Therefore it is wise to think about both genders as having the potential for developing problems with online sex.

Whether the OSA escalates to the status of a paraphilia-related disorder or to a paraphilia, the consequences can be serious. Golden (2001) notes that "While in fact some of these OSAs may not be illegal, when they are discovered, it may seem to those involved that a major loathsome crime has been committed" (p. 51).

The ripple effect of problematic OSAs can be devastating and pervasive. Not only does the person who suffers from this problem often require intensive intervention, it is also likely that interventions with family and community will be needed. The consequences of pedophilia and Internet use come together in the documentary *Capturing the Freidmans* (Jareki, 2003). In the documentary, the children who were allegedly victimized were shown sexual "games" masquerading as a teaching technique for learning how to use the computer. Observing the students' reaction to it may have been a covert grooming technique for the subsequent sexual abuse perpetrated by the teacher. The documentary powerfully depicts the vortex of family dysfunction and destruction as well as community hysteria that surrounds these difficult issues. Studies demonstrate that people with both paraphilia-related disorders as well as paraphilias have not only comorbid mental health problems (Kafka, 2000) but also have childhoods that are notable for sexual and physical abuse as well as early and inappropriate exposure to sexual material and over-sexualized environments (Carnes, 1983, 1991; Coleman, 1995).

A case illustration highlights the above discussion and raises many assessment and treatment issues:

> Carl is a 42-year old man who has been married eight years and has a two-year-old daughter. He has had trouble holding a job over the years but his wife, Mary, maintains a family business which allows him some structure and therefore he is able to contribute to it. Prior to the referral for marital therapy, he had been in treatment for depression for a year. He was seeing a therapist once a week and was being followed by a psychiatrist for medication. His wife, Mary, learned that he was having sex with a woman he had met online while she thought he was working. He claimed it was an innocent flirtation and did not mean anything, but his wife insisted that they get counseling. She wanted to salvage the marriage but was not sure it was possible. During the assessment phase with a marital therapist who had experience with hypersexuality, Carl revealed that he had a long-standing but secret obsession with exhibiting himself and had masturbated to this fantasy as frequently as five times a day, sometimes at work. It has recently escalated to the point where Carl had taken nude photos of himself and placed them on the Internet. He also spent as many as eight hours at a time in chat rooms, masturbating to images of a voyeuristic nature. He fantasized about contacting "young women" who will watch him masturbate and thinks about going to places where he may be seen masturbating. He denies he has ever actually acted on his fantasy and feels he never would but his habit has escalated over the past few years and his depression is getting worse.

ASSESSMENT CONSIDERATIONS

The assessment of Internet-related sexual behaviors, whether they are paraphilia-related behaviors or paraphilias, presents unique issues and raises difficult questions. For example, the assessment phase and treatment phase need to overlap in these cases, particularly in the area of attempting to contain some of the behaviors. In addition, the taxonomy, treatment methodologies and the law have not yet caught up with some of the issues that are emerging and get uncovered in an assessment. Foley (2002) has recently noted that some of his clients, with no prior history of sexual compulsions or sexual acting out, have eventually accessed the Internet to observe pictures of children although they claim not to have engaged in the behavior off-line. Fedoroff (2003) refers to these men as "victimless" pedophiles. However, in so far as the images are of real children, viewing these images may be seen as contributing to the victimization of children. How do we determine how likely it is that these people will act out with children as their inner resources are challenged? As we have seen earlier, recent observations within prison settings suggest that some men who have only been detected for downloading Internet "child porn" have, in fact, molested children (Hernandez, 2000, 2004). Thus, use of the Internet to access sexual images of children appears to be associated with actual molestation. In any case, those who use the Internet for the purpose of accessing sexual images of children clearly have a serious sexual problem whether or not they have, as yet, actually molested children. These clients are likely to appear more frequently at treatment programs over the next few years. At present, unfortunately, we know little about these offenders. It is also possible that now there is more information and education about treatment for paraphilias, more people may ask for help and treatment before they are arrested (Fedoroff, 2003).

While we struggle with these questions, guidelines and laws are just beginning to emerge that can inform us as we make assessments of people who have OSPs, particularly those who access sites involving children. Some people who access these sites may incorrectly assume that it is legal to download all forms of pornography without fear of prosecution. However, paradoxically the United States Communications Decency Act of 1996 protects the net server from prosecution for posting pornography online but does not protect the consumer when they download pornography depicting children (Foley, 2002). As we pointed out above, the assumption of anonymity and confidentiality online is an illusion. Foley (2002) points out that, according to the FBI, illegal sexual activity online includes: "producing or possessing child pornography; uploading and downloading child pornography; and soliciting sex with children"(Foley, 2002, p. 26.2).

In conducting an assessment of OSA it is helpful (and wise) to keep in mind that the sexual activity being scrutinized has been a closely guarded secret that has often been in place for years. People do not give up their secrets willingly. Golden and Cooper (2003) observe that "the subtleties and nuances of sexual compulsivity connected to the Internet are often masked in a routine mental health evaluation or may masquerade as something else entirely" (p. 28). Some of the common problems masking online sexual compulsivity include: marital discord, intimacy and attachment difficulties, lowered work productivity, alcohol or substance abuse, depression and anxiety. The case above underscores just how important an accurate assessment can be. Carl was being treated for depression for a year but his secrets had not been revealed to either his therapist or psychiatrist. Therefore, his treatment and medication were targeting only a part of his problem and thus were not nearly as effective as they might have been. It also speaks to the need for the assessor to be someone who is experienced and knowledgeable in the area of sexual compulsivity and who keeps up with the rapidly evolving area of OSA (Cooper & Griffin-Shelly, 2002).

At the outset of every assessment, it is critical to understand the context of the referral and what the consequences of the desired changes will mean to the life of the person. Experienced clinicians will factor in not only the implications of giving up the pleasure the OSP provided but also the many levels of resistance inherent in the stasis of the family system. For example, in the case outlined above, Mary had a history of sexual abuse and was somewhat relieved to have Carl's sexual interest channeled away from her. In addition, while both of them were dissatisfied with Carl's pervasive sense of inadequacy and recurrent failures in holding jobs, he got gratification from Mary's caretaking and her ability to pick up most of the responsibilities. While she complained about the stress of being a caretaker, Mary had difficulty relinquishing the overt power and control that it gave her and that she needed in order to feel safe in the relationship. Therefore it is important to understand these online sexual behaviors in terms of intrapsychic and dyadic consent (Golden, 2001).

Assessments of OSPs may coincide with the necessity for containment of the behavior. A simple first containment measure might be denying or limiting access to the computer. It is important however to assess what this would mean to the patient, family or employer. In the cases that include illegal behaviors, the legal system provides containment measures and consequences that have a power of their own depending upon the particular jurisdiction, and the judge, as well as the mood of the community. It is notable that systematic analyses have called into question the idea that incarceration without treatment is the most effective way to reduce recidivism (Hanson & Bussière, 1998). The relationship between the legal system and the perpetrator is an adversarial one. The relationship between a therapist and a client demands a supportive, nonjudgmental stance, which at the same time must not be seen as condoning the behavior. Not unexpectedly, those involved, other than the client, feel anger, revulsion and discomfort with the behaviors of the perpetrator. The therapist is also called upon to deal with these feelings in a therapeutic way. Galbreath *et al.* (2002) spell out what must be the common denominator for all professionals who work with people who have OSPs:

> When a person receives a paraphilic diagnosis such as pedophilia, for example, it is important for the clinician to appreciate that it is not his fault that he has such a condition. In growing up, no one would decide to be sexually oriented toward children. (p. 197)

It is an essential ingredient of the assessment, therefore, that the assessor is clearly seen as nonjudgmental, experienced and knowledgeable, and knows about the treatment possibilities. The assessor should also be willing to share information and observations with the client as questions or problems arise. The relationship between this type of client and the person doing the assessment will no doubt be a complicated dance to both obtain honesty and establish trust. Even when the assessment and treatment are conducted by different people, there is much overlap between the assessment and treatment phases in these cases.

It is important to point out that when people who have been online for sexual activity enter the criminal justice system, there are some issues that are both unique and intrinsic to a forensic evaluation. In these cases, the legal system itself presents boundary issues that are complex and important to keep in mind (Doren, 2002). For example, who actually makes the referral for assessment? Is it the legal system, a parent, spouse, employer or the patient? What then are the obligations of the assessor to share the information gathered with someone other than the patient? In assessing paraphilic behavior on the Internet, we must keep in mind that there may be a forensic element to some of these cases and thus the possibility that the assessor will have to appear in court. It is likely that the evaluation and its findings might also be called upon to serve as a guideline for decision making about length and type of incarceration or treatment, in response to which the client may be unhappy. It is prudent, therefore, to consider having a separate person be responsible for the treatment phase following the evaluation. Galbreath *et al.* (2002) consider the essential elements of a thorough evaluation in the cases of paraphilic activity on the Internet. We have expanded it to include assessment issues in all types of OSPs. First, review as much collateral information as is available. This would include but would not be limited to: all medical (including mental health) records; police and legal records; family members and employers; victim impact statements; copies of any Internet communications; and information from prior therapist or evaluators. Second, conduct face-to-face interviews focussing on: medical history; previous participation in therapy; family and relationship history; sexual development history including any history of sexual abuse; sexual behaviors with partners; masturbatory fantasies; use of phone sex or prostitutes and details of pornography use; and finally, Internet use and sites accessed. When assessing Internet use it is necessary to determine what OSA was engaged in (pictures, jpegs, live streaming videos, chat rooms, sexual bulletin boards, net groups), whether or not images were traded, and whether or not sites were accessed to contact people off-line.

In forensic situations, the courts often want to have psychological testing done, and while psychological tests may be helpful, good clinical observations are also necessary (Galbreath *et al.*, 2002). It is important to note that at the present time "assessment instruments cannot replace the personal interaction and clinical judgment of a trained therapist" (Delmonico, Griffin & Carnes, 2002, p. 150) because tests to evaluate OSAs are still in the very early stages of development (Foley, 2002).

The family, relationships and social milieu of the person requiring attention are also a critical part of the assessment process. The long-term recovery of the person will be enhanced if they are involved in a supportive and stable family or partnered relationship (Wincze, 2000). Also the traumas experienced by the person in the past and the present may also be experienced by family members and others and require attention (Christensen & Cramer Reu, 2002). Unfortunately, the system often overlooks or minimizes the impact on the family and others of an accusation of paraphilic behavior and the ensuing criminal investigations and legal process. We know that children exposed to sexual material beyond their developmental capacity to understand it are often left with negative consequences (Longo, Brown & Orcutt, 2002). Having a parent, relative or friend hauled off by the legal system, chronicling it in the media, exposing them to community censure, and generally terrorizing them can be a crippling life event. Therefore, as the family and social system's needs are assessed, preventive and palliative measures should be applied as soon as possible in the process. Social and legal policy would be well served by more attention to this issue.

Finally, in making an assessment of online sexual problems, the clinician should assess the presence of other comorbid states.

> In the few studies that systematically evaluated Axis 1 diagnoses in "sexually compulsive" males and females ... or paraphilia-related disorders ... one of the major findings is that most subjects with these disorders have multiple lifetime comorbid mood, anxiety, psychoactive substance abuse and/or impulse disorder diagnoses. (Kafka, 2000)

With the lifting of these often chronic issues, a person can bring much more resilience and perspective to the work of resolving the sexual acting out.

TREATMENT CONSIDERATIONS

Golden (2001) notes that treatment for online sexual compulsivity needs to be multimodal. Fedoroff (2003) suggests that the relapse rates for people with these problems can be reduced by modern specialized treatment. He adds that if there is a shared vision between therapist and patient and the goal of treatment is the "establishment of a lawful, happy, fulfilling sex life within the context of a meaningful and balanced lifestyle" (Fedoroff, 2003, p. 351), it will result in much higher motivation during the treatment. We must not underestimate that power of the therapeutic relationship and the "safe holding environment" it provides. At the same time, it is not unusual for patients to lie or withhold information from the therapist. When this occurs, understanding and support should also be given by the therapist.

At this time, the state of the art in the treatment of OSPs includes cognitive-behavioral, psychodynamic, medical and group components (Foley, 2002). Group therapy is valuable (Line & Cooper, 2002), and while sometimes therapist-run groups are not available in a particular community, 12-step groups (e.g. SA and SLAA) are not uncommon and even available online.

Cognitive-behavioral interventions are the most prevalent and therefore provide the greatest opportunity for research with sexual disorders (Delmonico et al., 2002; Fedoroff, 2003; Hanson et al., 2002; Marshall, Anderson & Fernandez, 1999). This approach includes, among others: procedures for keeping diaries of fantasies, thoughts and behaviors; understanding the behavioral chains that trigger sexual acting out; and teaching relapse prevention strategies. In addition, when the Internet user is accessing child pornography, he should be seen in the same light as a child molester and offered a full comprehensive sexual offender program (see Marshall et al., 1999 for a description). Such programs address self-esteem, cognitive distortions, schemas, empathy, intimacy, coping, deviant sexual interests and detailed relapse prevention plans (Carich & Mussack, 2001; Marshall, Serran & Moulden, in press).

If the OSA is potentially risky (e.g. loss of employment or professional license, multiple anonymous adult sexual contacts without precautions for STDs, severe sadomasochism or pursuing children for sexual contacts) the need for containment is urgent and might include an intensive course of treatment or even referral to a residential treatment program. The partner, spouse and family should also be referred for help for themselves and begin to be educated about what it means to have this problem, and what the treatment options are.

Psychodynamic psychotherapy may also be a helpful part of the equation in working with people who have OSP (Cooper & Marcus, 2003). As noted above, the therapeutic relationship may provide the first occasion the patient has ever had to reveal his secrets and have them reflected back in a nonjudgmental way. In therapy, both patient and therapist can discover the function secrets served in the life of the patient. Understanding what is behind the acting out and how it is a defensive structure against painful and difficult feelings will provide the patient with a solid foundation for recovery. It is to be expected that the intimacy of the therapeutic relationship will be difficult for a person who has carefully defended against a close meaningful relationship in which the self is exposed. As the secrets come out, the patient typically feels out of control and angry and acts this out in the therapy over and over again.

Transference and countertransference issues are always complex in therapy. Eroticizing the therapist is a common way transference manifests itself when working with a person with sexual problems. For example, when Carl began to keep diaries of his fantasies, thoughts and behaviors early in the treatment process, they were very detailed accounts, to the point where they appeared to have an exhibitionistic quality to them. It was easy to see that he was trying to repeat with the female therapist what he did online. Since she knew he had been rejected by both his parents as well as by many women, she had to be careful to be supportive while also helping him to contain himself. If she had rejected the diaries' content and was judgmental, it would have reinforced rather than contained his behaviors. Rejected, he also might have ended his therapy. In order for the therapist to provide an appropriate response to Carl's diaries she also had to be conscious of her feelings about them. It could have been easy for her to feel angry, exploited and victimized by being exposed to such details. If she had not understood her own reactions that session could have repeated many experiences Carl had had with women in the past. Seemingly small details such as timing of appointments, payments, the space within which the therapy takes place, as well as what the therapist may wear are all possible triggers for transference reactions and will be grist for the therapeutic mill. There are many opportunities when the therapist can both think and behave psychodynamically as well as behaviorally. They are not mutually exclusive styles.

In addition to the above, a comprehensive treatment package for OSPs has also included a 12-step program and a professionally led group if available in the community (Orzack & Ross, 2000). Such 12-step groups are said to decrease the client's sense of alienation and increase the realm of supports he has and, as a consequence, increase his full participation in a cognitive behavioral program (Orzack & Ross, 2000). Neverthless, it is important to assess the effectiveness of these additional groups and their degree of fit for individual goals. Apparently some of these self-led groups actually reinforce dysfunctional behavior rather than support change (Golden & Cooper, 2003).

The role of medication is an important adjunct to therapy and the choices have burgeoned just as choices on the Internet have in the past 20 years. The selective serotonin reuptake inhibitors have had an impact upon the standard of care for people suffering with hypersexuality, sexual compulsions and the comorbid states that accompany them (Nelson, Soutullo, DelBello & McElroy, 2002). They quiet the obsessional thinking in a remarkable way and give clients a sense of control over their thoughts and behaviors that they have never before experienced and thus provide growth in many areas of their lives. In cases of pedophilia, some patients may benefit from the use of antiandronergic medications which serve to lower the sexual appetite of the paraphilic person (Galbreath et al., 2002).

As we have mentioned above, there are also many comorbid conditions in people who have hypersexual habits on the Internet. It is essential to treat these problems as one would any other person with depression, anxiety or obsessive and compulsive habits. Sobriety from drugs and alcohol is essential. It is our observation that once these comorbid problems are treated and contained over a period of time, perhaps four or five years, the developmental steps that were missed because of drugs, alcohol, sexual abuse and chronic mental and emotional issues will begin to take place, allowing the person to have more resilience and control over their impulses.

CONCLUSIONS

We cannot help but wonder what the warrior Gilgamesh would think of the Internet and its possibilities. Could he have limited his sexual exploits to the Internet and been an occasional user or would he have used the Internet to enlarge upon his predatory proclivities? Even though we have evolved from writing on granite walls to watching a small flat screen, the need for sexual expression has remained a powerful force. It is only the venue that separates us from Gilgamesh.

Many of the debates about the Internet have the same tone as when the technology of movies, radios and television burst upon the public. Boundaries all over the world are being broken down; we have the potential to be closer to each other than ever before and perhaps it makes us all uncomfortable, this much intimacy with strangers. Maybe impersonal cybersex becomes an easier substitute.

Our warrior Gilgamesh was a sexual predator, a womanizer, before there were labels for these types of behavior. The Internet merely provides a novel and inventive venue for sexual activity in a way that has not been available before. Some are up to the challenge that the Internet lavishly and seductively offers, and some are not. None of us decide one day to be hypersexual any more than we decide how to be sexual in other realms. However, being aware of the potential for losing control and perhaps being in danger of doing something illegal, it "becomes an individual's responsibility to do something about it so as to ensure that he will not cause problems in the lives of others" (Galbreath et al., 2002, p. 196). By developing treatments and creating social policy to respond to these issues, we are not supporting the behavior; rather we are offering the possibility that the person can accept the responsibility to change these behaviors and find a functional and harmless way to fulfill their sexual and relational needs.

Treatment methodologies, research, taxonomy and social policy regarding the Internet are gaining momentum. The opportunities the Internet provides are developing faster than we can respond to them. However, it is remarkable how much more we know about these issues now and how much more we have to offer. It is often useful, in the course of therapy, to look back with the client to consider how much has changed since they first began the journey of recovery. It is equally important for those of us who are trying to keep up with the Internet, and feel it is out-running us, to also remember how far we have come since the journey began. For those of us who treat these clients and know how hard it is for them to deal with their personal issues, help cannot come soon enough.

REFERENCES

Carich, M.S. & Mussack, S.E. (2001). *Handbook for Sexual Abuser Assessment and Treatment.* Brandon, VT: Safer Society Press.
Carnes, P. (1983). *Out of the Shadows: Understanding Sexual Addiction.* Minneapolis: Compcare.
Carnes, P. (1991). *Don't Call it Love: Recovery from Sexual Addiction.* New York: Bantam Books.

Christensen, G.E. & Cramer Reu, H.E. (2002). Assessment and treatment for the non offending parent for the benefit of the victim—a dynamic continuum of reaction and response.
In B. Schwartz (ed.), *The Sex Offender: Current Treatment Modalities and Systems Issues*,
vol. **IV** (pp. 25.1–25.15). Kingston, NJ: Civic Research Institute.

Coleman, E. (1995). Treatment of compulsive sexual behavior. In R.C. Rosen & S.R. Lieblum
(eds), *Case Studies in Sex Therapy* (pp. 333–49). New York: Guilford Press.

Cooper, A. (1997). The Internet and sexuality: into the new millennium. *Journal of Sex Education and Therapy*, **22**, 5–6.

Cooper, A., Boies, S., Mahieu, M. & Greenfield, D. (1999). Sexuality and the Internet: the
next sexual revolution. In L. Szuchman & F. Muscarella (eds), *Psychological Perspectives on
Human Sexuality* (pp. 519–45). New York: John Wiley & Sons.

Cooper, A., Delmonico, D.L. & Burg, R. (2000). Cybersex users, abusers and compulsives:
new findings and implications. *Sexual Addiction and Compulsivity*, **7**, 5–29.

Cooper, A. & Griffin-Shelly, E. (2002). The Internet: the next sexual revolution. In A. Cooper
(ed.), *Sex and the Internet: A Guidebook for Clinicians* (pp. 147–68). New York: Brunner
Routledge.

Cooper, A. & Marcus, D. (2003). Men who lose control of their sexual behavior. In S. Levine
(ed.), *Handbook of Clinical Sexuality for Mental Health Professionals* (pp. 311–32). New York:
Brunner Routledge.

Cooper, A., Putnam, D.E., Planchon, L. & Boies, S.C. (1999). Online sexual compulsivity:
getting tangled in the net. *Sexual Addiction and Compulsivity*, **6**, 79–104.

Cooper, A., Scherer, C., Boies S.C. & Gordon, B. (1999). Sexuality on the internet: from sexual
exploration to pathological expression. *Professional Psychology: Research and Practice*, **30**,
154–64.

David, P.A., Hislop, C.R. & Dunbar, T. (1999). *Female Sexual Abusers*. Brandon, VT: Safer
Society Press.

Delmonico, D., Griffin, E. & Carnes, P. (2002). Treating online sexual behavior: when cybersex
is the drug of choice. In A. Cooper (ed.), *Sex and the Internet: A Guidebook for Clinicians*
(pp. 147–68). New York: Brunner Routledge.

Doren, D.M. (2002). *Evaluating Sex Offenders*. Thousand Oaks, CA: Sage Publications.

Egan, T. (2002, 23 October). Technology sent Wall Street into market for pornography.
New York Times, **1**, 20.

Fedoroff, J.P. (2003). The paraphilic world. In S. Levine (ed.), *Handbook of Clinical Sexuality
for Mental Health Professionals* (pp. 333–6). New York: Brunner Routledge.

Fedoroff, J.P., Fishell, A. & Fedoroff, B. (1999). A case series of women evaluated for paraphilic
sexual disorders. *Canadian Journal of Human Sexuality*, **5**, 127–40.

Finkelhor, D., Mitchell, K.J. & Wolak, J. (2000). Online victimization: a report on the nation's
youth. Durham, NH: National Center for Missing and Exploited Children: Crimes against
Children Research Center.

Foley, T.P. (2002). Forensic assessment of internet child pornography offenders. In
B. Schwartz (ed.), *The Sex Offender: Current Treatment Modalities and System Issues*, vol. **IV**
(pp. 26.1–26.18). Kingston, NJ: Civic Research Institute.

Galbreath, N.W., Berlin, F.S. & Sawyer, D. (2002). Paraphilias and the internet. In A. Cooper
(ed.), *Sex and the Internet: A Guidebook for Clinicians* (pp. 187–205). New York: Brunner-
Routledge.

Golden, G.H. (2001). Dyadic-dystonic compelling eroticism: can these relationships be
saved? *Journal of Sex Education and Therapy*, **26**, 50–8.

Golden, G.H. & Cooper, A. (2003). Summary of treatment and assessment issues in sexual
compulsivity. *Annals of the American Psychotherapy Association* **6**, 28–30.

Greenfield, D.N. (1999). *Virtual Addiction: Help for Netheads, Cyberfreaks, and Those Who Love
Them*. Oakland, CA: New Harbinger Publications.

Hanson, R.K. & Bussière, M.T. (1998). Predicting relapse: a meta-analysis of sexual offender
recidivism studies. *Journal of Consulting and Clinical Psychiatry*, **66**, 348–62.

Hanson, R.K., Gordon, A., Harris, A.J.R., Marques, J.K., Murphy, W.D., Quinsey, V.L. & Seto,
M. (2002). First report of the collaborative outcome data project on the effectiveness of
psychological treatment for sex offenders. *Sexual Abuse: A Journal of Research and Treatment*,
14, 167–92.

Hernandez, A.E. (2000, November). Self-reported contact sexual offenses by participants in the Federal Bureau of Prisons' Sex Offender Treatment Program: Implications for Internet sex offenders. Paper presented at the 19th Annual Research and Treatment Conference of the Association for the Treatment of Sexual Abusers. San Diego, CA.

Hernandez, A.E. (2004). Self-reported contact sexual crimes of federal inmates convicted of child pornography offenses. Unpublished paper, Federal Correctional Institute, Butner, NC.

Jareki, A. (2003). *Capturing the Friedmans.* Los Angeles: HBO.

Kafka, M.P. (2000). The paraphilia-related disorders: non-paraphilic hypersexuality and sexual compulsivity/addiction. In S.R. Lieblum & R.C. Rosen (eds), *Principles and Practice of Sex Therapy*, 3rd edn (pp. 471–503). New York: Guilford Press.

Lane, F. (2001). *Obscene Profits: The Entrepreneurs of Pornography in the Cyber Age.* New York: Routledge.

Leitenberg, H. & Henning, K. (1995). Sexual fantasy. *Psychological Bulletin, 117,* 469–96.

Lieblum, S.R. (1997). Sex and the net: clinical implications. *Journal of Sex Education and Therapy,* **22,** 21–7.

Line, B. & Cooper, A. (2002). Group therapy: essential component for success with sexually acting out problems among men. *Sexual Addiction and Compulsivity: Journal of Treatment and Intervention, 9,* 15–32.

Longo, R., Brown, S.M. & Orcutt, D.P. (2002). Effects of internet sexuality on children and adolescents. In A. Cooper (ed.), *Sex and the Internet: A Guidebook for Clinicians* (pp. 87–105). New York: Brunner Routledge.

Marshall, W.L., Anderson, D. & Fernandez, Y.M. (1999). *Cognitive Behavioural Treatment of Sexual Offenders.* Chichester, UK: John Wiley & Sons.

Marshall, W.L., Serran, G.A. & Moulden, H. (in press). Effective intervention with sexual offenders. In H. Kemshall & G. McIvor (eds), *Sexual Offending: Managing the Risk, Research Highlights in Social Work.* London: Jessica Kingsley.

McCabe, K. (2000). Child pornography and the Internet. *Social Science Computer Review,* **18,** 73–6.

Nelson, E.B., Soutullo, C.A., DelBello, M.P. & McElroy, S.L. (2002). The psychopharmocological treatment of sexual offenders. In B. Schwartz (ed.), *The Sex Offender: Current Treatment Modalities and System Issues*, vol. **IV** (pp. 13.1–13.30). Kingston, NJ: Civic Research Institute.

Orzack, M.H. & Ross, C.J. (2000). Should virtual sex be treated like other sex addictions? *Sexual Addiction and Compulsivity, 7,* 113–25.

Schneider, J.P. (2000). Effects of cybersex addiction on the family: results of a survey. *Sexual Addiction and Compulsivity, 7,* 31–58.

Wincze, J.P. (2000). Assessment and treatment of atypical sexual behavior. In S.R. Lieblum & R.C. Rosen (eds), *Principles and Practice of Sex Therapy*, 3rd edn (pp. 449–70). New York: Guilford Press.

Chapter 7

AN ATTACHMENT-THEORETICAL REVISION OF MARSHALL AND BARBAREE'S *INTEGRATED THEORY* OF THE ETIOLOGY OF SEXUAL OFFENDING

STEPHEN W. SMALLBONE

School of Criminology and Criminal Justice, Griffith University, Queensland, Australia

The observed heterogeneity of sexual offending behavior has presented a significant obstacle to the development and testing of general explanatory models. Numerous taxonomic schemes have been suggested as a means to identify more homogenous offense and offender subgroups. The most popular of these are rational, descriptive schemes based on victim age, victim gender and, particularly with respect to sexual offending against children, whether the offenses have occurred in familial or nonfamilial settings. Other taxonomic schemes have been empirically (e.g. Knight, Carter & Prentky, 1989) or theoretically derived (e.g. Hall & Hirschman, 1991). The prevailing consensus is that sexual offending behavior is multi-faceted and multi-determined, and that there may be different causal pathways associated with different forms of sexual offending (Hudson, Ward & McCormack, 1999). Taxonomic approaches may thus produce important contributions to knowledge about sexual offenses and sexual offenders. However, short of assuming that the various proposed types of sexual offending represent distinct and unrelated phenomena, which seems untenable, taxonomic approaches cannot *replace* knowledge about the more general features of the phenomenon. There remains a need to discover and better understand features that may be common to all, or at least to a majority, of sexual offenses.

Among the few attempts to articulate a general explanatory model of sexual offending, Marshall and Barbaree's (1990) *Integrated Theory* is arguably the most comprehensive. In short, the model proposes that human males are biologically prepared for sexual aggression, that positive psychosocial development generally serves to restrain this potential for sexual aggression, that adverse developmental outcomes interact selectively with negative socio-cultural cues to weaken

Sexual Offender Treatment: Controversial Issues. Edited by W.L. Marshall, Y.M. Fernandez, L.E. Marshall and G.A. Serran.   © 2006 John Wiley & Sons, Ltd.

these restraints, and that sexual offending behavior itself is precipitated in under-restrained individuals by transitory situational factors such as anger, intoxication and/or opportunity.

The development and application of attachment-theoretical conceptions of sexual offending behavior have arisen directly from Marshall and Barbaree's (1990) integrated theory and associated commentaries (e.g. Marshall, 1989, 1993). However, although there is now a considerable body of theoretical and empirical literature focusing on attachment and attachment-related problems among sexual offenders, attachment-theoretical models are not yet well developed, and direct empirical support for existing models has initially been mixed and at times inconsistent. In the main, this work has been limited to applying attachment perspectives to understanding offenders' psychosocial development. Attachment problems themselves have generally been conceived of as stable, trait-like characteristics. The other three aspects of Marshall and Barbaree's model—biological, socio-cultural and situational influences—have been largely ignored in attachment formulations. Existing approaches have therefore perhaps not yet fully exploited the potential of attachment theory for informing a dynamic, interactional model of sexual offending behavior—one that accounts for interactions of biological, psychological, social and immediate situational factors, and explains how these interactions produce sexual offending behavior. The broader body of attachment literature, encompassing biological, social and ecological perspectives, provides considerable scope for extending early ideas about the role of attachment insecurity and/or disorganization in sexual offending behavior.

This chapter aims to reconsider Marshall and Barbaree's integrated theory from an attachment-theoretical perspective. The chapter focuses specifically on physical-contact sexual offending by adult males against children and young people. The present work is thus more restricted in scope than is Marshall and Barbaree's (1990) integrated theory, which aims to explain sexual offending in general. On the other hand the present work aims to extend Marshall and Barbaree's theory in several specific ways. First, whereas Marshall and Barbaree concentrated on the common biological bases of sexual arousal and aggression, the revisions proposed here consider the common and distinct biological bases of sexual drive, sexual attraction, mate selection and parenting behavior. Second, the proposed revisions elaborate upon the role of human attachment in the organization of sexual and courtship behavior, and in the development of capacities for behavioral restraint, notably involving empathy and perspective-taking, emotional regulation and coercive versus cooperative interpersonal strategies. Third, I attempt to elaborate upon the role of immediate situational factors in the commission of sexual offenses against children. Rather than viewing the potential offense scene merely in terms of otherwise neutral opportunities that may be recognized and exploited only by "chronically vulnerable" men (Marshall, Anderson & Fernandez, 1999, p. 31), I consider instead how certain everyday adult–child interactions may precipitate inappropriate sexual responses. In this respect, the present emphasis is as much on acute, as it is on chronic, vulnerability.

Attachment theory may also have something to contribute to understanding the broader socio-cultural influences on sexual offending, insofar as it may draw attention to the multiplicity (some might say the *duplicity*) of modern cultural standards influencing human sexuality, attachment and parenting. Indeed, a general explanatory model of sexual offending would be incomplete without reference to the human societies in which it occurs and by which it is ultimately defined. A cultural analysis, for the present purposes, may for example ask questions about whether sexual offenses against children are influenced by the cultural promotion of youth and beauty as the male sexual ideal, or perhaps instead by the failure to promote aging and beauty as the adult attachment ideal. However, personal and space limitations do not allow a detailed discussion of this here. The chapter concentrates instead on biological, developmental and situational influences.

Since Marshall and Barbaree's (1990) model is concerned with etiology, the present emphasis is accordingly on the onset, rather than the maintenance, of sexual offending behavior. Although attachment and related behavioral systems may well play a continuing role in repeated patterns of sexual offending, it is also likely that many of the factors associated with the maintenance of the behavior are different from those associated with its onset. It has been noted that cognitive distortions and deviant sexual preferences, for example, may emerge as a *result* of repeated offending, and may therefore be less relevant in explaining its onset (Marshall *et al.*, 1999). Before working through the proposed revisions in some detail, then, I briefly review available evidence on the onset of sexual offending against children. Since it is also of course important to consider what these offenders actually *do*, I also briefly review available evidence on their modus operandi.

CHILD SEXUAL ABUSE: ONSET AND MODUS OPERANDI

Even a cursory reading of the sexual offending literature reveals widely held assumptions that adult child-sex offenders (CSOs) tend to begin offending, or at least that their sexual offense-related problems first emerge, in adolescence. Certainly there is evidence that, as is the case for nonsexual offending, involvement in sexual offending peaks during adolescence and early adulthood. However, unlike age trends for nonsexual offending, the age distribution for sexual offenders is markedly bi-modal, with a second, more prominent peak observed in the mid- to late-30s (Canadian Center for Justice Statistics, 1999, cited in Hanson, 2002). While some may interpret this as evidence of continuity from adolescence to middle-age, the low rates of adult sexual recidivism observed in adolescent CSOs, together with the low rates of adolescence-onset reported by adult CSOs, suggest that adolescent and adult CSOs may be largely distinct populations.

The most widely cited empirical basis to support assumptions about early onset among adult CSOs is Abel and his colleagues' confidential self-report study, in which a little over half of a sample of 561 "paraphiliacs" indicated that their deviant sexual interests had begun in adolescence (Abel *et al.*, 1987; Abel & Osborn, 1992). However, leaving aside complex questions about the relationship between deviant sexual interests and deviant sexual behavior, early onset was more characteristic of the victimless paraphilias (e.g. transvestism and fetishism) than of those sexual deviations seen in forensic settings. The only subgroup of child sexual offenders (CSOs) that tended to report adolescence-onset of deviant sexual interests was nonfamilial CSOs who had offended against males. For these offenders, who constituted about 20% of the CSOs in Abel *et al.*'s sample (and about 8% of the total sample), the mean self-reported age of onset of their deviant sexual interests was 18 years. The mean age of onset for nonfamilial CSOs (female victims) was 22 years, for familial CSOs (male victims) 24 years, and for familial CSOs (female victims) (who constituted 58% of all the CSOs in their sample) 27 years. Abel and his colleagues' data cannot therefore be taken to support an early-onset hypothesis even with respect to the emergence of deviant sexual interests, and certainly not of sexual offending behavior itself.

Most adult CSOs, it seems, do not commit their first sexual offense until their 30s, and many not until much later. In a large-scale correctional study, Hanson (2002) reported that the average age of sexual offense convictions for Canadian, British and US adult incest offenders was about 40 years, and for nonfamilial offenders about 37 years. Smallbone and Wortley (2004) reported the average age at *first* sexual offense conviction for some 360 Australian adult CSOs to be about 37 years. In the same study, confidential self-reports indicated that the average age at first sexual contact with a child was about 32 years. The age distributions for both the official and self-reported first sexual offense were normal, with very wide ranges (e.g. 10 to 63 years for first sexual contact with a child). Thus, late onset appears to be as common as early onset, but neither is as common as onset in early middle-age. As Hanson (2002) has argued, opportunities for sexual contact with children peak in middle-age. It is of course at this time in their lives that men are most likely to be in parental or step-parental roles, or to have established themselves in other trusted positions involving care-taking and authority with respect to children.

Modus operandi studies clearly show that CSOs typically have already established a relationship with a child before the first overt sexual contact with that child occurs (Elliot, Brown & Kilcoyne, 1995; Kauffman *et al.*, 1998; Smallbone & Wortley, 2000). This relationship is most often a parental, step-parental or other familial relationship. In nonfamilial settings too, CSOs very often have established a relationship with the child, and also often with the child's parent(s), before the first sexual contact takes place. Other common types of prior relationships established with child victims are quasi-parental relationships—nonfamilial CSOs are not uncommonly teachers, sporting coaches, priests and others whose routine activities bring them into emotional or physical connection with children, and whose role involves a similar mix of care-taking and authority as is found in formal parental roles.

A popular assumption, based on the stereotype of the predatory, determined "pedophile", is that CSOs consciously and actively join organizations or seek out relationships with single mothers in order to obtain sexual access to children. But this may often not be the case. Smallbone and Wortley (2000) found, for example, that while 20% of nonfamilial CSOs reported that they had offended in a child-related organization, only 1% said they had joined that organization for the express purpose of obtaining sexual access to children. Thus, rather than actively creating such opportunities, many CSOs may instead capitalize on the opportunities with which they are presented, perhaps responding to specific cues that are presented in certain environments, especially in circumstances in which their first sexual offense occurs.

Abrupt sexual assault by strangers certainly occurs, but is atypical. Instead, in both familial and nonfamilial settings, the relationship between a CSO and a future child victim tends to be based on an emotional attachment that has been established over time. Among Smallbone and Wortley's (2000) sample, 73% reported having known their victim(s) for more than one month prior to the first sexual contact, including 63% of the nonfamilial offenders. More than half of the combined CSOs said they had known the child for more than a year. The so-called "grooming" process tends to involve a graduation from attention-giving and nonsexual touching, through low-level sexual talk or touching, to increasingly more explicit sexual behaviors (Conte, Wolf & Smith, 1989; Smallbone & Wortley, 2000). Overt aggression and physical violence may occur during, or as a means to obtain, sexual contact, but this too is atypical (Smallbone & Milne, 2000; Smallbone & Wortley, 2000).

In summary, some adult CSOs begin sexual offending in adolescence, but most, apparently, do not. Evidence indicates instead that adult CSOs tend to commit their first sexual offense at a time in their lives when they are most likely to be involved in care-giving and authority relationships with young people—as a parent or step-parent, or in another role involving emotional connection and close and unsupervised physical proximity to children and young people. This may be a well-established (e.g. parent, teacher) or temporary guardianship role (e.g. babysitting for the children of a friend or acquaintance). Finally, CSOs tend to know the child for a considerable period of time before they become sexually involved with them, and prior to making the first overt sexual contact tend to engage in grooming behavior that, at least superficially, resembles adult courtship behavior.

Taken together this evidence suggests that, much like criminal behavior in general (see e.g. Felson & Cohen, 1980), sexual offending against children, at least initially, occurs with little deviation from routine activities—for either offenders or victims. General explanatory models must therefore account for how sexual offending against children arises in ordinary, routine circumstances and specifically, it seems, in circumstances where offenders are in parenting and other guardianship roles in relation to children and young people.

But what is it about parenting and related roles that could explain why some men are motivated to misdirect courtship and sexual behavior toward children and young people in their care? In the remainder of this chapter I attempt to come to grips with this difficult and disturbing question.

ATTACHMENT, SEXUALITY AND PARENTING

Bowlby regarded attachment, sexuality and parenting to be the three most important social behavioral systems for species survival. In the first volume of his trilogy on attachment theory, Bowlby (1969) commented that "although [they are] distinct behavioural systems, attachment behaviour and sexual behaviour . . . have unusually close linkages" (p. 230), and that in humans, "overlaps between attachment behaviour, parental behaviour, and sexual behaviour are commonplace" (p. 233). Although distinctions can be drawn in terms of their maturational stages, social function and eliciting conditions, the attachment, sexual and parenting behavioral systems share many behavioral components (e.g. kissing and embracing), and the three systems commonly serve both complementary and reciprocal functions within established adult pair bonds. Attachment, sexual and parenting behavior are all partly biologically determined, they are all shaped by individual psychosocial development, and they are all highly situation-dependent.

Biological Influences

Marshall and Barbaree (1990) argued that human males are biologically prepared for sexual aggression, pointing to common neurochemical, neuroanatomical and physiological bases for sexual arousal and aggression. According to their integrated theory, a universal developmental task for human males is to acquire inhibitory controls over their biologically endowed propensity for sexual aggression. An attachment-theoretical perspective broadens this focus to include other discrete aspects of sexual functioning as well, namely sexual attraction and mate selection. From this perspective, a key developmental task is to organize and integrate several distinct behavioral systems involved in attachment, sexual and parenting behavior.

Neurobiologists have recently proposed the existence of a neural "social motivation circuitry", responsible for a number of primary emotion-motivation systems that have evolved to direct different aspects of human social behavior (Panksepp, 1998). In particular, Fisher (1998; see also Fisher, Aron, Mashek, Li & Brown, 2002) has proposed that three distinct primary emotion-motivation systems—sexual drive, sexual attraction and mate selection (or adult attachment)—have evolved to direct mating, reproduction and parenting.

According to this model, sexual drive has evolved to motivate humans to seek sexual contact with nonspecific others. Thus, as Laws and Marshall (1990) have argued, humans are biologically prepared to respond sexually to a very broad range of potential sexual stimuli. In human males, the sexual drive system may be activated particularly by visual and tactile stimuli. The primary biological agents involved in sexual drive are the androgens and estrogens. Subjectively, sexual drive is characterized by cravings for sexual gratification.

Whereas sexual drive is largely nonselective, sexual attraction (sometimes referred to as romantic passion) is thought to have evolved separately for the purposes of directing sexual drive toward a more restricted range of objects. In evolutionary terms, sexual attraction is thought to serve the purpose of concentrating mating effort on genetically appropriate partners. In social terms, sexual attraction thus provides for courtship behavior to be focused on specific kinds of individuals. Both common and distinct patterns of sexual attraction have been observed in males and females: whereas both tend to be attracted for example to healthy, reliable, intelligent partners, males are more attracted than are females to the physical qualities of potential sexual partners, and especially to physical indicators of youth and beauty (Buss, 1994). The primary neurochemicals involved in sexual attraction are thought to be the catecholamines: specifically, increased central dopamine and norepinephrine, and decreased central serotonin. Subjectively, sexual attraction is characterized by feelings of exhilaration and intrusive thoughts about the love object.

Distinguishing between sexual drive and sexual attraction in this way has important implications for understanding the clinical constructs of deviant sexual preferences and deviant sexual fantasy. For example, despite the fact that few

CSOs have elevated blood testosterone levels, psychiatric approaches have traditionally concentrated on testosterone-reducing methods of pharmacological or surgical intervention for reducing deviant sexual preferences. According to the present model, testosterone reduction would reduce sexual drive, but would not directly alter patterns of sexual attraction. Perhaps this is why some CSOs who take anti-androgen medication, for example, report continued emotional and sexual attraction to children. On the other hand, clinical reports of the use of serotonin reuptake inhibitors with persistent CSOs show that, along with a general reduction in sexual drive, more specific changes in sexual attraction patterns and associated obsessive thinking can be achieved (Bradford, 1997). Perhaps the clearest distinction between sexual drive and sexual attraction can be seen in the results of clinical trials in which testosterone has been administered to men and women to *increase* sexual desire. These studies show that while increased sexual feelings and activity typically occur in these clinical patients, many are disappointed to find there is an absence of associated increases in sexual or romantic attraction to their sexual partners (Fisher *et al.*, 2002).

Psychological approaches to understanding deviant sexual fantasy may also benefit from the recognition that *non-deviant* sexual attraction too involves obsessive, intrusive thinking that is typically reported as involuntary and uncontrollable (Fisher *et al.*, 2002). Indeed, the fact that normal adult males are typically most attracted to youthful and physically beautiful sexual partners suggests that it is the *exploitation*, rather than the *recognition*, of young people's sexual appeal that characterizes sexual offending behavior. In this sense sexual offending against children is much more like theft or robbery than it is like non-criminal sexual deviations such as fetishism or transvestism. The question of why most men do not sexually exploit children and young people is not all that different from the question of why most do not rob banks. The answer to the latter question is surely not that most men have no attraction to, or do not occasionally entertain fantasies about, large sums of money!

A third emotion-motivation system—mate selection or adult attachment—is thought to have evolved for the purpose of cooperating with reproductive mates to ensure the survival of offspring. While in reproductive terms the essential task of mate selection is effective parenting, secure adult attachment also brings personal benefits to both members of the pair bond, including mutual support, happiness, physical and emotional intimacy, and of course consensual sexual partnership. Indeed the modeling of such relationship qualities may in turn be a critical aspect of effective parenting. Proceeding from sexual attraction to mate selection and adult attachment is not of course always desired, and even when it is desired the transition may be a difficult one. In contrast to the comparatively short-lived exhilaration of sexual attraction, adult attachment is characterized by more enduring (and perhaps less exciting) feelings of comfort, security and emotional union. This system is thought to involve yet another distinct system of neurochemical agents, namely the neuropeptides oxytocin and vasopressin.

The successful integration or organization of these three emotion-motivation systems clearly serves to maximize reproductive fitness in favorable environments. However, since in biological terms the systems appear designed with the potential to operate independently, in psychosocial terms the task of organizing the three systems presents profound developmental and social challenges.

Psychosocial Influences

The distinct biological bases for sexual drive, sexual attraction and mate selection provide for considerable flexibility in sexual, mating and parenting strategies. This makes good sense in evolutionary terms, since it makes successful reproduction possible in both high resource and low resource environments. Behavioral ecologists have argued that childhood attachment experiences effectively signal the availability of resources required for successful reproduction, and thereby "trigger" one of two prototypical reproductive strategies (Belsky, Steinberg & Draper, 1991). In low resource early attachment environments, where close relationships are experienced as rejecting, unreliable or coercive, a reproductive strategy tends to emerge that involves early-onset puberty, opportunistic or coercive sexual behavior, many short-term, unstable pair bonds, and low levels of parental investment. Conversely, high resource early attachment environments, where close relationships are experienced as safe, reliable and enduring, tend to trigger a reproductive strategy involving late-onset puberty, delayed overt sexual behavior, few high-quality pair bonds, few offspring and high levels of parental investment. While each may be adaptive in evolutionary terms, in psychosocial terms the former strategy is clearly associated with increased risks of engaging in opportunistic, exploitative and coercive sexual behavior.

The question of whether insecure childhood attachment "triggers" a particular reproductive strategy, or whether instead insecure attachment increases risks of certain negative developmental outcomes that in turn affect sexual and parenting behavior, may be merely one of interpretation. The evidence itself is clear. Secure childhood attachment has been empirically associated with empathy and perspective-taking, the capacity for autonomous affect regulation, cooperative interpersonal styles, satisfaction in intimate relationships, secure adult attachment styles and effective parenting. Conversely, insecure childhood attachment has been empirically associated with hostility, aggression, impulsivity, difficulties in regulating negative emotion, increased risks of sexual and physical victimization, coercive interpersonal styles, substance dependence, and anxious, fearful or dismissive adult attachment. Thus, early childhood experiences with primary care-givers appear to have far-reaching potential effects on individual functioning, and especially on interpersonal functioning, well into adulthood.

The urgent goal-directed sexual behavior that emerges during puberty does not arise in a psychosocial vacuum; patterns of individual and interpersonal functioning are already well established by that time. Thus, courtship (sexual attraction) and adult attachment (mate selection) behaviors are likely, at least initially, to be shaped largely by childhood attachment experiences. From adverse developmental circumstances, it is perhaps no surprise that courtship behavior may emerge as opportunistic or coercive, that difficulties in regulating the powerful emotions of sexual attraction may be experienced, and that less than optimal empathy and perspective-taking may be involved in intimate and sexual encounters.

Consistent with Marshall and Barbaree's integrated theory, an attachment conceptualization of sexual offending emphasizes problems in the development of capacities for behavioral restraint rather than the development of more specific disorders of sexual functioning (e.g. stable deviant sexual preferences). An attachment conceptualization would thus lead to three main predictions: (a) that CSOs would have experienced insecure childhood attachments, and that they would be likely to develop insecure adult attachments; (b) that they would demonstrate reduced capacities for behavioral restraint; and (c) that their under-restrained behavior would be manifest in circumstances that are not wholly restricted to their sexual offending behavior.

Despite retrospectivity and measurement problems, adult CSOs do appear to report insecure childhood and adult attachment, although some inconsistencies have been found in empirical investigations. Several studies have found CSOs to report less secure childhood attachments than nonsexual offenders (Marsa *et al.*, 2004; McCarthy, 2004; Smallbone & Dadds, 1998) and nonoffenders (Marsa *et al.*, 2004; Smallbone & Dadds, 1998). Familial CSOs seem to be more likely than nonfamilial CSOs to report insecure childhood attachments (Smallbone & Dadds, 1998; Smallbone & Wortley, 2000). Indeed, Marshall, Serran and Cortoni (2000) found that nonfamilial CSOs were no more likely than nonoffenders to report insecure childhood attachment. With respect to adult attachment, CSOs have been found to be more likely to report an insecure than a secure adult attachment style (Jamieson & Marshall, 2000; Ward, Hudson & Marshall, 1996), and to report less secure adult attachment than both nonsexual offenders and nonoffenders (Marsa *et al.*, 2004; Sawle & Kear-Colwell, 2001; Smallbone & Dadds, 1998).

Studies of attachment in children have identified three main mechanisms of behavioral restraint in interpersonal settings that are linked to insecure early attachment experiences—a reduced capacity for empathy and perspective-taking, difficulties in emotional self-regulation and the development of a coercive interpersonal style. Of these, empathy has been given the greatest attention in studies of CSOs. Notwithstanding serious problems in conceptualizing and measuring empathy (see Marshall, Hudson, Jones & Fernandez, 1995, for a review), some studies have found lower trait empathy in CSOs than in nonoffenders (Chaplin, Rice & Harris, 1995; Marshall & Maric, 1996). Lower trait empathy has been found in non-incarcerated, compared to incarcerated, CSOs (Marshall, Jones, Hudson & McDonald, 1993), and in criminally versatile, compared to specialized, sexual offenders (Smallbone, Wheaton & Hourigan, 2003). Several studies have found CSOs to be deficient in their empathy toward their own victims, but not toward other children who had suffered an accident, or who had been sexually abused by someone else (Fernandez, Marshall, Lightbody & O'Sullivan, 1999; Marshall, Champagne, Brown & Miller, 1997).

With the possible exception of anger, little direct attention has been given to emotional regulation problems and other mechanisms of behavioral restraint among CSOs. Once again, the results of empirical investigations of anger among sexual offenders are mixed. In one study, trait anger levels were found to be higher in CSOs than in rapists (Kalichman, 1991), but in another study the reverse was found (Hudson & Ward, 1997). In yet another study, no differences in trait anger were found between CSOs and rapists although, especially among CSOs, higher trait anger was associated with higher levels of verbal aggression used in their sexual offenses (Smallbone & Milne, 2000). Dalton, Blain and Bezier (1998) found that mean trait anger scores for sexual offenders (predominantly CSOs) did not differ from scores for normal males.

Although studies of restraint *mechanisms* among CSOs have tended to produce equivocal results, the criminal versatility observed among CSOs (see Simon, 2000, for a review) strongly suggests that these offenders are under-restrained in a variety of contexts in addition to their sexual offending behavior. In one study, every standard category of offense was represented in the criminal histories of some 360 CSOs (Smallbone & Wortley, 2004). For the recidivists in this study, convictions for nonsexual offenses typically preceded their self-reported first sexual contact with a child. Taken together, these results suggest that sexual offenses against children may be more likely for men who have already established patterns of serious rule-breaking, dishonesty, exploitation or aggression.

In summary, CSOs, especially familial CSOs, tend to report insecure childhood and adult attachment. They tend to be less than optimally empathic, especially toward their own victims, but are not necessarily high in trait anger. Criminal versatility among CSOs suggests that they are typically, but not universally, under-restrained in a broad range of contexts. Thus, while many CSOs may, as a result of negative socialization, be "chronically vulnerable" to recognizing and exploiting opportunities for sexual contact with children and young people, many apparently are not. Consistent with Marshall and Barbaree's integrated theory, this in turn suggests: (a) that vulnerability to commit sexual offenses against children may be very widespread among adult males; and (b) that there may be features of the situational context in which sexual offenses against children arise that may themselves exert a powerful influence.

Situational Perspectives

With its specific emphasis on situational influences, Marshall and Barbaree's (1990) integrated theory represents a significant departure from mainstream clinical approaches to sexual offending. With the other notable exception of Finkelhor's (1984) four preconditions model, clinical conceptions of sexual offending tend to be heavily biased toward dispositional explanations. References to situational factors are often either vague, or are merely extensions of person-centered conceptualizations (e.g. state anxiety or anger, without reference to specific eliciting conditions). Situational analyses of sexual offense environments tend to regard factors external to the offender as neutral and, perhaps to avoid controversies about moral agency, overlook the potentially dynamic situational contributions to sexual offending behavior. As indicated above, an important exception has been Finkelhor's (1984) work, which among other things identified a range of influences external to the offender, such as unusual sleeping arrangements in the home or an ill or distant mother. Certainly most empirical work has concentrated on within-individual factors such as sexual preferences, cognitive distortions, empathy deficits, and so on. Recent work on the development of risk prediction models too has concentrated on identifying individual-level predictors, though none of these has yet been shown to explain more than 10% of the variance in recidivism outcomes (Hanson & Bussière, 1998). And yet even if offender dispositions are assumed to be the most significant influence (a largely untested assumption), person–situation interactions still need to be understood. Even the most highly predisposed CSO requires the immediate presence of a victim before an offense can take place. But more is required than the mere presence of a victim. As criminologists Cohen and Felson (1979) have argued, any offense against a person requires three minimal elements—a potential offender, a suitable target and the absence of a capable guardian. It is a particular source of concern that in sexual offenses against children, the offender is very often the (not-so-capable) guardian as well.

To return to my earlier question, what is it about parenting and related roles that could explain why some men are motivated to misdirect courtship and sexual behavior toward children and young people in their care? From an attachment perspective, parenting behavior is at least partly governed by biological mechanisms evolved for the purpose of cooperating with reproductive mates, and is shaped psychologically by earlier attachment and other experiences. Parenting behavior directed toward children is largely a complementary arrangement. Whereas attachment (proximity-promoting) behavior in the child is activated by subjective distress and terminated once felt security is re-established, parenting (care-giving) behavior is in turn activated by the child signaling its distress and terminated by the child signaling its return to felt security. Within adult pair bonds, attachment and care-giving behavior are both complementary and reciprocal. Here each partner is at times the care-seeker, and at times the care-giver.

Adult pair bonds of course also commonly involve sexual behavior, and the "overlaps" that Bowlby (1969) described between the attachment, sexual and parenting behavioral systems can be most clearly observed within these relationships. Situational cues for each of these three systems are not always easy to distinguish, and chains of events can commonly ensue that involve all three behavioral systems operating more or less simultaneously. For example, distress may activate attachment (care-seeking) behavior in one partner, and this may bring the care-seeker and care-giver into close physical (and emotional) contact with one another. In some cases both partners may simultaneously play care-giving and care-taking roles, such as may occur when both experience the same upsetting event and turn to each other for comfort. In either case, physical and emotional intimacy arising from attachment and care-giving behavior may arouse sexual feelings. Indeed, research on reward mechanisms in the human brain shows that feelings of romantic or sexual attraction are *intensified* in times of adversity (Fisher *et al.*, 2002; Schulz, 2000).

Certain protections normally exist in adult pair bonds against the temporary disorganization of these three behavioral systems producing socially undesirable outcomes, such as coercive or non-mutual sexual behavior. These are primarily psychological, rather than biological, protections involving empathy and perspective-taking, a cooperative rather than a coercive interpersonal style, and the capacity for autonomous emotional regulation so that the powerful emotions of distress, sexual drive and sexual attraction can be reined in if necessary; for example, if one partner signals the wish not to proceed with physical, emotional or sexual contact. These capacities for behavioral restraint are of course subject to earlier social learning influences, the most important of which may be the primary attachment relationships.

The separate biological systems underlying human sexual drive, sexual attraction and mate selection, as we have seen, provide for behavioral diversity. Indeed, these systems can, and often do, operate both independently and simultaneously.

For example, humans can "express deep attachment for a long-term partner, while they feel romantic attraction for someone at the office or in their social circle, while they feel the sex drive toward stimuli unrelated to either partner" (Fisher *et al.*, 2002). Behavioral restraint, on the other hand, is largely a product of socialization. A particular biosocial tension may thus exist with respect to human male preferences for youthful and beautiful sexual partners, especially as they (and perhaps their sexual or attachment partners) age. Less restrained individuals are thus clearly at greater risk to direct their sexual attention toward younger people, even while maintaining sexual and attachment relationships elsewhere.

Parenting and related roles (teaching, coaching, and so on) routinely bring adult males into physical and emotional contact with children and young people. Since these roles are assumed (and are often in fact relied upon by significant others) to provide capable guardianship, the development of the relationship, as well as the moment-to-moment interpersonal interactions, usually proceed unsupervised. External controls are thus effectively absent. As unpalatable as it may seem, an attachment perspective suggests that a significant potential exists within these situations for sexual experiences and behavior to emerge. For example, a distressed male may direct his own attachment behavior toward a child or young person, thus bringing him, and perhaps both, into a more intense emotional interaction and a more intimate physical interaction. This may cue cognitive, affective and sensory sexual responses, which, if not restrained, may in turn precipitate overt sexual behavior. Similarly, care-giving behavior may be activated in the adult by the presence of a distressed child, and this too may increase emotional intensity and physical intimacy, again cueing sexual responses by way of the same mechanisms as occurs routinely in adult pair bonds. These circumstances may be more likely to arise when the adult male has no available adult partner to whom they are able to direct their attachment behavior, or if their attempts to direct attachment behavior toward their adult partner fail.

Person–situation Interactions

Men with insecure adult attachment styles may be especially vulnerable to an acute disorganization of attachment, sexual and parenting behavior. Vulnerability in adult males may be further exacerbated by experiences of sexual encounters with adults when they themselves were children, since this is likely to provide a concrete, rather than merely an abstract, cognitive representation of adult–child sexual interactions, and perhaps because, as with their own offending, their sexual victimization involved a similar disorganization of attachment, sexual and care-giving systems. Finally, vulnerability would be particularly exacerbated in men with a poorly developed repertoire for behavioral restraint.

An attachment-theoretical perspective thus suggests that, while the contribution made by psychosocial vulnerability factors will vary among individual CSOs, onset of sexual offending behavior against children is at least partly influenced by situational factors commonly found in potential offense scenes—specifically, in circumstances where adult males are in parenting and other guardianship roles. Direct empirical investigations are needed to confirm the relevance of these common situational influences, and to discover other immediate situational influences that may be more or less relevant in specific settings. For example in familial settings, as Finkelhor (1984) has suggested, there is a need to better understand the influence of marital problems, excessive alcohol use, an absent, ill, distant or unprotective mother, unusual opportunities for the offender to be alone with the child, unusual sleeping or rooming conditions in the home, and so on. In nonfamilial settings, it may be fruitful for example to examine the relationship between the offender and the child's usual guardians, as well as parental monitoring and supervision of the child. In institutional settings, a better understanding of the influence of institutional culture (e.g. the operation of policies and codes of conduct governing relationships between adults and young people) may be helpful. However, although the distinct constellation of situational influences will vary from offense to offense, an attachment-theoretical perspective suggests that there are common situational elements as well. As occurs routinely in adult pair bonds, these effectively involve an acute disorganization of specific cues for attachment, sexual and parenting behavior.

CONCLUSIONS

Marshall and Barbaree's (1990) integrated theory suggests that sexual offending behavior may best be understood in terms of distal and proximal interactions between biological, developmental, socio-cultural and immediate situational factors. In this chapter, I have sought to reconsider Marshall and Barbaree's integrated theory from an attachment-theoretical perspective, and in light of current evidence concerning sexual offending and sexual offenders. This evidence suggests that sexual offending against children: (a) generally arises at a time in men's lives when they are most likely to be in established or temporary roles of authority and care-taking with respect to children and young people; (b) is, at least initially, more likely to be a product generally of under-restrained behavior than it is more specifically of deviant sexual preferences established in adolescence; and (c) like other personal offenses, tends to occur with little deviation from routine activities for the offender or victim.

A number of specific conceptual revisions to Marshall and Barbaree's integrated theory have been proposed. First, I have argued that the focus on biological influences should be expanded beyond the common systems underlying sexual arousal and aggression to include consideration of the common and distinct biological systems underlying sexual drive, sexual attraction, mate selection (adult attachment) and parenting (care-giving) behavior. Second, I have argued that attachment theory provides a coherent conceptual framework for understanding the influence of childhood attachment on the development of key mechanisms of behavioral restraint (empathy and perspective-taking, emotional regulation, and a cooperative interpersonal style), and for drawing direct developmental and situational links between attachment, sexual and parenting behavior. Third, I have argued that situational analyses should move beyond individual-level conceptualizations to include frank analyses of the situational elements comprising victim–offender interactions, including those that comprise the physical and interpersonal environments in which offenses occur.

REFERENCES

Abel, G.G., Becker, J.V., Mittelman, M., Cunningham-Rathner, J.C., Roleau, J.L. & Murphy, W.D. (1987). Self-reported sex crimes of nonincarcerated paraphiliacs. *Journal of Interpersonal Violence*, **2**, 3–25.

Abel, G.G. & Osborn, C. (1992). The paraphilias: the extent and nature of sexually deviant and criminal behavior. *Clinical Forensic Psychiatry*, **15**, 675–87.

Belsky, J., Steinberg, L. & Draper, P. (1991). Childhood experience, interpersonal development, and reproductive strategy: an evolutionary theory of socialization. *Child Development*, **62**, 647–70.

Bowlby, J. (1969). *Attachment and Loss: Vol. 1. Attachment*. New York: Basic Books.

Bradford, J. (1997). Medical interventions in sexual deviance. In D.R. Laws & W. O'Donohue (eds). *Sexual Deviance: Theory, Assessment, and Treatment* (pp. 449–64). New York: Guilford.

Buss, D.M. (1994). *The Evolution of Desire: Strategies of Human Mating*. New York: Basic Books.

Chaplin, T.C., Rice, M.E. & Harris, G.T. (1995). Salient victim suffering and the sexual responses of child molesters. *Journal of Consulting and Clinical Psychology*, **63**, 249–55.

Cohen, L.E. and Felson, M. (1979). Social change and crime rate trends: a routine activity approach. *American Sociological Review*, **44**, 588–608.

Conte, J.R., Wolf, S. & Smith, T. (1989). What sexual offenders tell us about prevention strategies. *Child Abuse and Neglect*, **13**, 293–301.

Dalton, J.E., Blain, G.H. & Bezier, B. (1998). State-Trait Anger Expression Inventory scores of male sexual offenders. *International Journal of Offender Therapy and Comparative Criminology*, **42**, 141–8.

Elliot, M., Brown, K. & Kilcoyne, J. (1995). Child sexual abuse prevention: what offenders tell us. *Child Abuse and Neglect*, **19**, 579–94.

Felson, M. & Cohen, L.E. (1980). Human ecology and crime: a routine activity approach. *Human Ecology*, **8**, 389–406.

Fernandez, Y., Marshall, W.L., Lightbody, S. & O'Sullivan, C. (1999). The child molester empathy measure. *Sexual Abuse: A Journal of Research and Treatment*, **11**, 17–31.

Finkelhor, D. (1984). *Child Sexual Abuse: New Theory and Research*. New York: Free Press.

Fisher, H.E. (1998). Lust, attraction, and attachment in mammalian reproduction. *Human Nature*, **9**, 23–52.

Fisher, H.E., Aron, A., Mashek, D., Li, H. & Brown, L.L. (2002). Defining the brain systems of lust, romantic attraction, and attachment. *Archives of Sexual Behavior*, **31**, 413–19.

Hall, G.C.N. & Hirschman, R. (1991). Toward a theory of sexual aggression: a quadripartite model. *Journal of Consulting and Clinical Psychology*, **59**, 662–9.

Hanson, R.K. (2002). Recidivism and age: follow-up data from 4,673 sexual offenders. *Journal of Interpersonal Violence*, **17**, 1046–62.

Hanson, R.K. & Bussière, M.T. (1998). Predicting relapse: a meta-analysis of sexual offender recidivism studies. *Journal of Consulting and Clinical Psychology*, **66**, 348–62.

Hudson, S.M. & Ward, T. (1997). Attachment, anger, and intimacy in sexual offenders. *Journal of Interpersonal Violence*, **12**, 323–39.

Hudson, S.M., Ward, T. & McCormack, J.C. (1999). Offense pathways in sexual offenders. *Journal of Interpersonal Violence*, **14**, 779–98.

Jamieson, S. & Marshall, W.L. (2000). Attachment styles and violence in child molesters. *Journal of Sexual Aggression*, **5**, 88–98.

Kalichman, S.C. (1991). Psychopathology and personality characteristics of criminal sexual offenders as a function of victim age. Archives of Sexual Behavior, **20**, 187–97.

Kauffman, K.L., Holmberg, J.K., Orts, K.A., McGrady, F.E., Rotzein, A.L., Daleiden, E.L. & Hilliker, D.R. (1998). Factors influencing sexual offenders' modus operandi: an examination of victim-offender relatedness and age. *Child Maltreatment*, **3**, 349–61.

Knight, R.A., Carter, D.L. & Prentky, R.A. (1989). A system for the classification of child molesters: reliability and application. *Journal of Interpersonal Violence*, **4**, 3–23.

Laws, D.R. & Marshall, W.L. (1990). A conditioning theory of the etiology and maintenance of deviant sexual preference and behavior. In W.L. Marshall, D.R. Laws & H.E. Barbaree (eds), *Handbook of Sexual Assault: Issues, Theories, and Treatment of the Offender* (pp. 209–29). New York: Plenum.

Marsa, F., O'Reilly, G., Carr, A., Murphy, P., O'Sullivan, M., Cotter, A. & Hevey, D. (2004). Attachment styles and psychological profiles of child sex offenders in Ireland. *Journal of Interpersonal Violence*, **19**, 228–51.

Marshall, W.L. (1989). Intimacy, loneliness and sexual offenders. *Behaviour Research and Therapy*, **27**, 491–503.

Marshall, W.L. (1993). The role of attachments, intimacy, and loneliness in the etiology and maintenance of sexual offending. *Sexual and Marital Therapy*, **8**, 109–21.

Marshall, W.L., Anderson, D. & Fernandez, Y. (1999). *Cognitive Behavioural Treatment of Sexual Offenders*. Chichester: John Wiley & Sons.

Marshall, W.L. & Barbaree, H.E. (1990). An integrated theory of the etiology of sexual offending. In W.L. Marshall, D.R. Laws & H.E. Barbaree (eds), *Handbook of Sexual Assault: Issues, Theories, and Treatment of the Offender* (pp. 257–75). New York: Plenum.

Marshall, W.L., Champagne, F., Brown, C. & Miller, S. (1997). Empathy, intimacy, loneliness, and self-esteem in nonfamilial child molesters: a brief report. *Journal of Child Sexual Abuse*, **6**, 87–98.

Marshall, W.L., Hudson, S.M., Jones, R. & Fernandez, Y. (1995). Empathy in sex offenders. *Clinical Psychology Review*, **15**, 99–113.

Marshall, W.L., Jones, R., Hudson, S.M. & McDonald, E. (1993). Generalized empathy in child molesters. *Journal of Child Sexual Abuse*, **2**, 61–8.

Marshall, W.L. & Maric, A. (1996). Cognitive and emotional components of generalized empathy deficits in child molesters. *Journal of Child Sexual Abuse*, **5**, 101–11.

Marshall, W.L., Serran, G.A. & Cortoni, F.A. (2000). Childhood attachments, sexual abuse, and their relationship to adult coping in child molesters. *Sexual Abuse: A Journal of Research and Treatment*, **12**, 17–26.

McCarthy, J. (2004). The childhood attachment experiences of sex offenders: separating maternal and paternal attachment. Manuscript submitted for publication.

Panksepp, J. (1998). *Affective Neuroscience: The Foundations of Human and Animal Emotions*. New York: Oxford University Press.

Sawle, G.A. & Kear-Colwell, J. (2001). Adult attachment style and pedophilia: a developmental perspective. *International Journal of Offender Therapy and Comparative Criminology*, **45**, 32–50.

Schulz, W. (2000). Multiple reward signals in the brain. *Nature Reviews Neuroscience*, **1**, 199–207.

Simon, L. (2000). An examination of the assumptions of specialization, mental disorder, and dangerousness in sex offenders. *Behavioral Sciences and the Law*, **18**, 275–308.

Smallbone, S.W. & Dadds, M.R. (1998). Childhood attachment and adult attachment in incarcerated adult male sex offenders. *Journal of Interpersonal Violence*, **13**, 555–73.

Smallbone, S.W. & Milne, L. (2000). Associations between trait anger and aggression used in the commission of sexual offenses. *International Journal of Offender Therapy and Comparative Criminology*, **44**, 606–17.

Smallbone, S.W., Wheaton, J. & Hourigan, D. (2003). Trait empathy and criminal versatility in sexual offenders. *Sexual Abuse: A Journal of Research and Treatment*, **15**, 49–60.

Smallbone, S.W. & Wortley, R.K. (2000). *Child Sexual Abuse in Queensland: Offender Characteristics and Modus Operandi*. Brisbane: Queensland Crime Commission.

Smallbone, S.W. & Wortley, R.K. (2004). Onset, persistence and versatility of offending among adult males convicted of sexual offenses against children. *Sexual Abuse: A Journal of Research and Treatment* **16**, 285–298.

Ward, T., Hudson, S.M. & Marshall, W.L. (1996). Attachment style in sex offenders: A preliminary study. *Journal of Sex Research*, **33**, 17–26.

Chapter 8

COPING AND MOOD IN SEXUAL OFFENDING

GERIS A. SERRAN AND LIAM E. MARSHALL

Rockwood Psychological Services, Kingston, Ontario, Canada

Some sexual offenders appear to have little capacity for, or experience dealing with, emotions and fail to recognize emotions in themselves and others (Hudson *et al.*, 1993). It is not unusual for clients in our groups, when attempting to deal with the distress generated by addressing difficult issues in treatment, to become either angry or withdrawn. These responses to stress are also functionally related to offending (Pithers, Beal, Armstrong & Petty, 1989) and appear to influence treatment attrition.

Many sexual offenders describe the circumstances around the time of their offending as involving a great deal more stress than they normally experience. They also typically report poor attempts to cope with these difficulties. For example, many sexual offenders report loneliness, loss of work or anger, as pre-offence stressors (Hanson & Harris, 2000; Pithers *et al.*, 1989) and they often respond by increasing their use of alcohol or drugs (Hillbrand, Foster & Hirt, 1990), or attempting to use sex as a way of alleviating feelings of loneliness (Cortoni & Marshall, 2001). Thus sexual offenders appear to experience frequent mood altering stressors and while their attempts to cope with these stressors may provide short-term relief, their coping responses fail to address the problems and often make things worse.

In our treatment program some sexual offenders either drop out because they do not wish to deal with the negative emotions that can occur in treatment (e.g. as a result of having to face up to the harm they have caused) or remain in treatment but do not engage emotionally. Indeed, in a study on sexual offenders who refuse to participate in treatment, Mann and Webster (2002) report that fear of having to face emotional issues is a primary reason given for not entering treatment; it is our experience that some sexual offenders also drop out of treatment for the same reasons. Since research has demonstrated a relationship between treatment attrition and higher re-offence rates (e.g. Marques, Day, Nelson & West, 1994), we have begun to examine the occurrence, and the relationship between affect and coping in sexual offenders.

Sexual Offender Treatment: Controversial Issues. Edited by W.L. Marshall, Y.M. Fernandez, L.E. Marshall and G.A. Serran. © 2006 John Wiley & Sons, Ltd.

Coping has been defined as a response that attempts to ameliorate the negative impact of the stress generated by problems (Endler & Parker, 1989). Coping, which can be either cognitive or behavioral, is a capacity to respond and recover from the experience of stress. Vulnerable people are less capable of coping effectively with a stressor while those with greater resilience are more able to cope effectively. Vulnerability and resilience are influenced by both features of the person and features of their environment. For example, an individual's age, gender and personality features influence the capacity to respond effectively. Environmental factors (e.g. socio-cultural, socio-economic, available social services, literacy level) also influence the person's capacity. Many of the sexual offenders in our programs report dealing ineffectively with stress around the time they offended.

The regulation of affect appears to be impaired in sexual offenders (Ward & Hudson, 2000a). Some sexual offenders demonstrate intense emotional responses to stressors (e.g. sadness or anger) while others respond with blunted emotions. The problem for sexual offenders, then, appears to be related to the ends of an under-responsive/over-responsive dimension of affect. There are a number of possible explanations for these differences in affective responding, such as temperament or attachment style; however, a full examination of these differences is beyond the scope of this paper. Instead, we will focus on examining the role of coping and affect in sexual offenders.

RELEVANCE OF RELAPSE PREVENTION MODELS

Programs for sexual offenders that incorporate relapse prevention (RP) components are the most widely used treatment approaches (Laws, Hudson & Ward, 2000). These programs emphasize the importance of employing effective coping and suggest that it is the inability of sexual offenders to cope with high-risk situations (e.g. interpersonal conflicts and negative mood states) that put them at risk to re-offend (Pithers, Marques, Gibat & Marlatt, 1983). Unfortunately very little research has examined this idea that it is inadequate coping that increases the risk of sexual offending.

Central to this theory is the role that implementation of coping strategies and response to high-risk situations pose for offending behavior. RP also stresses the importance of an association between negative affect and relapse potential. Pithers *et al.* (1983) identified negative affect as an important trigger for re-offending. Subsequent reports (Ward & Hudson, 1998; Ward, Louden, Hudson & Marshall, 1995) have expanded upon our understanding of the process of offending and have led to criticisms of the original formulation of RP and a reconceptualization of the model (Hudson & Ward, 2000; Ward & Hudson, 2000b). Although this reconceptualization added a role in re-offending for positive affect, the revised model retained the idea that an inability to adequately cope with problems would increase the likelihood of a re-offense. The purpose of this chapter is to examine the limited research linking affect and coping to sexual offending and to offer some suggestions for further research. Certainly, the complexity of the literature in relation to these concepts has led to confusion and that has no doubt limited the research. More recent research (Cortoni & Marshall, 2001; Marshall, Cripps, Anderson & Cortoni, 1999; Marshall,

Serran & Cortoni, 2000; Ward *et al.*, 1995) has attempted to expand our understanding of the role that coping and various affective states play in offending, but further research is necessary.

The aim of an RP approach is to examine past offending in order to identify factors that increase the risk of offending. Among these factors are the events and situations that lead to an offense. Based on these analyses, the offender generates ways to either avoid or cope with these so-called "high-risk situations". Among these high-risk situations are events that present as stressful (e.g. interpersonal conflict) and, therefore, require a coping response. It is assumed that if the offender fails to cope appropriately, he will respond emotionally and these negative emotions will trigger thoughts of offending. The offender will then attempt to seek the opportunity to offend while engaging in cognitive distortions that justify offending (Laws, 1989; Pithers, Kashima, Cumming, Beal & Buell, 1988).

Once the client has identified his relevant high-risk situations or experiences, he is taught to respond more appropriately (i.e. cope effectively) when facing such situations in the future. If a client encounters a high-risk, stressful situation and is able to perform an effective coping response (e.g. resolving an argument assertively rather than aggressively), then the probability of a relapse decreases (Pithers *et al.*, 1983). Successful coping increases the individual's sense of self-efficacy and the belief that he can deal effectively with future high-risk situations. If the individual fails to effectively cope with a high-risk situation, he will feel a decrease in his sense of control, will feel more helpless and will be more likely to relapse. Thus, teaching the client adaptive coping is central to the process of preventing a re-offence (Pithers *et al.*, 1983). However, in the RP literature the focus has been on training the specific skills needed to deal with specific risk situations or experiences. Associated with this, RP approaches tend to emphasize the need to rely on past experiences to identify risk situations producing, as a result, a list of problematic situations and experience that, if avoided or dealt with effectively, is expected to minimize the chance of a re-offence. Very few programs appear to discuss more general coping styles (as opposed to specific coping skills), nor do they attempt to instill in the client a more generic disposition toward future risks that would permit a response to a risky situation that could not be anticipated on the basis of past experiences. We consider these two neglected issues to be quite critical to effective treatment.

COPING STYLES

Coping styles are referred to in the literature as characteristic or typical manners of confronting stressful situations and dealing with them (Folkman & Lazarus, 1980, 1985). Three consistently identified styles of coping have been identified: *task-focused* coping; *emotion-focused* coping; and *avoidance-focused* coping (Endler & Parker, 1990, 1994). Task-focused coping occurs when the individual believes they can change the situation. In this response to stressful circumstances, individuals adopt either behavioral strategies to deal directly with the problem, or cognitive strategies that reconceptualize the problem or minimize its effects. In fact, task-focused coping is essentially the same as the approach defined by D'Zurilla (1988) as "problem-solving". Emotion-focused strategies involve emotional responses to the problem, fantasizing or self-preoccupation. For example, individuals using these strategies may get angry and vent their anger on others, simply worry about the problem but do nothing, become depressed, or wallow in self-pity and see themselves as victims. Avoidance-focused coping involves techniques designed to escape or avoid the problem, using either distraction activities (such as watching TV, drinking alcohol, engaging in sex, or eating) or social diversion (such as phoning a friend).

Whether an individual possesses effective coping strategies is a major determinant of how well that person adjusts to difficult situations in life or deals effectively with stress. Coping strategies play a major role in an individual's well-being when faced with negative or stressful situations (Endler & Parker, 1989; McCrae & Costa, 1986; Miller, Brody & Summerton, 1988). Although most stressors typically elicit all three types of coping as an initial response, task-focused coping predominates when the person feels something constructive can be done, while emotion-focused coping predominates when the person feels the stressor is something that must be endured. Avoidance-focused coping generally occurs as a persistent response in persons who have no adequate coping skills.

Coping plays an important role in mediating between stressful events and outcomes such as anxiety, depression, psychological distress and physical problems (Billings & Moos, 1982, 1984; Endler & Parker, 1989). Research indicates that task-focused coping is significantly predictive of positive adaptation (Billings & Moos, 1984; Compas, Malcarne & Fondacaro, 1988; Endler & Parker, 1989, 1990; Mitchell, Cronkite & Moos, 1983). Emotion-focused coping, however, is related to depression, neuroticism, and may be a predictor of emotional distress. Although Folkman and Lazarus' (1986) concept of emotion-focused coping involves the management, palliation or expression of negative emotions, emotion-focused strategies which involve the expression of emotion, rather than the management of emotion, may be particularly problematic. The persistent adoption of avoidance-focused coping involving distraction techniques does nothing to alleviate the problem and generally leads to greater distress as the persistence of the problem is recognized. However, avoidance-focused coping that employs social diversions (i.e. contacting a support person) reduces stress and may lead to discussions that facilitate the adoption of task-focused solutions.

SEXUAL OFFENDING AND COPING

Research examining the coping strategies of sexual offenders suggests that these offenders tend to choose ineffective strategies, both general and situational. Neidigh and Tomiko (1991), in the first study specifically looking at this issue with sexual offenders, found that child molesters used more self-denigrating strategies when coping with daily stressors and more avoidance and self-denigration techniques when attempting to cope with an urge to offend. Similarly, Marshall and his colleagues (Marshall, Cripps, Anderson & Cortoni, 1999; Marshall, Serran & Cortoni, 2000) found that child molesters used significantly more emotion-focused strategies (e.g. blaming oneself, self-preoccupation and fantasizing) when compared to rapists, non-sex offenders and non-offenders. These studies demonstrate that child molesters in particular use ineffective coping styles, which serve to increase the amount of stress and negative affect they experience. This increase in negative affect increases their risk of offending.

Cortoni and Marshall (2001) investigated the possibility that sexual offenders use sex as a means of coping (i.e. as an avoidance-focused style). They found the typical response of both child molesters and rapists to stressful situations or negative emotions was to seek either appropriate or inappropriate sexual activity. Somewhat surprisingly, the use of sex as a coping strategy was found to significantly relate to *both* emotion-focused and avoidance-focused coping styles. Although ultimately ineffective, if these strategies serve to reduce personal discomfort, it is likely sexual offenders will continue to engage in such activities until they learn more effective alternatives.

In most of the research to date, however, and particularly in the relapse prevention literature, no distinction is made between the specific skills needed to cope with particular situations (e.g. being assertive with someone who is taking advantage of the person), and the person's more trait-like coping style which they bring to all situations. It seems to us that this distinction has important implications for treatment since it would seem to be most advantageous to both train specific skills and to modify the client's characteristic coping style. A thorough review of the sexual offender treatment literature revealed that almost all programs (certainly all cognitive behavioral programs) train clients in the skills necessary to deal with specific problematic situations, but we could find no evidence of attempts to modify the general coping styles of sexual offenders.

AFFECTIVE STATES

Howells, Day and Wright (2004) explored the literature detailing the importance of affect in sexual offending. Various researchers have demonstrated that negative affect in sexual offenders is associated with behaviors related to offending. As mentioned previously, negative emotional states (along with interpersonal conflict) have been identified in the traditional relapse prevention literature as the most frequently identified high-risk situations. Specifically, Pithers *et al.* (1983) analyzed the relapse episodes reported by sexually aggressive individuals, revealing that 75% of the relapses were precipitated by situations that evoked a negative mood state (e.g. boredom, frustration and anger). In subsequent research, Pithers *et al.* (1988) examined the immediate precipitants of sexual re-offending in 136 child molesters and 64 rapists. Ninety-four per cent of the rapists reported experiencing anger due to interpersonal conflict immediately before offending, while 46% of the child molesters reported feeling anxious and 38% reported feeling depressed prior to committing a sexual offense. This research, however, was conducted retrospectively, and may have been distorted due to poor recall or a self-justifying bias. It also fails to explain the process of re-offending and how these affective states influence the decision to offend.

Hanson and Harris (2000) identified acute changes in mood as one of the proximal dynamic factors that distinguished recidivists from nonrecidivists. They compared 400 recidivists and nonrecidivists by collecting data from community supervision appointments. The two groups did not differ on trait mood and emotion, but recidivists displayed an increase in negative mood states just prior to offending. The negative moods identified included: depression/discouragement/hopelessness; anxiety/worry/stress; frustration; loneliness; suicidal thoughts; and anger/hostility. Anger was one of the three strongest overall predictors of recidivism in this study.

The relationship between anger and offending is frequently stressed in the literature (Groth & Burgess, 1977; Knight & Prentky, 1990; Ward & Hudson, 2000a). Groth and Burgess (1977) reported that 40% of the rapists they interviewed were "anger rapists" and Knight and Prentky (1990) identify various sub-types of sexual offenders, including a globally and undifferentiated angry type and a vindictive group (anger focused on women). In view of these observations it is perhaps not surprising that anger toward women has been found to enhance sexual arousal to forced sex (Yates, Barbaree & Marshall, 1984).

What remains unclear, however, is how these affective states lead to offending. Perhaps negative affect resulting from a failure to cope effectively with a problem situation (e.g. interpersonal conflict, boredom or loneliness) results in the person seeking sexual relief from whomever is accessible as a way of reducing the negative mood state. This is the "sex as a coping strategy" model outlined by Cortoni and Marshall (2001). Or perhaps the negative affect simply serves on its own as a motivator to offend. This is essentially the model suggested by Groth (1979), although for him it is a chronic, rather than an acute, anger state that propels the rapist to assault. General psychological adjustment has not been linked to re-offending (Hanson & Bussière, 1998); therefore, negative affect in general does not appear to be the problem. Presumably, sexual offenders have not offended every time they experience a negative mood state, but when they do offend, it may be that their mood states are similar.

Negative Mood States and Deviant Fantasies

Earlier research suggested that sexual offenders may use sexual activity as a means of coping with their high-risk factors. Proulx, McKibben and Lusignan (1996) examined the relationship between sexual behavior, moods and other emotions following conflict in a group of sexual offenders. Using their *Fantasy Report*—a self-assessment method that examines conflicts and emotional states, sexual fantasies and masturbatory activities—Proulx *et al.* found that in rapists and child molesters, negative mood states and interpersonal conflicts increased the frequency of deviant sexual fantasies and associated masturbation. Anger, loneliness, and humiliation were most often reported by rapists as triggers of deviant fantasies, while loneliness and humiliation were reported by child molesters with female victims, and loneliness on its own was reported by child molesters with male victims. In Proulx *et al.*'s sample of rapists, when the factors that triggered deviant fantasies were present, nondeviant sexual fantasies were all but absent. When negative moods and conflicts were absent there was a greater frequency of normative fantasies and associated masturbation.

In a similar vein, Looman (1995) found that child molesters were more likely to fantasize sexually about a child as opposed to an adult if they felt depressed, had an argument with their partners, felt rejected or were angry. Dysphoria appeared to be a precursor to deviant sexual behaviors (i.e. deviant fantasizing and associated masturbation). Both Looman and Proulx *et al.* suggest that sexual offenders may engage in deviant sexual fantasies as a means of reducing their distress (i.e. coping with dysphoric moods). These studies provide support for the link between negative emotional states and the emergence of deviant sexual behaviors, although a causal relationship cannot be established between negative moods and offending behavior. One possible method of examining the causal relationship between negative moods and offending is to experimentally induce a negative mood among sexual offenders and examine its effect on various areas of functioning.

MOOD INDUCTION WITH SEXUAL OFFENDERS

A mood induction procedure (MIP) was developed by Emmett Velten in 1968 for his doctoral thesis. Despite the subsequent ubiquity of MIP research in other areas of psychology (e.g. risk taking behavior), and the relevance of mood to sexually deviant fantasizing and recidivism, there have been no applications of a MIP procedure with sexual offenders. This is surprising since Velten (1968) suggested that diagnosing sexual preferences may be enhanced by the use of his MIP procedure and there has been some research on sexual arousal and MIP, but only with nonoffenders. The results of these latter studies suggest that mood is related to sexual arousal with participants being more likely to report sexual arousal when in a negative mood (Laan, Everaerd, Van Berlo & Rijs, 1995; Mitchell, DiBartolo, Brown & Barlow, 1999).

We (Marshall, Marshall & Moulden, 2000) conducted a study that examined the possibility of inducing a negative mood using Velten's (1968) procedure with incarcerated sexual offenders. Because previous research has suggested the importance of negative moods in sexual offending (Hanson & Harris, 2000; Looman, 1995; McKibben, Proulx & Lusignan, 1994; Proulx *et al.*, 1996) any procedure that can induce negative moods in sexual offenders should prove invaluable in understanding the effects of such moods on these men. Previous research using the Velten procedure has shown that nonoffender respondents are susceptible to a MIP (e.g. Sinclair, Mark, Enzle, Borkovec & Cumbleton, 1994; Sinclair, Soldat & Ryan, 1997). In a meta-analysis of 11 different mood induction procedures used in 138 studies of adult nonclinical samples, Westermann, Spies, Stahl and Hesse (1996) found that the Velten MIP was at least as effective as other mood induction procedures and in some cases better.

Velten's (1968) procedure requires subjects to read cards, each of which has a simple statement such as "Sometimes I wonder if life is all that worthwhile" or "Things will go better and better today". These statements are designed to "induce" a positive or negative mood state. As noted, the evidence indicates that this simple mood induction procedure is effective. Marshall, Marshall and Moulden (2000) examined the effects of Velten's procedure in inducing a negative mood state in 22 sexual offenders. The MIP was found to induce mood changes in some, but not all, sexual offenders. Specifically, it was found that sexual offenders who reported offending while in a negative mood state were more likely to be susceptible to the MIP.

Interestingly, we had set out to examine the effects of the MIP on several areas of functioning and although we found that inducing a negative mood was possible in some sexual offenders, inducing the negative mood did not straightforwardly influence the areas of functioning we hypothesized would be affected by the MIP (i.e. self-esteem, anxiety and coping using sex). When we examined this lack of impact of the MIP on these areas of functioning what we found was that the respondents who were susceptible to the MIP were already displaying inadequate levels of functioning in the issues of concern. For example, the mean pre-MIP self-esteem score for the respondents who were susceptible to the procedure was more than two standard deviations below the normative mean and significantly lower than the participants who were not susceptible to the MIP. Respondents whose mood was lowered following the MIP also reported greater pre-procedure anxiety, and were more likely to report using sex as a coping mechanism.

While these results are preliminary they suggest that Velten's mood induction procedure has the potential to permit a better understanding of the role of mood in sexual offending. In particular, it appears that the qualities some sexual offenders possess may make them more susceptible to developing a transitory negative mood state than others, and this could serve as an indicator of their future risk. Research will need to clarify this possibility before firm conclusions can be drawn.

COPING WITH NEGATIVE MOOD STATES

Hanson and Bussière (1998) found that the overall level of distress is not what matters when predicting recidivism; rather, it is the mechanisms used by offenders to regulate these feelings that count. Hanson and Harris (2000), in examining the dynamic risk factors of sexual offenders who recidivated versus those who did not, determined that it was acute negative affect that distinguished the two groups. Thus, it is not depression per se that influences offending, but rather, it is a change in mood prior to the offence that has an impact. An offender who is generally angry is apparently not at higher risk, but if his anger suddenly worsens, this could trigger offending. This has implications for research and treatment strategies, in that "emergency" strategies might be required to manage acute changes in affect.

Marshall, Anderson and Fernandez (1999) suggest that negative moods create a vulnerability that can affect sexual offenders' ability to cope. In general, the failure to cope effectively has been related to feelings of depression and enhanced negative mood states (Bermond, Schuerman, Nieuwenhuyse & Fasotti, 1987). Wolf, Balson, Morse and Simon (1991) found that active behavioral coping was significantly related to enhanced mood and greater perceived social support, while avoidance coping was related to greater mood disturbance and lower social support. McCormick and Smith (1995) found that substance abusers who displayed more hostility and aggression were more likely than others to use escape/avoidance, confrontative and distancing coping styles when dealing with problems. These individuals reported more situations that triggered the use of substances and they expressed less confidence in dealing with these triggers.

One interesting concept is the idea that some individuals might be motivated to maintain negative emotions or mood states due to the reinforcement associated with those moods. For example, individuals displaying anger could more easily invoke control over others and a depressed mood might elicit comforting behaviors from others. Linked with sexual needs, these affective states could serve to influence the goal of the individual. In angry state, for example, a male appears to be more disposed to use force to gain the compliance of a potential sexual partner (Yates et al., 1984). A man who is transitorily depressed as a result of rejection by a woman may be more disposed to seek a nonthreatening target (e.g. a child) for sexual activity. Individuals also differ in their ability to regulate negative moods. For example, a pessimistic outlook on the ability to manage negative moods has been found to be predictive of depressive symptoms and maladaptive coping (Catanzaro, 1993). Although this issue has not been examined in relation to sexual offenders, general research suggests that negative mood regulation expectancies are substantially related to high levels of emotion-focused coping and an absence of task-focused coping (Flett, Blankstein & Obertynski, 1996). The magnitude of emotional responses, or affect intensity, is also strongly related to higher levels of emotion-focused and avoidance-focused coping. The ability to moderate emotional arousal is apparently essential before task-focused strategies can be applied; thus, individuals who experience problems doing so are unlikely to be successful at coping. Interestingly, it has been hypothesized that high affect intensity is related to poor self-regulation (Eisenberg & Fabes, 1992), in that such high affective states generate either over- or under-regulation, both of which are problematic.

SELF-REGULATION

The major criticism of most research and theories examining mood, affect and emotion in sexual offending is that it has focused solely on negative mood states and emotions, and has failed to describe *how* affective states lead to offending. Historically, the focus on negative affect made sense since traditional relapse prevention identified negative mood states as high-risk situations. However, Ward et al. (1995) identified two separate pathways to offending: a negative affect pathway as well as a positive affect pathway. The former is characterized by a diversity of negative affective states, implicit planning and substance abuse. In addition, in the negative affect pathway the offence is of relatively short duration. The pathway that is characterized by positive affective states, involves explicit planning, distorted thinking, deviant sexual fantasies and high sexual arousal, with the offence being of longer duration. Based on this descriptive model of the offence process, Ward and Hudson (2000a) developed the self-regulatory model of the relapse process.

According to Ward and Hudson (2000a), self-regulation consists of processes that allow an individual to engage in goal-directed actions, and involves inhibition as well as the enhancement or maintenance of specific behaviors. The goals, in this case, are related to the affective state, with the achievement of goals being associated with positive emotions, while failure is associated with negative emotions. In Ward and Hudson's model, two pathways are associated with avoidance goals, in that the goal is to not re-offend. The remaining two pathways are associated with approach goals, where sexual offending is the goal. In this model, dysfunctional self-regulation is associated with an increase in risk of relapse.

The *avoidant-passive* pathway involves the inability to control sexually deviant behaviors. Offenders under-regulate their behavior or emotions, resulting in a loss of control over behavior. Powerful negative affective states are often involved in this pathway, and individuals tend to be impulsive, experience low self-efficacy and lack effective coping strategies. The predominant affective state is likely to be negative because of the anxiety associated with possible relapse, and because they are unable to manage problems effectively. The *avoidant-active* pathway involves misregulation, where the offender actively attempts to control deviant thoughts and behaviors, but the strategies employed are not effective. For example, the offender might use substances or pornography hoping to quell deviant thoughts, which paradoxically increases the risk of offending. The predominant affective state is negative.

The remaining two pathways involve approach goals. The *approach-automatic* pathway involves the use of overlearned behavioral scripts and the behaviors appear impulsive. The primary affective state differs in that some individuals might be in a positive mood while others are in a negative mood. The presence of positive emotions is due to the anticipation of engaging in the deviant sexual activities. The final pathway, the *approach-explicit* pathway, involves intact self-regulation. In this pathway, the offender has deviant goals which he considers to be acceptable. Such goals are, therefore, associated with inappropriate beliefs about women and children. The predominant affective state may be positive or negative.

Initially, the two avoidance pathways are linked to negative affective states because the individual is attempting to avoid offending, while the two approach pathways may be characterized by positive or negative affect. In the latter two pathways, when the goal is to humiliate or retaliate, the emotional state will be negative, while if the goal is to develop an "affectionate" relationship with a child, the emotional state may be positive. As the relapse process unfolds, all offenders will experience positive emotions due to increased sexual arousal, and following the offence the emotional states should be negative for the avoidance pathways and positive for the approach pathways. The self-regulation theory does a good job of explaining various possible pathways to offending and also does a good job of explaining how different emotional states can influence behavior. However, empirical validation of this model is required, or we will fall into the same trap as we did with the original RP model; that is, unquestioned acceptance based on the appeal of the model.

COPING, AFFECT AND SEXUAL OFFENDER TREATMENT

The relapse prevention model has had a major impact on the design and implementation of treatment for sexual offenders. From this perspective, treatment programs have focused on self-management strategies designed to help sexual offenders manage specific high-risk situations. Skills acquisition is a major focus for most programs and emphasizes different, more effective coping responses. Although some research has explored the effectiveness of treatment through recidivism studies, only recently has any research examined whether there actually are changes in coping following treatment. These studies are briefly described below.

McKibben, Proulx and Lussier (2001) investigated the effectiveness of the coping skills employed by treated sexual offenders to deal with specific high-risk situations. McKibben *et al.* also examined the reasons why the offenders failed to utilize the effective skills they had learned in treatment. Included in this study were 32 treated sexual offenders, 18 of whom had child victims and 14 who had adult victims. McKibben *et al.* evaluated coping skills through the use of the *Coping Strategy Report* (CSR), a self-administered computerized questionnaire which they developed. The targeted "high-risk situations" involved negative mood states or interpersonal conflicts, and lapses were defined as engaging in deviant sexual fantasies. Since the subjects were all still incarcerated they had no opportunity to actually offend.

Self-reports, gathered over a three-month period after the end of treatment, provided an index of the number of high-risk situations and lapses. Interpersonal conflicts resulting in anger and feelings of inadequacy were reported more frequently than negative mood states. Treated offenders did frequently use adaptive coping strategies when faced with high-risk situations or a lapse, and they reported these strategies to be usually effective. However, treated participants did not always use adaptive coping skills in response to high-risk situations. Lack of will, ignorance of strategies and emotional disturbance were cited as the main reasons for not coping effectively with a negative mood, while anticipation of failure and emotional disturbance were the main reasons for failing to cope with interpersonal conflict. McKibben *et al.* suggested that it was critical to increase motivation to cope effectively and that treatment programs should stress "overlearning" of effective strategies.

McKibben *et al.*'s (2001) study focused on evaluating the use of coping skills that were learned during treatment to deal with specific high-risk situations. While the use of these specific skills is important, and is a feature of typical RP-based programs, changes in dysfunctional coping styles are also important since, as we have seen, research has shown that sexual offenders tend to have chronically poor coping styles. The following two studies address this issue.

Serran (2003) examined changes in both coping skills and coping styles following treatment of child molesters. Treated child molesters were compared to a waiting list group on their ability to effectively identify the skills necessary to cope with high-risk situations as well as their general coping styles and their likelihood of using sex as a coping strategy. The treatment program has been described elsewhere (Marshall *et al.*, 1999) and has a comprehensive range of targets including, of course, attempts to instill an effective coping style, training in identifying high-risk situations, and practice in the skills necessary to cope with these high-risk situations. Following treatment, it was found that child molesters identified more effective ways of coping with high-risk situations, and endorsed a more task-oriented coping style as well as social diversion strategies. Unfortunately, there was no change in emotion-focused coping styles, which remained problematic. As mentioned previously, emotion-focused strategies are linked to poor mental health and include self-oriented responses such as fantasizing, dwelling on the problem and self-blame. The use of this coping style in an attempt to attenuate a high-risk situation would place offenders at greater risk to re-offend. However, the acquisition of coping skills for specific problems and an increase in the use of a task-focused coping style should reduce the overall risk of these offenders. In addition, some promise has been shown in programs specifically focused on emotion control.

Roger and Masters (1997) developed a specific emotion control training program for sexual offenders that provided strategies designed to reduce rumination and increase adaptive coping. The focus in this program was on regaining control of attention and releasing "bottled up" emotion in a constructive manner. They found an increase in task-focused coping following treatment, and a decrease in emotion-focused coping style. Similarly, Feelgood, Golias, Shaw and Bright (2000) specifically focused their sexual offender treatment program on reducing emotional coping strategies and determined that these strategies were reduced following treatment. Interestingly, Stanton and Franz (1999) suggest that the coping literature has narrowly focused on the dysfunctional aspects of emotion-focused coping and failed to recognize the functionality of emotion. They suggest that specific emotion-focused coping, involving active efforts to recognize, understand and express emotion appear adaptive in managing stressful encounters. This is important since developmental research reveals that girls are exposed to wider range of emotion, resulting in more ease of effective emotional control, whereas men's emotional approach is more ruminative in nature (Brody, 1993).

IMPLICATIONS

What can be determined from the research on these issues? Clearly, a number of interrelated issues come into play, including our understanding of risk, mood, coping and sexual behavior, among other factors. We propose that coping and mood influence each other, such that negative mood can reduce an individual's ability to cope, and ineffective coping can increase negative mood. Various studies link problem-solving deficits and the use of emotion-focused coping to depressed mood and psychopathology, and negative mood also appears to influence the type of strategies employed.

Research suggests that affect, coping, and sexual offending are linked. Essentially, the inability to effectively cope with negative moods and stress appears to enhance these negative moods and, as a result, increase the likelihood that offenders will use sex as a coping strategy. Those offenders who are more likely to experience negative mood states (and who choose strategies such as emotion or avoidance coping) are also more likely to turn to sex to cope. Sexual gratification appears to decrease their negative emotions, but only in the short term. Because these offenders are not constructively dealing with their stress and negative emotions, they are not dealing with their problems in a constructive, task-focused manner. Therefore, sex becomes one of their primary (albeit ineffective) coping techniques. However, this decrease in negative mood and the associated pleasure of sex, produces a combination of negative reinforcement (i.e. escape from an aversive state) and positive reinforcement (the pleasure of sex), a combination that is almost certain to entrench the response as a characteristic reaction to stress (Domjan, 1998).

In other cases, positive affect also plays a direct role in offending, and occurs not only in response to the prospect of immediate gratification. This possibility has long been ignored, and only recently have positive pathways been incorporated into our understanding of offending. Sexual offenders appear to engage in abusive behavior to either attenuate a negative mood (as an ineffective means of coping) or to enhance a positive mood. Since those offenders who attempt to enhance a positive mood are more likely to plan their offences, perhaps it is the planning itself that increases positive affect, and not that positive affect increases the risk of offending. Treatment programs need to account for this possibility, which would require a modification to the original RP model. Since RP as a treatment model involves avoiding or coping with high-risk situations, it assumes that offenders are motivated to avoid offending, rather than considering that some offenders overtly plan to offend and do not experience any negative moods in the process. A different treatment strategy needs to be applied when positive moods are implicated in the offending process. Clearly, adopting a flexible approach to treatment is critical.

FUTURE RESEARCH

Despite the fact that research and theory have implicated both positive and negative affective states in sexual offending, and that treatment approaches to enhance effective coping appear promising, research remains unclear as to the processes that move offenders from affect states and poor coping to abusive acts. The relapse prevention model has been accepted for many years and only recently have researchers begun to critically examine it. In doing so, we have come to discover that there are diverse offending processes, with different offenders displaying differing emotional states and varying extents of planning in the lead-up to their offenses. All aspects of these differences require further research.

Affective states might differ at varying points during the offending process, and knowing this would increase our understanding the offender's goals at these various points. For those offenders attempting to avoid offending, equipping them with more appropriate coping strategies appears to be a relevant treatment goal. For those whose goals are supportive of offending, a more appropriate treatment approach may be to help them recognize the consequences of this goal and as a result encourage them to develop more appropriate goals. The recognition that positive emotional states also play an important role in offending leads to new venues for both researchers and treatment providers to explore and understand. As well, the intensity and type of emotion also appear to be relevant, but research has left these areas relatively unexplored. We look forward to seeing researchers explore the various issues raised in this chapter.

REFERENCES

Bermond, B., Schuerman, J., Nieuwenhuyse, B. & Fasotti, L. (1987). Spinal cord lesions: coping and mood states. *Tijdschrift voor Psychiatrie*, **29**, 365–73.

Billings, A.G. & Moos, R.H. (1982). Stressful life events and symptoms: a longitudinal model. *Health Psychology*, **1**, 99–117.

Billings, A.G. & Moos, R.H. (1984). Coping, stress, and social resources among adults with unipolar depression. *Journal of Personality and Social Psychology*, **46**, 877–91.

Brody, L.R. (1993). On understanding gender differences in the expression of emotion: gender roles, socialization, and language. In S.L. Ablon & D. Brown (eds), *Human Feelings: Explorations in Affect Development and Meaning* (pp. 87–121). Hillsdale, UK: Analytic Press Inc.

Catanzaro, S.J. (1993). Mood regulation expectancies, anxiety sensitivity, and emotional distress. *Journal of Abnormal Psychology*, **102**, 327–30.

Compas, B.E., Malcarne, V.L. & Fondacaro, K.M. (1988). Coping with stressful events in older children and young adolescents. *Journal of Consulting and Clinical Psychology*, **56**, 405–11.

Cortoni, F. & Marshall, W.L. (2001). Sex as a coping strategy and its relationship to juvenile sexual history and intimacy in sexual offenders. *Sexual Abuse: A Journal of Research and Treatment*, **13**, 27–43.

Domjan, M. (1998). *The Principles of Learning and Behavior*, 4th edn. New York: Brooks/Cole Publishing.

D'Zurilla, T.J. (1988). Problem-solving therapies. In K.S. Dobson (ed.), *Handbook of Cognitive Behavioral Therapies* (pp. 85–135). New York: Pergamon Press.

Eisenberg, N. & Fabes, R.A. (1992). *Emotion and its Regulation in Early Development*. San Francisco, CA: Jossey-Bass.

Endler, N.S. & Parker, J.D. (1990). Multidimensional assessment of coping: a critical evaluation. *Journal of Personality and Social Psychology*, **58**, 844–54.

Endler, N.S. & Parker, J.D.A. (1989). Coping with frustrations to self-realization: stress, anxiety, crises, and adjustment. In E. Krau (ed.), *Self-realization, Success, and Adjustment* (pp. 153–64). New York: Praeger Publishers.

Endler, N.S. & Parker, J.D.A. (1994). Assessment of multidimensional coping: task, emotion, and avoidance strategies. *Psychological Assessment*, **6**, 50–60.

Feelgood, S., Golias, P., Shaw, S. & Bright, D.A. (2000). Treatment changes in the dynamic risk factors of coping style in sexual offenders: a preliminary analysis. New South Wales Department of Corrective Services Sex Offender Programmes, Custody-Based Intensive Treatment (CUBIT), Sydney, New South Wales, Australia.

Flett, G.L., Blankstein, K.R. & Obertynski, M. (1996). Affect intensity, coping styles, mood regulation expectancies and depressive symptoms. *Personality and Individual Differences*, **20**, 221–8.

Folkman, S. & Lazarus, R.S. (1980). An analysis of coping in a middle-aged community sample. *Journal of Health and Social Behavior*, **21**, 219–39.

Folkman, S. & Lazarus, R.S. (1985). If it changes it must be a process: study of emotion and coping during three stages of a college examination. *Journal of Personality and Social Psychology*, **48**, 150–70.

Folkman, S. & Lazarus, R.S. (1986). Stress processes and depressive symptomatology. *Journal of Abnormal Psychology*, **95**, 107–13.

Groth, A.N. (1979). *Men Who Rape: The Psychology of the Offender*. New York: Plenum Press.

Groth, A.N. & Burgess, A.W. (1977). Rape: a sexual deviation. *American Journal of Orthopsychiatry*, **47**, 400–6.

Hanson, R.K. & Bussière, M.T. (1998). Predicting relapse: a meta-analysis of sexual offender recidivism studies. *Journal of Consulting and Clinical Psychology*, **66**, 348–62.

Hanson, R.K. & Harris, A.J.R. (2000). Where should we intervene? Dynamic predictors of sex offense recidivism. *Criminal Justice and Behavior*, **27**, 6–35.

Hillbrand, M., Foster, H. & Hirt, M. (1990). Rapists and child molesters: psychometric comparisons. *Archives of Sexual Behavior*, **19**, 65–71.

Howells, K., Day, A. & Wright, S. (2004). Affect, emotions and sex offending. *Psychology, Crime and Law*, **10**, 179–95.

Hudson, S.M., Marshall, W.L., Wales, D., McDonald, E., Bakker, L.W. & McLean, A. (1993). Emotional recognition skills of sex offenders. *Annals of Sex Research*, **6**, 199–211.

Hudson, S.M. & Ward, T. (2000). Relapse prevention: assessment and treatment implications. In D.R. Laws, S.M. Hudson & T. Ward (eds), *Remaking Relapse Prevention with Sex Offenders: A Sourcebook* (pp. 102–22). Thousand Oaks, CA: Sage Publications.

Knight, R.A. & Prentky, R.A. (1990). Classifying sexual offenders: the development and corroboration of taxonomic models. In W.L. Marshall & D.R. Laws (eds), *Handbook of Sexual Assault: Issues, Theories, and Treatment of the Offender* (pp. 23–52). New York: Plenum Press.

Laan, E., Everaerd, W., Van Berlo, R. & Rijs, L. (1995). Mood and sexual arousal in women. *Behaviour Research and Therapy*, **33**, 441–3.

Laws, D.R. (ed.) (1989). *Relapse Prevention with Sex Offenders*. New York: Guilford Press.

Laws, D.R., Hudson, S.M. & Ward, T. (eds) (2000). *Remaking Relapse Prevention with Sex Offenders: A Sourcebook*. Thousand Oaks, CA: Sage Publications.

Looman, J. (1995). Sexual fantasies of child molesters. *Canadian Journal of Behavioural Science*, **27**, 321–32.

Mann, R. & Webster, S. (2002, October). Understanding resistance and denial in incarcerated sexual offenders. Paper presented at the 21st Annual Research and Treatment Conference of the Association for the Treatment of Sexual Abusers. Montreal.

Marques, J.K., Day, D.M., Nelson, C. & West, M.A. (1994). Effects of cognitive-behavioral treatment on sex offender recidivism: preliminary results of a longitudinal study. *Criminal Justice and Behavior*, **21**, 28–54.

Marshall, L.E., Marshall, W.L. & Moulden H. (2000, October). Mood induction with sexual offenders. Paper presented at the 19th Annual Research and Treatment Conference of the Association for the Treatment of Sexual Abusers. San Diego.

Marshall, W.L., Anderson, D. & Fernandez, Y.M. (1999). *Cognitive Behavioural Treatment of Sexual Offenders*. Chichester, UK: John Wiley & Sons.

Marshall, W.L., Cripps, E., Anderson, D. & Cortoni, F. (1999). Self-esteem and coping strategies in child molesters. *Journal of Interpersonal Violence*, **14**, 955–62.

Marshall, W.L., Serran, G.A. & Cortoni, F.A. (2000). Childhood attachments, sexual abuse, and their relationship to adult coping in child molesters. *Sexual Abuse: A Journal of Research and Treatment*, **12**, 17–26.

McCormick, R. & Smith, M. (1995). Aggression and hostility in substance abusers: the relationship to abuse patterns, coping style, and relapse triggers. *Addictive Behaviors*, **20**, 555–62.

McCrae, R.R. & Costa, P.T. (1986). Personality, coping, and coping effectiveness in an adult sample. *Journal of Personality*, **54**, 385–405.

McKibben, A., Proulx, J. & Lusignan, R. (1994). Relationships between conflict, affect and deviant sexual behaviours in rapists and pedophiles. *Behaviour Research and Therapy*, **32**, 571–5.

McKibben, A., Proulx, J. and Lussier, P. (2001). Sexual aggressors' perceptions of effectiveness of strategies to cope with negative emotions and deviant sexual fantasies. *Sexual Abuse: Journal of Research and Treatment*, **13**, 257–73.

Miller, S.M., Brody, D.S. & Summerton, J. (1988). Styles of coping with threat: Implications for health. *Journal of Personality and Social Psychology*, **54**, 142–8.

Mitchell, R.E., Cronkite, R.C. & Moos, R.H. (1983). Stress, coping, and depression among married couples. *Journal of Abnormal Psychology*, **92**, 433–48.

Mitchell, W.B., DiBartolo, P.M., Brown, T.A. & Barlow, D.H. (1999). Effects of positive and negative mood on sexual arousal in sexually functional males. *Archives of Sexual Behavior*, **27**, 197–207.

Neidigh, L.W. & Tomiko, R. (1991). The coping strategies of child sexual abusers. *Journal of Sex Education and Therapy*, **17**, 103–10.

Pithers, W.D., Beal, L.S., Armstrong, J. & Petty, J. (1989). Identification of risk factors through clinical interviews and analysis of records. In D.R. Laws (ed.), *Relapse Prevention with Sex Offenders* (pp. 77–87). New York: Guilford.

Pithers, W.D., Kashima, K.M., Cumming, G.F., Beal, L.S. & Buell, M.M. (1988). Relapse prevention of sexual aggression. *Annals of the New York Academy of Sciences*, **528**, 244–60.

Pithers, W.D., Marques, J.K., Gibat, C.C. & Marlatt, G.A. (1983). Relapse prevention with sexual aggressives: a self-control model of treatment and maintenance of change. In J.G. Greer & I.R. Stuart (eds), *The Sexual Aggressor: Current Perspectives on Treatment* (pp. 241–59). New York: Van Nostrand Reinhold.

Proulx, J., McKibben, A. & Lusignan, R. (1996). Relationships between affective components and sexual behaviours in sexual aggressors. *Sexual Abuse: A Journal of Research and Treatment*, **8**, 279–90.

Rogers, D. & Masters, R. (1997). The development and evaluation of an emotional control training program for sexual offenders. *Legal and Criminological Psychology*, **2**, 51–64.

Serran, G.A. (2003). Changes in the coping strategies of extra-familial child molesters following cognitive behavioural relapse prevention treatment. Unpublished doctoral thesis. University of Ottawa, Canada.

Sinclair, R.C., Mark, M.M., Enzle, M.E., Borkovec, T.D. & Cumbleton, A.G. (1994). Toward a multiple-method view of mood induction: the appropriateness of a modified Velten mood induction technique and the problems of procedures with group assignment to conditions. *Basic and Applied Social Psychology*, **15**, 389–408.

Sinclair, R.C., Soldat, A.S. & Ryan, C.A. (1997). Development and validation of Velten-like image-oriented anxiety and serenity mood inductions. *Basic and Applied Social Psychology*, **19**, 163–82.

Stanton, A.L. & Franz, R. (1999). Focusing on emotion: an adaptive coping strategy? In C.R. Snyder (ed.), *Coping: The Psychology of What Works* (pp. 90–118). New York: Oxford University Press.

Velten, E.A. (1968). A laboratory task for the induction of mood states. *Behaviour Research and Therapy*, **6**, 473–82.

Ward, T. & Hudson, S. M. (1998). A model of the relapse process in sexual offenders. *Journal of Interpersonal Violence*, **13**, 700–25.

Ward, T. & Hudson, S.M. (2000a). A self-regulation model of relapse prevention. In D.R. Laws, S.M. Hudson & T. Ward (eds), *Remaking Relapse Prevention with Sex Offenders: A Sourcebook* (pp. 79–101). Thousand Oaks, CA: Sage Publications.

Ward, T. & Hudson, S.M. (2000b). Sexual offenders' implicit planning: a conceptual model. *Sexual Abuse: Journal of Research and Treatment*, **12**, 189–202.

Ward, T., Louden, K., Hudson, S.M. & Marshall, W.L. (1995). A descriptive model of the offense chain for child molesters. *Journal of Interpersonal Violence*, **10**, 452–72.

Westermann, R., Spies, K., Stahl, G. & Hesse, F.W. (1996). Relative effectiveness and validity of mood induction procedures: a meta-analysis. *European Journal of Social Psychology*, **26**, 557–80.

Wolf, T.M., Balson, P.M., Morse, E.V. & Simon, P.M. (1991). Relationship of coping style to affective state and perceived social support in asymptomatic and symptomatic HIV-infected persons: implications for clinical management. *Journal of Clinical Psychiatry*, **52**, 171–3.

Yates, E., Barbaree, H.E. & Marshall, W.L. (1984). Anger and deviant sexual arousal. *Behavior Therapy*, **15**, 287–94.

Chapter 9

SHAME AND GUILT IN CHILD MOLESTERS

MICHAEL PROEVE AND KEVIN HOWELLS
University of South Australia

The relevance of the emotions shame and guilt for sexual offenders has been noted previously in relation to the treatment components of victim empathy and relapse prevention. With regard to victim empathy, Roys (1997) argued that shame inhibits empathy, as its focus on self-worth dulls the person's capacity to experience other emotions. Therefore, the ability to share in another person's emotional experience is limited. She proposed that victim empathy interventions in sexual offender treatment might trigger a feeling of personal threat, which leads to the emotion of shame. Hanson (1997) similarly noted that exposure to victim suffering can increase victim blaming and cognitive distortions among sexual offenders. He implicated shame reactions in this process. Bumby (2000) also suggested that the self-oriented distress experienced by sexual offenders impedes empathy. Furthermore, perceived negative evaluation by others and personal distress experienced in shame leads to blaming the victim. This impairs empathy for the victim and may thereby increase the risk of re-offending. In contrast, the experience of guilt leads to an examination by the offender of the effects of the offence on the victim, reparative action, increased self-efficacy, increased ability to identify adaptive coping responses, and decreased risk of re-offending. The tendency to explore and identify the impact on the victim is increased. Bumby also reported that, in an empirical study of sexual offenders in outpatient treatment, there was a positive association between shame-proneness and measures of personal distress and externalization of responsibility. As proneness to guilt increased, so did level of empathic concern and perspective taking ability.

The role of shame in relapses was suggested by Hudson, Ward and Marshall (1992), within the framework of attribution theory. They argued that a sexual offender who responds to a lapse with an internal but controllable attribution should experience guilt, which should motivate a commitment to abstinence. However, a sexual offender who responds to a lapse with an internal uncontrollable attribution (e.g. "I have no willpower. I am a disgusting person") experiences shame.

Sexual Offender Treatment: Controversial Issues. Edited by W.L. Marshall, Y.M. Fernandez, L.E. Marshall and G.A. Serran.   © 2006 John Wiley & Sons, Ltd.

This could result in giving up attempts to cope, so that a complete relapse could occur.

Bumby, Marshall and Langton (1999) proposed a model of the influence of shame and guilt on sexual offending, which incorporated the effects of shame on empathy and on relapse. These authors suggested that the experience of shame following sexual offending results in decreased self-efficacy, decreased ability to use adaptive coping, increased personal distress, externalization of blame, increased cognitive distortions, and decreased victim-specific empathy, all of which increase the risk of re-offending.

In this chapter, we draw on general psychological literature to argue for the relevance of shame and guilt for child molesters. In order to explore this issue, we outline the concepts of shame and guilt, reasons for expecting shame to be common in child molesters, and the functions of shame. Because others have discussed the impact of shame and guilt on the treatment issues of empathy and relapse prevention, we emphasize the influence of shame and guilt as factors in readiness for treatment. We discuss approaches to treatment that are likely to decrease shame. Finally, we discuss methods of assessing shame and guilt, and evaluate their usefulness for child molesters.

CONCEPTS OF SHAME AND GUILT

Guilt and shame have been described as self-conscious emotions, which require recognition of the self as separate from others. In self-conscious emotions, the self evaluates itself against standards, rules and goals (Lewis, 1995). Commonly discussed characteristics of shame and guilt in the psychological literature include actions or action tendencies (Frijda, 1986), and characteristic cognitions. Shame and guilt can be distinguished according to cognitions and action tendencies.

Hiding oneself from others is a commonly described action or action tendency of shame (Tangney, Miller, Flicker & Barlow, 1996). Other actions described as characteristic of shame include externalizing strategies such as denying a negative action or characteristic, or blaming someone else for it. Externalization of blame has been found empirically to be associated with shame (Tangney, Wagner, Fletcher & Gramzow, 1992).

In contrast, action tendencies associated with guilt include confession (Barrett, 1995) and reparation (Frijda, 1986), which may take the form of apologizing, undoing damage or otherwise repairing the situation. Reparation has been found empirically to be an aspect of guilt experiences (Roseman, Wiest & Swartz, 1994).

Characteristic cognitions of guilt and shame have different foci; on actions in the case of guilt and on the self in the case of shame. When feeling guilty, relatively more emphasis is given to thoughts about an action than about the self (Lewis, 1995), including a focus on the negative consequences of the action for others (Barrett, 1995). The appraisal that one has violated a personal or moral standard has been noted in theoretical and empirical literature (Barrett, 1995; Wicker, Payne & Morgan, 1983). In addition, a person feeling guilty makes an appraisal that they are responsible for the violation of personal standards (Frijda, 1986).

Evaluation of the self may be the core cognition by which guilt may be distinguished from shame. Although people experiencing guilt may focus on aspects of the self that led to a failure of action, they do not make global negative evaluations of the self. In contrast, global negative evaluation of the self may be a core feature of shame (Lewis, 1995). The experience of shame involves judgement of the self as inferior, incompetent or bad in some way (Lewis, 1995; Tangney, 1990). The judgement of self in shame is in response to a specific failure or transgression, not the general negative self-evaluation across situations and over time that is low self-esteem (Tangney & Dearing, 2002). A second cognitive appraisal that has been described in shame is that people think of themselves as judged by others. This has been described as thinking of the self as seen through the eyes of another (Taylor, 1985), imagery of how the defective self appears to others (Tangney, 1990), or an appraisal by a person that other people think them a bad person and are looking at them (Barrett, 1995).

Different views of the relationship of the two types of self-evaluative appraisals to the experience of shame have been proposed. Taylor (1985) proposed that the self-consciousness involved in thinking of the self as seen through the eyes of another person is a necessary condition for shame. For Taylor, shame also requires the second type of appraisal: an adverse judgement of the self. Therefore, shame does not occur unless there is a negative view of the self through the eyes of others with which one identifies. Other authors have differed from Taylor in the relative importance given to each type of appraisal in shame. Tangney's (1990) emphasis is on the evaluation of self by that person as central to shame, with "self-consciousness" as a second element. In contrast, Crozier (1998) emphasized the importance of self-consciousness in shame. He proposed that, first, shame involves "taking an 'other' perspective on the self" (p. 273). Second, shame involves a negative judgement from this "other" perspective. Third, shame involves core features of the self. According to Crozier, it is not necessary that one accept the adverse self-evaluation in order to feel shame.

Gilbert (1998) described cognitive domains of external and internal shame. These domains correspond to the two types of shame cognition identified by other authors. External shame reflects a concern by a person with how others view them, a recognition that they are the object being looked at and judged by others. The experience of shame depends on how important the views of others are to the self. Negative self-evaluation can be identified with Gilbert's term "internal shame". The latter relates to an awareness of falling short of some internalized standard. Gilbert stated that internal and external shame cognitions are often highly correlated in the general population (see Goss, Gilbert & Allan, 1994). However, internal and external shame need not always be highly correlated. He cited the example of a pedophile who acknowledges that others see his actions as bad but has little internal shame.

SHAME IN CHILD MOLESTERS

We propose that there are features of sexual offending against children that promote shame, or external reasons for shame, and features of child molesters that promote shame, or internal reasons for shame. We suggest that, given external and internal reasons for shame, it is likely that child molesters would experience shame. We first discuss external reasons for shame.

Greenwald and Harder (1998) propose that both guilt and shame are adaptive and promote fitness. Guilt "functions as a signal, as a cognitive-emotional expectation, to regulate or prevent actions that would violate obligations to family, the larger social group and deities" (Greenwald & Harder, 1998, p. 228). Shame on the other hand, in its milder forms, also is adaptive, promoting attempts to repair or avoid damage to one's status or reputation (p. 229). Thus mild shame facilitates the maintenance of social bonds. Anticipatory shame serves to alert the person to the negative social consequences of transgressions, thus promoting relationships and status in the group. Both guilt and shame are adaptive according to Greenwald and Harder but have the potential to be destructive in extreme forms. These authors suggest there are four domains of shame experience, all of which relate to fitness: conformity, prosocial behaviour, sexuality and status/competition. Individual variation may exist in relation to sensitivity to shame in all these domains; thus one individual may be very low in shame in all domains, while another is high in all domains, and a third is shame-prone only in relation to a particular domain (Greenwald & Harder, 1998).

We know very little about sexual offenders' proneness to shame in these four domains. What is striking is that sexual offending has the capacity to activate multiple shame domains; particularly conformity, prosocial behaviour and sexuality and even, to some degree status/competition. The person who engages in sexual offending against a child, for example, breaks basic social rules and expectations and sets himself up as a social outcast (anti-social), fails to contribute to the social good and violates strongly engrained taboos about how sexuality is to be expressed. The behaviour is also likely to lower status (e.g. the low status of sexual offenders in prison) and reduce attractiveness to potential sexual partners. This analysis would suggest that sexual offending is a quintessential shame-eliciting form of behaviour. Other forms of offending and socially deviant behaviour rarely cross so many shame domains. Violence, for example, is not unequivocally non-conforming, probably is anti- rather than prosocial but does not infringe sexual taboos. Our suggestion that sexual offending represents an extreme form of shame-eliciting behaviour needs to be tested empirically. This could be done in a straightforward way by asking subjects to rate the degree of shame they might experience in relation to a set of hypothetical scenarios (e.g. "You have been accused of sexually touching a young girl, of being violent to your wife, of stealing money from your employer").

It is useful, however, to distinguish affective reactions (shame or guilt) to specific behaviours, to recorded offences and to a social identity as a sexual offender, and also to recognize that desynchronies of affective response are possible. A sexual abuse perpetrator, for example, may feel no guilt or shame in relation to particular acts (fondling a child sexually) but experience shame (but no guilt) in relation to officially recorded offences and also in response to his public identification as a sexual offender by the court and by his family, workmates and the wider community. Given the importance for shame of the theme of observation by others of the moral transgression, it might be expected that a social identity as a sexual offender is the primary elicitor of shame reactions in sexual offenders. The shame-inducing aspects of this social identity are likely to be reinforced by media coverage of the offences and the trial and also by subsequent treatment in the criminal justice system (e.g. by other inmates in prison).

If sexual offending is indeed a multi-domain infringement of social expectations and standards, why does shame or anticipated shame fail to control the deviant behaviour? Is the deficit located in the inability to experience anticipatory shame rather than in experiencing shame once the transgression has occurred and been observed by others? If so, we would need to further deconstruct the cognitive affective processes involved in using anticipated shameful outcomes as a self-regulation strategy and direct therapeutic attention at any deficits observed.

There may also be personal characteristics of child molesters, or *internal reasons*, that predispose them to the experience of shame. These characteristics may involve particular attachment styles that are more common in child molesters. Ward, Hudson and McCormack (1997) identified three insecure attachment styles hypothesized to lead to a lack of intimacy in adult relationships. Child molesters were found to be more likely than rapists to show a preoccupied attachment style (having a negative view of self and a positive view of others) or a fearfully attached style (negative self, negative others), and less likely to show dismissive styles (positive self, negative others). Non-violent offenders and non-sexual offenders were more likely than either group to show secure (positive self, positive others) attachment styles (Ward, Hudson & Marshall, 1996). Preoccupied attachment is characterized by relying on others for approval. There is a high level of loneliness and, commonly, sexual preoccupation. The fearful attachment style, while characterized by the desire for social contact and intimacy, is associated with the experience of distrust and fear of rejection, and a lack of concern about victims' feelings (Ward *et al.*, 1997).

Both the preoccupied and fearful attachment styles are characterized by a negative view of self, which would be expected to bring vulnerability to internal shame. In line with these expectations, Gross and Hansen (2000) found that fearful and preoccupied attachment styles were positively correlated with shame in a sample of university students. The secure attachment style was negatively correlated with shame and the dismissing style was unrelated to shame. Linking these findings to the literature on attachment style in sexual offenders suggests that child molesters would be expected to be vulnerable to the experience of (internal) shame.

Our suggestion is that there are sufficient reasons to expect child molesters to be likely to experience shame. A number of child molesters may not experience shame or guilt. They may have no particular negative feelings about themselves or their actions. However, many offenders who describe "feeling bad" are more likely to experience shame rather than guilt. We suggest here that characteristic aspects of the presentation of child molesters resemble the correlates of shame that have been found in empirical studies.

The correlates of shame and guilt have been the subject of a good deal of empirical research. Tangney and colleagues have studied the association of proneness to shame and to guilt with empathy and psychopathology, using self-report instruments that distinguish between guilt and shame (Tangney, 1990; Tangney, Wagner, Fletcher & Gramzow, 1992; Tangney, Wagner & Gramzow, 1992). In Gilbert's terms, these are measures of proneness to guilt and to internal shame. The measures are scenario-based instruments that assess the tendency to experience one emotion rather than the other given the same situation.

Tangney (1991) found that proneness to guilt was positively correlated with empathy, while shame-proneness was negatively correlated with empathy. Leith and

Baumeister (1998) found that guilt-proneness was positively correlated with perspective taking ability and total empathy, while shame-proneness was unrelated to perspective taking. However, shame-proneness was positively correlated with personal distress. In addition, proneness to guilt (controlling for shame-proneness), was inversely related or unrelated to measures of anger arousal, resentment, irritability, indirect hostility and a tendency to blame others for negative events. Shame-proneness was positively correlated with irritability, suspiciousness, resentment, anger arousal and externalization of blame for negative events (Tangney, Wagner, Fletcher & Gramzow, 1992). Externalization by blaming others may be a strategy for coping with shame, which protects a person's self-image and results in anger at others (Tangney & Dearing, 2002).

The correlates of shame-proneness identified in research with student populations have been afforded considerable attention in sexual offender research. Empathy is widely regarded as deficient in sexual offenders, and consequently their treatment invariably involves attention to empathy for their victims. However, the use of general measures of empathy has resulted in equivocal findings regarding empathy deficits in sexual offenders (Bumby, 2000). Recent consideration of victim-specific empathy as opposed to general empathy has been more fruitful. Marshall, Hamilton and Fernandez (2001) found that child molesters showed greater empathy for accident victims and sexual abuse victims than for their own victims. Furthermore, lower empathy was associated with greater distortions in beliefs about sex between adults and children. These findings are consistent with the findings from non-clinical populations of associations between shame-proneness, empathy and externalization. If child molesters experience greater shame, they would be expected to show greater externalization. Cognitive distortions shown by sexual offenders externalize in the sense that responsibility for sexual abuse is attributed to victims. Cognitive distortions may also involve denial or minimization of harm to victims; in other words failure to appreciate the victim's perspective. Such failures in perspective taking would be reflected in lower empathy for their own victims.

The associations of shame-proneness and guilt-proneness with forms of psychopathology have also received research attention. Shame-proneness is positively correlated with anxiety problems and depression (Allan, Gilbert & Goss, 1994; Tangney, Wagner & Gramzow, 1992).

FUNCTIONALITY OF SHAME FOR CHILD MOLESTERS

As for other emotions, it is likely that shame has evolved because of its functional nature. Greenwald and Harder (1998), for example, suggest that shame has evolved because it "plays an important part in promoting fitness through the regulation of behaviour in the areas of group identity, social bonding and competitive mating success" (p. 225). In considering the functions of shame, it is useful to distinguish the functions of the emotional state, including psychophysiological accompaniments, from the functions of behavioural emotional expressions of shame—what we might call its communicative functions. The display of emotions is believed to have informative, instrumental and evocative functions (Keltner & Harker, 1998).

Displays of shame, for example, inform others in the environment about the expressor's emotional state, likely cognitive appraisals and possible action tendencies. If we observe a sexual offender in a therapeutic group displaying shame when discussing his previous offences, we may infer from his expression of shame that he is distressed, that he evaluates his actions negatively to some degree, and even that he would prefer to avoid discussing the topic further. The display of shame may be instrumental in having an effect on the behaviour of observing others. The therapist's (or other group members') observation of shame in a group participant may lead them to change their behaviour towards him, in the direction of increased helping behaviour or reduced criticism. The evocative function of shame refers to the emotions evoked in the observer as a result of the observation of shame (Keltner & Harker, 1998). In a therapeutic group context it is possible to envisage diverse evoked emotional reactions ranging from increased sympathy to anger and hostility. If experienced and expressed shame potentially affect the behaviour of the individual perpetrator, other group members and the therapist, it follows that shame requires clinical assessment and monitoring.

Many of the communicative functions of shame can be seen as submissive behaviour (Gilbert, Pehl & Allan, 1994) or appeasement (Keltner & Harker, 1998), and may be common to many species. The non-verbal behaviours associated with shame are readily construed as submissiveness and may serve to reduce aggression and punitiveness, and increase affiliation, sympathy, liking and forgiveness on the part of others (Keltner & Harker, 1998). Given the high salience of sexual offending as a moral transgression it would follow that shame expression would be particularly functional for sexual offenders. There is clearly a need for empirical study of this topic.

Keltner and Harker (1998) in their review of the functions of shame suggest that both guilt and shame may follow serious moral transgressions and that both function to repair social relationships. They propose, however, that shame produces these effects through the non-verbal display of submissiveness, while guilt does so "through remedial behaviour, such as apologies, confessions and tending to others' pain" (p. 95). From a therapeutic perspective, therefore, guilt is more conducive to treatment readiness than is shame.

SHAME AND GUILT AS READINESS FACTORS

We propose that the emotions of shame and guilt are highly pertinent to the readiness of child molesters to engage in treatment. The construct of treatment readiness has been proposed as a framework for conceptualizing those factors that might diminish offenders' engagement in rehabilitation programs (Howells & Day, 2003). Treatment readiness is defined by Ward and colleagues (Ward, Day, Howells & Birgden, in press) as involving a number of internal and external factors, which collectively determine whether an individual offender engages in, and subsequently benefits from, treatment. Internal factors include beliefs about treatment, past experiences of programs, and offender goals. External factors include the extent to which treatment is coerced, the setting in which treatment is delivered and the availability of resources to support program delivery. An important component of the Ward *et al.* (in press) model of readiness comprises the affective reactions of the offender, particularly to his offending behaviour.

As Macdonald (1998) has insightfully pointed out, Goffman's (1963) early work has much to say about how individuals struggle to uphold their "identity claims", either having to manage the fact that their shameful qualities are already exposed for all to see or making efforts to prevent others knowing about such qualities. Many sexual offenders in treatment probably alternate between both strategies, at least in the early stages of therapy. They have already lost the battle to maintain a normal identity to some degree by virtue of being known to attend a sexual offender treatment group, but may still be endeavouring to protect their non-deviant identity by minimizing the extent or nature of their sexual deviance or by limiting the number of people who know about their offending behaviour. In effect, by less than full engagement in treatment they are struggling to prevent shame arising (Macdonald, 1998).

If a social identity as a sexual offender were the primary elicitor of shame it would be predicted that level of shame would vary over the course of an offending career. The transformation of social identity in many first conviction sexual offenders would appear to be massive and abrupt. One day he may be a respectable member of the local community, the next day a convicted pedophile or rapist. Repeat offenders, on the other hand, presumably learn to cope with this identity and its cognitive, affective and behavioural consequences.

How might guilt and shame affect readiness for treatment? In guilt, the individual's focus is on the act, whereas in shame it is on the self (Barrett, 1995). Guilt also involves a focus on the negative consequences of the act for others and an accompanying belief that one has violated a personal, moral standard. A number of action tendencies have been described for guilt, including apologizing, undoing damage and attempts to repair the damage done (Barrett, 1995; Frijda, 1986). These reactions may be conducive to engagement in therapy.

A person who feels guilty regards their action as wrong, and perceives themself as responsible for what occurred. In sexual offender treatment, therapists encourage clients to challenge their justifications about their actions, and to take responsibility for their offending. Sexual offender treatment may even be organized entirely around the notion of responsibility (e.g. Jenkins, 1990).

Shame can be distinguished from guilt in terms of the self-evaluative components of emotion. Global negative evaluations of the self characterize shame. The self is seen as inferior, incompetent or otherwise bad. Shame also involves an awareness of being judged by others, and seen as defective (Taylor, 1985). As discussed above, the action tendency associated with shame appears to be hiding oneself from others, whereas confession and reparation are more salient for guilt (Barrett, 1995). In this context, higher levels of guilt may be associated with increased levels of emotional self-disclosure.

If the action tendency associated with shame is to hide, while a requirement of therapy is to reveal information about the self and previous behaviour, then the high-shame individual is likely to find it difficult to fully engage in treatment. This difficulty may be amplified if the experience of shame is sometimes very brief, not consciously acknowledged and quickly transformed to other emotions such as anger, as some theorists have claimed (Macdonald, 1998). There appears to be increasing evidence that shame reduces the disclosure of emotional experiences to others, thereby preventing exploration and cognitive assimilation of such material (Macdonald, 1998; Stiles, 1987).

As we have discussed, experiences of shame can lead to withdrawal or to anger as a result of externalization. These coping strategies may also be evident in therapy situations. Withdrawal is manifested by such behaviours as missing sessions, arriving late, saying little, or abruptly changing the subject. Externalization in response to shame may be shown in behaviours such as questioning the therapist's skills, or becoming hostile during a productive session (Tangney & Dearing, 2002). Thus, coping strategies for shame also decrease responsivity to treatment.

An additional aspect of treatment readiness is motivation for treatment. The connection between shame and motivation can be understood through the concept of cognitive dissonance. The dissonance between a sexual offender's self-image and his evaluation of his sexually deviant behaviour may be the fuel for motivating behaviour change (Kear-Colwell & Pollock, 1997). In the experience of shame, cognitive dissonance is resolved by evaluating both self and sexually offensive behaviour negatively. Therefore, with little cognitive dissonance, there would be little motivation (Proeve, 2003).

If the experience of shame serves to reduce an offender's readiness for and responsivity to treatment, then shame itself needs to be a focus of treatment. This would require formally acknowledging the normality of shame reactions in the context of sexual offending, exploring the cognitive appraisals and schemata that constitute shame for individual clients, considering the effects of shame on the client's behaviour in therapeutic groups, and distinguishing the useful and damaging aspects of shame experiences. In addition, work on shame also suggests a need to look at non-specific aspects of treatment programs that might enhance or decrease shame. The therapists' style and attitudes to the client are likely to be crucial in ensuring that destructive shame is not the predominant emotional experience of sexual offenders in therapy.

DECREASING SHAME

As well as processes and interventions in sexual offender treatment that decrease shame, there are aspects of therapist style that are likely to increase shame. Serran, Fernandez, Marshall and Mann (2003) reviewed factors that have been found to facilitate or impede therapeutic change from the general psychotherapy literature. Of these factors that impede therapeutic change, confrontation has also been discussed in relation to sexual offender treatment. Although the use of strong confrontation has been common in treatment of sexual offenders, recent opinion has condemned its use (Kear-Colwell & Pollock, 1997; Serran *et al.*, 2003). Confrontation is likely to be experienced as an attack on the self, and therefore is likely to increase the level of shame experienced.

Other aspects of therapist style are likely to decrease shame in sexual offender treatment. Serran *et al.* (2003) listed the following therapist features that facilitate change: empathy, genuineness, warmth, respect, support, therapist self-disclosure, encouragement of emotional expressiveness, directiveness and use of humour. Of this list, warmth and respect expressed by the therapist, and communicating acceptance of the client, are likely to be particularly important in decreasing clients' shame. In agreement with Serran and colleagues, humour has been recommended in other therapeutic literature as an antidote to shame (Tangney & Dearing, 2002).

It is also helpful for decreasing shame that therapists distinguish between clients and their offensive actions. Jenkins (1998) proposed that the sexual offender "is assisted to separate his actions (what I have done) from his identity (who I am); to recognize that he may have done a terrible thing, but that he is not a terrible person" (p. 164). Another way to express this is to say that the offender is helped to change the focus away from condemnation of self, to condemnation of his actions, which is akin to moving from shame to guilt. Clients may find it easier to distinguish themselves from their actions when they understand and can label the concepts of shame and guilt. The suggestion by Tangney and Dearing (2002) that clients should be educated explicitly about the difference between shame and guilt may be useful also in the treatment of child molesters.

In addition, Marshall, Anderson and Fernandez (1999) have described direct interventions to enhance self-esteem. Such interventions include encouraging clients to increase social and pleasurable activities, having them write down positive and attractive features of themselves and pay frequent attention to them, and encouraging clients to attend to their appearance and self-presentation. The expected effect of these interventions in increasing positive evaluation of self should also be helpful in decreasing shame.

The general adoption of the therapist features and interventions described here should help to promote treatment readiness by decreasing the level of shame experienced by clients. The identification of high-shame individuals would be helpful for treatment planning, as such individuals may require additional intervention or different pacing of treatment. Suitable assessment measures for shame and guilt are necessary for the identification of shame issues. Reliable and valid measures of shame and guilt are also needed to evaluate interventions directed at shame and guilt.

ASSESSMENT OF SHAME AND GUILT

A number of instruments for the measurement of shame and guilt have been developed. In this section, available assessment approaches are reviewed with regard to their usefulness for assessing shame and guilt in child molesters.

Many of the available instruments are self-report measures of trait guilt or shame, or proneness to experience guilt and shame. Reviews of shame and guilt measures (Tangney, 1996; Tangney & Dearing, 2002) suggest that some dispositional measures confound the concepts they assess. Some instruments assess either shame or guilt only. The concepts of shame and guilt may be confounded in these instruments, in that items in some guilt inventories reflect judgements about the self and therefore may reflect shame. Another potential problem is distinguishing shame from self-esteem. The Internalized Shame Scale (ISS; Cook, 1988) includes items that may reflect self-esteem issues, and correlates substantially with measures of self-esteem. Self-reports may also invite denial of shame experiences, as some individuals may not recognize these experiences, or may be embarrassed by their feelings and as a result deny such experiences.

Scenario-based measures developed by Tangney and colleagues, which have been used in numerous studies, address these problems in that they distinguish between shame and guilt in response to particular events, they do not rely on respondents' ability to distinguish between abstract notions of shame and guilt, and they may circumvent denial of shame experiences because they require responses to specific situations rather than requiring acknowledgment of global tendencies to experience shame and guilt. The latest measure developed by this research group is the Test of Self-Conscious Affect, third version (TOSCA-3; Tangney, Dearing, Wagner & Gramzow, 2000). However, there is also a conceptual problem with this instrument, given that we have argued for the usefulness of Gilbert's notions of internal and external shame. The TOSCA-3 scenarios address action tendencies and cognitions relevant to internal shame, but there are no items that are characteristic of external shame. The only instrument designed to measure external shame is the Other As Shamer Scale (OAS; Goss et al., 1994). This instrument was paired with the Internalized Shame Scale (ISS) as a measure of internal shame. The conceptual problems of the ISS have already been discussed.

Both internal and external shame could be measured by combining the OAS and the TOSCA-3. However, some scenarios of the TOSCA-3 are designed for university students and may not be relevant for sexual offenders. A modified version of a scenario-based instrument for socially deviant populations, the TOSCA-SD (Hanson & Tangney, 1995) may be more relevant. However, the properties of this instrument have not been described in published research studies.

Measurement of dispositional shame and guilt in child molesters may be useful for assessing treatment readiness in that there will be some indication of the likelihood of shame reactions or appropriate guilt occurring when treatment is undertaken. An alternative approach is to measure state guilt and shame. Reviews of these instruments show similar problems to dispositional measures (Tangney, 1996; Tangney & Dearing, 2002). Some instruments confound shame and guilt, or shame and embarrassment. A self-report instrument that does distinguish shame and guilt but does not require respondents to distinguish the two concepts is the State Shame and Guilt Scale (SSGS: Marschall, Sanftner & Tangney, 1994). This instrument has good internal reliabilities for shame and guilt sub-scales. However, unless the instrument were used temporally close to treatment sessions, good test-retest reliabilities over a period of weeks would be required in order for it to be useful in assessing treatment readiness. Test-retest reliabilities for the SSGS have not been published.

For the purposes of assessing treatment readiness, an instrument for the measurement of shame and guilt should ideally be based on scenarios relevant to sexual offenders, including reference to their own and others' reactions to their offences, and action tendencies in response to offences. Internal and external shame, as well as guilt, should be assessed. Respondents should be asked for current reactions or feelings within the recent past, such as the past week. Unfortunately, such an instrument has not yet been developed.

Given the difficulties in assessing shame and guilt by self-report, one option is to assess shame and guilt through direct observation in therapeutic or interview settings. A precondition for this strategy is that associated behaviours can be defined. On occasion the client may directly verbally express shame or guilt in relation to events being discussed but, more typically, the clinician needs to assess these emotions from the non-verbal behaviours of the client. It is more likely that shame can be detected non-verbally than guilt. Actions associated empirically with guilt include apologizing and changing one's behaviour (Baumeister, Stillwell & Heatherton, 1995). However, apologizing has been found also to be associated with shame (Proeve, 2001), and changing one's behaviour can be observed only over a considerable period of time. In contrast, characteristic actions of shame include blushing and hiding behaviour (Wicker *et al.*, 1983), which may be readily observable. Keltner and Harker (1998) suggest that shame involves "a shrinking and folding in of the body, gaze aversion and motor avoidance, which may signify inferiority and withdrawal" (p. 81). Keltner and Harker reported the results of experimental studies that showed observers could identify displays of shame with above-chance accuracy, and could reliably distinguish shame from embarrassment. In assessment for treatment readiness, it may be possible to identify shame, if not guilt, through the non-verbal behaviours of the client.

CONCLUSIONS

Prominent clinicians and researchers in the field of sexual offender treatment have noted the relevance of shame and guilt for child molesters. However, the existing literature consists of theoretical articles arguing for the usefulness of attending to shame and guilt in sexual offenders as part of their treatment. In this chapter we have tried to bolster the case for considering shame and guilt in child molesters, by drawing on theoretical, experimental and clinical literature from outside the field of offender treatment. We have discussed the generally agreed profiles of these two emotions and have argued that, for shame, Gilbert's (1998) concepts of internal and external shame are usefully applied to child molesters. Drawing on the theoretical and empirical literature we suggest that the way in which sexual offending is viewed, along with the attachment styles common in child molesters, make it likely that these offenders would experience shame. Furthermore, interpersonal variables and psychopathology associated with shame and guilt, including empathy and anger, have been observed in sexual offenders. Shame is not only likely in child molesters, it may be functional in some ways when they enter group treatment. As a result of reviewing this literature, we conclude that shame and guilt require greater attention in the treatment of child molesters.

Within the framework of treatment readiness, shame is more likely among child molesters and reduces readiness for treatment, whereas guilt is conducive to engagement in treatment. Interventions and therapy processes that are likely to increase or decrease shame experiences are already known in sexual offender treatment. Interestingly, aspects of therapist style and specific interventions that are advocated as good practice for facilitating client change are also likely to decrease shame and promote treatment readiness. This is consistent in that the action tendency of hiding and avoidance, associated with shame, naturally impedes change. Keeping in mind the connection between therapy practices and shame may help sexual offender therapists stay alert to manifestations and changes in shame shown by their clients in treatment. It may be that high-shame individuals require interventions additional to these general approaches.

Developing familiarity with shame and guilt experiences, and developing interventions to influence these emotions, is dependent on the ability to identify and measure shame and guilt. Assessment is the most pressing issue in applying the concepts of shame and guilt to the treatment of child molesters. Existing instruments for assessing shame and guilt have significant shortcomings. There is a need for the development of specialized measures. Both self-report and therapist-rated approaches are needed, although the latter may perhaps be realistically restricted to the assessment of shame. Appropriate assessment of shame and guilt in child molesters will be the key to enhancing our understanding of these emotions and our interventions directed at them.

REFERENCES

Allan, S., Gilbert, P. & Goss, K. (1994). An exploration of shame measures: II: Psychopathology. *Personality and Individual Differences*, **19**, 293–9.

Barrett, K.C. (1995). A functionalist approach to shame and guilt. In J.P. Tangney & K.W. Fischer (eds), *Self-conscious Emotions: The Psychology of Shame, Guilt, Embarrassment, and Pride* (pp. 25–63). New York: Guilford Publications.

Baumeister, R.F., Stillwell, A.M. & Heatherton, T.F. (1995). Interpersonal aspects of guilt: evidence from narrative studies. In J.P. Tangney & K.W. Fischer (eds), *Self-conscious Emotions: The Psychology of Shame, Guilt, Embarrassment, and Pride* (pp. 255–73). New York: Guilford.

Bumby, K.M. (2000). Empathy inhibition, intimacy deficits, and attachment difficulties in sex offenders. In D.R. Laws, S.M. Hudson & T. Ward (eds), *Remaking Relapse Prevention with Sex Offenders: A Sourcebook* (pp. 143–66). Thousand Oaks, CA: Sage Publications.

Bumby, K.M., Marshall, W.L. & Langton, C. (1999). A theoretical model of the influences of shame and guilt on sexual offending. In B.K. Schwartz (ed.), *The Sex Offender: Theoretical Advances, Treating Special Populations and Legal Developments*, vol. **III** (pp. 5.1–5.12). Kingston, NJ: Civic Research Institute.

Cook, D.R. (1988). Measuring shame: the Internalized Shame Scale. In R.T. Potter-Efron & P.S. Potter-Efron (eds), *The Treatment of Shame and Guilt in Alcoholism Counseling* (pp. 197–215). New York: Haworth Press.

Crozier, W.R. (1998). Self-consciousness in shame: the role of the 'Other'. *Journal for the Theory of Social Behaviour*, **28**, 273–86.

Frijda, N.H. (1986). *The Emotions*. Cambridge: Cambridge University Press.

Gilbert, P. (1998). Shame and humiliation in the treatment of complex cases. In N. Tarrier, A. Wells & G. Haddock (eds), *Treating Complex Cases: The Cognitive Behavioural Therapy Approach* (pp. 241–71). London: John Wiley & Sons.

Gilbert, P., Pehl, J. & Allan, S. (1994). The phenomenology of shame and guilt: an empirical investigation. *British Journal of Medical Psychology*, **67**, 23–36.

Goffman, E. (1963). *Stigma: Notes on the Management of a Spoiled Identity*. London: Penguin Books.

Goss, K., Gilbert, P. & Allan, S. (1994). An exploration of shame measures: I: The 'other as shamer scale'. *Personality and Individual Differences*, **17**, 713–17.

Greenwald, D.F. & Harder, D.W. (1998). Domains of shame: evolutionary, cultural, and psychotherapeutic aspects. In P. Gilbert & B. Andrews (eds), *Shame: Interpersonal Behavior, Psychopathology, and Culture* (pp. 225–45). New York: Oxford University Press.

Gross, C.A. & Hansen, N.E. (2000). Clarifying the experience of shame: the role of attachment style, gender, and investment in relatedness. *Personality and Individual Differences*, **28**, 897–907.

Hanson, R.K. (1997). Invoking sympathy: assessment and treatment of empathy deficits among sexual offenders. In B.K. Schwartz & H.R. Cellini (eds), *The Sex Offender: New Insights, Treatment Innovations, and Legal Developments*, vol. II (pp. 1.1–1.12). Kingston, NJ: Civic Research Institute.

Hanson, R.K. & Tangney, J.P. (1995). *The Test of Self-Conscious Affect-Socially Deviant Populations (TOSCA-SD)*. Corrections Research, Department of the Solicitor General of Canada, Ottawa.

Howells, K. & Day, A. (2003). Readiness for anger management: clinical and theoretical issues. *Clinical Psychology Review*, **23**, 319–37.

Hudson, S.M., Ward, T. & Marshall, W.L. (1992). The abstinence violation effect in sex offenders: a reformulation. *Behaviour Research and Therapy*, **30**, 435–41.

Jenkins, A. (1990). *Invitations to Responsibility*. Adelaide, Australia: Dulwich Centre Publications.

Jenkins, A. (1998). Invitations to responsibility: engaging adolescents and young men who have sexually abused. In W.L. Marshall, Y.M. Fernandez, S.M. Hudson & T. Ward (eds), *Sourcebook of Treatment Programs for Sexual Offenders* (pp. 163–89). New York: Plenum Press.

Kear-Colwell, J. & Pollock, P. (1997). Motivation or confrontation: which approach to the child sex offender? *Criminal Justice and Behavior*, **24**, 20–33.

Keltner, D. & Harker, L. (1998). The forms and functions of the nonverbal signal of shame. In P. Gilbert & B. Andrews (eds), *Shame: Interpersonal Behavior, Psychopathology, and Culture* (pp. 78–98). New York: Oxford University Press.

Leith, K.P. & Baumeister, R.F. (1998). Empathy, shame, guilt, and narratives of interpersonal conflicts: guilt-prone people are better at perspective taking. *Journal of Personality*, **66**, 1–37.

Lewis, M. (1995). Self-conscious emotions. *American Scientist*, **83**, 68–78.

Macdonald, J. (1998). Disclosing shame. In P. Gilbert & B. Andrews (eds), *Shame: Interpersonal Behavior, Psychopathology, and Culture* (pp. 141–60). New York: Oxford University Press.

Marschall, D., Sanftner, J. & Tangney, J.P. (1994). *The State Shame and Guilt Scale*. George Mason University, Fairfax, VA.

Marshall, W.L., Anderson, D. & Fernandez, Y. (1999). *Cognitive Behavioural Treatment of Sexual Offenders*. Chichester, UK: John Wiley & Sons.

Marshall, W.L., Hamilton, K. & Fernandez, Y. (2001). Empathy deficits and cognitive distortions in child molesters. *Sexual Abuse: A Journal of Research and Treatment*, **13**, 123–30.

Proeve, M. (2001). Remorse: its description and its interpersonal effects. Unpublished PhD thesis, University of South Australia, Adelaide.

Proeve, M.J. (2003). Responsivity factors in sexual offender treatment. In T. Ward, D.R. Laws & S.M. Hudson (eds), *Sexual Deviance: Issues and Controversies* (pp. 244–61). Thousand Oaks, CA: Sage Publications.

Roseman, I.J., Wiest, C. & Swartz, T.S. (1994). Phenomenology, behaviors, and goals differentiate discrete emotions. *Journal of Personality and Social Psychology*, **67**, 206–21.

Roys, D.T. (1997). Empirical and theoretical considerations of empathy in sex offenders. *International Journal of Offender Therapy and Comparative Criminology*, **41**, 53–64.

Serran, G., Fernandez, Y., Marshall, W.L. & Mann, R.E. (2003). Process issues in treatment: application to sexual offender programs. *Professional Psychology: Research and Practice*, **34**, 368–74.

Stiles, W.B. (1987). I have to talk to somebody: a fever model of disclosure. In V.J. Derlaga & J.H. Berg (eds), *Self-disclosure: Theory, Research and Therapy* (pp. 257–82). New York: Plenum Press.

Tangney, J.P. (1990). Assessing individual differences in proneness to shame and guilt: development of the Self-Conscious Affect and Attribution Inventory. *Journal of Personality and Social Psychology*, **59**, 102–11.

Tangney, J.P. (1991). Moral affect: the good, the bad, and the ugly. *Journal of Personality and Social Psychology*, **61**, 598–607.

Tangney, J.P. (1996). Conceptual and methodological issues in the assessment of shame and guilt. *Behaviour Research and Therapy*, **34**, 741–54.

Tangney, J.P. & Dearing, R.L. (2002). *Shame and Guilt*. New York: Guilford.

Tangney, J.P., Dearing, R.L., Wagner, P.E. & Gramzow, R. (2000). *The Test of Self-Conscious Affect-3 (TOSCA-3)*. George Mason University, Fairfax, VA.

Tangney, J.P., Miller, R.S., Flicker, L. & Barlow, D.H. (1996). Are shame, guilt, and embarrassment distinct emotions? *Journal of Personality and Social Psychology*, **70**, 1256–69.

Tangney, J.P., Wagner, P., Fletcher, C. & Gramzow, R. (1992). Shamed into anger: the relation of shame and guilt to anger and self-reported aggression. *Journal of Personality and Social Psychology*, **62**, 669–75.

Tangney, J.P., Wagner, P. & Gramzow, R. (1992). Proneness to shame, proneness to guilt, and psychopathology. *Journal of Abnormal Psychology*, **101**, 469–78.

Taylor, G. (1985). *Pride, Shame, and Guilt: Emotions of Self-assessment*. Oxford: Clarendon.

Ward, T., Day, A., Howells, K. & Birgden, A. (in press). The multifactor offender readiness model. *Aggression and Violent Behavior*.

Ward, T., Hudson, S.M. & McCormack, J. (1997). Attachment style, intimacy deficits, and sexual offending. In B.K. Schwartz & H.R. Cellini (eds), *The Sex Offender: New Insights, Treatment Innovations, and Legal Developments*, vol. **II** (pp. 2.1–2.14). Kingston, NJ: Civic Research Institute.

Ward, T., Hudson, S.M. & Marshall, W.L. (1996). Attachment style in sex offenders: a preliminary study. *Journal of Sex Research*, **33**, 17–26.

Wicker, F.W., Payne, G.C. & Morgan, R.D. (1983). Participant descriptions of guilt and shame. *Motivation and Emotion*, **7**, 25–39.

PART II

TREATMENT

Chapter 10

NEW IDEAS IN THE TREATMENT OF SEXUAL OFFENDERS

TONY WARD* AND DAWN FISHER[†]
* Victoria University of Wellington, New Zealand
[†] University of Birmingham and Llanarth Court Hospital, Wales, UK

This is an exciting time for those of us researching and working clinically with sexual offenders. In the last ten years or so a diverse range of theoretical and therapeutic innovations have emerged, extending from a consideration of the developmental precursors of sexual crimes (Keenan & Ward, 2003) to the espousal of public health models of intervention (Laws, 2000). New ideas are particularly important in science and practice as they open up areas for exploration and help to focus treatment on the causes of sexually abusive behavior. In our view the recent arrival on the theoretical horizon of positive approaches to practice, combined with new developments in evolutionary theory, is particularly promising. Gene-culture theory is a flexible evolutionary model that claims the evolution of human beings is propelled by genetic, individual learning and cultural processes and that, therefore, the explanation of human traits is likely to involve these three sets of processes (Odling-Smee, Laland & Feldman, 2003). Genetic factors may result in a predisposition to seek certain types of goods, while learning events in an individual's lifetime, within a particular cultural context, provide socially constructed ways of achieving these valued experiences, activities and outcomes. From a correctional perspective, this means that the causes of sexually aggressive behavior are likely to have a naturalistic basis and that motivational and cognitive biases lead individuals to seek basic human goods in socially unacceptable ways. An intriguing aspect of this naturalistic picture is the powerful influence of genetic and cultural processes; neither dominates the other, giving both biological and social learning oriented researchers an important role in accounting for sexually abusive behavior.

The stipulation that human beings are "naturally inclined" (i.e. it is part of their nature) to seek certain primary goods means that the achievement of these goods is likely to result in higher levels of well-being and reduced risk of psychopathology

Sexual Offender Treatment: Controversial Issues. Edited by W.L. Marshall, Y.M. Fernandez, L.E. Marshall and G.A. Serran. © 2006 John Wiley & Sons, Ltd.

and antisocial behavior (Emmons, 1999). This view has direct implications for the rehabilitation of offenders and highlights the critical role of the therapeutic alliance and positive treatment approaches in facilitating an offence-free lifestyle. The natural predisposition to seek goods such as friendship, community connectedness, personal autonomy and self-esteem points to the importance of structuring treatment around the acquisition of a new personal identity and lifestyle rather than simply risk reduction and management (Maruna, 2001). In other words, there is a clear relationship between this theory of human nature, the etiology of sexual offending, the aims of rehabilitation, the treatment strategies employed, the style of therapy, and the role of therapist factors in the change process.

Therefore, in this chapter we will attempt the rather ambitious task of demonstrating how these ideas are linked, and moreover, how collectively they can both accommodate existing insights into the treatment process and also lead to new interventions. First, we will briefly outline gene-culture co-evolutionary theory in order to provide the theoretical underpinning to positive treatment practices, and contrast it with evolutionary psychology. Second, we will explicate the notion of natural human goods and discuss their key features. Third, the etiological implications of primary goods are explicitly addressed and by way of illustration, related to deviant sexual arousal. Fourth, positive treatment approaches that are consistent with the idea of primary goods are examined, with particular emphasis placed on Haaven and Coleman's "new me, old me" theory and Ward and Stewart's good lives model. Fifth, we discuss how a naturalistic positive model is able to explain why therapist factors and the quality of the therapeutic alliance are important determinants of treatment outcome. Finally, we conclude the chapter with some comments on future research direction for positive practice models.

GENE-CULTURE CO-EVOLUTION THEORY

There are three essential elements in Darwin's ideas about natural selection (Darwin, 1859). First, individual members of a species all vary with respect to their physical and psychological traits. Second, some individual members of a species will demonstrate variations which make them better able to survive or adapt to changing environmental conditions. For example, the faster antelope is more likely to escape predatory lions. Third, those individuals who are better equipped to survive will be more likely to breed and in doing so will pass on these characteristics to their progeny. Consequently, these inherited characteristics will become more common within that species.

In addition to natural selection, Darwin also discerned one other important process in evolution—sexual selection. This is the idea that male and female members of a particular species will demonstrate distinct preferences in their choice of mates based upon the physical or behavioral characteristics of such organisms. Consequently, individuals with characteristics or traits that are highly preferred in mates will leave behind more offspring and these characteristics will become more frequent in the population. For example, in certain species of birds (e.g. peacocks), the females demonstrate a preference for males with extravagant, brightly colored plumage.

There are different ways of applying evolutionary theory to human behavior. These include sociobiology, human behavioral ecology, memetics, evolutionary psychology and gene-culture co-evolution theory. Each has its strengths and weaknesses and is the focus of continued research and theoretical development (Laland & Brown, 2002). For reasons that are not entirely clear, evolutionary psychology has had the most influence in psychology and is the approach underpinning the majority of the current evolutionary work in the sexual offending area (e.g. Quinsey, 2002). We do not have the space to systematically critique evolutionary psychology here so we will simply summarize our concerns (see Ward & Siegert, 2002, for a more detailed critique).

Critique of Evolutionary Psychology

First, there is evidence from cognitive neuropsychology and developmental psychology that our minds are not massively modular in the way depicted by evolutionary psychology (Buller & Hardcastle, 2000). Rather, a critical human adaptation appears to be our cognitive plasticity and ability to learn from experience and each other (Clark, 2003); and this capacity is likely to involve domain general learning mechanisms (Griffiths & Stotz, 2000). Second, we actively engineer or construct our environment by using technology and social learning, and therefore any explanation of robust human characteristics will necessarily involve cultural factors (Odling-Smee et al., 2003). Third, our minds are constructed throughout the process of development and are not preformed in any meaningful sense, rather they emerge out of a matrix of developmental resources. This means that social scaffolding by parents, peers and other social actors plays a critical role in the development of the mind (Sterelny, 2003). Contrary to the claims of evolutionary psychology, we do not house ancient minds within modern skulls but rather inherit the capacity to acquire a mind (Clark, 2003). Thus we argue that human beings' ability to construct and in turn be shaped by their environment(s), in conjunction with their cognitive and behavioral plasticity and the role of culture and social learning in creating minds, means that it is a mistake to view human nature as biologically fixed in the way evolutionary psychology does. Clark (2003) noted that human beings do not have a set nature with a "simple wrap-around of tools and culture; the tools and culture are as much determiners of our natures as products of it" (p. 86).

In view of these considerations we argue that any evolutionary explanation of sexual offending will need to be based on a triple inheritance or gene-culture co-evolutionary model: covering genetic, ecological and cultural inheritances (Odling-Smee et al., 2003). Of course this argument means applying the tenets of a model designed to explain human evolution to understanding sexually deviant behavior. This is a reasonable extension as long as it is clear that the primary aim is to account for population level characteristics (i.e. the traits that human beings as a whole exhibit), and as consequence of this, explain the variety of sexual behaviors (including offending) and strategies apparent in human beings. Thus the causes of sexual offending will be derived from genetically encoded cognitive and motivational predispositions, specific learning experiences, cultural processes, and the impact each of these sets of influences have on the environment in which individuals live.

Gene-culture Co-evolutionary Theory and Niche Construction

The version of gene-culture co-evolution theory we prefer is that developed by Odling-Smee *et al.* (2003) and is best defined by its focus on the construct of *niche construction*. According to Odling-Smee *et al.*, niche construction occurs when organisms alter the environment and thereby modify the relationship between their characteristics and the features of the environment. A good example is the leaf-cutter ant. These ants store plant material in their nests in order to cultivate a specific type of fungus (i.e. they construct fungal gardens), which they use as a food source. The process of constructing this niche results in systematic changes to the soil and ecosystem within and around the nest and also alters the selection environment of their offspring. This alteration may effectively reduce selection pressures (i.e. reduce the pressure on organisms to adapt or be eliminated) in ways that benefit or harm the long-term survival chances of the ant and its offspring. Examples of niche construction in human beings are the building of houses, implementation of farming practices and the development of technology. All these changes modify the niche in which human beings live their lives and thereby change the relationship or match between themselves and features of the environment.

According to Odling-Smee *et al.*, there are three types of processes involved in niche construction in a population of diverse phenotypes (living organisms): *genetic processes*, *ontogenetic processes* (individual learning within a lifetime) and *cultural processes*. Each of these processes is associated with unique ways of acquiring, storing and transmitting information, and also with distinct means of interacting with the environment. An example of genetic processes is that of the orb-web spider where the spinning of webs on a nightly basis is thought to be rigidly determined by genes (Avital & Jablonka, 2000). An example of ontogenetic or learning processes is the use of pine needles by woodpecker finches in the Galapagos Islands to dislodge insects from the bark of trees. This behavior is thought to be relearned by each generation of finches on a trial and error basis (Avital & Jablonka, 2000) and enables the finches to exploit resources (i.e. create a new niche) that were not previously available to them, thereby creating "a stable selection favoring a bill able to manipulate tools rather than the sharp, pointed bill and long tongue characteristic of woodpeckers" (Odling-Smee *et al.*, 2003, p. 22). The advantage of an ontogenetic process such as learning is that organisms are able to rapidly adapt to changing circumstances and not rely on inbuilt genetic solutions. Odling-Smee *et al.* state that this type of learning may well be regulated by a general principle such as the law of effect, and therefore actions that are followed by a positive outcome are more likely to be repeated in the future. An example of cultural processes in animals is the discovery by macaque monkeys that washing potatoes nested in the sand improves their edibility (Avital & Jablonka, 2000). A human example is the cultural discovery of dairy farming practices resulting in the widespread development of lactose tolerance (Durham, 1991).

The existence of culturally stored knowledge means that organisms do not have to learn all the information critical for survival themselves and therefore do not have to repeat the (often painful and occasionally deadly) mistakes made by those who have gone before them. This knowledge confers greater flexibility on a species and the opportunity to gradually develop increased technological expertise and environmental control.

These three types of behavioral strategies are hypothesized by Odling-Smee *et al.* to causally affect and interact with each other and, in some instances, may reduce or exacerbate selection pressures. For example, the development of medications in human beings to cure hereditary diseases means that individuals with these diseases are able to survive and reproduce, reducing the evolutionary pressure to select for genes that protect individuals from developing the disease in the first place. In other words, a cultural response is able to solve the problems and reduce the need for a genetic solution. However, in some situations cultural responses may in effect exacerbate problematic situations and prevent the chances of genetic solutions even appearing. A good example is the pollution of waterways, the air and the earth.

The three types of processes outlined above are thought to result in the modification of the environment and are also implicated in the creation of three quite different types of inheritance: genetic inheritance, cultural inheritance and ecological inheritance (the altered ecological niche). *Genetic inheritance* consists in the genetic resources (i.e. the genome) available to the next generation, and is responsible for some of the cognitive, motivational and behavioral characteristics comprising the nature of the species in question. *Cultural inheritance* consists in the knowledge, values, practices and technology passed on to offspring by way of social learning (i.e. imitation and modeling). *Ecological inheritance* refers to the changed environment and ecology passed on to the new generation and, as such, constitutes a new selection environment; this is the constructed niche and is built by the three sets of processes described above. An interesting observation is that the availability of an externally structured learning environment makes the reliance of young organisms on innate genetic programs such as mental modules less essential and, in a sense, can be seen as an external nervous system or knowledge resource (Sterelny, 2003). Each of these inheritance systems makes a potentially valuable contribution to the offspring of the organisms in question and may equip them to successfully exist within their niche or, in some situations, result in additional problems. The crucial point is that the selection environment is fundamentally altered in some way, thereby modifying the relationship between the traits of the organism and the features of the environment. There are two basic types of niche construction: (1) inceptive niche construction, the original modification of the environment and (2) counteractive niche construction, modification in an attempt to counteract a previous change or problem. In addition, organisms may choose to alter an existing niche or to move and create a new one.

Applying Gene-culture Co-evolutionary Theory to Sexual Offending

We will now apply these ideas to the example of rape in order to grasp their significance for the field of sexual offending. From the perspective of the niche construction model we assume that there are three sources of cognitive and behavioral strategies involved in human mating behavior: (soft) genetic constraints or predispositions, individual learning processes and cultural resources and processes. In addition, we assume that the population of human beings is characterized by cognitive flexibility and behavioral plasticity. In other words, while there may be soft (i.e. modifiable) genetic predispositions that kick off human development and the construction of different capacities, the final architecture of our minds and capacities is strongly affected by social learning and scaffolding. Our minds are constructed during development rather than simply unfolding when triggered by environmental cues.

An example of a genetic predisposition might be males' hypothesized tendency to seek impersonal sex and also to attempt to exert power and control over females (Ellis, 1989). An example of an ontogenetic process leading to impersonal sex could be learning to use sex as a way of coping with negative mood states and feelings of inadequacy (Marshall & Barbaree, 1990). An example of a relevant cultural process might be the portrayal of females as sexual objects and males as sexually entitled to have sex when and where they want (Polaschek & Ward, 2002). These three sets of processes will individually, and in interaction, result in the construction of the mating domain; that is, the individual, social, physical (e.g. nightclubs, bars) and cultural environment where sexual interests, meanings and opportunities converge. A given individual will enter this arena with combinations of these sets of factors, typically resulting in varying degrees of rape-proneness (Sanday, 2003). For some males, the weak genetic predisposition toward sexual promiscuity may interact with a learning environment where females are routinely ridiculed and presented as inferior, and a culture where females are not valued and are underrepresented in positions of power and influence. In other cases, this weak predisposition may be modified by socialization in a household where sex is viewed as an essential component of intimacy and females are viewed as equal to males. Furthermore, this strong individual learning experience could offset any culturally entrenched hostility toward woman, or alternatively, be strengthened in cultures (or subcultures) where the relationship between males and females is more harmonious.

Counteractive niche construction in a rape-prone society is possible at each of the three levels outlined earlier. First, it may be possible for genes that code for sexual co-operation (assuming that this makes sense) to be selected if females consistently reject aggressive and sexually promiscuous males. In this scenario, the mating domain (i.e. constructed niche) has been modified to make it less likely aggressive sexual behavior will result in reproductive success, and this change is hypothesized to select out males with rape-supportive dispositions. Second, individuals might decide to cease their sexually aggressive behavior following powerful learning experiences; for example, consistent rejection by females or becoming aware of the suffering they have inflicted on others. In this situation, the salient causal factor is offenders' specific learning experiences rather than genetic or cultural factors. Third, at a cultural level there may be a commitment to rehabilitation and also changes to the way sexuality is represented, and the way males and females are socialized. The impact of such a cultural change is likely to be pervasive and alter the context in which males are socialized, thereby lessening the likelihood of developing rape-supportive attitudes and beliefs.

HUMAN GOODS

The broad evolutionary model outlined above is useful for researchers and clinicians working with sexual offenders because of its multifaceted nature. The view of human mating behavior, and its pathological variants, is directly related to biological, learning and cultural factors and as such provides a rich basis for the explanation of sexual offending. The nature of the genetic processes informing human niche construction and ongoing behavior is not entirely clear but is likely to include the capacity to identify with other people and thereby view them as intentional agents who act on the basis of desires, beliefs and goals (Tomasello, 1999). This ability, in conjunction with human beings' cognitive and behavioral plasticity, opens up the possibility of cultural learning and inheritance. It is also likely that perceptual and cognitive biases such as being attentive to socially salient events and the predisposition to form causal inferences in certain situations play a role in the construction of the mind and the human environment (Sterelny, 2003). Finally, basic human needs are plausibly construed as adaptations or inherited characteristics and function to motivate infants and adults toward experiences and activities likely to improve their chances of survival and reproductive success (Deci & Ryan, 2000). The outcome of such experiences will be the formation of reliable beliefs and the acquisition of competencies required to function independently in the world. These basic needs are satisfied when certain (i.e. primary) goods are secured; for example, intimate relationships, a sense of autonomy and enjoyable physical activities. In other words, needs function as indicators that orientate human beings toward certain activities and objects (e.g. food, mastery experiences, relationships) that benefit them and contribute to their well-being. The relationship between needs and primary goods is like that of a drive toward its object; the attainment of the object satisfies the drive and thus reduces the likelihood of the person being harmed (through starvation, neglect and so on). In our view, the natural inclination to seek primary goods, and the relationship between these goods and human well-being, are of paramount importance in understanding both adaptive and maladaptive behavior (including offending). Such needs and their attendant goods structure actions and constitute one of the major sources of human strivings and meaning.

We define primary goods as actions, states of affairs, characteristics, experiences and states of mind that are intrinsically beneficial to human beings and are therefore sought for their own sake rather than as means to some more fundamental ends (Deci & Ryan, 2000). Primary goods are viewed as objective and tied to ways of living that if pursued involve the actualization of potentialities that are distinctively human (Kekes, 1989). Primary goods emerge out of basic needs, while secondary goods provide concrete ways of securing these goods; for example, certain types of work, relationships or language ability. The nature of primary goods sought by individuals and their weightings are formed in specific cultural contexts and represent individuals' interpretations of interpersonal and social events. The type of secondary or instrumental goods utilized by individuals reflects their specific learning and cultural experiences.

We argue that there are a plurality of primary human goods and that each of these makes a crucial contribution to the quality of individuals' lives and their subsequent levels of well-being. A close review of the research and theoretical literature from anthropology, psychology, philosophy, social policy, sociology and biology suggests there are at least ten types of primary human goods (Arnhart, 1998). Our list of the ten primary human goods is:

- life (including healthy living and functioning)
- knowledge
- excellence in play and work (including mastery experiences)
- excellence in agency (i.e. autonomy and self-directedness)
- inner peace (i.e. freedom from emotional turmoil and stress)
- friendship (including intimate, romantic and family relationships)
- community
- spirituality (in the broad sense of finding meaning and purpose in life)
- happiness (including pleasure)
- creativity.

We argue that psychological, social and lifestyle problems can emerge when these goods are pursued in problematic ways. To capture the relationship between goods striving and subsequent levels of personal and social adjustment one of us has introduced the concept of the good lives model (Ward & Stewart, 2003). This refers to each individual's implicit (typically with offenders) or explicit plan for living their life. It is hypothesized that ideally each good lives model (GLM) will contain all the primary human goods outlined above. However, it is expected that people will weigh or value the distinct goods rather differently: one person might value relationships most and use this as the overarching value or pivot around which their life is planned. For another person, work and the associated goods of competency and achievement might be most important. It is anticipated that the overarching good and the resultant GLM reflecting its priority will have a direct impact on the type of personal identity constructed (and meaning experienced) by an individual (Ward & Stewart, 2003). The critical thing is that all the primary goods are contained within a GLM, but the structure of each person's GLM will vary depending on the specific weightings they place on the component goods. In addition, the pluralistic nature of the GLM means that there is no right way to live a life. That is, for any individual, there are a number of plans for living they could reasonably follow that would result in comparable levels of well-being.

Human Goods and Etiology

An important question concerns the relationship between human goods and sexual offending: Why do individuals who are striving for personally important goals commit harmful actions? There are two parts to the answer to this question. First, it is important to understand the relationship between internal and external conditions and the achievement of valued outcomes. The successful implementation of a person's GLM depends on their possessing certain capabilities and internal resources. For example, the establishment and maintenance of an intimate relationship requires that the person in question has the ability to discuss their feelings with a partner, recognize and acknowledge the partner's needs, resolve conflict, learn to share activities and interests, and so on. In addition, external requirements include exposure to appropriate role models as a child, access to possible partners, opportunities to engage in certain types of activities (e.g. movie theatres, sporting events). In other words, the possession of capabilities and skills, in addition to learning opportunities and resources, are essential preconditions for the securing of primary human goods. While inherited motivational biases in the form of a tendency to seek primary goods will focus attention on certain types of activities, the ability to secure these goods is entirely dependent on individuals having the requisite capacities and opportunities. This is where individual learning histories and social/cultural factors scaffold or structure learning experiences and, as such, partially determine the shape and content of a person's life plan (i.e. GLM). Dynamic risk factors, or criminogenic needs (Ward & Stewart, 2003), are usefully construed as distortions in the conditions required to achieve primary human goods and therefore can be viewed as internal or external obstacles that prevent basic needs from being met in an optimal manner.

The cultural aspect of sexual offending behavior is evident in conditions such as the structure and nature of people's learning opportunities and the prevailing norms and institutions associated with sexuality and gender roles. The internal dimension of these factors is reflected in the values, beliefs, attitudes and competencies an individual acquires, while the external dimension is evident in the type of social environment confronting individuals (e.g. existence of rigid sex roles, opportunities for employment, male-dominated power structures).

Second, in the case of criminal behavior, it is hypothesized that there are four major types of difficulties with the structure and content of GLMs: (1) problems with the means used to secure goods, (2) a lack of scope, (3) the presence of conflict among goals (goods sought) or incoherence, (4) or a lack of the necessary capacities to form and adjust a GLM to changing circumstances (e.g. impulsive decision making). Each of these structural flaws may individually be causally related to sexually abusive behavior or work in combination with the others.

The problem of inappropriate means occurs when the way an individual seeks to achieve a primary good is counterproductive and actually lessens the chances of the good being realized. An offender might seek the primary human goods of relatedness and agency in a sexual relationship with a child or through coercive sex with an adult. Clearly this is an inappropriate way of seeking these valued states and is unlikely to result in higher levels of well-being because, for example, intimacy can only be maximized in a relationship characterized by equality (Marshall, 1996). The problem of scope occurs when an individual does not seek the full range of primary human goods thought to be essential components of a fulfilling life, and is therefore unlikely to experience adequate levels of well-being. An individual's obsession with achieving a sense of control and power over their partner would almost certainly fail to achieve the goods associated with intimacy and ultimately result in the destruction of their relationship. The problem of incoherence occurs when there is a conflict within a person's GLM, one that involves dissonance between the way they pursue distinct human goods. Thus, someone could seek the goods of play (leisure) and relatedness through associating with a group of heavy-drinking male friends. Their predilection for drinking and late-night partying may conflict with his attempt to cultivate a loving and intimate relationship with his partner. Finally, the problem of lack of capacity to form, develop and adjust a GLM to changing circumstances would leave an offender feeling out of control of his life. An impulsive individual would be unable to shape his life to any significant degree and would be vulnerable to the influences of rapidly changing circumstances and the wishes and whims of others. Each of these problems in individuals' GLM is directly related to their specific learning experiences and the broader social and cultural environment in which they are raised.

The above considerations enable us to understand why individuals might choose to commit sexual offences and how the pursuit of primary human goods could underpin sexually abusive actions. In other words, focusing on the reasons or goals that ground the actions of sexual offenders makes their behavior intelligible and can also provide a more effective means of motivating them to enter treatment. Thus the problem does not reside in the primary human goods that underlay sexual offending, but in the way individuals seek these goods. We will illustrate this with an example of a factor frequently invoked as a cause of some types of sexual offending, deviant sexual preferences and arousal (for a detailed treatment of the relationship between etiology and the GLM, see Ward & Marshall, 2004).

The presence of deviant sexual arousal indicates that an individual has developed deviant sexual interests in either children or coercive sex, or other abnormal sexual activities. This arousal may reflect entrenched deviant sexual preferences or more state-dependent arousal. The GLM is able to account for the fact that individuals who have sex with children or coercive sex with adults may not all have a sexual preference for such activities. The nature of the goods involved can point to the function or purpose of the illegal sexual activity and its value to the offender. For some offenders sexual contact with children may be a consequence of a decision to seek an intimate relationship with a child, sex being a component of such a relationship. For another, the primary end or good might be establishing a sense of autonomy or power. Thus, from a GLM perspective, the individual may be seeking a number of primary goods through sex; for example, physical satisfaction (goods of healthy living), intimacy (relatedness) and emotional regulation (inner peace). The same principle holds for other types of sex offenders, such as rapists. For some offenders, rape might be associated with a misguided attempt to establish or cement an intimate relationship (e.g. women like and respond to "rough" sex), while another individual could rape as a way of punishing women for their perceived rejection of him (e.g. be seeking the goods of agency or emotional regulation).

The four types of problems that may arise in a GLM provide a useful way to clarify the possible kinds of difficulties with offenders' sexual preferences. Sexual contact with a child or the rape of another adult are examples of seeking the goods of healthy functioning or relatedness through inappropriate means. Lack of scope might be evident in sexual arousal that is generated by faulty assumptions about a child by ignoring the presence of other goods that should be considered when engaging in a sexual encounter with someone else (e.g. the goods of intimacy and community). Conflicting goals or incoherence might be evident in sexual arousal and preferences that conflict markedly with each other or else tend to undermine other important goods; for example, the development of a loving intimate relationship, autonomy (i.e. ending up in prison), and the good of the community. Finally, the offender may lack the necessary capacities to develop appropriate sexual arousal to consenting adults, perhaps because of faulty beliefs, lack of normal fantasies, or poor knowledge of sexuality.

Human Goods and the Treatment of Sex Offenders

There has been a sea change in the way psychology approaches research and treatment over the last few years and a positive, more constructive way of solving basic human behavioral and mental health problems has emerged. The name given to this emphasis on human strengths, resilience and flourishing is *positive psychology*. The interest in positive psychology is apparent in the large numbers of scholarly articles and books recently published on the subject, addressing both basic and applied psychological issues (e.g. Aspinwall & Staudinger, 2003; Keyes & Haidt, 2003). What these publications have in common is a determination to view human beings as psychological agents who strive to interpret their world and lives in a meaningful and growth-oriented manner.

In a similar vein, recent work in the sexual offending area has taken a more holistic perspective and is based on the idea that the concept of wellness should drive rehabilitation efforts alongside that of risk management (e.g. Ellerby, Bedard & Chartrand, 2000; Freeman-Longo, 2001). This work is particularly exciting and based on the idea that human needs or goods are important treatment targets and that sexual offending may reflect problematic ways of achieving these goods. Thus these models stress the importance of helping offenders to function in more balanced and integrated ways and to work towards establishing a constructive and positive view of how their lives could be different. We will briefly outline two of these approaches.

A particularly noteworthy example of an early positive approach comes from the treatment of developmentally disabled sexual offenders; more specifically the model developed by Haaven and Coleman (2000). In this model treatment is based around the distinction between a "new me" and an "old me". The "old me" constitutes the individual who committed sexual offenses and encompasses values, goals, beliefs and ways of living that directly generate offending behavior. The construction of a "new me" involves the endorsement of a new set of goals that specify a "good life" for the individual; that is, a life in which important primary goods are achieved in ways that are socially acceptable and personally fulfilling. The setting of new goals and ways of living highlights the internal (i.e. skills, beliefs, attitudes) and the external (i.e. access to resources, opportunities, social supports) conditions necessary to achieve them. The offender is hypothesized to construct a more adaptive personal identity through the adoption of a new plan for living. This plan is tailored to his interests, abilities, preferences and needs and is designed to mesh with the environments he is likely to be living in. Therapy, then, is based on instilling the competencies required to meet the goals, instituting the conditions and structuring the environment in ways consistent with living a more fulfilling life.

According to Ward and Stewart's (2003) good lives theory, treatment plans for sexual offenders should be explicitly constructed in the form of a good lives conceptualization that takes into account their preferences, strengths, primary goods and relevant environments, and specifies exactly what competencies and resources are required to achieve these goods. This crucially involves identifying the internal and external conditions necessary to implement the plan and designing a rehabilitation strategy to equip the individual with these required skills, resources and opportunities. Such an approach to offender rehabilitation is significantly contextualized, and promotes the importance of personal identity and its emergence from daily living (and actions). It is also clearly value-laden in the sense that primary human goods represent outcomes that are beneficial to human beings and their absence harmful (to the individual and to others).

The argument is that rehabilitation should be tailored to the individual offender's particular GLM and should seek to install the internal and external conditions that will enable its realization. The detection of dynamic risk factors, or criminogenic needs, signals that there are problems of scope, coherence, inappropriate means and planning deficits in the distinct domains of a person's life. Risk analysis simply informs therapists that there are problems in the way offenders seek human goods and the aim of assessment is to clarify the nature and extent of these difficulties. Questions such as "How have you gone about achieving X (e.g. establishing close relationships) in your life? Which strategies have worked the best? Which have worked least well?" are particularly useful in helping to document these problems in offenders' GLMs. Such questions allow for the assessment of each individual's conception of a good life and facilitate an understanding of the individual's strategies for realizing primary goods.

Treatment should proceed on the assumption that effective rehabilitation requires the acquisition of competencies and external supports, and opportunities to live a different kind of life. Ward and Stewart argue that therapy should focus first on identifying the various obstacles preventing offenders from living a balanced and fulfilling life, and then seek to equip them with the skills, beliefs, values and supports needed to counteract their influence. For example, assessment might reveal that an offender has limited strategies for achieving the human good of inner peace (affect regulation), confuses intimacy and sex, and overvalues the goods of physical satisfaction (health/living good) and play. A treatment plan constructed along the lines of the GLM would aim to provide the offender with a wider range of strategies for achieving emotional balance (e.g. keeping an emotion diary, talking with friends), and seek other means of achieving physical stimulation, pleasure and sense of adventure/play (e.g. engage in challenging sports such as rock climbing or hiking). Additionally, the difference between the goods of friendship and sex would be distinguished and alternative types of activities devised to achieve these distinct goods. This could also involve acquiring the skills and confidence necessary to achieve greater levels of intimacy with adults.

Human Goods and the Therapeutic Relationship

The role of the therapeutic alliance in determining treatment outcome has been a focus of recent research in both the sexual offending and general psychotherapy domains. Marshall *et al.* (2003) argue that increasing sexual offenders' self-esteem, working collaboratively on developing treatment goals, and specific therapist features such as displays of empathy, warmth, encouragement and rewards for progress, enhance the change process in sex offenders. Research into the therapeutic alliance in psychotherapy supports this contention; Ackerman and Hilsenroth (2003), in their review of therapist characteristics and techniques that facilitate the development of the bond between therapist and patients, cite trustworthiness, honesty, respectfulness, warmth, interest and openness as being particularly important.

What is the relationship between these factors and primary human goods? We suggest that it is much easier to establish a strong therapeutic alliance if a therapist has a positive attitude toward offenders. Therapist and process variables reflect underlying assumptions about forgiveness, intrinsic value and the nature of unjustified harm (i.e. evil). It is not possible for therapists to quarantine ethical or moral issues from therapeutic ones when working with individuals who have committed sexual offences against children or adults. The fact that an offender has harmed another human being and been punished is likely to evoke therapist beliefs about the nature of unjustified harm (i.e. evil), and also related issues such as forgiveness and revenge. It would be a mistake to simply argue that therapy can proceed without a consideration of such issues.

The source of therapists' attitudes toward the offender arguably resides in their conception of the nature and value of human beings, and the extent to which engaging in harmful actions diminishes that value. We propose that the quality of the therapeutic alliance is a function of two key factors: the model of rehabilitation underpinning treatment and the moral status of the offender in the eyes of the therapist. Rehabilitation that revolves around risk management may fall into the trap of viewing the offender as essentially a bearer of risk, and focus primarily on reducing that risk. While this is a necessary treatment aim it can easily slide into quite confrontational and pejorative attitudes toward offenders and create problems in maintaining good rapport (Ward & Stewart, 2003). A positive treatment approach that is focused on constructing a "new me" or promoting good lives among offenders makes it easier for the therapist to avoid this mistake. The view that offenders, along with all human beings, are predisposed to actively seek relationships and other human goods provides a theoretical basis for positive treatment methods and generates the kind of attitudes that are likely to create a strong therapeutic alliance.

The perceived moral status of the offender is determined by therapists' conception of human nature as essentially good, bad or mixed (Kekes, 1990). According to the first perspective, human beings are believed to be essentially good and commit harmful actions only if they fail to cultivate more prosocial values and the abilities required to achieve their goals (human goods) in adaptive and socially acceptable ways. From the second perspective some people are thought to be fundamentally bad and born criminals, and it is these characteristics that cause them to initiate harmful acts while the third perspective regards people as equally capable of beneficial or harmful actions by virtue of their natural dispositions and characteristics. In our opinion, a mixed view of human nature as involving both dispositions to behave in ways that increase human welfare and to act in ways that reduce human welfare is more consistent with the scientific evidence (i.e. anthropological, psychological, biological, and so on) and everyday knowledge. This means that individuals have innate tendencies to behave both altruistically and aggressively or selfishly toward their fellow human beings.

A model of etiology based on natural goods and a subsequent view of human nature as partially comprising a set of predispositions to seek social and personal goods can make it easier for therapists to reconcile conflicting views of the offender's actions. That is, the tension between perceiving that the offender has severely harmed another individual and the belief that he has intrinsic value by virtue of his capacity for caring, loving, and so on; basically wanting the things we all seek and need. His harmful behavior is understood as reflecting acquired traits such as ignorance, greed or selfishness rather than an inborn and unchangeable set of flaws. Thus he is viewed as capable of modifying his abusive actions through the acquisition of new competencies, different values and the opportunity to live a different kind of life. The mixed view of human nature makes it possible to adopt a positive attitude toward offenders without minimizing their tendencies to behave in a harmful manner.

CONCLUSIONS

In this chapter we have examined the relationship between new ideas in five areas recently applied to the sexual offending domain: evolutionary models of human behavior, natural human goods, the etiological role of primary goods, positive or constructive approaches to the treatment of sex offenders, and the therapeutic alliance. One of our tasks was to demonstrate how these ideas can be coherently linked, using the notion of natural human goods as a connecting thread. The basic argument was that the tendency of human beings to seek primary goods is weakly genetically encoded while the realization of these goods in ways of living is strongly influenced by individual learning experiences within a specific cultural context. In other words, understanding the phenomena of sexual offending requires us to take into account the goods individuals are attempting to seek through such actions. Additionally, it was hypothesized that problems in the structure of offenders' GLMs mean that they fail to achieve these primary goods in socially acceptable and, often, personally fulfilling ways.

If the argument outlined in this chapter is a valid one, then we would argue that it is a mistake to construct etiological explanations of sexual offending in exclusively learning, cultural or biological terms. We are complex animals whose characteristics reflect both universal and local influences and, alongside genetic changes, culture exerts an independent causal influence on the evolution of these traits. Furthermore, treatment models should incorporate these insights and seek to build on our natural dispositions without insisting that biology is destiny. It is important to accept we have a rather malleable nature, but a nature it is. To ignore offenders' natural dispositions runs the risk of ultimately frustrating and distorting the treatment process in ways that are counterproductive.

REFERENCES

Ackerman, S.J. & Hilsenroth, M.J. (2003). A review of therapist characteristics and techniques positively impacting on the therapeutic alliance. *Clinical Psychology Review*, **23**, 1–33.

Arnhart, L. (1998). *Darwinian Natural Right: The Biological Ethics of Human Nature*. Albany, NY: State University of New York Press.

Aspinwall, L.G. & Staudinger, U.M. (eds). (2003). *A Psychology of Human Strengths: Fundamental Questions and Future Directions for a Positive Psychology*. Washington, DC: American Psychological Association.

Avital, E. & Jablonka, E. (2000). *Animal Traditions: Behavioural Inheritance in Evolution*. Cambridge, UK: Cambridge University Press.

Buller, D.J. & Hardcastle, V.G. (2000). Evolutionary psychology meets developmental neurobiology: against promiscuous modularity. *Brain and Mind*, **1**, 307–25.

Clark, A. (2003). *Natural-born Cyborgs: Minds, Technologies, and the Future of Human Intelligence*. New York: Oxford University Press.

Darwin, C. (1859). *On the Origin of Species by Means of Natural Selection, or Preservation of Favoured Races in the Struggle for Life*. London: Murray.

Deci, E.L. & Ryan, R.M. (2000). The "what" and "why" of goal pursuits: human needs and the self-determination of behavior. *Psychological Inquiry*, **11**, 227–68.

Durham, W.H. (1991). *Coevolution: Genes, Culture, and Human Diversity*. Stanford, CA: Stanford University Press.

Ellerby, L., Bedard, J. & Chartrand, S. (2000). Holism, wellness, and spirituality: moving from relapse prevention to healing. In D.R. Laws, S.M. Hudson & T. Ward (eds), *Remaking Relapse Prevention with Sex Offenders: A Sourcebook* (pp. 427–52). Thousand Oaks, CA: Sage.

Ellis, L. (1989). *Theories of Rape: Inquiries into the Causes of Sexual Aggression*. New York, NY: Hemisphere Publishing Corp.

Emmons, R.A. (1999). *The Psychology of Ultimate Concerns*. New York: Guilford.

Freeman-Longo, R.E. (2001). *Paths to Wellness: A Holistic Approach and Guide for Personal Recovery*. Holyoke, MA: NEARI Press.

Griffiths, P.E. & Stotz, K. (2000). How the mind grows: a developmental perspective on the biology of cognition. *Synthese*, **122**, 29–51.

Haaven, J.L. & Coleman, E.M. (2000). Treatment of the developmentally disabled sex offender. In D.R. Laws, S.M. Hudson & T. Ward (eds), *Remaking Relapse Prevention with Sex Offenders: A Sourcebook* (pp. 369–88). Thousand Oaks, CA: Sage.

Keenan, T. & Ward, T. (2003). Developmental antecedents of sexual offending. In T. Ward, D.R. Laws & S.M. Hudson (eds). *Sexual Deviance: Issues and Controversies* (pp. 119–34). Thousand Oaks, CA: Sage.

Kekes, J. (1989). *Moral Tradition and Individuality*. Princeton, New Jersey: Princeton University Press.

Kekes, J. (1990). *Facing Evil*. Princeton, NJ: Princeton University Press.

Keyes, C.L.M. & Haidt, J. (eds). (2003). *Flourishing: Positive Psychology and the Life Well-lived*. Washington, DC: American Psychological Association.

Laland, K.N. & Brown, G.R. (2002). *Sense and Nonsense: Evolutionary Perspectives on Human Behaviour*. Oxford, UK: Oxford University Press.

Laws, D.R. (2000). Sexual offending as a public health problem: A North American perspective. *The Journal of Sexual Aggression*, **5**, 30–44.

Marshall, W.L. (1996). Assessment, treatment, and theorizing about sex offenders: developments over the past 20 years and future directions. *Criminal Justice and Behavior*, **23**, 162–99.

Marshall, W.L. & Barbaree, H.E. (1990). An integrated theory of the etiology of sexual offending. In W.L. Marshall, D.R. Laws & H.E. Barbaree (eds), *Handbook of Sexual Assault: Issues, Theories, and Treatment of the Offender* (pp. 257–75). NY: Plenum Press.

Marshall, W.L., Fernandez, Y.M., Serran, G.A., Mulloy, R., Thornton, D., Mann, R.E. & Anderson, D. (2003). Process variables in the treatment of sexual offenders. *Aggression and Violent Behavior: A Review Journal*, **8**, 205–34.

Maruna, S. (2001). *Making Good: How Ex-convicts Reform and Rebuild their Lives*. Washington, DC: American Psychological Association.

Odling-Smee, F.J., Laland, K.N. & Feldman, M.W. (2003). *Niche Construction: The Neglected Process in Evolution*. Princeton, NJ: Princeton University Press.

Polaschek, D.L.L. & Ward, T. (2002). The implicit theories of potential rapists. What our questionnaires tell us. *Aggression and Violent Behavior*, **7**, 385–406.

Quinsey, V.L. (2002). Evolutionary theory and criminal behaviour. *Legal and Criminological Psychology*, **7**, 1–13.

Sanday, P.R. (2003). Rape-free versus rape-prone: how culture makes a difference. In C.B. Travis (ed.), *Evolution, Gender and Rape* (pp. 337–61). Cambridge, MA: MIT Press.

Sterelny, K. (2003). *Thought in a Hostile World: The Evolution of Human Cognition*. Oxford: Blackwell Publishing.

Tomasello, M. (1999). *The Cultural Origins of Human Cognition*. Cambridge, MA: Harvard University Press.

Ward, T. & Marshall, W.L. (2004). Good lives, aetiology, and the rehabilitation of sex offenders: a bridging theory. *Journal of Sexual Aggression*, **10**, 153–69.

Ward, T. & Siegert, R.J. (2002). Toward a comprehensive theory of child sexual abuse: a theory knitting perspective. *Psychology, Crime, and Law*, **8**, 319–51.

Ward, T. & Stewart, C.A. (2003). The treatment of sex offenders: risk management and good lives. *Professional Psychology: Research and Practice*, **34**, 353–60.

Chapter 11

SEXUAL OFFENDER TREATMENT FOR PSYCHOPATHS: IS IT HARMFUL?

HOWARD BARBAREE*, CALVIN LANGTON*, AND EDWARD PEACOCK[†]
* University of Toronto and the Centre for Addiction and Mental Health, Canada
[†] Correctional Service of Canada

The present chapter will address an important controversy that has become prevalent in recent discussions concerning the treatment of sexual offenders. The suggestion has been made that modern cognitive-behavioral treatment for sexual offenders may be "harmful" to psychopaths. According to this hypothesis, cognitive-behavioral treatment might provide psychopathic individuals with an opportunity to learn manipulative or other interpersonal skills that would make them more effective in gaining access to victims, thereby increasing their risk for sexual and other serious recidivism after their release. This chapter will focus on the empirical data relevant to this hypothesis. Specifically, we will focus on the effects of modern sexual-offender specific cognitive-behavioral treatment on recidivism in psychopathic sexual offenders.

PSYCHOPATHY

A detailed discussion of historical and current conceptions of psychopathy is beyond the scope of this chapter (see Hare, 1996; Blackburn, 1994; and Coid, 1993 for reviews). While there is continuing debate in the literature concerning the etiology and dynamics of this personality deviation, there is now widespread consensus among authorities concerning its core attributes (Hare, 1996; 1998). Hare (2003) has described the psychopath as: (1) interpersonally grandiose, egocentric, manipulative, dominant, forceful, exploitative and cold-hearted; (2) affectively shallow and labile, unable to form long-lasting personal bonds, devoid of principles or goals, and lacking empathy and genuine guilt or remorse; (3) their lifestyle is impulsive, unstable and sensation-seeking; they readily violate social norms and fail to fulfill social obligations and responsibilities, both explicit and implied.

Sexual Offender Treatment: Controversial Issues. Edited by W.L. Marshall, Y.M. Fernandez, L.E. Marshall and G.A. Serran. © 2006 John Wiley & Sons, Ltd.

The Psychopathy Checklist-Revised (PCL-R) is a reliable and valid measure of psychopathy in adult male forensic populations (Hare, 2003). Based on a semi-structured interview and a review of collateral documents, subjects are assigned ratings of 0 (absent), 1 (some indication), or 2 (present) on each of the 20 PCL-R items, tapping such psychopathic features as superficial charm, pathological lying, conning and manipulative behaviors, impulsivity, irresponsibility and callousness. The total score is obtained by summing the items, resulting in scores ranging from 0 to 40. In forensic evaluations, where the possibility of a false positive is more problematic, the conventional cut-off score supporting the diagnosis of psychopathy is a score of 30. In research studies, where the problem of a false positive is not so serious, many research studies have used 25 as a cut-off score. Using the more conservative cut-off score of 30, approximately 20% of North American male offenders and approximately 10% of North American male forensic patients would be diagnosed as psychopathic (Hare, 2003). Among the samples that form the basis of standardization of the PCL-R 2nd Edition (Hare, 2003), the following describes the percentages of sexual offender subgroups who score above the cut-off score of 30: 6% of extra-familial child molesters and mixed extra- and intra-familial molesters, 11%; of intra-familial (incest) child molesters, 36% of rapists, 64% of men who both rape adults and molest children.

In their recent meta-analysis of the world's literature on sexual offender recidivism, Hanson and Morton-Bourgon (2004) have identified the PCL-R as one of the strongest predictors of recidivism among sexual offenders. Therefore, while psychopaths represent a minority of participants in sexual offender treatment, they have been identified as being among the higher-risk participants. As a consequence, the effective treatment of the psychopathic sexual offender would result in a significant reduction to their risk for future sexual violence, and would contribute significantly to the overall benefits of sexual offender treatment. If, on the other hand, treatment of psychopaths is ineffective or, worse, if the treatment of psychopaths increases their risk for recidivism, the implications for sexual offender treatment would be profound.

TREATMENT OF PSYCHOPATHS

Classic early works expressed the strong view that psychopathy is untreatable (Cleckley, 1941; Hare, 1991; McCord & McCord, 1964; Suedfeld & Landon, 1978). It is, therefore, not surprising that there is a pervasive feeling of pessimism in the field with respect to the treatment of the psychopath, and many authorities argue that the pessimism is justified by the empirical evidence (e.g. Gacono, Nieberding, Owen, Rubel & Bodholdt, 2001; Meloy, 1995; Reid & Gacono, 2000). Quite apart from the issue of treatment outcome, psychopaths are not considered to be good candidates for treatment due to their disruptive and negative behavior in treatment. Hildebrand, de Ruiter and Vogel (2004), for example, claim that psychopaths are highly resistant to treatment and they cause disruptions and display various negative behaviors during treatment.

The results of a recent meta-analysis suggest that such statements do not accurately reflect the outcomes of research on treatment interventions involving psychopaths. Salekin (2002) reviewed 42 published studies and concluded that there was evidence psychopathy was amenable to treatment since 60% of the studies (excluding single case reports) reported some degree of treatment success. Salekin noted that the treatments that were successful were ones involving considerable direct contact between the participating psychopaths and the mental health professionals providing treatment. Therapeutic communities were not successful in producing change in psychopaths and they involved little or no direct contact with mental health professionals. Intensive long-term treatments appeared to be more effective than less intensive short-term ones. For example, treatments that involved an average of four sessions per week for at least one year were the most effective with 91% showing improvement compared to a 61% success rate for treatments of less than six months' duration (Salekin, 2002).

While Salekin's review provides some encouragement for those who involve psychopaths in treatment, we should not be entirely convinced by his conclusions. Salekin's meta-analysis combined studies that differed greatly in terms of methodological rigor, conceptualization and measurement of psychopathy, outcome measures employed and treatment methods. Importantly, less than 15% of the studies examined recidivism as an outcome measure. Nevertheless, the findings from this meta-analysis suggest that treatment interventions involving intensive interactions with mental health professionals over a relatively long period may have a positive impact on psychopaths. Given that psychopathic offenders are high-risk and high-needs individuals, this finding appears consistent with well-established principles (risk-needs) of effective correctional programming (Andrews & Bonta, 2003).

IS TREATMENT OF PSYCHOPATHS HARMFUL?

In the present chapter, we are not going to focus on the question of treatment efficacy with psychopaths, although our focus is related to this. Beyond pessimism that treatment of psychopaths might not be effective, there have been suggestions in the literature that sexual offender treatment may actually be harmful, making the psychopath more likely to re-offend. For example, Hart and Hare (1997) reviewed the treatment literature on psychopaths and suggested it was possible that "group therapy and insight-oriented programs help psychopaths to develop better ways of manipulating, deceiving, and using people but do little to help them to understand themselves" (p. 31). In fact, there is one influential published study providing empirical evidence that treatment made psychopaths worse. Rice, Harris and Cormier (1992) reported the 10-year recidivism rates of violent offenders treated in a maximum-security psychiatric hospital. Inpatients treated in a therapeutic community were compared with matched subjects sampled from a correctional setting. Comparing the groups overall, there were no differences in recidivism. However, separating the groups into psychopathic and non-psychopathic subgroups, treated psychopaths were more likely to re-offend than untreated psychopaths, whereas treated non-psychopaths were less likely to re-offend than untreated non-psychopaths.

A recent narrative review of psychopathy and treatment conducted by D'Silva, Duggan and McCarthy (2004) addressed the central question posed in this chapter. These investigators examined the evidence to support the belief that treatment of psychopaths is counterproductive because it actually results in increased re-offending. They identified 24 published and unpublished treatment outcome studies that used the PCL-R (or its variants) to assess psychopathy. They then systematically evaluated the studies in relation to several basic methodological criteria. D'Silva *et al.* judged all of the studies to have important methodological limitations. Only three of the studies had a control group of untreated high-scoring psychopaths and all of these studies were assessed as having important design flaws. Six other studies did not have a control group, but compared two groups of high-scoring psychopaths, and 14 additional studies used correlational designs. Results from D'Silva *et al.*'s review upheld the oft-cited finding in the literature that those with higher PCL-R scores have poorer outcomes. This observation was based on evidence that the high-scoring psychopaths remained in treatment for less time, showed poorer response to treatment, and had higher recidivism rates. However, not all of the studies included in D'Silva *et al.*'s review found that high PCL-R scores were universally associated with poorer outcomes. There were three studies for which the results either directly or indirectly suggested that treatment had some positive effects with these offenders (Gretton, McBride, Hare & O'Shaughnessy, 2000; Reiss, Meux & Grubin, 2000; Yates & Nicholaichuk, 1998). D'Silva *et al.* (2004) concluded that there was insufficient high-quality data to support the view that treating psychopaths makes them worse. These authors highlighted the need for more methodologically rigorous studies, especially the need for studies directly comparing treated psychopaths with untreated psychopaths.

For the remainder of the chapter, we will review in detail research we have conducted on this issue, specifically in the context of sexual offender treatment. All participants in this research were men who underwent sexual offender specific treatment at the Warkworth Sexual Behavior Clinic (WSBC), a modern cognitive-behavioral treatment program with a heavy emphasis on the principles of relapse prevention that operates in a prison within the Correctional Service of Canada. Three separate studies will be described in detail.

Seto and Barbaree (1999)

Six years ago, Seto and Barbaree (1999) reported unexpected results in a follow-up study of 224 sexual offenders who were treated in the prison-based program. Consistent with findings from other psychotherapy research, we predicted that good treatment behavior would be associated with lower recidivism during the average follow-up period of 32 months. Ratings combined indices of clinical change with observations of behavior in group therapy sessions; the ratings were completed by research assistants who reviewed the clinical notes and treatment reports in the WSBC files. Each item was anchored by behavioral exemplars (e.g. an offender would be coded as very disruptive if he consistently interrupted others, made threats or other intimidating gestures, or left abruptly during a group therapy session). In addition, separate from these ratings by research assistants, ratings of motivation for treatment and overall degree of change were jointly made by the group therapist and program director on a 5-point scale (from "low" to "high"). The joint clinician ratings were made at the end of the participants' involvement in treatment, before they were released from prison. All ratings were made without knowledge of recidivism outcomes. From a psychometric point of view, the set of treatment ratings had good scale properties, and ratings by the research assistants all had acceptably high inter-rater reliabilities.

Surprisingly, our prediction was not supported: good treatment behavior was not associated with less recidivism. Instead, it was associated with greater recidivism, especially among individuals scoring high on psychopathy. Men who scored 15 or higher on the PCL-R and who behaved better in treatment were more likely to commit a new offense than other offenders, and almost four times as likely to commit a new serious offense.

We posited two plausible explanations for this finding. The first of these pointed to the oft-cited abilities of the psychopath to con and manipulate others. According to this explanation (the "psychopath as manipulator" hypothesis), our measure of treatment behavior identified a subset of psychopathic offenders who were particularly skilful and effective at manipulation and exploitation. In treatment, these individuals displayed the ability to ascertain what was appropriate, and then exhibit behavior that would contribute to positive ratings by therapists (e.g. making positive contributions in group sessions, interacting appropriately with other group members and therapists, and asking for additional help to satisfactorily complete homework assignments). Once released to the community, these same individuals apparently used these skills to gain access to potential victims.

Our second explanation (the "treatment causes harm" hypothesis) posited that treatment might actually provide psychopathic individuals with an opportunity to learn interpersonal skills that serve to increase their risk for serious recidivism. According to this explanation, psychopathic individuals who were most affected by treatment while incarcerated (i.e. by learning more effective interpersonal skills) would as a consequence be more effective in gaining access to victims after their release. As noted, this "treatment causes harm" hypothesis had been articulated previously (Hart & Hare, 1997).

Prominent and influential authorities in the field put the Seto and Barbaree (1999) study and the Rice *et al.* (1992) study together to argue that treatment for the psychopathic sexual offender may be harmful. Rice and Harris (2003), in a presentation to a meeting of the New York Academy of Science, presented these two studies as providing support for their argument that psychological treatment of sexual offenders may be harmful. In a review of a book describing a community treatment approach for sexual offenders, Rice (2000) referred to these two studies in her criticism that the author appeared not to be aware of the "possibility that treatment could cause harm". In an article in a British legal journal describing how the criminal justice system should respond to psychopaths, Hill (2003) cited Seto and Barbaree (1999) to support his conclusion that treatment programs for psychopaths that are empathy-oriented might very well produce harm in the form of higher re-offense rates. He suggested that psychopaths can "learn the words but not 'the music'".

The Seto and Barbaree (1999) findings attracted attention outside the usual academic arena. In the *National Post*, a conservative Canadian national daily newspaper, columnist Norman Doidge (2000) wrote an article entitled "Beyond therapy: some evil can't be cured". He cited the Seto and Barbaree study as an unwitting replication of Rice *et al.* (1992) and concluded that psychopaths undergoing treatment re-offend at higher rates than psychopaths who are not treated. Finally, as an unusual indication of the widespread influence of the Seto and Barbaree finding, a term paper on "Recidivism of sexual offenders" (Hammet, undated) available on the web to plagiarizing undergraduate students included a detailed description of Seto and Barbaree (1999) on its first page.

If either of our explanations of the Seto and Barbaree findings received empirical support, the results would have serious implications for work in our field. Sexual offender evaluations are routinely conducted by psychologists and psychiatrists to inform courts in Sexually Violent Predator applications in the United States and in Dangerous Offender Hearings in Canada. Such proceedings have direct and considerable effects on the long-term detention or liberty of the individuals involved and the decisions have implications for the safety of the public. The Seto and Barbaree (1999) finding, and subsequent inferences, place all treated sexual offenders who score high on the PCL-R in a serious double bind. Any evidence they exhibit of treatment compliance and success can be interpreted as indicating increased risk for serious re-offense. If the "treatment causes harm" hypothesis is supported by further empirical data, psychopathic sexual offenders might reasonably be prevented from taking psychological treatments. The potential impact of the Seto and Barbaree (1999) findings on current practice in the field, and on individual offenders, is profound. Considering this impact, it is extremely important to subject the study, the findings and related inferences to very careful scrutiny.

Other researchers had examined the relationship between sexual offender treatment behavior and recidivism, with quite different results. Marques and her colleagues (Marques, Day, Wiederanders & Nelson, 2002; Marques, Nelson, West & Day, 1994) reported that sexual offenders who participated in an institutional treatment program and obtained good post-treatment scores (on phallometrically measured sexual arousal, self-reported attitudes and beliefs about sexual offending, and ratings of their relapse prevention assignments) were *less* likely to re-offend than those who did not obtain positive post-treatment scores, even after statistically controlling for actuarially estimated risk to re-offend. While these published findings were opposite to those of Seto and Barbaree (1999), other studies have reported no relationship between treatment behaviour and recidivism. For example, Quinsey, Khanna and Malcolm (1998) found that clinician ratings of treatment gain were unrelated to recidivism among 193 sexual offenders treated at a correctional psychiatric centre, even though the treated offenders showed significant improvements on within-treatment measures. As a more directly relevant example, Looman, Abracen, Serin and Marquis (in press) attempted but failed to replicate the Seto and Barbaree (1999) finding in a sample of sexual offenders treated at a correctional psychiatric centre. Using a PCL-R cut-off score of 25 to identify psychopaths, Looman *et al.* showed that psychopathy was significantly related to serious recidivism, but offenders who performed well in treatment did not significantly differ from those who did less well, in terms of their rates of serious recidivism during the follow-up period.

Barbaree (in press)

Given these conflicting results, the relationship between treatment behavior and re-cidivism among sexual offenders needed further investigation. Barbaree (in press)[*] described the results of an extended follow-up of the sample studied by Seto and Barbaree (1999). In this later study, there were two important methodological differences from the earlier study. First, the average time-at-risk for recidivism was increased to just over five years from the earlier 2.5 years. Second, for the Barbaree (in press) study, a national database of criminal charges and convictions was used, maintained by the Canadian Police Information Centre (CPIC) of the Royal Canadian Mounted Police. Data on recidivism outcome was sought from CPIC in order to identify recidivism that might not have been recorded by the Correctional Service of Canada or the National Parole Board, which were the sources used in Seto and Barbaree (1999). Using CPIC, which records every criminal charge and conviction registered in the courts in Canada, was an important methodological improvement over Seto and Barbaree (1999).

In the Barbaree (in press) study, offenders retained their membership in one of four groups from the earlier study, based on whether their scores on the PCL-R and on the measure of treatment behavior fell above or below the median of that measure (median PCL-R score = 15, median treatment behavior score = 0.70). There was a significant difference among the four groups in the proportion of men who committed a new offense during the follow-up period. Men who scored high on psychopathy were more likely to re-offend than men who scored low on psychopathy. However, in contrast to the Seto and Barbaree (1999) finding, treatment behavior had no relationship to general recidivism. Interestingly, and contrary to what might be expected for psychopaths, there was no significant overall group difference when only serious re-offenses were considered.

The groups significantly differed in time-at-risk with those in the two high psychopathy groups having the shortest time-at-risk. To control for this potential confound, we examined recidivism using Kaplan-Meier survival analysis, which takes time-at-risk into account. Men in the high PCL-R/good treatment behavior group re-offended at a significantly faster rate than men in the low PCL-R/good treatment behavior group, indicating a significant effect of psychopathy among the good treatment behavior groups. There were no other significant differences between groups in any of the other pair-wise comparisons.

Clearly the results reported by Barbaree (in press) differed from those reported by Seto and Barbaree (1999). There are at least two possible explanations for this difference. The first is the difference between studies in time-at-risk; that is, Barbaree

---

[*] Portions of this article were presented at the 2001 Annual Research and Treatment Conference of the Association for the Treatment of Sexual Abusers in San Antonio, Texas (Barbaree, Seto, Langton & Peacock, 2001).

(in press) had a longer follow-up period. However, analyses of data from various fixed duration follow-up periods found significant effects for psychopathy at 5- and 6-year follow-up periods but not at three years (i.e. the time at risk in the Seto & Barbaree study), and the effects of treatment behavior and the interaction between treatment behavior and psychopathy were not significant at any fixed follow-up period. Therefore, the differences could not be attributed to different durations of follow-up.

The second plausible explanation for the difference between the two reports is the source of recidivism data. More comprehensive recidivism data acquired from CPIC increased the rate of recidivism across all psychopathy-treatment behavior groups, indicating that the recidivism data we had for our 1999 report was incomplete. While the number of additional offenders who were identified as serious recidivists using CPIC data did not significantly differ across the four groups, none of the analyses we conducted using CPIC data replicated our 1999 result. Therefore, it must be concluded that the difference between the current findings and those we reported in 1999 were due to differences between an incomplete and a more complete recidivism data set.

In retrospect, the strength of inferences made and the degree of attention paid to the Seto and Barbaree (1999) finding were at odds with the strength of the data presented. First, while the data were only correlational in nature, the notion that "treatment causes harm" was a causal inference. Second, the 1999 finding was relatively weak from a statistical point of view. In both the original and the current study, the various psychopathy and treatment behavior sub-groups differed in their time-at-risk, likely due to the fact that both psychopathy and treatment behavior influenced parole decisions. The appropriate analyses of these data would have corrected for time-at-risk. In the 1999 study, the statistical analysis comparing recidivism rates among the four groups resulted in a significant χ^2 but it did not correct for time-at-risk. When we presented the statistical analysis correcting for time-at-risk, the results did not meet traditional criteria for rejection of the null hypothesis.

> In both survival curves, men who were higher in psychopathy and better in treatment behavior *tended* to recidivate at a faster rate than men in the other groups; despite the relatively low base rates, this trend approached *(but did not achieve)* statistical significance for serious recidivism . . . (Seto & Barbaree, 1999; p. 1244; parenthetic remark added)

In conclusion, there are no analyses of the current and improved (CPIC) data set that replicate the result we reported in 1999, nor are there any analyses of the CPIC data that warrant the conclusions drawn in our 1999 report. Specifically, there is no evidence that those offenders high in psychopathy and good in treatment behaviour re-offended at a greater rate than other offenders, beyond the well-known effect of psychopathy on recidivism. To state more explicitly, there is no support in these data for the notion that psychopaths who perform well in treatment should be considered at higher risk for re-offense compared with psychopaths who perform badly in treatment. Finally, there is no evidence in our data that psychological treatment caused psychopathic sexual offenders to re-offend at a higher rate.

Langton (2003)

In the conduct of his doctoral dissertation, Calvin Langton (2003)[*] examined the "treatment causes harm" hypothesis in a study that contained a number of improvements over Seto and Barbaree (1999) and Barbaree (in press). First of all, Langton used a much larger sample. Included in his sample of 476 sexual offenders were 202 from the sample of 216 described in Seto and Barbaree (1999). Second, as a result of his larger sample, Langton was able to use a more traditional cut-off score for psychopathy (score of 25) rather than that (score of 15) used by Seto and Barbaree (1999) and Barbaree (in press). Third, Langton's *Response to Treatment* scale was a revised and improved version of the scale used in the two earlier studies. Fourth, the average time-at-risk (time to first conviction) for the sample was lengthened to almost six years.

Langton (2003) was also able to retain the improvements in methodology achieved by Barbaree (in press). Recidivism outcome was determined using the national data base (CPIC), and Langton used statistical analyses that controlled for time-at-risk. A series of Kaplan-Meier survival analyses were conducted to examine differences in the failure rates between mutually exclusive groups (based on the independent variables, psychopathy and treatment behavior) using serious recidivism as the dependent variable. Offenders were assigned to one of four groups according to their ratings on the Response to Treatment variable (using the median value for the sample, good response = scores < 2.43; poor response = scores ≥ 2.43) and the PCL-R (low = scores < 25; high = scores ≥ 25). The survival curves for the four groups are plotted in Figure 11.1.

The only observed significant difference indicated that the high PCL-R–poor response group had more failures than did the two low PCL-R groups. Although the high PCL-R–good response group appears to have re-offended at a somewhat faster rate than the two low PCL-R groups, these differences are non-significant. While there is a clear psychopathy effect as would be expected, there is no evidence that psychopaths with better treatment behavior show higher rates of recidivism than other groups.

Overall Recidivism Among Psychopaths

Finally, we will attempt here to determine the meaning of the observed recidivism rate among the psychopaths treated at the WSBC. The purpose of this evaluation is to examine the possibility that our treated sample of psychopaths exhibited a rate of recidivism greater than an appropriate benchmark. If this is found to be the case, then the hypothesis that our treatment produced an increased risk among psychopaths would be supported. On the other hand, if the recidivism rate of our sample of psychopaths is found to be equivalent to, or lower than, the appropriate benchmark, then the hypothesis would not be supported. We chose to use a benchmark provided by actuarial methodology.

---

[*] Portions of this dissertation were presented at the 2002 Annual Research and Treatment Conference of the Association for the Treatment of Sexual Abusers in Montreal, Quebec (Langton, Barbaree, Seto, Harkins & Peacock, 2002).

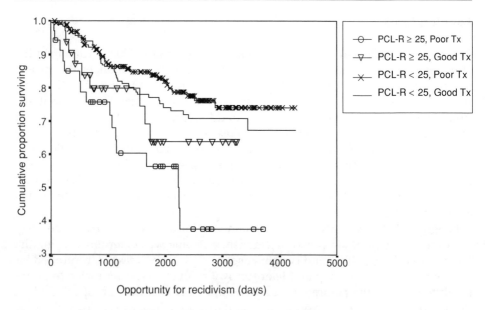

Figure 11.1   Kaplan-Meir Survival Curves for each of the four psychopathy-treatment behavior subgroups in Langton (2003). © 2003 by the author. Reproduced with permission.

A number of actuarial instruments for use with sexual offenders are currently available. Of those with evidence of long-term predictive validity, one of the most promising appears to be the Rapid Risk Assessment of Sexual Offense Recidivism (RRASOR; Hanson, 1997). Actuarial methods provide probabilistic estimates of risk based on empirically established relationships between certain risk scores and the likelihood of re-offense over the long term. A probabilistic estimate of risk indicates the percentage of individuals with a given "risk score" who have re-offended within a defined period of opportunity (i.e. time-at-risk) in the samples used in the development of the test. The RRASOR manual (Hanson, 1997) provides a probabilistic estimate of the percentage of each score value group (groups are determined by their RRASOR scores) that can be expected to recidivate in a particular period of time (five and ten years). The samples of subjects forming the standardization samples for the RRASOR included both treated and untreated subjects, with somewhat less than half of the standardization sample being involved in sexual offender treatment.

In order to ensure that these percentage estimates are stable, Doren (2004) sought and acquired data from the authors of ten recent studies of the RRASOR. Importantly for this investigation, the recidivism represented in these studies was contemporaneous with recidivism in the WSBC sample. Of the ten samples, four are Canadian, and two are from Ontario. Therefore, these data are closely related to the WSBC sample in terms of time-frame, geography and legal jurisdiction. Doren (2004) reported that the percentage recidivism associated with each score value of the RRASOR in these recent studies replicated those provided earlier by Hanson (1997) and that the percentage estimates for each score value of the RRASOR were stable over a wide range of sample base rates.

Table 11.1 Expected rates and observed rates of recidivists among psychopathic subjects in the WSBC treated sample

	Actuarial rates of recidivism	Actuarial rates of recidivism	WSBC	Expected number of recidivists	Expected number of recidivists	WSBC
RRASOR Scores	Doren (2004)	Hanson (1997)	N Psychopaths	Doren (2004)	Hanson (1997)	Observed recidivists
0	3.8%	4.4%	8	0.30	0.35	0
1	9.3%	7.6%	22	2.05	1.67	1
2	11.5%	14.2%	11	1.27	1.56	3
3	27.7%	24.8%	9	2.49	2.23	2
4	33.8%	32.7%	8	2.70	2.62	2
5	47.2%	49.8%	3	1.42	1.49	1
		TOTALS:	61	10.23	9.93	9

Table 11.1 presents our calculations of the expected recidivism rates for non-psychopathic sexual offenders, derived from both Doren (2004) and Hanson (1997), compared to the actual observed rates of recidivism from the WSBC sample of treated psychopaths. The first three columns are self-explanatory. The fourth column indicates the number of WSBC psychopathic subjects in each RRASOR score category. Columns 5 and 6 represent the expected number of WSBC recidivists in each RRASOR score category, calculated from either Doren's (2004) or Hanson's (1997) percentage of recidivists in each score category. The final column reports the actual number of recidivists in each RRASOR score category observed among WSBC treated psychopaths.

As can be seen, actuarial methodology estimates that we should have between nine and ten recidivists among the 61 psychopaths in our sample. The actual number of recidivists we observed among our treated psychopaths was nine. The observed value was then compared with the expected value using Fisher's Exact Test and, not surprisingly, the comparison was not significant. According to this analysis, recidivism among our psychopaths is exactly what would be predicted on the bases of the actuarial levels of risk for the sample. This finding provides no support for the hypothesis that our cognitive-behavioral treatment has caused an increase in recidivism in this group.

CONCLUSIONS

The present chapter reviewed evidence concerning the effects of sexual-offender specific treatment on recidivism in psychopaths. Suggestions have been made in the literature that psychological treatments may have the effect of increasing psychopathic sexual offenders' ability to manipulate and gain access to potential victims and thereby increase their risk for recidivism. The first of a number of reports from follow-up studies of a sample of sexual offenders treated at the Warkworth Sexual Behavior Clinic (Seto & Barbaree, 1999) suggested that psychopaths who had seemingly done well in treatment were at higher risk for recidivism. Later reports

(Barbaree, in press; Langton, 2003), based on more complete recidivism data and improved research methodology, indicated that psychopaths who did well in treatment were no more likely to re-offend than psychopaths who did poorly. Finally, the overall rate of recidivism among psychopaths in the WSBC treatment sample was found to be almost precisely what would have been predicted using actuarial methodology. The present chapter, therefore, found no evidence in support of the notion that cognitive-behavioral treatment causes psychopaths to re-offend at a higher rate than they would without treatment.

REFERENCES

Andrews, D.A. & Bonta, J. (2003). *The Psychology of Criminal Conduct*, 3rd edn. Cincinatti, OH: Anderson Publishing.

Barbaree, H.E. (in press). Psychopathy, treatment behavior, and recidivism: an extended follow-up of Seto and Barbaree (1999). *Journal of Interpersonal Violence*.

Barbaree, H.E., Seto, M.C., Langton, C.M. & Peacock, E.J. (2001, October). Psychopathy, treatment behavior and sexual offender recidivism: an extended follow-up. Paper presented to the Annual Meeting of the Association for the Treatment of Sexual Abusers. San Antonio, Texas.

Blackburn, R. (1994). *The Psychology of Criminal Conduct: Theory, Research and Practice*. Chichester, England: John Wiley & Sons.

Cleckley, H. (1941). *The Mask of Sanity*. St Louis, MO: Mosby.

Coid, J. (1993). Current concepts and classifications of psychopathic disorder. In P. Tyrer & G. Stein (eds), *Personality Disorder Reviewed* (pp. 113–64). London Royal College of Psychiatrists: Gaskell Press.

Doidge, N. (2000). Beyond therapy: some evil can't be cured. *National Post*, Friday, 7 January.

Doren, D.M. (2004). Stability of the interpretative risk percentages for the RRASOR and Static-99. *Sexual Abuse: A Journal of Research and Treatment*, **16**, 25–36.

D'Silva, K., Duggan, C. & McCarthy, L. (2004). Does treatment really make psychopaths worse? A review of the evidence. *Journal of Personality Disorders*, **18**, 163–77.

Gacono, C., Nieberding, R., Owen, A., Rubel, J. & Bodholdt, R. (2001). Treating conduct disorder, antisocial, and psychopathic personalities. In J.B. Ashford, B.D. Sales *et al.* (eds), *Treating Adult and Juvenile Offenders with Special Needs* (pp. 99–129). Washington, DC, USA: American Psychological Association.

Gretton, H.M., McBride, M., Hare, R.D. & O'Shaughnessy, R. (2000, November). Psychopathy and recidivism in adolescent offenders: a ten year follow-up. Paper presented at the 19th annual conference of the Association for the Treatment of Sexual Abusers (ATSA), San Diego, CA.

Hammet, K. (undated) Recidivism of sexual offenders. Go to http://www.collegetermpapers.com/TermPapers/Sociology/Recidivism_of_Sex_Offenders.

Hanson, R.K. (1997). The development of a brief actuarial risk scale for sexual offense recidivism (User report 1997-04). Ottawa: Department of the Solicitor General of Canada. (Public Works and Government Services Canada; Cat. No. JS4-1/1997-4E; ISBN: 0-662-26207-7)

Hanson, R.K. & Bussière, M.T. (1998). Predicting relapse: a meta-analysis of sexual offender recidivism studies. *Journal of Consulting and Clinical Psychology*, **66**, 348–62.

Hanson, R.K. & Morton-Bourgon, K. (2004). *Predictors of Sexual Recidivism: An Updated Meta-analysis*. Public Works and Government Services Canada. Cat. No.: PS3-1/2004-2E-PDF. ISBN: 0-662-36397-3.

Hare, R.D. (1991). *Manual for the Revised Psychopathy Checklist*. Toronto, ON: Multi-Health Systems.

Hare, R.D. (1996). Psychopathy: A clinical construct whose time has come. *Criminal Justice and Behavior*, **23**, 25–54.

Hare, R.D. (1998). Psychopaths and their nature: implications for the mental health and criminal justice systems. In T. Millon, E. Simonson, M. Burket-Smith & R. Davis (eds), *Psychopathy: Antisocial, Criminal and Violent Behavior* (pp. 188–212). New York: Guilford Press.

Hare, R.D. (2003). *Hare Psychopathy Checklist-Revised (PCL-R): 2nd Edition Technical Manual*. Toronto: Multi-Health Systems Inc.

Hart, S.D. & Hare, R.D. (1997). Psychopathy: assessment and association with criminal conduct. In D. Stoff, J. Breiling & J.D. Maser (eds), *Handbook of Antisocial Behavior* (pp. 22–35). New York: Wiley.

Hildebrand, M., de Ruiter, C. & Vogel, V. (2004). Psychopathy and sexual deviance in treated rapists: association with sexual and nonsexual recidivism. *Sexual Abuse: A Journal of Research and Treatment*, **16**, 1–24.

Hill, S. (2003). Psychopathy and the criminal justice system. *Justice of the Peace*, **167**.

Langton, C.M. (2003). Contrasting approaches to risk assessment with adult male sexual offenders: an evaluation of recidivism prediction schemes and the utility of supplementary clinical information for enhancing predictive accuracy. Unpublished doctoral dissertation. University of Toronto, Canada.

Langton, C., Barbaree, H., Seto, M., Harkins, L. & Peacock, E. (2002, October). How should we interpret behavior in treatment? Paper presented to the Annual Research and Treatment Conference of the Association for the Treatment of Sexual Abusers. Montreal.

Looman, J., Abracen, J., Serin, R. & Marquis, P. (in press). Psychopathy, treatment change and recidivism in high risk high need sexual offenders. *Journal of Interpersonal Violence*.

Marques, J., Day, D.M., Wiederanders, M. & Nelson, C. (2002, October). Main effects and beyond: new findings from California's Sexual Offender Treatment and Evaluation Project (SOTEP). Paper presented at the 21st Annual Research and Treatment Conference of the Association for the Treatment of Sexual Abusers, Montréal.

Marques, J., Nelson, C., West, M.A. & Day, D.M. (1994). The relationship between treatment goals and recidivism among child molesters. *Behaviour Research and Therapy*, **32**, 577–88.

McCord, W. & McCord, J. (1964). *The Psychopath: An Essay on the Criminal Mind*. New York: Can Nostrand-Reinhold.

Meloy, R. (1995). Antisocial personality disorder. In G. Gabbard (ed.), *Treatments of Psychiatric Disorders*, 2nd edn (pp. 2273–90). Washington DC: American Psychiatric Press.

Quinsey, V.L., Khanna, A. & Malcolm, P.B. (1998). A retrospective evaluation of the Regional Treatment Centre Sexual Offender Treatment Program. *Journal of Interpersonal Violence*, **13**, 621–44.

Reid, W.H. & Gacono, C. (2000). Treatment of antisocial personality, psychopathy, and other characterologic antisocial syndromes. *Behavioral Sciences and the Law*, **18**, 647–62.

Reiss, D., Meux, C. & Grubin, D. (2000). The effect of psychopathy on outcome in high security patients. *American Academy of Psychiatry and the Law*, **28**, 309–14.

Rice, M.E. (2000). Book review of "Child sexual abuse: A community treatment approach". *Psychiatric Services*, **51**, 398.

Rice, M.E. & Harris, G.T. (2003). The size and sign of treatment effects in sex offender therapy. *Annals of the New York Academy of Sciences*, **989**, 428–40.

Rice, M.E., Harris, G.T. & Cormier, C.A. (1992). An evaluation of a maximum security therapeutic community for psychopaths and other mentally disordered offenders. *Law and Human Behavior*, **16**, 399–412.

Salekin, R.T. (2002). Psychopathy and therapeutic pessimism: clinical lore or clinical reality? *Clinical Psychology Review*, **22**, 79–112.

Seto, M.C. & Barbaree, H.E. (1999). Psychopathy, treatment behavior, and sexual offender recidivism. *Journal of Interpersonal Violence*, **14**, 1235–48.

Suedfeld, P. & Landon, P.B. (1978). Approaches to treatment. In R.D. Hare & D. Schalling (eds), *Psychopathic Behavior: Approaches to Research* (pp. 347–78). New York: Wiley.

Yates, P. & Nicholaichuk, T. (1998). The relationship between criminal career profile, psychopathy, and treatment outcome in the Clearwater sexual offender program. *Canadian Psychology*, **39**, 97.

Chapter 12

SCHEMA-DRIVEN COGNITION IN SEXUAL OFFENDERS: THEORY, ASSESSMENT AND TREATMENT

RUTH E. MANN* AND JO SHINGLER†
* HM Prison Service, London, England
† Hampshire Probation Service, England

This chapter discusses the role of cognition in sexual offending. In particular, we will challenge the traditionally held notion that "cognitive distortions" (e.g. Abel *et al.*, 1989; Murphy, 1990) should be the primary focus for assessment and treatment with sexual offenders. Instead, we propose that an information processing perspective should be adopted in trying to understand the role of cognition in sexual offending (e.g. Langton & Marshall, 2000). Such a perspective ensures that assessment and treatment go beyond surface-level cognition, enabling both the clinician and the offender to understand how offence-enabling cognitions arise, how information processing errors occur and how these issues are linked to sexual offending.

THE COGNITIVE DISTORTION MODEL: A CRITIQUE

The dominant model for understanding the role of cognition in sexual offending has been the "cognitive distortion" model. This appears to have first been described by Finkelhor (1984). Finkelhor proposed four stages to offending: motivation to abuse; overcoming internal inhibitors; overcoming external inhibitors; and overcoming victim resistance. Finkelhor's "four preconditions" model has been influential in the sexual offender treatment field. The focus of concern here is the second precondition which refers in particular to cognitive methods of overcoming inhibitors to offending. Finkelhor proposed that most offenders know that sexual abuse is wrong and harmful, and therefore in order to act out their desire to abuse they need to overcome such inhibitory cognitions. The most effective way of doing this is to employ countering cognitions that excuse or justify a sexually abusive act.

Sexual Offender Treatment: Controversial Issues. Edited by W.L. Marshall, Y.M. Fernandez, L.E. Marshall and G.A. Serran.   © 2006 John Wiley & Sons, Ltd.

Excuses are a category of causal attribution, where the actor admits a bad act but gives an external reason for its occurrence, thus denying personal responsibility (Scott & Lyman, 1968). *Justifications* have been distinguished from excuses (Scott & Lyman, 1968) as referring to explanations that agree the act was committed but deny it was wrong.

The problem with the "cognitive distortion" model is that it has led assessors and clinicians to place considerable emphasis on these types of statements within treatment programmes. The usual goal of treatment, based on this model, is to eliminate excuses and justifications from an offender's account of his abusive behaviour. When the more general psychological literature on excuses is examined, a different view emerges. It appears that excuses are in fact likely to serve a positive function, making it easier for a transgressor to ensure that he avoids repetition of a harmful act. Furthermore, excuse-making is a normal social activity, which takes place in order to avoid social censure. This is accepted in everyday walks of life, but when sexual offenders are the ones making excuses, the process is frowned upon and viewed as dangerous.

Snyder and Higgins (1988) reviewed a large body of research showing that the process of excuse-making is healthy, and leads to better performance and a greater sense of well being. For example, clients in therapy progress from internal-stable-global (ISG) attributions of their problems to external-variable-specific (EVS) attributions as their mental health improves (Peterson & Seligman, 1981). An EVS attributional style for bad performances correlates with longevity in athletes (Seligman, 1986). Snyder and Higgins (1988) concluded that, "EVS as compared to ISG styles relate to superior (a) athletic performance, (b) selling, (c) anagram-solving performance, (d) college performance, (e) persistence in manuscript submission and (f) psychotherapy outcome" (p. 28). Snyder and Higgins (1988) also pointed to programmes where the object is to improve the functioning of clients by teaching them to favour external and unstable causal explanations over internal stable ones. For example, children who were seen as helpless in their arithmetic skills were trained to attribute their failures to lack of effort and subsequently improved in their performance (Dweck, 1975). Excuses in a variety of contexts therefore seem to be adaptive responses to failures or mistakes. Furthermore, there is also the question of whether excuses are always conscious distortions of the truth. It may be that behaviours do have external and unstable causes, and so to assume that any explanation with these properties is an excuse and therefore a lie might be an unjust conclusion.

Given the extent of research on excuses in the social psychological literature, it is surprising that research into the excuses of sexual offenders has not tested hypotheses based on this more general work. Sexual offenders' excuses are almost universally assumed to be "bad things" indicating that these offenders have failed to take responsibility for their actions. It is consistently claimed that treatment for sexual offenders should focus on increasing the internality and stability of their explanations for their offending (Loza & Clements, 1991; Marshall, Anderson & Fernandez, 1999). As early as 1968, McCaghy recommended that, "Of primary importance to therapists is that offenders assume full responsibility for their behaviour without relying on . . . rationalizations" (p. 47). In fact, these recommendations are contradicted by the general psychological literature, which suggests, as above, that internal and stable explanations for offending would reduce rather than promote efforts towards self-improvement.

A recent study by Maruna (2001) indicated that making external attributions for offending can have a positive effect on desistance from crime. He compared the self-narratives of 30 career criminals (not sexual offenders) who had desisted from crime for more than 12 months, with 20 similar offenders who readily admitted that they were continuing to offend. Maruna described the narratives of the persistent offenders as being characterized by a "condemnation script". Their explanations for their offending tended to be external, stable and uncontrollable. The desisting group also attributed their earlier offending to external factors, but they saw these factors as unstable. They believed that their "real me" was not an offender but rather that they had been forced into crime against their better self by external circumstances. Thus, their ability to attribute their offending to unstable causes allowed them to successfully desist from crime. Maruna did note that many of the desisters suffered from a "conflicted locus of control", on the one hand trying to take responsibility for their offending, on the other hand continuing to excuse it (e.g. "Obviously I'm not making excuses, but the drugs made me do it"). What is clear is that in Maruna's study, desisting "interviewees rarely attributed negative behaviours to underlying personality defects of character weaknesses" (Maruna, 2001, p. 136). As a result, Maruna cautioned that it is not possible to conclude that "internalizing shame" (i.e. making an internal stable attribution for behaviour) is a necessary or even helpful stage of offender reform. The findings of Maruna's study, therefore, support the argument that excuses for offending may have a healthy function, and may promote change in offenders.

The social psychological literature sees excuses as occurring *post hoc*. If this is correct, then given our brief review, there may be little need to challenge the excuses of sexual offenders. The social psychological literature, and the study by Maruna (2001), would suggest that excuses should be encouraged, or at least allowed, rather than challenged. On the other hand, if we accept Finkelhor's (1984) view that excuses and justifications precede offending and are part of the process that allows offending to take place, then they should indeed be addressed in treatment.

AN ALTERNATIVE MODEL: INFORMATION PROCESSING AND SCHEMAS

A schema-based theory of cognition in sexual offending is based on the hypothesis that certain dysfunctional cognitive schemas bias information processing in such a way as to make sexual assault a likely behavioural response. In this theory, a schema is seen as a *structure*, with cognitive *contents*, which influences and directs the *processing* of information. The contents of a schema have in common their adherence to a certain theme (e.g. power, respect, suspiciousness, revenge) and may include rules, attitudes, self-verbalizations, beliefs or assumptions. The contents of a schema may or may not be available to conscious awareness. The contents of a dysfunctional schema are hypothesized to assume global and stable attributes to life and other people. Schema contents are said to originate from trying to make sense of early life experiences, particularly ambiguous or traumatic experiences where a rational explanation is not possible, given the level of knowledge of the child.

The schema is the organizing framework for processing new information. Given that sexual offences occur in interpersonal contexts, relevant schemas will particularly affect the processing of social and interpersonal information. The more ambiguous or threatening the situation, the more likely it is that the schema will be used as a heuristic for perceiving and interpreting the situation and focusing attention. Thus a schema results in consistency of processing across situations, yielding largely schema-confirming results each time.

In this model, underlying dysfunctional schemas guide the processing of negative or ambiguous life events to produce cognitive outputs (surface cognitions) which interpret the situation as threatening in some way. These thoughts, in the context of other risk factors related to sexual offending (e.g. lack of intimacy, lifestyle impulsivity, poor self-management, deviant sexual interest) increase the likelihood of sexually assaultative behaviour being selected as the appropriate behavioural response.

Implications of the Schema-based Information Processing Approach

If the above model is accepted, assessment should no longer focus on cognitive distortions, excuses and justifications. Instead, attempts should be made to identify the contents of underlying schemas. These schemas should be examined to see if they are translated into surface cognitions and how they influence perceptions related to sexual abuse.

The primary focus of treatment should, therefore, be on underlying schemas and their contents. Otherwise, however successfully particular surface cognitions are challenged in treatment, these same surface cognitions and other related products of the underlying and unchallenged schema will emerge in subsequent ambiguous or threatening situations. Excuses and justifications produced *at the time of* offending are seen as the products of underlying schemas. Excuses and justifications produced *after* offending are not legitimate targets for treatment given the theory of excuse-making outlined above. Thus this treatment approach would tolerate external, unstable attributions for offending in favour of developing acknowledgement of information processing errors occurring as a result of biased schemas.

RESEARCH INTO SCHEMA-LEVEL COGNITION IN SEXUAL OFFENDERS

Schema contents have not been comprehensively examined in sexual offenders, although in the last 15 years, several authors have pointed to the relevance of the notion and have offered ideas about how distorted schemas may operate in this population. The development of knowledge has been hampered by different definitions of schema or the use of different terms from author to author. For example, Hanson (1998) used the term "script" interchangeably with "schema"; Ward and

Keenan (1999) rejected the term "schema" in favour of "implicit theory" but essentially addressed the same notion. What little research there has been to date has established the presence of three schemas related to sexual offending; namely, hostile masculinity, sexual entitlement and suspiciousness of women. Several additional schemas can be reasonably hypothesized to be relevant on the basis of recent exploratory research.

Hostile Masculinity Schema

Malamuth, Heavy and Linz (1993) suggested that certain childhood environments (e.g. violence between parents) are related to the development of aggressive adversarial schemas about intimate relationships between men and women. Association with delinquent peers and the socio-cultural environment, which in the Western world values qualities such as power and toughness, reinforce the development of these attitudes. At the same time, pro-social protective skills, such as the ability to manage frustration and to negotiate conflict, do not develop. The consequent pattern of attitudes is termed the "hostile masculinity schema". If, at the same time, a boy learns the sexual promiscuity path, which places undue emphasis on sexual conquest as a source of identity, the interaction between this path and the hostile masculinity schema would lead to sexual aggression. Malamuth et al.'s (1993) data on men who rape acquaintances supported their model, indicating that sexual aggression resulted from a combination of high levels of hostile masculinity and sexual promiscuity. Hostile masculinity without sexual promiscuity was related to non-sexual aggression against women.

Suspiciousness Schema

Malamuth and Brown (1994) identified a further schema in their evaluation of sexually aggressive males. Participants were shown a video of a man making sexual advances to a woman who responds in one of four ways: friendly, seductive, assertively rejecting or hostile. Results showed that the sexually aggressive men perceived the hostile responses as being seductive, and the seductive reaction as being negative and hostile. Thus a "suspiciousness schema" hypothesis was confirmed: sexually aggressive men seem to believe that women are game-playing deceptive people who use aggression as a form of seduction, and who are deceitful when they behave seductively. The more highly aggressive the man, the greater was his level of suspiciousness.

Sexual Entitlement Schema

Although they did not conceptualize this as a schema, Hanson, Gizzarelli and Scott's (1994) notion of sexual entitlement appears to fit the definition. A questionnaire measuring this construct, among others, was administered by Hanson et al. to incest offenders and two comparison groups: non-offending males and male batterers. An overall difference on the measure between groups was attributable to a mixture of the incest offenders showing more child abuse-supportive beliefs and scoring more highly on the sexual entitlement sub-scale. Items related to sexual entitlement included "A person should have sex whenever it is needed" and "Women should oblige men's sexual needs". Sexual entitlement could be considered to be a schema (or part of a schema) rather than an attitude because it is specifically concerned with the relationship between the self and others.

Other Hypothesized Schemas Related to Sexual Offending

Beck (1999) proposed seven schemas related to (non-sexual) violence: (1) authorities are controlling and punitive; (2) spouses are deceitful; (3) outsiders are hostile; (4) nobody can be trusted; (5) I need to fight back; (6) physical force gets respect; and (7) if you don't get even people will walk over you. Although Beck described these beliefs as separate schemas, they could also be seen as beliefs contained within one "hostile world" schema. Hanson (1998) proposed that sexual offenders have "sex offence" schemas containing the following elements: egocentric self-perception, sex over-valued in the pursuit of happiness (including a link between sex and power), and an ability to justify to oneself that some people deserve to be victimized. Ward and Keenan (1999) analysed questionnaire items used to measure cognitions in sexual offenders and proposed five "implicit theories" (a similar concept to schema) that seem to be common in child molesters: (1) children as sexual objects; (2) entitlement; (3) dangerous world; (4) uncontrollable world; and (5) the belief that sexual activity with children is not harmful. Some of these theories could equally legitimately be classed as offence-supportive attitudes (e.g. children as sexual objects, and the belief that sex with children is not harmful). But the notions of entitlement, dangerous world and uncontrollable world are more accurately described as schemas.

   Myers (2000) compared "life maps" (i.e. autobiographies) of rapists, child molesters and non-sexually violent offenders in terms of themes to do with their views of themselves and the world. She found very different patterns among the three groups. Rapists showed clear patterns (or schemas) of distrust of women and need for control. The clearest patterns for child molesters in contrast were worthlessness and a passive "victim stance". Violent offenders were similar to rapists in their need for control, but did not show the "distrust of women" schema. Sexual entitlement was observed among more of the rapists than among the child molesters but did not occur in the violent offenders. A schema for violent offenders that was not observed for child molesters or for rapists was to see themselves as protectors of others.

   Mann (2004) identified four schemas related to sexual offending. The descriptions given by a sample of offenders of their information processing at the time of offending were utilized to develop a questionnaire. Factor analysis revealed two main factors, each with two second-order factors. Two "dominance" schemas were identified, with one theme concerning a desire for vengeance, and the other concerning a need to be respected by others. Two "disadvantaged" schemas involved feeling damaged by the actions of other people, and seeing the self as controlled by past negative experiences. Cluster analysis of 482 sexual offenders, with a roughly equal proportion of child molesters and rapists, revealed four clusters of offenders based on schema scores.

1. *Low schema-reporting* (n = 175). These offenders did not indicate that any of the four schemas were characteristic of their thinking. Offenders who clustered in this group were either low-risk offenders or those who demonstrated social desirability biases in their questionnaire responses. This group was least pathological on a range of other measures such as submissiveness, self-esteem, impulsivity, ruminations, sexual entitlement and minimization of offending.
2. *Average schema-reporting* (n = 92). This cluster contained offenders who indicated that one schema may be characteristic of their thinking. This cluster showed few discriminating characteristics on other psychometric measures relevant to sexual offending, apart from low emotional openness and a greater tendency to accept rape myths.
3. *Submissive cluster* (n = 151). This cluster was characterized by particularly low levels of the dominance schemas. Analysis of cases falling into this cluster revealed that a pattern of submissiveness was notably evident both in the lead-up to their offending and in their daily lives. This cluster showed characteristics consistent with very low levels of dominance on other psychometric measures, such as submissiveness and low self-esteem.
4. *Hypercharged cluster* (n = 62). This cluster was characterized by all four schemas being "primed" (i.e. reported as characteristic thinking patterns). This cluster contained primarily men at high risk of further violence, as opposed to men at high risk of further sexual offending; it was also more likely to contain rapists than child molesters. This cluster showed significantly more dysfunction in other areas relevant to sexual offending, such as aggressiveness, impulsivity, ruminations, sexual entitlement, and poor self-esteem and perspective-taking.

Mann (2004) observed from case study analysis that the four schemas all appeared to play a role in sexual offending but could not be identified as exclusively or directly related to sexual offending. That is, schema-related cognitions could be seen in the offence chain, but were not major motivators for offending; other factors (such as sexually deviant interests) were more clearly observed immediately prior to the decision to offend. Furthermore, sexual offenders and non-sexual violent offenders did not differ in their mean scores on the self-report measure, suggesting that the schemas may be an aspect of all serious (i.e. violent) offending, rather than being specific to sexual offending.

ASSESSING SCHEMAS

The measurement of schema-level cognition is a challenge. Schemas are usually seen as affecting information processing in a way that is outside conscious awareness (A.T. Beck, 1996), although Beck's cognitive therapy approach also assumes that schema-related biases can be brought under conscious control with effort. If schemas are not usually within conscious awareness, it is not clear whether they can be directly measured by self-report methodologies. It may be that less direct methodologies, such as Stroop tasks, memory tasks, repertory grids, sentence completion tasks or even projective tests, are more appropriate. On the other hand, even though schemas may be out of conscious awareness, the beliefs and attitudes that make up their contents should resonate with a sense of familiarity, because they should reflect frequently experienced surface cognitions. The cognitive therapy approach does make considerable use of attitude scales, believing that schemas can be inferred from responses to attitude items. In discussing this matter, Welburn, Coristine, Dagg, Pontefract and Jordan (2002) argued that, "It is not unlikely that there would be some conscious awareness of the schema, particularly when they result in numerous negative experiences" (p. 520). Clearly, self-report measures have considerable advantages in cognitive measurement: they are economical, easy to administer and score, and have the potential for standardization across studies. In addition, they do not require substantial training to administer or score. However, they tend not to produce very rich data, can be susceptible to social desirability biases and do not uncover unexpected information (Segal & Shaw, 1988). In conclusion, self-report measures may produce some helpful information but for an in-depth analysis of schema-level cognition (particularly at the present early stage of research) more innovative assessment methodologies are needed.

Schemas can also be assessed through procedures such as autobiographical exercises or through deconstruction of everyday events (particularly where these led to maladaptive behavioural or emotional responses).

Life Maps

"Life maps" or "life histories" are a useful tool for identifying recurring thinking patterns. Through life maps, sexual offenders and therapists can begin to identify the schemas most relevant to the individual's sexual offending and general dysfunction, in addition to identifying any patterns of thinking that have had a positive effect on his life. The life map exercise involves individuals charting significant life experiences, identifying high points and low points and, where possible, identifying the accompanying thoughts and emotions. This exercise emphasizes historical events over current events. Young (1990) described how the development of maladaptive schemas seems to result from ongoing patterns of everyday unpleasant experiences. Young also suggested the method of eliciting personal histories from clients in order to establish the weight of evidence clients have for their maladaptive schema. Similarly, Winter and Kuiper (1997) suggested that by tracing the development of cognitions and life experiences, the therapist has more access to, and a clearer understanding of, patterns of dysfunctional thinking and how they function.

Once completed, group members talk through their life maps, and therapists and peers have the opportunity to ask questions or give feedback designed to help the individual understand his thinking patterns more clearly. For example, having described an instance of being bullied at school, an individual might report revenge-oriented thinking in response to this. If later he describes an instance of being cheated on by his partner, it would be sensible to ask if the revenge-oriented thoughts re-emerged at this time. Questioning such as this results in an assessment of the extent to which a thinking pattern endures over time. Once this exercise is completed in the group, there should be a reasonably good awareness of the particular schemas relevant for each individual.

Another way by which schemas can be identified clinically is by having group members give examples of times at which a particular schema has been activated. This enables the identification of self-talk, or surface cognitions, accompanying a particular schema. For example, if an individual identified an "entitlement" type schema as relevant to him, he could be asked to give examples of where this schema was activated in recent months, in his past life and in a situation that was directly linked with his sexual offending. This enables an exploration of the way in which the schema operated, and how it was associated with sexual offending. It also provides information about the types of situations that trigger the schema, which is crucial for learning to improve schema-management.

TREATMENT APPROACHES

The aim of an intervention is not to "change" schemas, but to help individuals recognize their schemas and view them as hypotheses to be tested rather than as absolute truths. Attempting to aim to "change" schemas in the course of a time-limited and structured group program is unlikely to be successful, and this is probably true of any therapy program. Schemas are hypothesized to be "extremely stable and enduring themes that develop during childhood and are elaborated upon throughout an individual's lifetime" (Young, 1990, p. 9). As such, it is considered more appropriate to aim for schema recognition and management, rather than schema removal or change.

The purpose, then, is to strike a balance on the dialectic of acceptance and change (see Linehan, 1993); offenders are encouraged to accept the existence of their dysfunctional schemas, and understand their role both in their sexual offending and in other areas of their lives. Clients need to be equipped with the skills necessary to recognize their schemas, so they have an awareness of when their dysfunctional schemas are operating; and they need to have the skills to dispute their schemas in order to reduce their influence on their information processing. The emphasis is on the importance of self-awareness and cognitive restructuring. This usually involves four stages of therapy: (1) explaining the concept of schema; (2) recognizing schemas, (3) learning techniques for managing schema-related cognition; and (4) role-playing schema management in the context of ambiguous or threatening life situations.

Explaining the Concept of Schemas

We have found that the use of analogy has been particularly helpful in explaining the concept of schemas. For example, it can be useful to refer to the saying "looking at the world through rose-coloured spectacles" and asking clients to consider the meaning of this saying (i.e. that this is someone who takes a positive outlook on everything). Making use of humour, clients can be encouraged to consider what someone who was wearing rose-coloured spectacles might think if someone cheated on them (e.g. "Everyone needs some variety in life"), or stole from them ("I've got loads of stuff, I won't miss one TV"). This analogy can then be extended by suggesting that clients consider their own schemas as spectacles which colour the way they see the world. When wearing particular pairs of spectacles, situations are interpreted in different ways. To illustrate this, different situations (such as "a confident person chats you up"; "someone hugs you"; "your partner argues with you for not phoning") are explored as they would be seen through different pairs of schema-spectacles. To further increase the power of the analogy, sunglasses with different coloured lenses can be used as "props".

In such therapeutic exercises, it is essential that a spirit of openness and co-operation is employed. The exercises aim to make learning about what is a sensitive and emotionally charged subject as light-hearted and engaging as possible.

Schema Recognition

After the concept of schemas has been understood, the next stage is for clients to begin to identify and then recognize their own schemas. Clients are encouraged to look for patterns in their thinking, and to label their patterns in a way that makes sense to them. Therapists intervene only to encourage clients to identify the entire range of their schemas. Therapists do not offer ideas for labelling schemas—this is left entirely to clients.

Clients can also be encouraged to keep schema diaries. In his diary, the client might be asked to record particularly difficult situations he had to deal with outside of the therapy context. He would record the nature of the event, the schema that was triggered by the event, the schema-related self-talk that he used and his behavioural response. Such a task facilitates recognition of typical schema-related self-talk.

Schema Management

The primary treatment tool used in working to manage schemas is a modified form of cognitive therapy, namely schema-focused therapy (J.S. Beck, 1996; Padesky, 1994; Young, 1990). Schema-focused therapy was first developed for use with personality disordered clients (Young, 1990), for whom traditional cognitive therapy had not proved successful. The issues affecting personality disordered clients in cognitive therapy, as described by Young, are applicable to sexual offenders. For example, many sexual offenders struggle to articulate emotions, have difficulty in identifying self-talk, find it hard to trust people in authority (such as court-mandated therapists) and have difficulties with intimacy and building relationships (e.g. Marshall, 1989, 1993). Consequently, the application of schema-focused cognitive therapy means that therapists must pay more attention to the therapeutic alliance, such as therapeutic warmth, empathy, specific positive reinforcement (Marshall et al., 1999), and validation (Linehan, 1993).

Additionally, schema-focused therapy involves challenging schema-related behaviour that is displayed in the context of an interaction in the group. Therapists need to remain alert at all times to the possibility of schema processes operating, and be prepared to highlight them respectfully and without accusation or confrontation. It is not uncommon for seemingly straightforward and unthreatening occurrences (such as a brief introduction to a session, the introduction of a new topic, the absence of a regular therapist, a group starting late) to become "hijacked" by the activation of one or more schemas. It is at these moments that some of the most valuable work in terms of recognizing and modifying schemas can be accomplished.

Fundamentally, cognitive therapy involves helping clients consider that their beliefs are hypotheses to be tested, rather than absolute truths. Exercises that can facilitate such self-challenge include: (1) considering the advantages and disadvantages of holding the dysfunctional belief; (2) thinking about consequences of their schema in the past, as well as current and potential future consequences of continuing to process information via their schema; and (3) collecting evidence for and against the schema-related beliefs. It must be emphasized that it is crucial that clients are required to list the evidence supporting the schema; not to do so would be invalidating (see Linehan, 1993).

Role-play

Role-play is used to help the individual to develop the skills required for disputing his schema-related self-talk. Role-plays usually involve the therapist (or a group member, if treatment is group-based) taking on the schema of the client in focus and speaking from that (dysfunctional) position. The client in focus is required to argue against his schema (as portrayed by the other person), so that he can develop, practise and strengthen alternative self-talk to reduce the impact of his schema on his information processing. The most effective scenarios on which to base role-play are those that are ambiguous (i.e. those that have more than one likely meaning), but that would activate the dysfunctional schema. It is sensible to avoid role-play scenarios that would activate a negative interpretation in most people, such as "Your partner forgets your birthday", or "Your partner insults you in front of your family". Neither is it appropriate to use scenarios in which the (usually) dysfunctional schema may be helpful, for example, "Someone threatens you". Role-play should not be used to help group members to reconstrue childhood negative or abusive experiences. These exercises are not about changing the past but about managing schemas when they interfere in a potentially unhelpful way with information processing. A more sensible approach to early negative experiences is that of acceptance.

During role-plays, the therapist should act as a coach to help the individual to focus through the role-play. Role-play is experienced as challenging and anxiety provoking by most people; when the role-play is focused around an area as sensitive and emotionally demanding as dysfunctional schemas, the need for careful management is paramount. Therapists should intervene if the individual appears to be getting stuck, or if he starts to experience intense emotion. Therapists should approach role-play as an opportunity for group members to learn new skills. Role-plays should be set up according to the existing skills of the individual to be moderately challenging, without being an impossible task. Role-play is not about testing the individual but about enabling him to develop new skills and improve existing ones.

CONCLUSION

This chapter has argued that an understanding of the role of cognition in sexual offending should be based on an information processing approach rather than the cognitive distortion model. If the information processing approach is adopted, this has implications for assessing and treating sexual offenders; and novel methodologies need to be developed in both arenas. At present, a variety of dysfunctional schemas are possibly relevant to sexual offending, but the exact nature and role of such schemas needs further investigation. Treatment for sexual offenders should cease to focus on excuses and justifications for offending and should adopt the methods of cognitive therapy for working with underlying core beliefs about the self, others and the world. Until this is achieved, sexual offenders may complete treatment programs without having effected any fundamental changes in the cognitive structures which at least partly enabled sexual offending to take place.

ACKNOWLEDGEMENT

The authors would like to acknowledge the contribution of Professor Clive R. Hollin (University of Leicester) to the development of the ideas contained in this chapter.

REFERENCES

Abel, G.G., Gore, D.K., Holland, C.L., Camp, N., Becker, J.V. & Rathner, J. (1989). The measurement of the cognitive distortions of child molesters. *Annals of Sex Research*, **2**, 135–53.

Beck, A.T. (1996). Beyond belief: a theory of modes, personality, and psychopathology. In P.M. Salkovskis (ed.), *Frontiers of Cognitive Therapy* (pp. 1–25). New York: Guilford Press.

Beck, A.T. (1999). *Prisoners of Hate: The Cognitive Basis of Anger, Hostility and Violence*. New York: HarperCollins.

Beck, J.S. (1996). Cognitive therapy of personality disorders. In P.M. Salkovskis (ed.), *Frontiers of Cognitive Therapy* (pp. 165–81). New York, Guilford Press.

Dweck, C.S. (1975). The role of expectations and attributions in the alleviation of learned helplessness. *Journal of Personality and Social Psychology*, **31**, 674–85.

Finkelhor, D. (1984). *Child Sexual Abuse: New Theory and Research*. New York: Free Press.

Hanson, R.K. (1998, September). Working with sex offenders. Keynote address at the annual conference of the National Organization for the Treatment of Abusers, Glasgow, Scotland.

Hanson, R.K., Gizzarelli, R. & Scott, H. (1994). The attitudes of incest offenders: sexual entitlement and acceptance of sex with children. *Criminal Justice and Behavior*, **21**, 187–202.

Langton, C.M. & Marshall, W.L. (2000). The role of cognitive distortions in relapse prevention programs. In D.R. Laws, S.M. Hudson & T. Ward (eds), *Remaking Relapse Prevention with Sex Offenders: A Sourcebook* (pp. 167–86). Thousand Oaks, CA: Sage Publications.

Linehan, M.M. (1993). *Cognitive Behavioural Treatment of Borderline Personality Disorder*. New York: Guilford Press.

Loza, W. & Clements, P. (1991). Incarcerated alcoholics and rapists' attributions of blame for criminal acts. *Canadian Journal of Behavioural Science*, **23**, 76–83.

Malamuth, N.M. & Brown, L.M. (1994). Sexually aggressive men's perceptions of women's communications: testing three explanations. *Journal of Personality and Social Psychology*, **67**, 699–712.

Malamuth, N.M., Heavy, C.L. & Linz, D. (1993). Predicting men's antisocial behaviour against women: the interaction model of sexual aggression. In G.C.N. Hall, R. Hirschmann, J.R. Graham & M.S. Zaragoza (eds), *Sexual Aggression: Issues in the Etiology, Assessment and Treatment* (pp. 63–97). Washington, DC: Taylor & Francis.

Mann, R.E. (2004). An investigation of the nature, content and influence of schemas in sexual offending. PhD thesis in preparation, University of Leicester, England.

Marshall, W.L. (1989). Intimacy, loneliness and sexual offenders. *Behaviour Research and Therapy*, **27**, 491–503.

Marshall, W.L. (1993). The role of attachments, intimacy and loneliness in the etiology and maintenance of sexual offending. *Sexual and Marital Therapy*, **8**, 109–21.

Marshall, W.L., Anderson, D. & Fernandez, Y.M. (1999). *Cognitive Behavioural Treatment of Sexual Offenders*. Chichester, England: John Wiley & Sons.

Maruna, S. (2001). *Making Good: How Ex-convicts Reform and Rebuild Their Lives*. Washington, DC: American Psychological Association.

McCaghy, C.H. (1968). Drinking and deviance disavowal: the case of child molesters. *Social Problems*, **16**, 43–9.

Murphy, W.D. (1990). Assessment and modification of cognitive distortions in sex offenders. In W.L. Marshall, D.R. Laws & H.E. Barbaree (eds), *Handbook of Sexual Assault: Issues, Theories, and Treatment of the Offender* (pp. 331–42). New York: Plenum Press.

Myers, R. (2000). Identifying schemas in child and adult sex offenders and violent offenders. Unpublished MSc thesis, University of Leicester, England.

Padesky, C.A. (1994). Schema change processes in cognitive therapy. *Clinical Psychology and Psychotherapy*, **1**, 267–78.

Peterson, C. & Seligman, M.E.P. (1981). Helplessness and attributional style in depression. *Tiddsskrift for Norsk Psykologforening*, **18**, 53–9.

Scott, M.B. & Lyman, S.M. (1968). Accounts. *American Sociological Review*, **33**, 46–62.

Segal, Z.V. & Shaw, B.F. (1988). Cognitive assessment: issues and methods. In K.S. Dobson (ed.), *Handbook of Cognitive-behavioural Therapies* (pp. 39–81). New York: Guilford Press.

Seligman, M.E.P. (1986, July). Explanatory style: depression, Lyndon Baines Johnson and the Baseball Hall of Fame. Paper presented at the 94th Annual Convention of the American Psychological Association, Washington, DC.

Snyder, C.R. & Higgins, R.L. (1988). Excuses: their effective role in the negotiation of reality. *Psychological Bulletin*, **104**, 23–35.

Ward, T. & Keenan, T. (1999). Child molesters' implicit theories. *Journal of Interpersonal Violence*, **14**, 821–38.

Welburn, K., Coristine, M., Dagg, P., Pontefract, A. & Jordan, S. (2002). The Schema Questionnaire—short form: factor analysis and relationship between schemas and symptoms. *Cognitive Therapy and Research*, **26**, 519–30.

Winter, K.A. & Kuiper, N.A. (1997). Individual differences in the experience of emotions. *Clinical Psychology Review*, **17**, 791–821.

Young, J.E. (1990). *Cognitive Therapy for Personality Disorders: A Schema-focused Approach*. Sarasota, FL: Professional Resource Press.

and relationships, competencies, and specifically exactly what competencies and resources are required to achieve these goods. This crucially involves identifying the internal and external conditions necessary to implement the plan and the offender's rehabilitation strategy to equip the individual with these required skills, resources, and opportunities. Such an approach to offender rehabilitation is significantly contextualized, and devalues the importance of personal identity and its embeddedness in daily living (and activities). Less attention is also paid to the idea that primary human goods represent influences that are beneficial to human beings and their absence is harmful to the individual and to others.

The argument is that rehabilitation should establish human and undermine dynamic risk factors (CRN) and should seek to install the internal and external conditions that will enable its realization. The detection of dynamic risk factors, or criminogenic needs, signals that there are problems of scope, coherence, inappropriate means, and planning deficits in the distinct domains of a person's life. Risk analysis simply informs therapists that there are problems in the way offenders seek human goods and the aim of assessment is to clarify the nature and extent of these difficulties. Questions such as 'How have you gone about achieving X?' problems relationships in your life? Which strategies have worked the best? Which have worked least well? are particularly useful in helping to document these problems or indicators. Such questions allow for the assessment of each individual's conception of a good life and facilitate an understanding of the individual's strategies for realizing primary goods.

Treatment should proceed on the assumption that effective rehabilitation requires the acquisition of competencies and capabilities to pursue and enjoy a satisfying and different kind of life. Ward and Stewart argue that therapists should focus first on identifying the obstacles preventing offenders from living a satisfying and fulfilling life, and then seek to equip individuals with the skills, beliefs, values and supports needed to counteract their influence. For example, assessment might reveal that an offender has limited strategies for achieving the human good of inner peace (affect regulation), intimacy, and sex, and uses physical goods of physical satisfaction (health, living, sex). A treatment plan constructed along the lines of the GLM would aim to provide the offender with a wider range of strategies for achieving emotional balance (i.e. keeping an emotion diary, talking with a friend), and seek other means of achieving physical stimulation, pleasure and sense of accomplishment (through challenging sports such as mountaineering or hiking). Additionally, the difference between the goods of friendship and sex would be distinguished and alternative types of activities devised to achieve these distinct goods. This could also involve acquiring the skills and competency necessary to achieve greater levels of intimacy with adults.

Human Goods and the Therapeutic Relationship

The role of the therapeutic alliance in determining treatment outcome has been a focus of recent research in both the sexual offending and general psychotherapy domains. Marshall et al. (2003) argue that increasing sexual offenders' self-esteem, working collaboratively on developing treatment goals, and specific therapist

Chapter 13

FOCUSING ON THE POSITIVE AND AVOIDING NEGATIVITY IN SEXUAL OFFENDER TREATMENT

YOLANDA M. FERNANDEZ

Rockwood Psychological Services, Kingston, Ontario, Canada

In any therapeutic endeavor the responsibility for the effectiveness of treatment ultimately lies in the hands of the therapists delivering treatment. The literature on therapist characteristics has clearly identified both therapist characteristics and techniques that predict beneficial changes in treatment as well as those that are related to negative treatment outcome. Unfortunately, many treatment programs directed toward problems that have typically been considered distasteful (e.g. addictions, sexual deviance) have historically disregarded this research and taken on an approach to treatment that is harsh and confrontational. For example, both Salter (1988) and Wyre (1989) claim that since sexual offenders typically lie and present defensively in treatment, the approach to them must be aggressively confrontational with all decisions about the goals of treatment being made exclusively by the therapist. This aggressive approach is likely to be experienced by the client as denigrating and may result in hostile interactions between therapist and client. As a result clients may become pessimistic about their capacity to change. Such a disregard for the influence of well-documented therapist characteristics would seem likely to reduce any benefits that may otherwise result from treatment.

Contrary to this negative approach to treatment, recent data have shown that a confrontational approach to treatment increases resistance among sexual offenders and results in reduced gains in treatment (Beech & Hamilton-Giachritsis, in press; Drapeau, in press; Marshall *et al.*, 2002). Unfortunately, however, while sexual offender treatment providers may publicly advocate a more positive approach to treatment our experiences with training therapists suggest the contrary. In an attempt to combat this problem the present chapter will focus on what therapists should do to "keep it positive" in sexual offender treatment programs.

Sexual Offender Treatment: Controversial Issues. Edited by W.L. Marshall, Y.M. Fernandez, L.E. Marshall and G.A. Serran. © 2006 John Wiley & Sons, Ltd.

AVOIDING NEGATIVITY

Avoiding a Confrontational Approach

If there was only one thing we could recommend to sexual offender therapists it would be to avoid an aggressive confrontational approach with clients. Therapists inevitably serve as models to their clients, thus their actions should exemplify prosocial behaviors and attitudes. If the therapist is aggressive and confrontational they can expect this to elicit either the same responses from assertive clients or withdrawal from the therapeutic process by the unassertive clients. Although a confrontational approach is sometimes rationalized as "being honest" (Egan, 1970) the fact is that those clients who are struggling to come to grip with issues related to inappropriate sexual behavior are taking responsibility for their difficulties. Even sexual offender clients who are defensive about what they did are at least acknowledging by their defensiveness that they consider their offenses to be unacceptable.

An aggressively confrontational approach appears to assume that if clients are forced by the therapist to face their problems "head on" they will "see the error of their ways" and make the necessary changes. This approach, however, ignores research suggesting that clients join treatment at, and progress through, various stages of change during which they are more or less ready to directly face their problems (Prochaska & DiClemente, 1982). DiClemente (1991) has indicated that a confrontational therapeutic style is particularly damaging to clients who are in the "precontemplation" stage of change. Many sexual offenders are referred for treatment while still at this preliminary stage, which is characterized by client resistance to recognizing and modifying a problem. DiClemente suggests that harsh challenges at this stage will increase resistance, denial and non-compliance and reduce self-esteem.

Research in the more general psychotherapeutic literature has suggested that a number of process variables, including confrontation, negatively affect treatment outcome (Liberman, Yalom & Miles, 1973). Liberman et al. describe the most damaging type of therapist as the "aggressive stimulator", who is distinguished by a harsh confrontational style of challenging. Cormier and Cormier (1991) note that, when faced with a forceful confrontational therapist, clients typically: (a) discredit or vigorously challenge the therapist; (b) devalue the issue; or (c) acquiesce and then dismiss the issue as irrelevant. In support of Cormier and Cormier's assertion, confrontation has been linked to problems within the treatment context. For example, Patterson and Forgatch (1985) reported that increased non-compliance in clients was significantly related to the degree of confrontation in therapy. Nichols and Taylor (1975) found that in a comparison of six therapeutic communities, therapists who characteristically resorted to an aggressive confrontational style had less effective outcomes than supportive and less aggressive group leaders. Unfortunately when, as Cormier and Cormier suggest, clients acquiesce to confrontational therapists it serves to further reinforce the belief among those therapists that a confrontational style is effective. However, outcome research supports the contention that the apparent treatment gains of clients exposed to confrontational challenging are either superficial or do not generalize outside of the treatment context.

Within the alcoholism literature, Miller, Benefield and Tonigan (1993) found that a confrontational style was predictive of more clients drinking at one-year follow-up. Similarly, in a study by Miller and Sovereign (1989) alcoholic clients who received treatment from a confrontational therapist demonstrated increased resistance to therapy, higher levels of denial and increased drinking at follow-up. Of particular relevance to sexual offender therapists, however, is a study by Thornton, Mann and Williams (2000). They found that although subjects assigned to a "hostile and cold" therapist demonstrated apparent reductions in levels of denial and minimization, as well as in levels of pro-offending attitudes, they did not show similar reductions in related but less directly targeted areas such as entitlement thinking, distrust of women, subjective personal distress and impulsiveness. In contrast, the subjects assigned to a "warm and supportive" therapist demonstrated treatment gains in all of these and other areas. Although preliminary, this study suggests that confrontational therapists may be misled regarding the effectiveness of their style by apparent (but likely superficial) gains in more obvious treatment targets, while extended gains in related areas are missed.

Aggressive confrontational approaches are sometimes justified by the assertion that forensic clients are "different" from other consumers of psychological interventions (see Salter, 1988), which effectively translates to "more in need of confrontation". However, the few studies that have explored this issue with forensic and specifically sexual offender populations have not supported this contention. Annis and Chan (1983) reported that a confrontational approach was particularly detrimental to non-sexual offenders who were low in self-esteem, a characteristic observed in many sexual offenders involved in treatment (Marshall, Anderson & Champagne, 1997). This finding was supported by Beech and Fordham (1997) who found a similar negative relationship between therapist confrontation and low self-esteem among sexual offenders involved in treatment. A study by Drapeau (in press) reported that a non-confrontational style was influential in engaging a group of child molester clients in treatment. The child molester clients who perceived their therapist as rejecting and unable to limit confrontation withdrew from treatment participation. Interestingly, several of the child molester subjects in Drapeau's study reported that they relied on their perceptions of the therapist to determine whether or not to involve themselves in treatment. Therapists who displayed firm but supportive challenges engaged the clients whereas those who were seen as confrontational engendered client withdrawal.

In their evaluation of the effects of various therapist behaviors on treatment-induced changes among sexual offenders, Marshall *et al.* (2002) showed that a confrontational style was significantly negatively related to beneficial changes. A non-confrontational, but challenging, style was significantly positively related to treatment-derived benefits across a broad range of treatment targets. These differences were consistently observed across five different prison-based treatment programs.

As mentioned those who favor an aggressively confrontational approach sometimes claim that their clients are "different" from clients with other, perhaps less obviously harmful, problems. The available research on forensic and sexual offender populations has not supported this conclusion. It is our opinion that clients striving to address problems that appear morally reprehensible to others are equally, if not more, in need of therapists who model the qualities associated with positive treatment outcome in the general literature.

Avoiding a Collusive Approach

Our experience of training therapists has suggested that encouraging therapists to avoid a confrontational approach has sometimes been misinterpreted as an endorsement of the opposite approach; that is, of an approach that is too soft, and essentially collusive with clients. An unconditionally supportive stance toward offenders is definitely not recommended. Therapists who are overly compassionate, do not challenge and do not set firm boundaries, are at risk of becoming collusive and are doing a disservice to their clients. The term "collusive" is used here to describe behaviors that encourage a sexual offender's distorted, exculpatory and self-protective views of his offenses. Collusive therapists tend to construe their clients as victims and, as a result, do not require offenders to take responsibility for their own behaviors. Time is often spent exploring issues that the clients may see as excuses for their behavior instead of identifying factors that may have influenced the offender's decision to offend. Therapists who adopt a collusive approach may feel uncomfortable challenging in a firm but supportive manner. These therapists may have a strong need to be liked by their clients and may worry that offenders will be angry with them if they tackle difficult issues. Alternatively, they may be afraid that challenges may alienate them from the clients. Firm but non-confrontational challenging is an appropriate and important aspect of sexual offender treatment. Beech and Hamilton-Giachritsis (in press) note that in highly cohesive groups appropriate challenges by members and therapists are more likely to be accepted because participants feel supported rather than attacked. The unfortunate outcome of a collusive approach to therapy is that by taking responsibility for client change, or by attempting to solve the clients' problems for them, collusive therapists may inadvertently encourage clients to believe that their behavior is out of their control. Ultimately clients are left without a sense of accountability for past and future choices.

Controlling Anger and Hostility

The expression of anger and hostility toward clients in treatment is typically associated with a harsh confrontational style, although it can be an occasional lapse in judgment in otherwise appropriate therapists. Understandably, when working with a population such as sexual offenders, who have engaged in behaviors causing significant harm to other people and particularly to children, it may be difficult at times to suppress feelings of anger when the client blames his victim. In addition, it has been suggested that confrontation from clients is associated with strong emotional reactions in therapists (Breer, 1996; Lea, Auburn & Kibblewhite, 1999) which generate thoughts of retaliation and punishment (Mitchell & Melikian, 1995). Controlling anger and hostility may be even more difficult when clients are entrenched in cognitive distortions, maintaining a victim stance, are derogatory toward their victims or very negative toward treatment. However, therapists should note that expression of their negative feelings can have a detrimental impact on therapy. Strupp (1980) found that therapist expressions of anger and hostility were related to client negativity. Anger and hostility in the therapeutic context have been associated with a disrupted therapeutic relationship and diminished progress in treatment (Cullari, 1996; Fremont & Anderson, 1986). Expressions of anger by the therapist during therapy, however, may occasionally be difficult to avoid and it may, at times, be useful to express frustration toward a particularly uncooperative client. Clients should understand that their behavior can at times be distressing to others. However therapists should work to constrain expressions of anger until a strong therapeutic alliance has been established and keep such expressions to a minimum thereafter. When, for various reasons, the therapist has engaged in an angry or hostile interaction the therapist should acknowledge the inappropriateness of their own actions and apologize, but use it as an opportunity to help the client recognize the way his behavior can affect others.

EMPHASIZING THE POSITIVE

Using More Positive Language in Therapy

Historically sexual offender treatment programs have outlined their treatment strategies in what is predominantly negative language. A primary focus in treatment is often on eradicating problematic issues rather than strengthening existing resources. As Marshall *et al.* (in press) note, program manuals typically describe *eliminating* negative attitudes, *reducing* cognitive distortions, *extinguishing* deviant sexual interests and having clients *avoid* people, places and things that are considered to increase risk for reoffending. Even words used by therapists to describe fairly normal processes reflect this negative approach. For example, cognitive distortions are sometimes referred to as "stinking thinking" in sexual offender treatment manuals, which suggests that engaging in distortions is both aberrant and restricted to offenders when, in fact, all people distort some aspects of their experience. The word "grooming", which refers to non-violent behaviors offenders use to gain cooperation from victims, has similar negative connotations. Using the word "grooming" as a descriptor of what are ostensibly courting behaviors fails to acknowledge that many of these activities would be considered appropriate were they not used in the context of an abusive encounter. The message given to the offender is that the problem is the behavior rather than the inappropriateness of the target person. As a result some offenders conclude they should never engage in such "grooming" behaviors and, as a result, may be at a loss to know how to pursue appropriate adult interactions in a suitable manner.

In contrast, adopting more positive language in therapy can help offenders identify their existing strengths and find ways to adapt these strengths to meet their needs more appropriately. One particularly valuable way to do this is to refrain from describing clients as "sexual offenders", "rapists", "child molesters" or whatever legal/forensic term is applicable. Distinguishing people from their behaviors has a long tradition in behavioral research and treatment (Kazdin, 1978), and avoids all the problems inherent in labeling (Fink & Tasman, 1992). It is also important not to allow clients to label themselves, as one of the consequences of a client calling himself a sexual offender (or even worse one of the more derogatory colloquial descriptors) is that he will be likely to experience shame and see himself as unchangeable. When people experience shame for certain actions this reduces their efforts at change whereas experiencing guilt motivates change (Tangney & Dearing, 2002). Having our clients describe themselves as persons who have committed a sexual offense (rather than as a sexual offender) is not only likely to engender guilt but also makes it easier to convince them that they have areas of strength that can be built upon.

Instilling Hope and Belief in Client Change

It is surprising that some therapists working with sexual offenders hold the belief that treatment is ineffective. It is difficult to understand why someone would choose to provide treatment they believe is ineffective and it is doubtful that these negative attitudes are lost on the clients. Rejection of the client and low interest displayed by the therapist are variables that have been related to negative treatment outcome (Lambert, 1983). Interestingly, Ricks (1974) demonstrated that a group of disturbed boys treated by an uninterested therapist were more likely to develop schizophrenia than those treated by an interested and involved therapist. Clients' perceptions of the therapist's involvement, emotional engagement and positive feelings have been found to determine their view of the value of treatment and their willingness to engage in the therapeutic process (Saunders, 1999). Seligman (1990) examined studies of treatment derived from various psychotherapeutic orientations and showed that positive outcomes were significantly related to an emphasis on client support, display of interest in the client, acceptance of the client's beliefs and values, and an ability to engage clients.

The failure of therapists to instill hope in treatment participants appears to result in clients believing that they do not have the ability to change and is related to a lack of motivation by clients to make the necessary changes in their lives (Snyder, 2000). Frank (1989) has suggested that hope is the primary factor in producing treatment gains. Clients low in hope have been shown to readily give up when they perceive that their pathway to a goal has been blocked by obstacles (Snyder, 2000). Snyder suggests that therapists who do not encourage every effort by clients to practice new skills fail to increase the client's "agentic thinking" or self-efficacy, which is one of the three elements identified as crucial to effective functioning in hope theory. In support of this, one of the aspects of group process linked to treatment changes in sexual offenders was instilling hope in group members (Beech & Fordham, 1997).

Particular ways of construing a client's past actions may also have a negative impact on sexual offenders' sense of hope and belief in change. For example, sexual offender treatment programs typically have clients identify the goals they were seeking in their offending behavior (e.g. sexual gratification, desire for power and control, seeking acceptance). All too often these goals are presented to sexual offenders as unacceptable when, in fact, they are normative goals; it is the way in which these goals are pursued that is unacceptable. Interpreting these goals for the client as reflecting normative needs should serve to instill hope in the offender that he can meet his needs in a more effective and appropriate manner.

Interpersonal Skills

Beech and Hamilton-Giachritsis (in press) note that the activation of good group processes in sexual offender treatment has to be therapist-led. It is difficult to imagine how this could be done by therapists who are deficient in interpersonal skills. Numerous authors have concluded that the success of therapy is very much dependent on the therapists' interpersonal skills (Beck, Rush, Shaw & Emery, 1979; Egan, 1998; Frank 1971; Kleinke, 1994; Kohut, 1990; Lambert, 1989; Luborsky, 1984; Rogers, 1975). Certainly, a number of interpersonal skills have been identified in the literature as having a positive impact on therapy. These include empathy, genuineness, warmth, respect, supportiveness, confidence, emotional responsivity, self-disclosure, open-ended questioning, directiveness, flexibility, encouraging active participation and rewarding behavior (for a summary of research on these interpersonal skills see Marshall *et al.*, 2002). Additionally, numerous studies have confirmed a relationship between the interpersonal skills of the therapist and maximizing the therapeutic alliance (see Ackerman & Hisenroth [2003] for a review) and the quality of the therapeutic alliance has been shown to account for as much as 25% of the variance in treatment effectiveness (Morgan, Luborsky, Crits-Christoph, Curtis & Solomon, 1982).

In sexual offender research, Beech and Fordham (1997) reported that among community-based sexual offender programs in the United Kingdom the greatest magnitude of treatment changes was found in groups that were well organized, well led, cohesive, encouraged the open expression of feelings, produced a sense of group responsibility and instilled a sense of hope in members. A later study found that leader support, described as the help and friendships shown by group leaders, was related to group cohesion and expressiveness as well as other positive group processes (Beech & Hamilton-Giachritsis, in press). Beech and Hamilton-Giachritsis further reported that cohesion and expressiveness accounted for over 40% of the variance in the effectiveness of treatment. Drapeau (in press) indicated that a sample of 24 child molesters identified the therapist as more important than the specific techniques used in treatment, although they saw the techniques as essential. Many of Drapeau's participants said they assessed the quality of the treatment program based on their perception of the therapists' competence. Positively valued therapists were viewed as displaying leadership, confidence, strength, competence and persuasiveness when necessary.

Collaboration and Approach Goals

For the past decade correctional psychology has been dominated by the risk management model (Andrews & Bonta, 1998; Ashford, Sales & Reid, 2001), which focuses on reducing further crime and gives little attention to improving clients' quality of life.

Ward and his colleagues (Ward, 2002; Ward & Marshall, in press; Ward & Stewart, 2003) have pointed to the relevance for sexual offender treatment of research on the "good lives" (Deci & Ryan, 2000; Emmons, 1996). As Ward and others have noted, sexual offenders appear to seek the satisfaction of normative needs (e.g. sex, control, physical contact) but do so in inappropriate ways (i.e. forced sex or sex with a minor). Construed in this way, men who sexually offend are understood to be unable to satisfy their needs so the task of treatment becomes teaching them the attitudes, perceptions, thoughts, feelings and skills necessary to meet their needs in prosocial ways. To this end the emphasis in treatment should be on developing a satisfying and fulfilling future life for sexual offenders, the thesis being that a fulfilled and happy person is unlikely to enact behaviors that are hurtful to others. Ward's model of the "good lives" serves as an exemplary approach to achieving the goals of providing sexual offenders with a satisfying and more fulfilling future. Consistent with this is Mann's (2000) contention that approach goals are to be the preferred targets of sexual offender treatment.

Mann (2000) outlined her concerns with traditional relapse prevention strategies which concentrate on avoidance-based goals (i.e. things and situations to avoid in order to reduce risk of reoffending) but that often fail to appeal to offenders or inspire a dedication to improving their lives in other ways. She pointed to an extensive body of literature (Emmons, 1996; Gollwitzer & Bargh, 1996) demonstrating that avoidance goals are rarely maintained whereas approach goals are more likely to endure. In addition, people who have predominantly avoidance goals are less psychologically healthy, less happy and less successful than those who have approach goals. In terms of treatment, Cox, Klinger and Blount (1991) demonstrated that alcohol abusers who worked toward avoidance goals were more likely to relapse than those whose targets were appealing approach goals. Comparing sexual offenders who were assigned to relapse prevention programs that either focused on avoidance or approach goals, Mann, Webster, Schofield and Marshall (in press) found that those with approach goals were more engaged in treatment, completed more homework assignments, were more willing to disclose problems, and were judged to be more genuinely motivated to live an offense-free life.

The need to work collaboratively with sexual offenders in all aspects of treatment has been described elsewhere in this volume (see Chapter 12) so we will not elaborate too extensively here. However, it is clear that not allowing offenders to select some aspects of their treatment objectives that are personally meaningful may increase resistance and lower motivation to pursue other, possibly crucial, goals. This was supported in Drapeau's (in press) study in which child molester subjects reacted negatively if they felt they were denied participation in early decision making in treatment or if they felt pressure or coerced. When clients were excluded from decision making they became oppositional and resistant because they felt this was their only viable course of action.

Finally, the language we use influences not only the clients' perceptions but also how we view aspects of treatment. Negative labels for the components of treatment (e.g. "relapse *prevention*", "deviant sexual interests") may inexorably draw us to focus on negative (or avoidance) goals rather than on more healthy goals, and may cause us to ignore areas of strength in our clients. Renaming relapse prevention strategies as "self-management" or "respectful living", or renaming the components of treatment that target deviant sexual arousal as "healthy sexual functioning", may be more attractive to resistant clients.

CONCLUSIONS

Early studies of sexual offender treatment focused primarily on techniques and virtually ignored the influence of the therapist. Studying procedures makes good theoretical sense in identifying effective strategies but makes somewhat less sense if the goal is to enhance the quality of care provided (Okiishi, Lambert, Nielsen & Ogles, 2003). Clinical trials research that attempts to minimize the contribution of individual therapists in order to discern the impact of specific techniques on out-come reduces the relevance for clinical practice. Recently reported studies have demonstrated the effectiveness of cognitive-behavioral group-based treatment for sexual offenders (Hanson *et al.*, 2002). As a result it may now be time to turn our attention to those who provide the treatment in an effort to further refine and improve our ability to provide effective treatment. In the present paper we have focused on characteristics and behaviors associated with a positive approach to sexual offender treatment. It is our hope that this paper underscores the need to carefully choose and train therapists in any setting, but particularly those who work with sexual offenders. Ultimately, the most effective and empirically validated pro-cedures that focus on positive goals and emphasize our clients' strengths, delivered by the most skilled and well trained therapists, should result in maximum treat-ment benefits for both our clients and those unidentified, potential future victims.

REFERENCES

Ackerman, S.J. & Hilsenroth, M.J. (2003). A review of therapist characteristics and techniques positively impacting the therapeutic alliance. *Clinical Psychology Review*, **23**, 1–33.

Andrews, D.A. & Bonta, J. (1998). *The Psychology of Criminal Conduct*, 2nd edn. Cincinnati, OH: Anderson Publishing Co.

Annis, H.M. & Chan, D. (1983). The differential treatment model: empirical evidence from a personality typology of adult offenders. *Criminal Justice and Behavior*, **10**, 159–73.

Ashford, J.B., Sales, B.D. & Reid, W.H. (2001). Political, legal, and professional challenges to treating offenders with special needs. In J.B. Ashford, B.D. Sales & W.H. Reid (eds), *Treat-ing Adult and Juvenile Offenders with Special Needs* (pp. 31–49). Washington, DC: American Psychological Association.

Beck, A.T., Rush, P.J., Shaw, B.F. & Emery, G. (1979). *Cognitive Therapy for Depression*. New York: Guilford Press.

Beech, A. & Fordham, A.S. (1997). Therapeutic climate of sexual offender treatment pro-grams. *Sexual Abuse: A Journal of Research and Treatment*, **9**, 219–37.

Beech, A.R. & Hamilton-Giachritsis, C.E. (in press). Relationship between therapeutic climate and treatment outcome in group-based sexual offender treatment programs. *Sexual Abuse: A Journal of Research and Treatment*.

Breer, W. (1996). *The Adolescent Molester*, 2nd edn. Springfield, IL: Charles C. Thomas.

Cormier, W.H. & Cormier, L.S. (1991). *Interviewing Strategies for Helpers*. Pacific Grove, CA: Brooks / Cole.

Cox, W.M., Klinger, E. & Blount, J.P. (1991). Alcohol use and goal hierarchies: systematic motivational counseling for alcoholics. In W.R. Miller & S. Rollnick (eds), *Motivational*

Interviewing: Preparing People to Change Addictive Behavior (pp. 260–271). New York, NY: Guilford Press.

Cullari, S. (1996). *Treatment Resistance: A Guide for Practitioners*. Boston: Allyn & Bacon.

Deci, E.L. & Ryan, R.M. (2000). The "what" and "why" of goal pursuits: human needs and the self-determination of behavior. *Psychological Inquiry*, **11**, 227–68.

DiClemente, C.C. (1991). Motivational interviewing and the stages of change. In W.R. Miller & S. Rollnick (eds), *Motivational Interviewing: Preparing People to Change Addictive Behavior* (pp. 191–202). New York: Guilford Press.

Drapeau, M. (in press). Research on the processes involved in treating sexual offenders. *Sexual Abuse: A Journal of Research and Treatment*.

Egan, G. (1970). *Encounter: Group Processes for Interpersonal Growth*. Pacific Grove, CA: Brooks / Cole.

Egan, G. (1998). *The Skilled Helper: A Problem-management Approach to Helping*. Pacific Grove, CA: Brooks / Cole.

Emmons, R.A. (1996). Striving and feeling: personal goals and subjective well being. In P.M. Gollwitzer & J.A. Bargh (eds), *The Psychology of Action* (pp. 313–37). New York: Guilford Press.

Fink, P.J. & Tasman, A. (eds) (1992). *Stigma and Mental Illness*. Washington, DC: American Psychiatric Press.

Frank, J.D. (1971). Therapeutic factors in psychotherapy. *American Journal of Psychotherapy*, **25**, 350–61.

Frank, J.D. (1989). Non-specific aspects of treatment: the view of the psychotherapist. In M. Sheppherd & N. Satorius (eds), *Non-specific Aspects of Treatment* (pp. 95–114). Toronto: Hans Huber.

Fremont, S. & Anderson, W. (1986). What client behaviours make counselors angry? An exploratory study. *Journal of Counseling and Development*, **65**, 67–70.

Gollwitzer, P.M. & Bargh, J.A. (eds) (1996). *The Psychology of Action*. New York: Guilford Press.

Hanson, R.K., Gordon, A., Harris, A.J.R., Marques, J.K., Murphy, W., Quinsey, V.L. & Seto, M.C. (2002). First report on the collaborative outcome data project on the effectiveness of psychological treatment for sex offenders. *Sexual Abuse: A Journal of Research and Treatment*, **14**, 169–94.

Kazdin, A.E. (1978). *History of Behavior Modification: Experimental Foundations of Contemporary Research*. Baltimore: University Park Press.

Kleinke, C.L. (1994). *Common Principles of Psychotherapy*. Pacific Grove, CA: Brooks / Cole.

Kohut, H. (1990). The role of empathy in psychoanalytic cure. In R. Langs (ed.), *Classics in Psychoanalytic Techniques*, rev. edn (pp. 463–73). Northvale, NJ: Aronson.

Lambert, M.J. (1983). Comment on "A case study of the process and outcome of time-limited counselling". *Journal of Counseling Psychology*, **30**, 22–5.

Lambert, M.J. (1989). The individual therapist's contribution to psychotherapy process and outcome. *Clinical Psychology Review*, **9**, 469–85.

Lea, S., Auburn, T. & Kibblewhite, K. (1999). Working with sex offenders: the perceptions and experiences of professionals and paraprofessionals. *International Journal of Offender Therapy and Comparative Criminology*, **43**, 103–19.

Liberman, M.A., Yalom, I.D. & Miles, M.B. (1973). *Encounter Groups: First Facts*. New York: Basic Books.

Luborsky, L. (1984). *Principles of Psychoanalytic Psychotherapy: A Manual for Supportive/ Expressive Treatment*. New York: Basic Books.

Mann, R.E. (2000). Managing resistance and rebellion in relapse prevention intervention. In D.R. Laws, S.M. Hudson & T. Ward (eds), *Remaking Relapse Prevention with Sex Offenders* (pp. 187–200). Thousand Oaks, CA: Sage Publications.

Mann, R.E., Webster, S.D., Schofield, C. & Marshall, W.L. (in press). Approach versus avoidance goals in relapse prevention with sexual offenders. *Sexual Abuse: A Journal of Research and Treatment*.

Marshall, W.L., Anderson, D. & Champagne, F. (1997). Self-esteem and its relationship to sexual offending. *Psychology, Crime and Law*, **3**, 81–106.

Marshall, W.L., Serran, G., Moulden, H., Mulloy, R., Fernandez, Y. M., Mann, R. & Thornton, D. (2002). Therapist features in sexual offender treatment: their reliable identification and influence on behaviour change. *Clinical Psychology and Psychotherapy, 9,* 395–405.

Marshall, W.L., Ward, T., Mann, R.E., Moulden, H.E., Fernandez, Y. M., Serran, G. & Marshall, L.E. (in press). Working positively with sexual offenders: maximizing the effectiveness of treatment. *Journal of Interpersonal Violence.*

Miller, W.R., Benefield, R.G. & Tonigan, J.S. (1993). Enhancing motivation for change in problem drinking: a controlled comparison to two therapist styles. *Journal of Consulting and Clinical Psychology, 61,* 455–61.

Miller, W.R. & Sovereign, R.G. (1989). The check-up: a model for early intervention in addictive behaviours. In T. Loberg, W.R. Miller, P.E. Nathan & G.A. Marlatt (eds), *Addictive Behaviours: Prevention and Early Intervention* (pp. 219–31). Amsterdam: Swets & Zeitlinger.

Mitchell, D. & Melikian, K. (1995). The treatment of male sexual offenders: countertransference reactions. *Journal of Child Sexual Abuse, 4,* 87–93.

Morgan, R., Luborsky, L., Crits-Christoph, P., Curtis, H. & Solomon, J. (1982). Predicting outcomes of psychotherapy by the Penn Helping Alliance Rating Method. *Archives of General Psychiatry, 39,* 397–402.

Nichols, M.P. & Taylor, T.Y. (1975). Impact of therapist interventions on early sessions of group therapy. *Journal of Consulting and Clinical Psychology, 31,* 726–9.

Okiishi, J., Lambert, M.J., Nielsen, S.L. & Ogles, B.M. (2003). Waiting for Supershrink: An empirical analysis of therapist effects. *Clinical Psychology and Psychotherapy, 10,* 361–73.

Patterson, G.R. & Forgatch, M.S. (1985). Therapist behaviour as a determinant for client non-compliance: a paradox for the behaviour modifier. *Journal of Consulting and Clinical Psychology, 53,* 846–51.

Prochaska, J.O. & DiClemente, C.C. (1982). Stages of change in the modification of problem behaviors. In M. Hersen, R.M. Eisler & P.M. Miller (eds), *Progress in Behavior Modification,* vol. 28 (pp. 183–218). Sycamore, IL: Sycamore Publishing.

Ricks, D. (1974). Supershrink: methods of a therapist judged successful on basis of adult outcome of adolescent patients. In D. Ricks, M. Roff & A. Thomas (eds), *Life History Research in Psychopathology* (pp. 73–94). Minneapolis: University of Minnesota Press.

Rogers, C.R. (1975) Empathic: an unappreciated way of being. *Counseling Psychologist, 5,* 2–10.

Salter, A.C. (1998). *Treating Child Sex Offenders and Victims: A Practical Guide.* Newbury Park, CA: Sage Publications.

Saunders, M. (1999). Clients' assessments of the affective environment of the psychotherapy session: relationship to session quality and treatment effectiveness. *Journal of Clinical Psychology, 55,* 597–605.

Seligman, L. (1990). *Selecting Effective Treatment.* San Francisco: Jossey-Bass.

Snyder, C.R. (2000). *Handbook of Hope: Theory, Measures, and Applications.* New York: Academic Press.

Strupp, H.H. (1980). Success and failure in time-limited psychotherapy: a systematic comparison of two cases. *Archives of General Psychiatry, 37,* 595–603.

Tangney, J.P. & Dearing, R.L. (2002). *Shame and Guilt.* New York: Guilford Press.

Thornton, D., Mann, R.E. & Williams, F.M.S. (2000). Therapeutic style in sex offender treatment. Available from Offending Behaviour Programmes Unit. HM Prison Service, room 725, Abell House, John Islip St., London, SW1P 4LH.

Ward, T. (2002). Good lives and the rehabilitation of offenders: promises and problems. *Aggression and Violent Behavior: A Review Journal, 7,* 513–28.

Ward, T. & Marshall, W.L. (in press). The role of good lives features in the etiology of sexual offending. *Journal of Sexual Aggression.*

Ward, T. & Stewart, C.A. (2003). Good lives and the rehabilitation of sexual offenders. In T. Ward, D.R. Laws & S.M. Hudson (eds) *Sexual Deviance: Issues and Controversies* (pp. 21–44). Thousand Oaks, CA: Sage Publications.

Wyre, R. (1989). Working with the paedophile. In M. Farrell (ed.), *Understanding the Paedophile* (pp. 17–23). London: ISTD / The Portman Clinic.

Chapter 14

PREPARATORY PROGRAMS FOR SEXUAL OFFENDERS

LIAM E. MARSHALL* AND HEATHER M. MOULDEN[†]

* Rockwood Psychological Services, Kingston, Ontario, Canada
† University of Ottawa, Canada

Sexual offending has received considerable attention since the middle of the 20th century and advances have been made in important areas. For example, empirically based risk measures for recidivism and theories on the etiology of sexual offending have aided persons working with convicted sexual offenders. A meta-analysis of the impact of sexual offender treatment has shown modern cognitive-behavioral therapy to be effective (Hanson et al., 2002). However, even optimistic accounts suggest that approximately one out of every ten sexual offenders will reoffend even after participating in sexual offender treatment. Considering the cost to innocent women and children, this finding suggests that further improvements to treatment for sexual offenders can and should be made. However, treatment providers for sexual offenders typically have very limited resources. Therefore, there are limitations on the improvements that can be made to treatment.

There is a number of ways in which treatment for sexual offenders could be made more effective; for example, a better understanding of the factors related to the client, therapy and the environment within which therapy occurs could all contribute to more effective interventions. Clearer evidence on the factors related to etiology and recidivism, therapeutic techniques and the role of the therapist in therapy are but a few of the areas that may improve effectiveness, and indeed, these areas have recently received some empirical attention.

Specialized preparatory programs designed to enhance the effects of subsequent treatment have, in other areas of psychological treatment, demonstrated a beneficial effect. Research has demonstrated that programs designed to introduce and prepare participants for treatment increase the effectiveness for various psychological problems in both individual treatment (Davidson, 1998; Hoehn-Saric et al., 1964; Larsen, Nguyen, Green & Attkisson, 1983) and group treatment (see Mayerson, 1984). For example, clients subsequently receiving treatment for depression and

Sexual Offender Treatment: Controversial Issues. Edited by W.L. Marshall, Y.M. Fernandez, L.E. Marshall and G.A. Serran. © 2006 John Wiley & Sons, Ltd.

anxiety at a community mental health center were randomly assigned to receive either a pre-treatment preparatory program or no pre-treatment intervention. Individuals participating in the pre-treatment program reported more realistic expectations for therapy, and greater symptom reduction at one-month follow-up compared to the group who received no such intervention (Zwick & Attkisson, 1985).

Additional studies have demonstrated that pre-treatment interventions to prepare clients for group therapy produce positive effects on self-disclosure (Garrison, 1978; Whalen, 1969), self-exploratory verbalizations (Annis & Perry, 1977, 1978; Garrison, 1978; Heitler, 1973), perceived personal value, investment and participation (Conyne & Silver, 1980; Corder, Haizlip, Whiteside & Vogel, 1980), and increased motivation (Curran, 1978; Strupp & Bloxom, 1973). It seems likely that these positive effects of preparatory interventions would be transferable to treatment for sexual offenders and enhance their gains from subsequent full treatment programs.

In order for a pre-treatment program for sexual offenders to be valuable certain conditions must be present: sexual offender treatment must reduce reoffending but not be 100% effective, and there must be identifiable blocks to sexual offenders profiting maximally from sexual offender treatment which can be overcome with a preparatory program. These conditions are clearly met. As noted above, the available research on recidivism among sexual offenders suggests that at least one out of every ten sexual offenders will reoffend after participating in treatment. When they first enter treatment, sexual offenders typically present with some degree of resistance which in most cases diminishes over the course of treatment. It seems reasonable to suggest that this initial resistance may be reduced by a preparatory program designed specifically to address the causes of resistance and that the subsequent more rapidly achieved full participation in treatment should produce greater benefits.

Resistance can take many forms (denial, minimizations, disengagement, hostility, etc.) and presents obstacles to helping sexual offenders address the issues that may reduce their chance of reoffending. In our interviews with sexual offender treatment candidates, and in our therapy programs in federal prisons in Canada, we find that most sexual offenders present with at least some resistance. For example, they express concerns about particular aspects of treatment such as having to face difficult issues and discussing very personal matters in a group, and they also express uncertainty about what treatment involves and whether or not it is likely to be effective. They wonder if treatment providers will treat them with contempt and how long they will be involved in treatment. The level of most of our clients' self-esteem is substantially below the normative average (Marshall, Champagne, Brown & Miller, 1997; Marshall & Mazzucco, 1995), and there is evidence that this also blocks clients' participation in treatment (Marshall, Anderson & Champagne, 1997). Despite being incarcerated for the commission of a crime, some even question the need for change. Many who enter treatment seem to lack motivation and focus and therefore a great deal of time is spent simply engaging these clients. This means that instead of the initial aim of treatment being the achievement of the overall goals, we have to spend time motivating our clients.

Many of the sexual offenders who participate in our treatment programs present with resistance in the form of myths about sexual offender treatment. Beliefs such as "treatment does not work" or "participating in treatment will make me feel worse about myself" cause offenders to be wary both before and after entering therapy. Some of the sexual offenders we interview claim they learned these myths from other offenders or even non-therapy staff. Research from Her Majesty's Prison Service in England has examined the reasons sexual offenders give for not entering treatment (Mann & Webster, 2002). In Mann and Webster's study, sexual offenders who entered treatment were compared both with sexual offenders who admitted to at least some aspect of their offences but refused treatment, and with sexual offenders who denied having committed an offence and also refused treatment. The most common blocks to entering treatment cited by these sexual offenders were: lack of trust in key professionals; bad experiences within the prison system related to being a sexual offender; lack of awareness of the effectiveness of treatment; concern over possible side-effects; and a belief that therapy would focus solely on offence-related details.

Based on this evidence, it seemed to us that gaining access to sexual offenders when they are first incarcerated, and dispelling these myths and any concerns they have about participating in treatment, should be helpful. In addition, combining these efforts with motivating sexual offenders to believe that change is needed and will be beneficial to them should enhance the effects of subsequent treatment and thereby further reduce reoffending.

In the Ontario region of the Correctional Service of Canada all sexual offenders are first placed in an induction center where they receive a thorough assessment over a period of approximately four months. The induction center assesses the offender on a variety of indices of risk and needs, and then sends him to an appropriate security-level institution where his risk can be managed and his rehabilitation needs can be addressed. Although offenders undergo a rigorous and extensive assessment, they usually have a significant amount of unstructured time which they spend in their cell. This presented an opportunity to implement a preparatory program.

The preparatory program we implemented is predicated on the assumption that early intervention, focused on orientating sexual offenders to treatment and motivating them to believe that change is both necessary and beneficial, will allow the full focus of subsequent, comprehensive treatment programs to be the attainment of the targets of sexual offender treatment. Our hypothesis is that sexual offenders who complete the motivational pre-treatment program will participate more effectively in subsequent full treatment programs than will those sexual offenders who do not participate in the preparatory program. Also we propose that the preparatory program subjects will benefit more from their subsequent treatment in terms of earlier release and lower recidivism rates than will those clients who simply participate in a full treatment program.

This chapter, then, will describe the procedures and processes used in our preparatory program, which will be followed by a brief summary of an evaluation of its effects. First, the components and procedures of the program will be described. Then, we will examine process-related issues such as therapist characteristics and therapeutic style. Finally, we will examine the outcome of the preparatory program as it relates to both pre- and post-release.

THE ROCKWOOD PSYCHOLOGICAL SERVICES PREPARATORY PROGRAM

In the general treatment literature, pre-treatment can consist of interviews, information sessions, videos or pamphlets. Because we are preparing sexual offenders for group treatment, we chose to run our preparatory program in a group treatment format that focuses on issues relevant to maximizing treatment responsiveness. Our preparatory program, due to space and budget limitations, includes six to eight offenders at any one time. A cognitive-behavioral approach is used and treatment involves two 2.5-hour sessions per week. The program is approximately six to eight weeks in length dependent upon when the client is transferred to his home institution. Treatment is available to any sexual offender willing to participate in treatment, providing there is space available and he is not appealing his conviction. The program is run in an "open" or "rolling" format. That is, the length of time in treatment, and the stage of treatment an offender is in, varies within the group. The open format is particularly helpful to the preparatory program because participants are transferred to their next institution at different times and it allows the flexibility to deal with cases needing urgent attention.

The primary aim is to prepare the client to participate more effectively in subsequent treatment than he would have without the preparatory program. This is accomplished by informing clients on treatment and its effectiveness, and aiding adjustment to working in a group situation. As space becomes available, newly incarcerated sexual offenders are interviewed to determine suitability for the preparatory program. Consistent with Correctional Service of Canada guidelines, sexual offenders do not have to admit to their crimes to enter our program. However, most of the offenders who deny they committed their crimes are also appealing their conviction and, consequently, are not suitable for the program. Once clients are deemed suitable, every effort is made to get them to take responsibility for entering the program; that is, it is offered to them but the choice is theirs.

The initial interview provides an opportunity to allay many of the concerns sexual offenders have about participating in treatment. One of the primary concerns expressed is for personal safety. We assure the participants that we do all we can to protect their safety and that we will work with them to keep them as safe as possible. They are encouraged to give any suggestions that they think will enhance safety. To date we have had no problems in this regard.

Topics of the Program

When clients enter the preparatory program they are provided with an orientation to the program and to the subsequent full sexual offender treatment programs available in the institutions to which they will be sent. Typically, clients are given two sessions to get adjusted to the group and to see how it functions before they do their first in-group exercise; that is, a brief disclosure of their offence. Clients are required, however, even from the outset to contribute to all discussions.

Once a client does an in-group exercise (e.g. disclosure), the therapist asks each other group member for comments about the positive things the target offender did in his exercise (i.e. "What did you like about [offender's name]'s exercise?"). The other group members are then to describe how the group member met the targets of the exercise (e.g. taking responsibility in a disclosure) or treatment in general (e.g. providing evidence of change). This strategy helps group members to understand the goals of the assignments in a non-threatening way and shapes them toward satisfactory participation. Criticism of a group member's assignment is rarely done and is usually reserved for the most problematic clients or those who have a strong therapeutic alliance with, and confidence in, the therapist. Throughout the preparatory program every effort is made to make the client feel comfortable, to encourage responsibility-taking and to enhance his sense of self-worth.

All participants in the preparatory program are required to complete a disclosure of their offence and a life history. Disclosure is the first exercise because most sexual offenders expect to have to discuss their offence and it is an exercise that reveals some of the resistance that sexual offenders display. It also helps prepare them for subsequent full treatment programs. The disclosures in our preparatory program are done in many ways. The therapists are flexible in the way they deliver each aspect of the preparatory program in order to accommodate a wide variety of learning styles and levels of readiness for treatment. Many of our participants are entering treatment and prison for the first time and consequently they tend to be very nervous and defensive. Therefore, we try to help them adjust by being as flexible as possible in the delivery of the program. For example, although participants usually give an unprompted verbal account of their offence, we have allowed the most apprehensive offenders to write, and then read aloud, their disclosure.

Some of the clients we see in the preparatory program are experiencing overwhelming outside issues, which makes the goal of our efforts simply their stabilization in order that they can function in prison and participate in their subsequent full treatment program. We have had clients whose fear, loneliness or depression has been so strong that they have difficulty getting through each session. For these clients we have found that simply having a group to go to twice a week, where they can talk about the difficulties they are facing and gain support from the other offenders and the therapist, can transform them into effective group members who are then able to focus on the goals of sexual offender treatment. We believe this is accomplished because our approach repeatedly emphasizes the positive aspects of our clients and deals with them in a supportive, but firm manner (see Marshall *et al.* [in press] for details of this overall approach).

Life history is the second exercise in the preparatory program because it can give the offender a break from offence-related discussions; some offenders immediately connect aspects of their life history to their offending, however, most are not treatment-sophisticated enough to be able to do this without guidance. We encourage clients to use the life history as an opportunity to talk about their strengths as well as the problems that have occurred throughout their lives. As a result they come to recognize that the focus of therapy is not just on their offences but on helping them to build more fulfilling lives for the future that exclude offending. Mann and Webster (2002) point out that many treatment refusers say they would enter treatment if the focus was not just on their offence, but also on all aspects of their life. The life history provides an opportunity to explore the offender's lifelong patterns of behaviour that led him to have difficulties without emphasizing or even discussing his offending.

Many participants have completed their assessment at the induction center and are transferred to their home institution by the time they complete these two exercises (i.e. disclosure and life history). If participants are in the program longer than it takes for them to complete the disclosure and life history exercises, then they also complete a victim empathy component and describe the four stages of offending outlined by Finkelhor and Araji (1986). We do an empathy exercise that focuses on victims in general rather than their own in order to allow the offenders to consider the effects of sexual abuse without being defensive. Finkelhor and Araji's four stages of offending exercise begins the process of developing an offence pathway analysis. In this exercise the offender is asked to explore the reasons why he wanted to offend, the cognitive distortions he used to justify his offending to himself, how he overcame victim resistance, and how he created an opportunity to offend. As mentioned, these are the most common exercises group members do after disclosure and life history; however, the therapist is able to select whatever assignment or exercise would be of most value to the specific offender. Therapists primarily focus on those needs that present the most significant blocks to the offender participating effectively in subsequent treatment.

There are a number of treatment targets that complement these exercises and the attainment of treatment goals. Issues that research has shown to be relevant to sexual offenders, such as loneliness, jealousy, coping and mood management, and intimacy and attachment typically arise within the context of the preparatory program. These issues are not given the same focus as occurs in subsequent full programs but if one or more of them is particularly problematic for an offender then he may be assigned a specific exercise to begin to deal with that issue. For example, since most clients have very low self-esteem, most are required to complete an exercise on their positive qualities (see Marshall, Champagne, Sturgeon & Bryce [1997] for details).

Goals of the Program

There are a number of goals of the preparatory program: demonstrating that treatment can be a positive experience, orienting participants to working a group setting, helping clients to become more comfortable discussing their offences, beginning to identify victim harm, beginning to explore the reasons for offending, and enhancing motivation. Some of the sexual offenders we see in our preparatory program display little optimism about their future and this seems to diminish their motivation for engaging fully in treatment. One area that has received theoretical interest recently, that is related to internal motivation, is hope theory (Snyder, 2000), and we (Moulden & Marshall, in press) have made a preliminary application of this theory to sexual offender treatment. Essentially this theory suggests that if a person can be convinced he has the capability of achieving his goals and can develop plans for doing so, his feelings of hope will be maximized and his likelihood of success will be high. Part of the goal of our preparatory program, then, is to increase hope defined in these terms.

There are a number of basic goals for a pre-treatment program with sexual offenders from a hope theory perspective. The first is to increase the client's belief in his capacity to achieve the goals of treatment. Strategies aimed at increasing this belief involve discussing the therapy process and revealing to clients what therapy will be about. In doing so, we make explicit the process of change and the client's role and responsibility for that change. Another technique is to watch for skills and strengths within the client and then identify them to him. For some clients, recognizing the positive skills they possess is a novel task, and may be difficult at first. This exercise provides clients with a sense of personal control and responsibility.

A primary aim of our pre-treatment program is to reduce resistance. Initially many of our clients see treatment as something forced upon them, and from which they will derive few if any benefits. Part of reducing resistance is to begin to personalize the general treatment plans and exercises. In doing so, the personal benefits are highlighted, and the client begins to recognize the value of the goals of therapy. As part of this aim, we assist our clients in identifying their personally relevant goals and sub-goals. Some of these goals are to some extent imposed (e.g. not reoffending) but many clients, when given the opportunity, are able to identify important and clinically relevant sub-goals, such as anger-management, intimacy issues or personal growth issues. In this phase of pre-treatment, the therapist is looking for examples in the offenders' lives of previous successes and it may be necessary to remind participants of these experiences (see Michael, 1999). These strategies are aimed at increasing the offender's hope about his ability to engage in therapy, experience something positive from the therapy process, and envision real changes for his future. The pre-treatment program is also a time to discuss the potential pathways to the goals our clients have defined. These pathways are the plans for how the offender will achieve his goals. Examples of such pathways are effectively participating in treatment programs, applying for employment, upgrading education or seeking a relationship.

Most sexual offenders are trying to reach the goal of not offending in one step, rather than working on more manageable sub-goals. However, the larger goal of not offending often seems overwhelming to the client and the pathways to get there unclear. In our treatment programs we refer to the maintenance of non-offending status as self-management, which may be more accurately conceptualized as a collection of sub-goals (e.g. avoiding high-risk situations, contacting supports, communicating effectively and fostering a healthy lifestyle that is exclusive of offending). Although there is moral value for change being rooted in recognizing harm to others, offenders are more likely to be internally motivated to change due to the achievement of personally valued outcomes. Such outcomes are the focus of various positive approaches to sexual offending therapy, such as the good lives model, approach goals in relapse prevention, and motivational interventions (see Marshall *et al.* [in press] for an integration of these approaches).

Thus far we have discussed what we do in the preparatory program. However, what is arguably more important is how we do it. We will now turn to examining the delivery of the program. First we will examine therapist qualities that have been shown to affect treatment outcome and then therapist style.

Process Issues

There is an extensive body of literature demonstrating the impact of the therapist on the outcome of treatment (Marshall, Fernandez *et al.*, 2003). Negative therapist behaviors such as anger and hostility, confrontation, rejection of the client, low levels of interpersonal skills, and manipulation of the client for therapist needs have been associated with poor outcome in general psychotherapy (Cullari, 1996; Fremont & Anderson, 1986; Strupp, 1980) and in the treatment of sexual offenders (Marshall *et al.*, 2002). In particular, Marshall *et al.* (2002) demonstrated that a confrontational approach actually made sexual offenders worse on several of the targets of treatment. These findings are consistent with research on the treatment of addictions. For example, compared with a group of alcoholics treated in a supportive but firmly challenging way, those in a confrontationally oriented group presented with greater resistance and denial, and relapsed at a higher rate (DiClemente, 1991; Miller, Benefield & Tonigan, 1993; Miller & Sovereign, 1989). Furthermore, confrontation has been shown to be associated with non-compliance and to be particularly damaging to clients with low self-esteem (Annis & Chan, 1983; Cormier & Cormier, 1991; Patterson & Forgatch, 1985). As a consequence we avoid confrontation and seek to establish a supportive and collaborative relationship with our clients based on the motivational model described by Miller and Rollnick (2000). Positive therapist behaviors such as confidence, respectfulness, flexibility and supportiveness have been shown to predict positive outcome (Rabavilas, Boulougouris & Perissaki, 1979; Salzman, Luetgert, Roth, Creaser & Howard, 1976; Strupp, 1980).

Recent studies by Marshall and his colleagues (Marshall, Serran *et al.*, 2002, 2003) have demonstrated the importance of the therapist in sexual offender treatment. The features of therapists that Marshall *et al.* found contributed most strongly to positive treatment changes were warmth, empathy, rewardingness and directiveness. Marshall *et al.* showed that these four therapist characteristics accounted for between 30% and 60% of the variance in the attainment of a broad range of treatment targets. These positive therapist characteristics are rigorously applied in our preparatory program.

Within the motivational style the therapist helps a client to change through acceptance of him as a whole person with strengths who has, nevertheless, engaged in an unacceptable behavior. We require clients to describe themselves as someone who has committed a sexual offence rather than as a sexual offender, hoping in this way to have the offender see himself as someone who has positive qualities as well as someone who has engaged in unacceptable behaviors. In this style the therapist is encouraging and supportive, but also challenges the client in an effort to engender cognitive dissonance in order to motivate change. Dependent on the stage of change the client is in (see Prochaska & DiClemente, 1984, 1992) supportive challenges can consist of questions asked in the spirit of genuine inquiry (e.g. clarification of something the client said). If the client–therapist alliance is strong, challenges can be more direct. This would most often be the case when an offender has been in a program for long enough to have built rapport with the therapist.

We have so far presented a rationale for, and the procedures and processes used in, our preparatory program for sexual offenders. While these seem sound, the most important measure of the success of the preparatory program is its effect on sexual offenders' subsequent participation in full treatment and post-release recidivism. Because the program has been running for more than seven years we are able to report some preliminary outcome data.

OUTCOME OF THE PREPARATORY PROGRAM

We are currently in the process of fully evaluating the impact of our pre-treatment program on participation in the subsequent full treatment program and outcome. To date we have received positive feedback from the therapists in the subsequent programs, and the program appears to be meeting the goals of the Correctional Service of Canada. Therapists facilitating the subsequent programs report that those offenders who have participated in the preparatory program are better prepared for treatment and participate more effectively than do sexual offenders who have not participated in the preparatory program. These therapists have referred to improved self-disclosure, advanced understanding of both static and dynamic risk factors, increased responsibility and appropriate group behavior (i.e. appropriate challenging and responsiveness to feedback, respectful of other group members, less resistance). Thus, there seems to be evidence that the skills and positive personal benefits resulting from pre-treatment generalize to the full treatment programs, facilitating the acquisition of skills and increasing motivation for change.

Examination of the preparatory program by researchers within the Correctional Service of Canada also shows that the program has utility. In a yet-to-be-published study, two groups of sexual offenders who had completed full treatment programs were compared: (1) those who had participated in the preparatory program; and (2) a matched group of sexual offenders who did not participate in the preparatory program. These two groups were matched on variables such as age at intake, date of intake, length of sentence and risk assessment scores. These two groups were also matched on phallometrically assessed sexual deviance, victim type and number of victims. It is important to note that because the preparatory program had only limited spaces, the selection of clients was random, based solely on who could be contacted on any particular day. The comparison group willingly entered treatment when they arrived at their home institution so initial acceptance of the need for treatment did not appear to differentiate the two groups. Indeed, some quite resistant men were convinced to enter the preparatory program.

Compared with those sexual offenders who did not participate in the pre-treatment program, the preparatory participants displayed greater treatment readiness, were more likely to be accepted for a subsequent lower intensity program, received earlier parole and were less likely to be returned to custody or recidivate. Sexual offenders who participated in the preparatory program were returned to custody half as often as the matched group who similarly completed a full treatment program but did not enter the preparatory program. The sexual recidivism rate for the preparatory program sexual offenders was found to be 1% compared to 5% for the matched group who received full treatment but did not participate in the preparatory program. The preparatory program clients also reoffended in non-sexual ways at a lower rate; 4% compared to 13%.

It is important to note here that these results are based on a smaller than ideal sample size ($n = 188$) who have been released to the community for between two and seven years. However, statistically significant differences have been found between these two groups and therefore there is reason to believe that these differences will be maintained with a larger sample size over a longer period of follow-up.

CONCLUSIONS

There is clear utility in enhancing the effects of treatment for incarcerated sexual offenders. One method of accomplishing this goal is to give sexual offenders early intervention that aims at reducing resistance and increases hope and motivation for change. The Rockwood Psychological Services Sexual Offender Preparatory Program is one such program that has demonstrated the value of an early motivational preparatory program with incarcerated sexual offenders. Sexual offenders participating in this preparatory program have been judged by subsequent therapists to be better participants in full sexual offender treatment programs. Early data suggest that they show greater benefits from treatment, in terms of parole and recidivism, than do those sexual offenders who have not participated in the preparatory program. Although further examination of the benefits of the preparatory program will need to be done, the present results are encouraging.

REFERENCES

Annis, H.M. & Chan, D. (1983). The differential treatment model: empirical evidence from a personality typology of adult offenders. *Criminal Justice and Behavior*, **10**, 159–73.

Annis, L.V. & Perry, D.F. (1977). Self-disclosure modeling in same-sex and mixed-sex unsupervised groups. *Journal of Counseling Psychology*, **24**, 370–2.

Annis, L.V. & Perry, D.F. (1978). Self-disclosure in unsupervised groups: effects of videotaped models. *Small Group Behavior*, **9**, 102–8.

Conyne, R.K. & Silver, R.J. (1980). Direct, vicarious, and vicarious-process experiences: effects on increasing therapeutic attraction. *Small Group Behavior*, **11**, 419–29.

Corder, B.F., Haizlip, T., Whiteside, R. & Vogel, M. (1980). Pre-therapy training for adolescents in group psychotherapy: contract, guidelines, and pretherapy preparation. *Adolescence*, **15**, 699–706.

Cormier, W.H. & Cormier, L.S. (1991). *Interviewing Strategies for Helpers*. Pacific Grove, CA: Brooks/Cole.

Cullari, S. (1996). *Treatment Resistance: A Guide for Practitioners*. Boston: Allyn & Bacon.

Curran, T. (1978). Increasing motivation to change in group treatment. *Small Group Behavior*, **9**, 337–48.

Davidson, M.A. (1998). The effects of pre-therapy information audiotape on client satisfaction, anxiety level, expectations, and symptom reduction. *Dissertation Abstracts International*, **58**(8-B), 4441.

DiClemente, C.C. (1991). Motivational interviewing and the stages of change. In W.R. Miller & S. Rollnick (eds). *Motivational Interview: Preparing People to Change Addictive Behavior* (pp. 191–202). New York: Guilford Press.

Finkelhor, D. & Araji, S. (1986). Explanations of pedophilia: a four factor model. *Journal of Sex Research*, **22**, 145–61.

Fremont, S. & Anderson, W. (1986). What client behaviors make counselors angry? An exploratory study. *Journal of Counseling and Development*, **65**, 67–70.

Garrison, J. (1978). Written vs. verbal preparation of patients for group psychotherapy. *Psychotherapy: Theory, Research, and Practice*, **15**, 130–4.

Hanson, R.K., Gordon, A., Harris, A.J.R., Marques, J.K., Murphy, W., Quinsey, V.L. & Seto, M.C. (2002). First report of the collaborative outcome data project on the effectiveness of psychological treatment for sex offenders. *Sexual Abuse: A Journal of Research and Treatment*, **14**, 169–94.

Heitler, J.B. (1973). Preparation of lower-class patients for expressive group psychotherapy. *Journal of Consulting and Clinical Psychology*, **41**, 251–60.

Hoehn-Saric, D.S., Frank, J., Imber, S., Nash, E., Stone, A. & Battle, C. (1964). Systematic preparation of patients in psychotherapy: I. Effects on therapy behavior and outcome. *Journal of Psychiatric Research*, **2**, 267–81.

Larsen, D.L., Nguyen, T.D., Green, R.S. & Attkisson, C.C. (1983). Enhancing the utilization of outpatient mental health services. *Community Mental Health Journal*, **19**, 305–20.

Mann, R.E. & Webster, S. (2002, October). Understanding resistance and denial. Paper presented at the 21st Annual Research and Treatment Conference of the Association for the Treatment of Sexual Abusers. Montreal, Canada.

Marshall, E.L., Anderson, D. & Champagne, F. (1997). Self-esteem and its relationship to sexual offending. *Psychology, Crime and Law*, **3**, 81–106.

Marshall, W.L., Champagne, F., Brown, C. & Miller, S. (1997). Empathy, intimacy, loneliness, and self-esteem in nonfamilial child molesters. *Journal of Child Sexual Abuse*, **6**, 87–97.

Marshall, W.L., Champagne, F., Sturgeon, C. & Bryce, P. (1997). Increasing the self-esteem of child molesters. *Sexual Abuse: A Journal of Research and Treatment*, **9**, 321–33.

Marshall, W.L., Fernandez, Y.M., Serran, G.A., Mulloy, R., Thornton, D., Mann, R.E. & Anderson, D. (2003). Process variables in the treatment of sexual offenders: a review of the relevant literature. *Aggression and Violent Behavior: A Review Journal*, **8**, 205–34.

Marshall, W.L. and Mazzucco, A. (1995). Self-esteem and parental attachments in child molesters. *Sexual Abuse: A Journal of Research and Treatment*, **7**, 279–85.

Marshall, W.L., Serran, G., Fernandez, Y.M., Mulloy, R., Mann, R.E. & Thornton, D. (2003). Therapist characteristics in the treatment of sexual offenders: tentative data on their relationship with indices of behaviour change. *Journal of Sexual Aggression*, **9**, 25–30.

Marshall, W.L., Serran, G., Moulden, H., Mulloy, R., Fernandez, Y.M., Mann, R.E. & Thornton, D. (2002). Therapist features in sexual offender treatment: their reliable identification and influence on behaviour change. *Clinical Psychology and Psychotherapy*, **9**, 395–405.

Marshall, W.L., Ward, T., Mann, R.E., Moulden, H., Fernandez, Y.M., Serran, G.A. & Marshall, L.E. (in press). Working positively with sexual offenders: maximizing the effectiveness of treatment. *Journal of Interpersonal Violence*.

Mayerson, N.H. (1984). Preparing clients for group therapy: a critical review and theoretical formulation. *Clinical Psychology Review*, **4**, 191–213.

Michael, S. (1999). The effects of expressive and hopeful writing on coping with traumatic events. Unpublished master's thesis, University of Kansas, Lawrence.

Miller, W.R., Benefield, R.G. & Tonigan, J.S. (1993). Enhancing motivation for change in problem drinking: a controlled comparison of two therapist styles. *Journal of Consulting & Clinical Psychology*, **61**, 455–61.

Miller, W.R. & Rollnick, S. (2000). *Motivational Interviewing: Preparing People to Change Addictive Behavior*, 2nd edn. New York: Guilford Press.

Miller, W.R. & Sovereign, R.G. (1989). The check-up: a model for early intervention in addictive behaviors. In T. Loberg, W.R. Miller *et al.* (eds), *Addictive Behaviors: Prevention and Early Intervention* (pp. 219–31). Lisse, Netherlands: Swets & Zeitlinger.

Moulden, H.M. & Marshall, W.L. (in press). Hope in the treatment of sexual offenders: the potential application of hope theory. *Psychology, Crime, and Law*.

Patterson, G.R. & Forgatch, M.S. (1985). Therapist behavior as a determinant for client noncompliance: a paradox for the behavior modifier. *Journal of Consulting and Clinical Psychology*, **53**, 846–51.

Prochaska, J.O. & DiClemente, C.C. (1984). *The Transtheoretical Approach: Crossing Traditional Boundaries of Therapy*. Homewood, IL: Dow Jones-Irwin.

Prochaska, J.O. & DiClimente, C.C. (1992). Stages of change in the modification of problem behaviors. In M. Hersen, R.M. Eisler & P.M. Miller (eds), *Progress in Behavior Modification*, vol. 25 (pp. 183–218). Sycamore, IL: Sycamore Publishing.

Rabavilas, A.D., Boulougouris, I.C. & Perissaki, C. (1979). Therapist qualities related to outcome with exposure in vivo in neurotic patients. *Journal of Behaviour Therapy and Experimental Psychiatry*, **10**, 293–4.

Saltzman, C., Luetgert, M.J., Roth, C.H., Creaser, J. & Howard, L. (1976). Formation of therapeutic relationship: experiences during the initial phase of psychotherapy as predictors of treatment duration and outcome. *Journal of Consulting and Clinical Psychology*, **44**, 546–55.

Snyder, C.R. (ed.) (2000). *Handbook of Hope: Theory, Measures, and Applications*. New York: Academic Press.

Strupp, H.H. (1980). Success and failure in time-limited psychotherapy: a systematic comparison of two cases. *Archives of General Psychiatry*, **37**, 595–603.

Strupp, H. & Bloxom, A.L. (1973). Preparing lower class patients for group psychotherapy: development and evaluation of a role-induction film. *Journal of Consulting and Clinical Psychology*, **41**, 373–84.

Whalen, C. (1969). Effects of a model and instructions on group verbal behaviors. *Journal of Consulting and Clinical Psychology*, **33**, 509–21.

Zwick, R. & Attkisson, C.C. (1985). Effectiveness of a client pre-therapy orientation program. *Journal of Counseling Psychology*, **32**, 514–24.

Chapter 15

PUTTING "BEHAVIOR" BACK INTO THE COGNITIVE-BEHAVIORAL TREATMENT OF SEXUAL OFFENDERS

YOLANDA M. FERNANDEZ*, JO SHINGLER[†] AND WILLIAM L. MARSHALL*
* Rockwood Psychological Services, Kingston, Ontario, Canada
[†] Hampshire Probation Service, England

Cognitive-behavioral therapy has now been generally accepted as the most effective approach to treating sexual offenders (Hanson & Bussière, 1998; Hanson et al., 2002). In contrast, early behavioral treatment programs construed the actions of sexual offenders in very simple and strictly behavioral terms. The basis for these early programs was a belief that interest in deviant sexual acts was developed through experience, particularly by the processes of classical conditioning (Laws & Marshall, 2003). As a result early behavioral treatment focussed almost exclusively on behavioral techniques aimed at addressing deviant preferences, primarily through aversive therapy. Deviant stimuli were associated with distressing agents such as nausea-inducing drugs, electric shocks, foul odours or unpleasant covert images.

However, as the field of sexual offender treatment progressed it became obvious there was a need for additional components. Treatment programs became more comprehensive, including components to enhance normative sexual arousal, broaden sexual knowledge, improve social skills, decrease cognitive distortions and enhance empathy (Marshall & Laws, 2003). Certainly this broadening of treatment targets resulted in considerably more comprehensive and effective treatment programs, but as the field has embraced a more "cognitive" approach it appears that, with the exception of specific techniques aimed at modifying deviant sexual interests, many sexual offender treatment programs have become so heavily cognitive that the utilization of behavioral strategies has been either seriously neglected or abandoned altogether. Even the use of behavioral techniques to address deviant sexual interests appears to have waned. This is not to say that the cognitive aspects of sexual offender treatment are unimportant. To the contrary

Sexual Offender Treatment: Controversial Issues. Edited by W.L. Marshall, Y.M. Fernandez, L.E. Marshall and G.A. Serran.   © 2006 John Wiley & Sons, Ltd.

cognitions play a significant role in both offending behavior and strategies to control sexual behavior (Fernandez, Anderson & Marshall, 1999; Langton & Marshall, 2000; Murphy, 1990; Segal & Stermac, 1990). For example, recent groundbreaking ideas have focussed on the role of cognition in both the etiology and treatment of sexual offending (Ward & Keenan, 1999). We are not suggesting that therapists return to the simple reliance on behavioral techniques; however, we do believe that sexual offender therapy would benefit from a better balance between cognitive and behavioral strategies.

First, we feel a need to point to some errors in the way behavior therapy and behavior therapists have been construed. When behavior therapy first became popular, many people saw it as a rather cold inhuman approach in which the therapist somewhat indifferently applied procedures to the client (see Kazdin [1978] for a discussion of these objections). While it is true that some uses of behavioral principles have rightly been criticized (Winett & Winkler, 1972), it is evident that most applications of behavioral principles have been delivered by a warm and caring therapist (Schaap, Bennun, Schindler & Hoogduin, 1993) and have been implemented in a collaborative way with the client (Spiegler & Guevremont, 1998).

The appropriate utilization of behavioral techniques can lead to significant and lasting change just as the inappropriate application of these procedures can be counter-therapeutic. In fact much of everyday social intercourse involves the relatively unsystematic use of behavioral principles. Our point in this chapter is that many cognitive-behavioral treatment programs for sexual offenders do not apply behavioral procedures appropriately and neglect to apply them to aspects of treatment that would markedly benefit from their application. For instance, it is clear that participatory learning is more effective than allowing clients to passively observe what is happening in group treatment (Spiegler & Guevremont, 1998). Despite this many sexual offender treatment programs fail to fully engage each client in discussions and have limited behavioral practices both within the treatment setting and in the client's everyday world.

Behaviorism was the fundamental philosophy that originally guided modern attempts to modify various human problems, and guided much research in basic psychology for many years. Behavior therapy was initially restricted to the application of procedures derived from classical and operant conditioning. B.F. Skinner developed the notion of "operant conditioning", which describes how behavior is changed as a result of the associated consequences. Simply put, those behaviors that are followed by outcomes viewed as favourable by the subject (e.g. receiving food when hungry) will increase in frequency and intensity, whereas those behaviors associated with outcomes viewed as unfavourable by the subject (e.g. not getting food) will decrease in frequency and intensity. Pavlov's demonstrations of what came to be called "classical conditioning" showed that associations also form between stimuli. By repeatedly pairing a previously neutral stimulus with one that automatically elicited a response, the previously neutral stimulus would then likewise elicit the response (see Laws & Marshall [1990] for detailed descriptions of both classical and operant conditioning).

Radical behaviorists (e.g. John B. Watson) suggested that psychology should limit itself to the study of observable behaviors rather than investigate consciousness. However, the extreme views of radical behaviorists fell out of favour as cognitive theorists demonstrated that schemata and interpretations of events are major factors influencing human behavior. Consequently, many behavior therapists began paying attention to thoughts, perceptions, judgements, self-statements and assumptions (Mahoney, 1974). Cognition and behavior are now generally accepted as continually and reciprocally influencing each other with new behavior altering thinking and new modes of thinking facilitating new behaviors (Meichenbaum, 1995). Generally, the cognitive paradigm has blended with the behavioral culminating in the cognitive-behavioral approach. That said, as behavior therapy has become more cognitive it has been suggested that it may be important to make a distinction between the processes that underlie improvement and the procedures that set these processes in motion. In fact, some theorists believe that behavioral procedures are more powerful than strictly verbal ones in affecting cognitive processes (Bandura, 1977). As such, sexual offender treatment programs may benefit from renewing their focus on some of the fundamental strategies of the behavioral approach. To that effect, other therapeutic approaches such as *functional analytic psychotherapy* and *dialectical behavior therapy* have successfully integrated behavioral psychology and psychotherapy.

INTEGRATION OF BEHAVIORAL PRINCIPLES AND THERAPY

Functional Analytic Psychotherapy

Functional analytic psychotherapy (FAP) is a radical behavioral approach to psychotherapy (Kohlenberg & Tsai, 1994). Kohlenberg and Tsai claim that criticisms of behavior therapy are not valid if the approach is applied with "compassion, sensitivity and an understanding of the client's perspective". The main thrust of this therapy is based on instrumental conditioning through reinforcement contingencies. As Kohlenberg and Tsai put it,

> you and I and our clients act the way we do because of the contingencies of reinforcement we have experienced in past relationships. Based on this theory, it follows that clinical improvements, healing or psychotherapeutic change, all of which are certain acts of the clients, also involve contingencies of reinforcement that occur in the relationship between the client and the therapist. (p. 177)

Contingent reinforcement, as described here, refers to the process by which a behavior emerges or is suppressed as a result of the consequences that follow the emission of the behavior. Behaviors that are followed by consequences that are desirable to the person will increase in frequency or intensity, whereas those that are followed by an undesirable consequence will reduce in frequency or intensity.

To illustrate this let us consider the following example. If, when a client is verbally challenged he responds with anger and hostility, and this causes the other person to back down (reinforcement of the client's behavior), a response of anger and hostility will become entrenched as the client's typical response to all challenges. In this example if, instead of backing down, the therapist remains firm but empathic toward the client, then his angry response is not being reinforced and should extinguish. This latter idea that an unreinforced behavior should disappear is based on the human and animal learning literature describing the processes of extinction (Bouton, 1994; Falls, 1998). Not only do behaviors extinguish when the responses they previously elicited are explicitly nonreinforced, they also extinguish when they are ignored. So, for example, if when challenging a client another group member offers a remark that colludes or supports the target client's distortions, the therapist should behave as though the collusive group member had not spoken and continue to question the target client. Only when the otherwise collusive group member offers a more appropriate response should his remark be acknowledged and praised. Thus the therapist, using simple contingency manipulation (i.e. changing their response to the clients' behaviors), can markedly influence behavior in the direction of less disruptive, more appropriate actions and remarks. Behaviors such as listening and responding appropriately to challenges should be reinforced, perhaps by nodding and verbal encouragement.

There is no guarantee, however, that changes resulting from this sort of contingency management will generalize to the client's behavior outside the therapy room. In fact, the evidence suggests that in the absence of direct attempts to produce generalization, it is unlikely that changes in the treatment context will appear in the client's daily life (Spiegler & Guevremont, 1998). Thus, having clients practice outside the treatment setting what they learn in treatment is essential if generalization is to occur. Between sessions practice not only increases skill levels, it also promotes generalization to the client's everyday life.

Generalization is a nonassociative process in which the tendency is to respond similarly in like circumstances. Clearly there is an evolutionarily adaptive advantage to generalization. There is survival value in recognizing a snake as a snake regardless of its color or size. In everyday life, generalization across varying stimuli should produce meaningful and predictable patterns of responses even if the original stimuli are not perfectly reproduced (Barker, 2001). Kohlenberg and Tsai (1994) suggest that the therapeutic environment mirrors that of the real world in its "functional similarity"; that is, the therapeutic environment is similar to the everyday environment to the extent that it elicits the same behaviors. For example, interacting with the group therapist (i.e. someone in a position of authority), should elicit behavior from clients that is similar to what they would demonstrate in interacting with their employer in the workplace (i.e. another authority figure). If the client typically responds to authority by becoming oppositional and aggressive, this will likely happen within the context of the group as well. Similarly, if he typically becomes passive and introverted in the face of authority, he is likely to respond in this manner to the therapist. By responding to clients in a manner that is different from their previous experiences (e.g. responding respectfully, empathetically and encouragingly) clients should begin to change their behavior accordingly.

However, as noted above, for these changes to be evident outside the therapeutic environment, the therapist must program the practice of the new responses in the client's everyday life. This will frequently require the therapist to seek the cooperation of others. For example, in a prison-based treatment program, the therapist could ask prison officers to change the way they respond to the client's hostile responses; in a community program the therapist could elicit the cooperation of the client's employer. In addition, role-play rehearsals of appropriate behaviors can provide the opportunity to refine responding before it is practiced in the real world. However, programmed between-sessions practice of all newly acquired behaviors is essential if generalization from the therapy setting to the real world is to occur.

Kohlenberg and Tsai (1994) also describe the importance of context in defining a behavior as problematic or not (i.e. that you cannot judge behavior as normal/abnormal in the absence of context). What is acceptable behavior in one context (e.g. forcefulness in a contact sport) may not be acceptable in another context (e.g. during sexual behavior). With sexual offenders, while clearly the behavior that brought them to treatment (i.e. sexually offending behavior) is problematic regardless of context, other behaviors may not be as easy to define. For example, looking at adult pornography might be progress for a child abuser, but possibly risky for a rapist who objectified women.

In order to promote generalization from the therapeutic environment into the "real world" Kohlenberg and Tsai's (1994) FAP emphasizes the use of *natural* reinforcers over *contrived* reinforcers. Use of natural reinforcers, Kohlenberg and Tsai claim, is likely to maximize generalization. Natural reinforcers occur typically and reliably in the natural environment, whereas contrived ones generally do not. Fining a client for not making eye contact is contrived; smiling and showing interest when he does make eye contact is natural. Contrived reinforcers can be effective when the environment is restricted, but they are less effective when the changed behaviors are expected to generalize to everyday life. Verbal reinforcement of a behavior (e.g. "I'm pleased you used assertiveness skills there") is unlikely to occur in the natural environment, whereas taking clients seriously and listening to their needs is more likely to occur in both therapy and the natural environment. Therefore, if the therapist follows a behavior by attending and smiling, this is more likely to produce generalization outside the therapy room.

Kohlenberg and Tsai comment that most people find some sort of social cues reinforcing. If we think about our own lives, we can all think of people we prefer to spend time with, and those we avoid. Those we choose to spend time with are those that provide us with the reinforcement we find valuable, be that time to talk, being confided in, being listened to, or whatever. These reinforcers are made use of in Kohlenberg and Tsai's program by using them strategically to effect change. A skilled and responsive therapist is likely to use social reinforcers (e.g. nodding, smiling, providing time to talk in the groups, listening) in every interaction with clients. These reinforcers will be effective when they occur in response to functional and socially "acceptable" behaviors. Therapists who pay less attention to such behaviors may, unwittingly, both produce a reduction in cooperative behavior and reinforce dysfunctional and socially disabling behaviors (e.g. interrupting, shouting, failing to listen to others, egocentrism). The aim in paying more attention to these issues is to make more strategic use of contingencies to generate prosocial behavior change in clients. Kohlenberg and Tsai note there is a "need to structure therapy so that genuine reactions to client behavior naturally reinforce improvements as they happen... a sensitive and genuine therapist can naturally reinforce improvements as they occur" (1994; p. 180).

Dialectical Behavior Therapy

Dialectical behavior therapy (DBT) was designed for use with clients suffering from *borderline personality disorder*. In her description of DBT, Linehan (1993) makes use of both direct and indirect behavioral approaches. She comments that, in the use of contingency management, "The aim is to harness the power of therapeutic contingencies to benefit the patient" (p. 294). Again reinforcement contingencies are constantly being used within the context of therapy. The aim of a skilled therapist is to be aware of the role of contingencies and to use them strategically to bring about desired therapeutic change. Linehan also points out that "contingency procedures require the therapist to carefully monitor and organize his/her own interactions with the patient so that behaviors targeted for change are not inadvertently reinforced while positive, adaptive behaviors are ignored" (Linehan, 1993, p. 294). This emphasizes the need for therapists to be aware of the contingencies maintaining problem behaviors and to constantly monitor the client's behavior and their own responses to the client's behavior in order to make the best use of contingency management. As an example, social cues such as verbal encouragement, smiling and nodding may be reinforcing for some individuals but less effective for others. Drawing attention to a shy person by praising them for group participation may have the unintended effect of making the person withdraw further. More subtle encouragement for tentative signs of participation may be more effective with such shy clients. Therapists who consistently monitor clients' responses to the therapist's own behaviors will readily recognize the need to find alternative ways for reinforcing the shy client's participation, such as a meaningful glance in their direction or verbal praise in private.

APPLICATION TO SEXUAL OFFENDER TREATMENT

Having identified other therapeutic approaches that make clear use of behavioral strategies, the next step is to consider how this approach might be used within the context of group work with sexual offenders.

Modifying Deviant Interests

The explicit use of behavioral procedures in the treatment of sexual offenders has been prominent in attempts to modify sexual interests or preferences. All the procedures that have been developed or adopted for this use explicitly rest on behavioral principles; typically operant or Pavlovian conditioning processes. Aversive therapies of various kinds (electric, olfactory or covert) were derived from research investigating methods of eliminating avoidance or escape behaviors in infrahuman animals (Laws & Marshall, 2003). However, in the application of these methods to the modification of deviant sexuality, basic principles of learning were frequently ignored or the procedures employed were often rather naive.

Carefully constructing aversive procedures and utilizing naturalistic stimuli and relevant aversive consequences are likely to maximize the effectiveness of behavioral techniques. Early applications of covert sensitization, for example, included as stimuli only the terminal aspects of offending behavior (e.g. having sex with a child). A better strategy would be to develop stimuli that describe the chain of behaviors and thoughts the client typically engages in leading to an offense. Other aversive procedures similarly depict the terminal offense behavior or simply images of potential victims with no accompanying descriptions of a chain of behaviors. As for aversive consequences, it is quite surprising that electric shocks to peripheral body parts (arms or legs) had any effect in reducing deviant sexual interests. It is doubtful that such procedures generated conditioned aversion (Marshall & Eccles, 1993) and there is no evidence that the effects (whatever they were) of reduced deviant interests, manifest in the treatment setting, ever generalized to the client's real world. Using more naturalistic stimuli and relevant consequences should increase the probability of generalization to the real world.

There is unfortunately little evidence (except for single case studies and one group study by Quinsey, Chaplin & Carrigan, 1980) that any aversive procedures generate the desired effects of reduced deviant responding, and what evidence does exist is all based on laboratory-assessed responding rather than documentations of real-life changes. As a result we discourage the use of overt aversive procedures, particularly electric aversion which brings with it images redolent of *Clockwork Orange*. Also punishment often evokes aggression that may be displaced toward innocent people (Sherman, 1990), or it may generate oppositional behaviors (Schmauk, 1970).

Covert sensitization readily allows the construction of stimuli that match the typical sequence of behaviors that precede offending, and permits the use of relevant consequences. For example, an offender's sequence may begin by fantasizing deviant sex or by feeling bored. He may then initiate a chain of behaviors (e.g. the steps involved in seeking out a victim or setting up the opportunity to offend against a readily available victim) that finally end with sexual assault. Consequences that are negative but realistic to the particular offender (e.g. detection, arrest, public exposure, rejection by family and friends, imprisonment and possibly being beaten), could then be used in conjunction with the sequence described in the stimuli. The negative consequences would serve both as punishers (that would be unlikely to generate aggression since they are self-administered) and as ways to interrupt the sequences of offense-directed behaviors. These consequences could be introduced earlier and earlier in the stimulus sequence over time until the punishers would interrupt the sequence at the first thought of offending. Evidence from the general learning literature indicates that interventions that abort behavioral chains at the earliest step in the chain are maximally effective (Domjan, 1998).

If any aversive procedures (covert or overt) are to be used, then the human and infrahuman literature (Axelrod & Apsche, 1983) indicates that the durability of their effects is dependent upon increasing competing behaviors. In the absence of training alternative, competing behaviors, aversive therapy effects have been shown to be short-lived (Linscheid, Hartel & Cooley, 1993). Fortunately, sexual offender treatment programs include training in appropriate ways to meet sexual and relevant needs in prosocial ways (e.g. enhancing attractiveness to adult consenting partners, self-confidence boosting, relationship skills training). However, these elements of treatment are not always well integrated with procedures to change sexual interests. These latter procedures are often completed as a separate module without placing them in the context of training clients in the skills and attitudes necessary to function effectively and prosocially. The tendency to modularize treatment has the danger of not allowing the client to recognize that all elements of treatment are aimed at the goal of providing him with the behavioral, affective and cognitive skills necessary for living effectively in ways that are acceptable to others. This is particularly true for those procedures that attempt to change expressions of sexual interest, which are all too often conducted apart from the rest of therapy in the context of the single goal of altering deviant arousal.

As already noted, employing naturalistic events is likely to maximize the effectiveness of any treatment procedure. Masturbation is a naturally occurring behavior that is practiced almost universally (Hatfield & Rapson, 1996) and is said to play a fundamental role in the emergence of sexual preferences (Abel & Blanchard, 1974; Kinsey, Pomeroy & Martin, 1948; McGuire, Carlisle & Young, 1965). Procedures that associate appropriate sexual fantasies (i.e. consenting sex between adults) with arousal generated by masturbation (so-called "masturbatory reconditioning") are popular but do not rest on well-documented evidence (Laws & Marshall, 1991). However, if practiced correctly and diligently, there is every reason to suppose these procedures will enhance a client's attraction to prosocial sexual activities and partners.

Satiation therapy (Marshall, 1979; Marshall & Lippens, 1977), relies on first generating a refractory (i.e. sexually unresponsive) state in the client by having him masturbate to orgasm. In the post-orgasm refractory state the client repeatedly rehearses his deviant fantasies thereby associating these unacceptable fantasies with a state of sexual unresponsiveness. This satiation procedure has solid supportive evidence (Laws & Marshall, 1991; Marshall & Laws, 2003).

One significant advantage of treatment procedures that rely on masturbation, other than the naturalistic relevance, is that they allow the combination of procedures to eliminate attraction to deviant acts (i.e. satiation) with procedures to enhance attraction to prosocial sex (i.e. masturbatory reconditioning). This meets the requirement already noted that procedures that reduce certain behaviors should always be combined with procedures that increase alternative competing behaviors. Such a combination also makes it easier for the therapist to encourage the client to see all aspects of treatment as an integrated attempt to change his behavior. Because masturbation is a naturally occurring behavior, these procedures can be practiced in the client's environment thereby increasing the likelihood that the changes will generalize to his everyday life. Since they are self-controlled procedures, the client can re-initiate them in the future should there be a re-emergence of his deviant desire. Indeed, with the elimination of any behavior, we can expect spontaneous recovery of the response (Barker, 2001) particularly when the client is under stress (Jacobs & Nadel, 1985) or otherwise upset. However, studies of basic learning processes also indicate that when an extinguished behavior remains unrewarded, instances of spontaneous recovery will eventually disappear (Falls, 1998). Thus so long as a sexual offender refrains from enacting (either overtly or in fantasy) his deviant behavior for some considerable time (perhaps two to three years) it should no longer be a threat to him. In addition, extinction is not simply the passive loss of a behavior; it is always the replacement of the response by some other response (Bouton, 1994); the goal of treatment in the case of sexually offensive behavior is that the problematic behavior will be replaced by prosocial sexual interests.

Although sexual offending seems certain to be associated with thoughts or fantasies about the deviant acts, since all behaviors are associated with relevant thoughts (Ingram, 1986), quite a number of treatment programs have no component that directly assesses or targets sexual interests. Since a substantial number of sexual offenders report ongoing deviant sexual thoughts or fantasies, and associated urges (Abel *et al.*, 1987), it would seem essential to target these deviant interests in treatment. Unless treatment providers can demonstrate that other aspects of their program have an effect on reducing deviant sexual thoughts (see Marshall [1997] for an example of such a demonstration), they should be obliged to directly target these problems.

In summary, then, there are numerous well-defined behavioral procedures that aim at changing deviant sexual interests and one or more should be part of an overall treatment program for sexual offenders. However, there has been a serious neglect of research attention on the evaluation of the effectiveness of these procedures with sexual offenders. It is time those who treat sexual offenders provide either empirical justifications for not addressing deviant sexual interests, or generate evaluations of the effectiveness of the procedures they use to target deviant interests.

Additional Use of Behavioral Procedures

In addition to the use of contingency management, extinction, generalization techniques and the modification of deviant fantasies, other aspects of sexual offender treatment would benefit from increased reliance on behavioral procedures. First programs could include more treatment exercises that are based on behavioral techniques such as modeling, and behavioral rehearsal (or role-playing). In addition to the task of identifying both problematic behaviors and improved strategies for behaving more effectively, clients could further internalize these gains through *in vivo* enactment of the newly identified appropriate strategies and behaviors. As noted earlier, therapists should also more actively use behavioral procedures such as contingency management, reinforcement and extinction in order to influence and shape the behavior of their group members both within and outside of the group setting.

Modeling, Behavioral Rehearsal and Role-playing

Treatment methods which have been found to be most beneficial with criminal offenders, including sexual offenders, involve modeling, graduated practice, behavioral rehearsal, reinforcement and training in both problem-solving and moral reasoning (Andrews & Bonta, 1994). Modeling by the therapist should include alternative, prosocial and more effective thinking and behaviors. It should, of course, take place in all interactions between therapists and group members, and explicitly through statements to do with personal attitudes. For example, the therapist should consistently display empathy toward group members and others since one of the primary targets of sexual offender treatment is to increase each offender's capacity to be empathic, particularly toward their own victims.

Additionally, clients should be instructed to practice or rehearse alternative thinking and behaviors outside the treatment group. These practice opportunities should be individualized for each group member and involve assignments related to areas of deficit for that person. The group member should work out, with the therapist and the group, a way of putting a new skill into practice. These newly identified skills may first be rehearsed within the safety of the group context. For example, once the improved behavior has been identified the therapist may begin by modeling the appropriate behavior during the session. The client should then be required to practice the new skills by mimicking the therapist's behavior during a short role-play, also within the session. If the client has difficulty with the rehearsal it can be broken down into smaller components and the client can practice each section, gradually shaping the overall behavior. All behavioral rehearsals should be immediately followed by reinforcing feedback from both the therapist and group. Eventually, clients should be instructed to practice their skills outside the therapeutic context and report back to the group on their progress. Our treatment manual describes several *in vivo* exercises that are rehearsed within the group and then assigned for outside practice between sessions (Mann & Fernandez, 2001). By doing this we are trying to encourage therapists to incorporate the steps beyond simply having clients identify what they should do. It is rehearsing the newly identified behaviors, first within the group context and eventually within a more "natural" environment, that provides confidence that the offenders will be able to generalize treatment gains to their everyday lives. It should be noted here that in this section we are not recommending the use of offense re-enactment role-plays. Pithers (1997) has outlined the potential problems associated with offense re-enactments and research has shown that the potential benefits are not worth the risk (Webster, Bowers, Mann & Marshall, 2005).

Contingency Management, Reinforcement and Extinction

It is imperative that therapists have a firm understanding of the nature of reinforcement, punishment, shaping and extinction. It should be considered a prerequisite that the therapist is sufficiently familiar with these processes in order to implement them strategically and effectively. Although most therapists claim to have an understanding of reinforcement and punishment principles we have been consistently surprised during our training sessions by how many professionals demonstrate a poor understanding of these issues, often describing or using the techniques ineffectively or incorrectly. This is most clearly illustrated by an adherence to an aggressively confrontational approach to sexual offender treatment despite clear evidence against the value of such an approach. For example, punishment procedures of any kind should be avoided as they are both less effective than reinforcement and, as we have seen, are likely to generate hostile or oppositional responding. Furthermore, there is now clear evidence that confrontation in sexual offender therapy reduces the likelihood of generating the sought after changes in treatment (Marshall *et al.*, 2003).

The first step in using contingency management is assessment. It is not possible to manipulate contingencies until you have identified what contingencies are in operation. The first step then is to identify behaviors that are problematic for the individual and, as a consequence, necessitate change. Additionally, therapists should look for behaviors that are adaptive and need to be maintained or enhanced through shaping. Context is an important consideration, as goals should be based on individual needs, deficits and strengths. Therapists should watch for conditions under which both problematic and adaptive behaviors appear. They should consider if problem behaviors are being (unwittingly) reinforced and conversely if adaptive behaviors are being punished.

The second step is to behaviorally define the target behavior. It is important to describe the behavior non-judgementally in behavioral terms. This allows for clearly defined goals. As an example, identifying a client's behavior as "resistant" does not indicate what aspects of his behavior are problematic and need to change. It also has the effect of "labeling" the client in a negative way that is likely to influence the therapist's response. A better alternative is to describe the behaviors in observational terms, such as "staring out of the window during sessions; not completing homework assignments; arguing with group members". This allows the therapist to more clearly target the problem and define behaviorally what would constitute an improvement.

As a third step the therapist should examine their own behavior to ensure they are not emitting behaviors (overt or subtle) that may be maintaining clients' problem behaviors or undermining prosocial change. It is important to keep in mind that "every therapist response observed or experienced by the patient can be neutral, punishing or reinforcing" (Linehan, 1993). As noted earlier, reinforcers should be as natural as possible. However, it is imperative that therapists evaluate the effect of the reinforcer they choose. Reinforcement and punishment are defined functionally; that is, not by the therapist's intention but rather by the outcome. Kohlenberg and Tsai (1994) note that, "If therapists have been emitting behavior that they think is reinforcing, it would be important for them to actually observe whether they are in fact increasing, decreasing or having no effect on a particular client behavior" (p. 188).

New, more effective behaviors are best developed through shaping. Shaping refers to rewarding small steps toward the target behavior until eventually only the target behavior is rewarded. For example, in attempting to have a client who is minimizing all aspects of his offense move toward accepting full responsibility, it is necessary to encourage him for each admission of some degree of responsibility. Failing to notice subtle changes in the right direction can mean the therapist misses valuable opportunities for learning. Each step toward the new behavior should be reinforced. This can be done during behavioral rehearsals and role-plays within the group sessions. However, it is important not to overdo rewards for initial first steps as this may be so satisfying to the client that he will see little point in making additional progress. Additionally, problematic group behaviors can be targeted using the Premack Principle (i.e. a high probability behavior can be used as a reinforcer for a low probability behavior). For example, if a client is demonstrating resistance in group by not completing homework assignments the therapist can suggest trading something desirable, such as a few minutes of group time to discuss personal issues, as a reward for compliance.

Extinguishing maladaptive behaviors can be more challenging. Withdrawing reinforcement for a problematic behavior (e.g. by ignoring the behavior) should eventually extinguish it; however, it is important to remember that when reinforcement for a maladaptive behavior is withheld the behavior will probably get worse before it gets better (this is known as an extinction burst). Additionally once reinforcement has been withdrawn for the maladaptive behavior the therapist should work to find opportunities to reinforce competing adaptive behaviors.

CONCLUSIONS

It seems that many putatively cognitive-behaviorally based treatment programs for sexual offenders have become considerably more cognitive and less behavioral over time. We believe that a better balance between cognitive and behavioral techniques (e.g. modeling, behavioral rehearsal, contingency management, reinforcement, shaping and extinction) will facilitate the acquisition of treatment gains and provide therapists with strategies for influencing and managing within-group behaviors. In addition, efforts to ensure generalization of treatment gains to the client's natural environment need to be given careful consideration. Designing interventions that are likely to maximize generalization is necessary and it is essential to provide clients with opportunities to practice new skills in their everyday life. Behavioral procedures should begin with a thorough analysis of behavior problems and the contingencies that maintain them at the early stages of treatment. Behavioral strategies should be evaluated on an on-going basis during treatment to ensure they are effective. Approaching group treatment with behavioral techniques in mind requires commitment, effort, flexibility and creativity from the therapist. We believe, however, that the effects on group participation, cohesion and long-term outcome are well worth the effort.

REFERENCES

Abel, G.G. & Blanchard, E.B. (1974). The role of fantasy in the treatment of sexual deviation. *Archives of General Psychiatry*, **30**, 467–75.

Abel, G.G., Becker, J.V., Mittelman, M.S., Cunningham-Rathner, J., Rouleau, J.J. & Murphy, W.D. (1987). Self-reported sex crimes of nonincarcerated paraphiliacs. *Journal of International Violence*, **2**, 3–25.

Andrews, D.A. & Bonta, J. (1994). *The Psychology of Criminal Conduct*. Cincinnati, OH: Anderson Press.

Axelrod, S. & Apsche, J. (eds) (1983). *The Effects of Punishment on Human Behavior*. New York: Academic Press.

Bandura, A. (1997). *Social Learning Theory*. Englewood Cliffs, NJ: Prentice-Hall.

Barker, L. (2001). *Learning and Behavior: Biological, Psychological, and Sociocultural Perspectives*, 3rd edn. Upper Saddle River, NJ: Prentice Hall.

Bouton, M.E. (1994). Conditioning, remembering, and forgetting. *Journal of Experimental Psychology: Animal Behavior Processes*, **20**, 219–31.

Domjan, M. (1998). *The Principles of Learning and Behavior*, 4th edn. Pacific Grove, CA: Brooks/Cole Publishing.

Falls, W.A. (1998). Extinction: a review of theory and the evidence suggesting that memories are not erased with nonreinforcement. In W.O'Donohue (ed.), *Learning and Behavior Therapy* (pp. 205–29). Boston: Allyn & Bacon.

Fernandez, Y.M., Anderson, D. & Marshall, W.L. (1999). The relationship among empathy, cognitive distortions, and self-esteem in sexual offenders. In B.K. Schwartz (eds), *The Sex Offender: Theoretical Advances, Treating Special Populations and Legal Developments*, vol. **III** (pp. 4.1–4.12). Kingston, NJ: Civic Research Institute.

Hanson, R.K. & Bussière, M.T. (1998). Predicting relapse: a meta-analysis of sexual offender recidivism studies. *Journal of Consulting and Clinical Psychology*, **66**, 348–62.

Hanson, R.K., Gordon, A., Harris, A.J.R., Marques, J.K., Murphy, W., Quinsey, V.L. & Seto, M.C. (2002). First report of the Collaborative Outcome Data Project on the effectiveness of psychological treatment for sex offenders. *Sexual Abuse: A Journal of Research and Treatment*, **14**, 169–94.

Hatfield, E. & Rapson, R.L. (1996). *Love & Sex: Cross-cultural Perspectives*. Boston: Allyn & Bacon.

Ingram, R.E. (1986). *Information Processing Approaches to Clinical Psychology*. New York: Academic Press.

Jacobs, W.J. & Nadel, L. (1985). Stress-induced recovery of fears and phobias. *Psychological Review*, **92**, 512–31.

Kazdin, A.E. (1978). *History of Behavior Modification: Experimental Foundations of Contemporary Research*. Baltimore: University Park Press.

Kinsey, A.C., Pomeroy, W.B. & Martin, C.E. (1948). *Sexual Behavior in the Human Male*. Philadelphia: Saunders.

Kohlenberg, R.J. & Tsai, M. (1994). *Functional Analytic Psychotherapy: A Guide for Creating Intense and Curative Therapeutic Relationships*. New York: Plenum Press.

Langton, C.M. & Marshall, W.L. (2000). The role of cognitive distortions in relapse prevention programs. In D.R. Laws, S.M. Hudson & T. Ward (eds), *Remaking Relapse Prevention with Sex Offenders: A Sourcebook* (pp. 167–86). Thousand Oaks, CA: Sage Publications.

Laws, D.R. & Marshall, W.L. (1990). A conditioning theory of the etiology and maintenance of deviant sexual preference and behavior. In W.L. Marshall, D.R. Laws & H.E. Barbaree (eds), *Handbook of Sexual Assault: Issues, Theories, and Treatment of the Offender* (pp. 209–29). New York: Plenum Press.

Laws, D.R. & Marshall, W.L. (1991). Masturbatory reconditioning with sexual deviates: an evaluative review. *Advances in Behaviour Research and Therapy*, **13**, 13–25.

Laws, D.R. & Marshall, W.L. (2003). A brief history of behavioral and cognitive-behavioral approaches to sexual offender treatment: Part 1. Early developments. *Sexual Abuse: A Journal of Research and Treatment*, **15**, 75–92.

Linehan, M.M. (1993). *Cognitive-behavioral Therapy for Borderline Personality Disorders*. New York: Guilford Press.

Linscheid, T.R., Hartel, F. & Cooley, N. (1993). Are aversive procedures durable? A five year follow-up of three individuals treated with contingent electric shock. *Child and Adolescent Mental Health Care*, **3**, 67–76.

Mahoney, M.J. (1974). *Cognition and Behavior Modification*. Cambridge, MASS: Balinger Press.

Mann, R.E. & Fernandez, Y.M. (2001). SOTP Rolling Programme: Treatment Manual. Unpublished manuscript.

Marshall, W.L. (1979). Satiation therapy: a procedure for reducing deviant sexual arousal. *Journal of Applied Behavior Analyses*, **12**, 10–22.

Marshall, W.L. (1997). The relationship between self-esteem and deviant sexual arousal in nonfamilial child molesters. *Behavior Modification*, **21**, 86–96.

Marshall, W.L. & Eccles, A. (1993). Pavlovian conditioning processes in adolescent sex offenders. In H.E. Barbaree, W.L. Marshall & S.M. Hudson (eds), *The Juvenile Sex Offender* (pp. 118–42). New York: Guilford Press.

Marshall, W.L. & Laws, R.D. (2003). A brief history of behavioral and cognitive-behavioral approaches to sexual offender treatment. Part 2. The modern era. *Sexual Abuse: A Journal of Research and Treatment*, **15**, 93–120.

Marshall, W.L. & Lippens, K. (1977). The clinical value of boredom: a procedure for reducing inappropriate sexual interests. *Journal of Nervous and Mental Diseases*, **165**, 283–7.

Marshall, W.L., Serran, G.A., Fernandez, Y.M., Mulloy, R., Mann, R.E. & Thornton, D. (2003). Therapist characteristics in the treatment of sexual offenders: tentative data on their relationship with indices of behavior change. *Journal of Sexual Aggression*, **9**, 25–30.

McGuire, R.J. Carlisle, J.M. and Young, B.G. (1965). Sexual deviations as conditioned behavior: a hypothesis. *Behavior Research and Therapy*, **3**, 185–90.

Meichenbaum, D.H. (1995). Cognitive-behavioral therapy in historical perspective. In B. Bongard & L.E. Beutler (eds), *Comprehensive Textbook of Psychotherapy: Theory and Practice* (pp. 140–58). New York: Oxford University Press.

Murphy, W.D. (1990). Assessment and modification of cognitive distortions in sex offenders. In W.L. Marshall, D.R. Laws & H.E. Barbaree (eds), *Handbook of Sexual Assault: Issues, Theories, and Treatment of the Offender* (pp. 331–42). New York: Plenum Press.

Pithers, W.D. (1997). Maintaining treatment integrity with sexual abusers. *Criminal Justice and Behavior*, **24**, 34–51.

Quinsey, V.L., Chaplin, T.C. & Carrigan, W.F. (1980). Biofeedback and signaled punishment in the modification of inappropriate sexual age preferences. *Behavior Therapy*, **11**, 567–76.

Schaap, C., Bennun, I., Schindler, L. & Hoogduin, K. (1993). *The Therapeutic Relationship in Behavioral Psychotherapy*. New York: John Wiley & Sons.

Schmauk, F.J. (1970). Punishment, arousal, and avoidance learning in sociopaths. *Journal of Abnormal Psychology*, **76**, 325–35.

Segal, Z.V. & Stermac, L.E. (1990). The role of cognition in sexual assault. In W.L. Marshall, D.R. Laws & H.E. Barbaree (eds), *Handbook of Sexual Assault: Issues, Theories, and Treatment of the Offender* (pp. 161–74). New York: Plenum Press.

Sherman, W.M. (1990). *Behavior Modification*. New York: Harper & Row.

Spiegler, M.D. & Guevremont, D.C. (1998). *Contemporary Behavior Therapy*, 3rd edn. Pacific Grove, CA: Brooks/Cole Publishing.

Ward, T. & Keenan, T. (1999). Child molesters: implicit theories. *Journal of Interpersonal Violence*, **14**, 821–38.

Webster, S.D., Bowers, L.E., Mann, R.E. & Marshall, W.L. (2005). Developing empathy in sex offenders: the value of offence re-enactments. *Sexual Abuse: A Journal of Research and Treatment*, **17**, 63–77.

Winett, R.A. & Winkler, R.C. (1972). Current behavior modification in the classroom: be still, be quiet, be docile. *Journal of Applied Behavior Analysis*, **5**, 499–509.

Chapter 16

COLLABORATION IN CLINICAL WORK WITH SEXUAL OFFENDERS: TREATMENT AND RISK ASSESSMENT

JO SHINGLER* AND RUTH E. MANN[†]

* Hampshire Probation Service, England
[†] Offending Behaviour Programmes Unit, HM Prison Service, London, England

Collaboration between client and therapist has not traditionally been seen as a necessary endeavour in sexual offender treatment. Salter (1988), in her influential early text describing sexual offender treatment, explicitly rejects collaboration:

> The rules must be different with child sexual abuse. It is to be expected that the client will have goals the therapist does not share, and the therapist is expected to override the client's wishes . . . It is the therapist who must set out the goals of therapy. (Salter, 1988, p. 88)

This paper will argue that Salter's position is unnecessarily restrictive, and that to reject the idea of collaboration forcefully is likely to damage the client's participation and ultimate achievement of treatment goals. We agree that many sexual offenders have different goals from their therapists, particularly early in treatment. However, we contend that collaboration is so advantageous that it should be attempted even in these circumstances. We argue that the more the therapist and the client can find common ground, treat each other with respect and show mutual commitment to the therapeutic process, the more likely it is that the ultimate goals of sexual offender treatment will be realized. While we advocate collaboration throughout the assessment and treatment of sexual offenders, here we will particularly focus on the task of dynamic risk assessment as a previously unrecognized opportunity for collaborative working.

Sexual Offender Treatment: Controversial Issues. Edited by W.L. Marshall, Y.M. Fernandez, L.E. Marshall and G.A. Serran.   © 2006 John Wiley & Sons, Ltd.

COLLABORATION

We use the term "collaboration" to refer to a practice in which the therapist works with the client to define together the nature of the client's problems and to agree on a process for working towards solutions to the problems. Collaboration requires that the client be fully and respectfully involved in all decisions and all therapeutic endeavours. The therapist and the client participate equally in agreeing to the content and structure of therapy.

Collaboration is particularly emphasized in three approaches applicable to sexual offender treatment. In cognitive therapy, relapse prevention and motivational interviewing, collaboration is seen as essential. To illustrate, we briefly review the use of collaboration within these three approaches.

Cognitive Therapy

Cognitive therapy is one of the best documented and evaluated psychological therapies for emotional, behavioural and personality disorders. Cognitive therapy originated in the work of Aaron T. Beck, with clients suffering from depression (Beck, Rush, Shaw & Emery, 1979). Since that time, the principles of cognitive therapy have been applied to a wide range of psychological, emotional and behavioural problems (Salkovskis, 1996).

Collaboration is a key aspect of cognitive therapy. The notion of "collaborative empiricism" is at the centre of this approach (Beck, 1976). Cognitive therapy is viewed as team-work, where the therapist and client decide together what is to happen next in therapy. J. Beck (1995) also highlights the importance of helping clients determine the accuracy and utility of their ideas, rather than expecting them to accept the viewpoint of the therapist.

Throughout J. Beck's (1995) recommendations for clinical practice, clinicians are asked to consider the extent to which they are working collaboratively with clients. Tips are given to help therapists demonstrate to the client that they are interested in collaborating. For example, therapists are encouraged to ask their clients for feedback, either verbally during the session, or written between sessions.

Collaboration may seem easy to establish with depressed or anxious clients, who are desperate to change and have volunteered for therapy. Clients such as these clearly differ in many important respects from those faced by practitioners in the sexual offender field. Sexual offenders are typically not voluntary clients, and at best have limited motivation to change. In these respects, they may be more similar to personality disordered clients than those suffering from mood disorders. Beck and Freeman (1990) emphasize the importance of collaboration in cognitive therapy with personality disordered clients, stating that the "cardinal principle of CT is instilling a sense of collaboration and trust in the client" (p. 66). Beck and Freeman liken this in importance and approach to therapeutic empathy, where therapists make an effort to see things from the clients' perspective. They note the importance of remaining non-judgemental, and recommend avoiding the use of labels as an important part of this.

The work of Jeffrey Young and of Marsha Linehan, both of whom have been pioneers in the application of cognitive therapy to personality disordered clients, also have ideas to offer to those working with sexual offenders. Young (1990) highlights some of the difficulties of applying "straight" cognitive therapy to those with personality disorders. For example, such individuals often cannot access thoughts and feelings easily; there are often difficulties in forming a collaborative working alliance with the client; the client may not have clearly identifiable problems on which therapy can focus; and the individual may not be motivated to complete personal assignments and work on developing self-control strategies. The features of personality disordered clients, then, appear remarkably similar to those presented by sexual offenders. Young's (1990) schema-focussed approach works with these difficulties, not by de-emphasizing collaboration, but rather by *increasing* the role of the therapeutic alliance as a vehicle for change.

Linehan (1993) has applied what she calls "dialectical behavior therapy" (DBT) in her work with borderline personality disordered clients. Despite the difficulties faced in developing a therapeutic alliance with such clients, Linehan emphasizes the importance of collaboration: "Collaborative behaviors are viewed in DBT both as essential to treatment and as a goal of treatment" (Linehan, 1993, p. 132).

In summary, collaboration between therapist and client is a cornerstone of cognitive therapy for all types of disorders. In fact, the more difficult and resistant clients are seen to be, the more collaboration is emphasized as essential to treatment success.

Motivational Interviewing

Motivational interviewing (MI) is an approach that was developed not as a standalone therapy but rather as an adjunct to other approaches. MI was designed to help people prepare for treatment. Originally developed for people with addictive behaviours, MI has since been applied to a wide range of behavioural and health disorders, including offending (Mann, Ginsburg & Weekes, 2002). A collaborative approach is a cornerstone of MI and this is particularly emphasized in the pre-treatment assessment stage. In the first MI sourcebook, Miller and Rollnick (1991) devoted a chapter to the practice of sharing the results assessment with the clients, in a way that would encourage them to co-operate with change rather than resist it. In essence, the approach they recommend is collaborative:

> There is [an] important potential use of pre-treatment assessment which is too often overlooked. This is to use evaluation results as a part of motivational counseling. Providing the client with a thorough summary of findings can be very helpful in building motivation and strengthening commitment to change. (Miller & Rollnick, 1991, pp. 89–90)

Miller and Rollnick (1991) have extensively discussed how to prepare clients for assessment, what to include in assessment, how to assess motivation and how to present findings in a motivational manner. Many of their recommendations are incorporated into the guidelines for risk assessment with sexual offenders that are described below.

Relapse Prevention

Relapse prevention (RP) is a treatment approach that was originally developed to facilitate the maintenance of behaviour change in people with addictive behaviours such as smoking or substance misuse (Marlatt & Gordon, 1985). Early results indicated that RP was effective in minimizing relapse after treatment had successfully accomplished the goal of reducing various addictive behaviours (Dimeff & Marlatt, 1995). In a particularly relevant passage from their book, Marlatt and Gordon noted that in RP:

> The therapist relates to the client as a colleague instead of the usual doctor-client relationship. By doing so, the client begins to adopt the role of objective observer, working along with the therapist as a co-investigator. Instead of feeling one-down and guilty in the eyes of the therapist, the client begins to get some distance from the problem and is more likely to see it objectively and to realise that some control over the behaviour is possible... The decrease in guilt and self blame that derives from this more objective approach is less likely to trigger defensive mechanisms such as denial and resistance to treatment. Increasingly as a result, the client begins to accept greater responsibility for the behaviour and the habit change endeavour. This increased sense of personal responsibility can be enhanced further if the client and therapist work together in the choice of treatment goals... and individualised treatment methods. (Marlatt & Gordon, 1985, p. 225)

While RP methods have been adopted wholesale by sexual offender treatment providers (Laws, 1989), its philosophy has not been so successfully embraced. Sexual offender treatment providers have too frequently omitted the collaborative aspects of the approach (see Mann [2000] for a discussion of this problem), apparently because collaboration does not fit with entrenched assumptions (see comments by Salter [1988] cited earlier). Some experts in the field are now questioning the value of RP in sexual offender treatment (Laws, Hudson & Ward, 2000); perhaps these doubts would not have arisen, had sexual offender therapists delivered RP in the collaborative spirit intended by Marlatt and Gordon (1985).

COLLABORATION WITH SEXUAL OFFENDERS

Collaboration is not an aspect of treatment that has received much attention in the sexual offender literature. However, in recent years, there has been more emphasis in this field on treatment process, therapeutic style and the importance of treatment values, such as honesty, genuineness and mutual respect between therapists and clients. For instance, Marshall, Anderson and Fernandez (1999) included a chapter devoted to the importance of a positive and respectful atmosphere in sexual offender treatment. Several studies (Beech & Fordham, 1997; Marshall et al., 2002, 2003) have shown that a more respectful and empathic approach to working with sexual offenders facilitates the attainment of within-treatment goals (e.g. reduced distortions, acceptance of responsibility, recognition of victim harm, increased coping skills, improved relationship style, identification of offending patterns and the generation of relapse prevention plans). In addition, Marshall et al. (1999) noted that "therapists spend far too much time focussing on clients' deficiencies and not enough time encouraging them to believe in their strengths and capacities to change" (p. 7). This strategy of focussing on deficits conveys to clients that the therapist believes they are broadly dysfunctional. Marshall *et al.* (1999) noted that, "Inadvertently communicating this message to our clients may convince them that they do not have the strengths necessary to meet their needs in prosocial ways, which may persuade them that they are unable to avoid future offending" (p. 42).

In contrast, collaboration communicates to clients that the therapist believes they are capable of understanding and solving their own problems. The collaborative therapist indicates to the client that he has the strengths and potential to change and assists the client in finding the strategies to do so. In this way, the therapist is able to communicate optimism about the future, which is an attribute of a therapist that has been shown to relate to treatment effectiveness (Beech & Fordham, 1997).

In practice, working collaboratively requires being fully open with clients about all aspects of treatment. This includes discussing the content of treatment, therapeutic strategies, the time scale, possible outcomes and the likely implications of those outcomes. Collaborative therapists state clearly the estimated completion date of therapy and engage clients in problem solving any potential negative consequences of this. Respecting the client's freedom to choose is essential in establishing a commitment to change (Miller & Rollnick, 1991; Linehan, 1993) and in building a collaborative relationship.

As well as preparing clients for therapy with open discussions, collaboration requires maintenance of this approach throughout therapy. Therapists should be explicit about the aims, goals and content of therapeutic exercises. Clients should not feel misled into participation, or uncertain and anxious. For example, in one treatment program, an exercise was observed in which one client was instructed to do what he could (without physical contact) to get another seated group member to stand up. Before this exercise, group members were to be told that they were participating in an "ice-breaker", but at the end of the exercise it was revealed that it was actually about understanding how sexual offenders use non-physical means of overcoming victim resistance (Finkelhor, 1984). This example illustrates clearly a non-collaborative approach. To reformulate this exercise in collaborative terms, we would omit instructions that undermine the exercise and say to clients, "We are going to look at how we communicate and the strategies we use to persuade people."

In what is, in many ways, an unequal relationship, therapists must do what they can to promote a sense of team-work with their clients. This means taking clients' concerns seriously, and enabling them to have as much control over their therapy as is possible. It means ensuring that clients are fully and respectfully consulted about all therapeutic processes. If clients ask personal questions that the therapist finds inappropriate, the therapist must find a respectful way to explain why they will not answer; for example, "I can understand why you want to ask me about myself, as this relationship probably seems quite unequal—I do the asking and you do the talking. Part of my role as your therapist, however, is to be a bit more distant than say a friend or relative might be, so I can help you get some distance from your problems. If I start sharing personal information with you that distance might start to reduce, and I might become less effective." Collaboration is also not about agreeing to the treatment goals prioritized by the client, if these are inappropriate, such as "understanding why my victim led me on". Situations like this could be avoided by being more specific in the initial request for client-identified goals; for example, "What aspects of your own thinking, emotions or behaviour would you like to work on?" If offence-supporting goals persist, therapists must explain clearly why they consider the goal to be unhelpful, and work towards identifying a mutually agreed-upon goal; for example, "I can't agree to working on that goal, as it is more about your victim's behaviour than yours. Let us focus on things you might like to change about yourself, to avoid getting into this position again."

Collaborative therapists facilitate discussion about any objections the client has to any aspects of therapy. This does not mean changing the structure or content of therapy, but it does mean hearing the client's objections without defensiveness. Being fully collaborative also means being prepared to change things to accommodate the client so long as those changes do not result in negative consequences. This is not to say that changes should always be made on request. When the request is unreasonable or cannot be met, this should be explained fully and clearly. In addition, therapists must be honest when decisions are made in the interests of the therapist; for example, "We can't move the sessions to the afternoon because I have to leave the prison at lunchtime." A collaborative relationship means that both clients and therapists have needs that affect their therapeutic relationship and these are made clear. Where possible, all needs are met and respected.

Barriers and Solutions to Collaboration

Given that collaboration is so important, so widely emphasized across well-respected treatment approaches for other problems and so clearly relevant to sexual offender treatment, we can only wonder why it is not an accepted approach with sexual offenders. Unlike cognitive therapy texts, which commonly devote careful consideration to gaining compliance and informed consent, sexual offender treatment texts have not given these issues much emphasis. Indeed, one of the most recent and otherwise comprehensive texts (Marshall *et al.*, 1999) does not mention how compliance is gained or how consent should be sought. The quotation cited at the beginning of this paper from Salter (1988), in fact, indicates how explicitly these notions have been rejected by some clinicians.

Young (1990) commented on the difficulties in working collaboratively with clients with personality disorders, and how some of their behaviours actively work against attempts at collaboration. Such clients are typically overly dependent on, or demanding of the therapist, or refuse to actively engage in treatment. Beck and Freeman (1990) discussed some of the barriers to collaborative working with such clients. Since many of these problems also seem to occur in the therapist–client relationship with sexual offenders' treatment, so we will review the barriers identified by Beck, as well as the barriers we have identified in our clinical practice.

The first potential barrier is that the client may lack the skill to be collaborative. He may not have had experiences encouraging the development of these skills. His distorted thinking may prevent him from trusting the therapist. Many sexual offenders have experienced physical, emotional or sexual abuse as children (Smallbone & Dadds, 2000; Starzyk & Marshall, 2003; Williams & Finkelhor,

1990) and have subsequent attachment difficulties as adults (Marshall, 1989; Ward, McCormack & Hudson, 1995). These experiences, particularly if they involved abuse of trust by an adult care-giver or person in authority, are likely to influence the level of trust with which the sexual offender client approaches treatment. Collaborative therapists approach new therapeutic relationships with empathy and understanding, being prepared to invest time in building the relationship. Collaborative therapists are prepared to openly discuss problems within the therapeutic relationship, and are prepared to adapt their therapeutic style to benefit the client.

Beck and Freeman's (1990) second point is that therapists may lack the skill to develop collaboration. Therapists may lack skills in working with particular aspects of a disorder, or with the behaviour the client presents in sessions. Alternatively, therapists may lack skill in building relationships, and their approach to their role may interfere with their ability to collaborate.

Pithers (1997) discussed some of the ways in which therapists working with sexual offenders may fail to develop therapeutic rapport with clients. In particular, Pithers pointed to problems resulting from therapists adopting hostile societal beliefs about sexual offenders. When this happens, therapists may not act towards their clients in ways that respect their dignity. Such a stance is clearly at odds with the collaborative approach, and is likely to reinforce and accentuate the sexual offender's own hostile, victimized view of the world. Pithers (1997) described some examples of this process in practices designed to enhance victim empathy. In cases such as this, the role of supervision is essential in facilitating skill development in a non-collaborative therapist.

Third, Beck and Freeman (1990) suggested that environmental factors may interfere with efforts to change and may reinforce dysfunctional behaviour. For example, individuals in the client's life may reinforce their dysfunctional thinking, or they may not support the individual in his quest for change. More specifically with sexual offenders, friends and family may reinforce the client's view of himself as a victim, and they may want to see the offender as not fully responsible for his offences. In addition, sexual offenders in prison are often vilified by their peers and even by prison staff. A recent Joint Prison Probation Inspectorate report of English and Welsh prisons (HM Inspectorate of Prisons, 2001) found that prisoners who refuse sexual offender treatment do so mainly because they feel the environment of prison is at odds with the values of treatment. The inmates feared being identified as sexual offenders, and they were afraid to enter treatment. Where possible, steps must be taken to educate significant people outside of the therapeutic relationship in the nature of sexual offending and sexual offender treatment. In English and Welsh prisons that run sexual offender treatment, "staff awareness training" is an annual requirement. The *Thames Valley Sex Offender Groupwork Programme*, a community program run largely in the South of England, includes a short program for partners of sexual offenders participating in the main program (Still, Faux & Wilson, 2001).

Fourth, clients' ideas and beliefs regarding their potential to fail in therapy, Beck and Freeman (1990) point out, may contribute to non-collaboration. This may be mirrored by a general belief that whatever they do is doomed to fail. Research within HM Prison Service (Mann & Beech, 2002; Mann & Shingler, 1999) has found that sexual offenders hold schemas (i.e. basic styles of thinking) of hostility, grievance and revenge and the perception of themselves as disadvantaged. In particular, the last of these patterns is an obstacle to collaboration. Clients with these problems tend not to believe they will succeed in therapy and they find it difficult to accept that they are at least partly responsible for their success or failure. This habitual lack of a sense of self-efficacy reduces the effort made in therapy. Adding to this lack of self-efficacy, the usual approach to sexual offender treatment is to communicate to the client that the pathways to success are likely to be difficult. Indeed, sexual offender clients are often told in many relapse prevention programmes that they are certain to frequently lapse into abuse-supportive beliefs, fantasies and behaviours and they are bound to encounter numerous risky situations from which they must escape. It is hard to communicate such a message in a way that also implies that the therapist believes in the clients' ability to manage their lives in an offence-free style. Thus, some programs may be discouraging collaboration through the construction of this barrier to change.

Fifth, the beliefs clients have regarding the effects of changed attitudes and behaviours on others (e.g. friends and family) may reduce compliance. Typically clients wish to maintain important relationships and some worry that this support will not be maintained if they make radical changes. This appears to be particularly true for sexual offenders who deny having committed an offence. Research within HM Prison Service (Lord & Willmot, in press) has identified the most common reason for denial being that the sexual offender is anxious about the reactions, and possible loss, of family and friends as a result of their admission of guilt. Furthermore, therapists tend to encourage sexual offenders to be more open with their family and friends about their offending and their risk factors, and offenders are asked to engage their support network in monitoring and supporting the relapse prevention plan. Offenders who feel insecure in their personal relationships are likely to fear the effects of such disclosures, and may instead prefer to continue to deny the problem.

Further barriers to collaboration may be related to the client's view of change. Sexual offenders often lack intrinsic motivation to change. For example, they may have been ordered to enter therapy, a lack of motivation may be part of their presenting problems, or it may be that they view their problems as external to themselves, and so do not see a need to change them. A collaborative therapist understands and accepts this dilemma. Alternatively, the goals of therapy may be felt to be unrealistic either by the client or by the therapist. Working collaboratively does not mean doing what the client says, or allowing them to set goals for themselves that are unachievable. In fact, quite the opposite; therapists must help clients to recognize the impracticality of some of their goals and assist them to arrive at a set of goals that are attainable within the limits of their capacities. Collaboration is not the *opposite* of the approach to therapy described by Salter (1988). Collaboration means the search for mutually agreed-upon goals.

It is particularly important to explicitly define mutually agreed-upon goals. Clients and therapists may believe that the goals are implicit in the list of presenting problems, but they may have different views of what the goals are unless they are made explicit. For example, sexual offenders may assume that the therapist is interested in improving the quality of their lives, but the therapist may be focussed on reducing the risk of further offending. In order for proper collaboration to be achieved, both clients and therapists must discuss and then agree upon the goals that are set for therapy, and therapists must pay particular attention to the clients' goals, rather than just working toward their own. This does not mean that goals should be rigid. In fact, part of working collaboratively is to frequently review goals, both to assess progress and to establish whether a particular goal is still meaningful now that some changes have been made. Explicit discussion and formulation of goals ensures that both therapists and clients are clear about what they can expect to achieve. When goals remain implicit, the therapist cannot be sure that the client is working towards the same things.

Frustration with therapy can also be a barrier to collaboration. The client or therapist may be frustrated about lack of progress. This is likely to result in negative thoughts and a sense of hopelessness. This may also arise if the therapist or client has unrealistic ideas about change (i.e. expecting clients to change too quickly). It is therefore important for the therapist to explain to clients the likely time it will take to achieve the goals of treatment. The expected time to achieve the various goals of treatment needs to be discussed and timelines established collaboratively. High risk offenders in particular may be discouraged by observing that they are spending more time in treatment than are lower risk offenders. As a result they may conclude that their problems are intractable unless they have extensive and collaborative discussions with the therapist about the expected schedule for successful treatment. It is during the pre-treatment risk assessment that these discussions should commence. Clients who have their expectations structured more accurately from the outset, and who have the rationale for these expectations explained to them, are less likely to become discouraged.

Barriers to collaboration are not solely located within the therapeutic relationship. Therapists may believe there are statutory barriers to collaborations; for example, rules that prevent them from being fully open with clients, or procedures that require the use of non-collaborative terminology. For example, English and Welsh probation officers working with clients in the community may know, but have to withhold, information about their clients obtained from police surveillance. This creates a barrier to the free discussion of all the information relevant to risk. Similarly, clients in the community are aware of the role of their probation officer in sharing information about risk with other agencies, including the police, and may therefore be motivated to conceal risky thoughts or urges from the person who is their main contact for support. These issues must be approached collaboratively. Clinicians must be open about their role, as well as their limits and responsibilities. They must discuss with the client any need to share information with other agencies and, where possible, encourage the clients to liaise with the other agencies.

RISK ASSESSMENT

"Risk" assessment is a term used for any procedure that aims to predict how likely it is that an offender will offend again. Risk assessment may focus on either static or dynamic factors. Most static risk factors are not amenable to change and include features such as previous offences. Dynamic risk scales consist of factors predictive of recidivism that are amenable to change and that can be targeted by intervention. For instance, commonly agreed-upon dynamic risk factors for sexual offending include deviant sexual preferences, pro-criminal attitudes, anti-social peers, lifestyle impulsivity, poor coping skills and intimacy deficits (Harris & Hanson, 1999). Dynamic risk assessment frameworks for sexual offenders include the Sex Offender Need Assessment Rating (Hanson & Harris, 2001) or Thornton's Structured Risk Assessment (SRA; Thornton, 2002).

In this paper, we will describe how collaboration can be integrated into the application of a dynamic risk assessment framework. The risk assessment procedure we will use as our framework for illustrating a collaborative approach is the Structured Assessment of Risk and Need (SARN; Webster *et al.*, 2004), which was developed from Thornton's SRA. Briefly, SARN consists of two parts: the Risk Matrix 2000, which is a static scale (Thornton, 2002), as well as a dynamic scale. The dynamic scale consists of 16 risk factors divided into four domains: sexual interests, pro-offending attitudes, socio-affective functioning, and self-management. Each offender is assessed for the presence and strength of each of the 16 risk factors leading to the offender's crime and occurring in the offender's general life.

While interviews with the offender are identified as part of the data collection process for this and other similar dynamic risk instruments, little or no guidance is given in the manuals about how to involve the offender in the process. Risk assessment scales often appear as procedures that are "done to" an offender, and which can easily be done without his knowledge or his co-operation. The implication is that risk assessment scales are completed by a detached evaluator, and conducted for the purposes of informing criminal justice decisions, rather than being tools to assist treatment planning or assess post-treatment improvements.

In HM Prison Service, SARN is used as a way of assessing treatment needs prior to interventions being implemented and then as a way of examining progress following treatment. Early experience of introducing SARN into the overall treatment process in HM Prisons indicated that offenders found the process disheartening. They felt they participated in group treatment, developed good rapport and a collaborative relationship with treatment facilitators, and then received a report post-treatment that seemed detached from the treatment process. In particular, they considered the reports to contain conclusions about their risk and need about which they had not been consulted. The early application of the SARN procedure within HM Prisons, therefore, appeared to undermine trust and rapport. In response, we began to look for ways of incorporating risk assessment into the collaborative process of treatment that would respect the dignity and autonomy of the offenders.

Collaboration in Sexual Offender Risk Assessment

Turning to look more specifically at sexual offender risk assessment, Proulx, Tardif, Lamoureux and Lussier (2000) highlighted the importance of offenders being engaged in the process of risk assessment: "First an offender has to understand the recidivism risk factors in his offending process. Second he has to learn the skills to cope appropriately with these risk factors. These two dimensions are necessary to reduce the risk of recidivism in sexual aggressors" (pp. 479–80).

Proulx *et al.* (2000) suggested that one reason why an offender fails to accept his risk factors or identify coping strategies is the failure of the assessor to develop a collaborative relationship with the client. Thus, in their view, a co-operative or collaborative approach between client and assessor is essential if risk assessment is to lead to effective treatment and the development of adequate relapse prevention plans. When risk assessment is not done collaboratively, it leads to post-treatment management structures that are *imposed* on the client, which seems likely to generate resentment and oppositional behaviour. Collaborative approaches to risk assessment should, therefore, facilitate greater co-operation by the client as well as encourage post-discharge supervisors to work collaboratively with the client.

Post-treatment supervision, which of course is aimed at keeping risk to a minimum, can also be made more effective by adopting a collaborative approach. This should involve making clear the roles and responsibilities of the supervisor, including the supervisor's statutory responsibilities. For example, if supervisors are required to pass on information about escalating risk to the police, this should be made clear at the outset as should the definition of "escalating risk" for that client. If and when this risk behaviour manifests itself, a collaborative supervisor will inform the client that the behaviour must be reported and, if possible, discuss with the client how they should go about informing the relevant authorities. The advantages of the collaborative approach are that the client is informed about procedures and has the opportunity to provide information about escalating risk that might not otherwise be available. As many supervisors will retain responsibility for a client following any breach action, taking the collaborative approach reduces the likelihood of damaging the relationship, as might occur if the client felt misled or deceived.

Guidelines for Collaborative Risk Assessment with Sexual Offenders

Collaborative techniques will be successful only if the assessor is genuinely committed to the philosophy of the collaborative approach. As discussed earlier, noncollaborative assessment or treatment is similar to traditional medical treatment, where the client has little or no say and the expert provides a diagnosis and cure. In this approach, there is no negotiation about treatment goals, and the client is not usually made fully aware of the basis for the expert's decisions. Consequently, in this approach, therapists impose their own goals on clients and there is no discussion or attempt to establish mutual goals, or even to explain the relevance of particular interventions. The only input from the client is to provide information about the nature of the problem.

In contrast, collaborative assessors are genuinely committed to working openly with their clients. The collaborative assessor believes that this is the only way in which the client can develop autonomy and self-respect. Such an assessor also understands that for a relationship to be collaborative, it must be perceived in this way by the client as well as by the assessor. The collaborative assessor therefore seeks constant feedback from the client. Given the potential barriers outlined above, and their collective potential for undermining collaborative work, the achievement of a collaborative approach requires considerable effort by the assessor.

First it is necessary to clearly introduce and explain the assessment plan. This includes illustrating how the assessment will proceed and being clear about the form of the final report and how it will be used. It is also important to explain how the assessment can benefit the client. In the application of SARN within HM Prison Service, we changed the language of "dynamic risk assessment" and refer instead to "treatment need assessment". This is a more accurate reflection of the goal of dynamic risk assessment. The assessor should explicitly emphasize their own commitment to working collaboratively and why this is valuable. Since the collaborative approach to assessment is likely to take longer than the usual approach, it is important to enter the collaborative process wholeheartedly, and to commit to the spirit of collaboration.

Whenever any initial negative reactions are evident, these must be dealt with openly. Some clients within the criminal justice system have had negative prior experiences with professionals. A comment inserted inaccurately into an early report may be repeated endlessly in subsequent reports. Clients, especially those in prison, are used to being interviewed and asked questions such as "Do you feel remorse for your crime?" or "Do you have deviant sexual fantasies?" The process of collaborative formulation may be new to them, and they may initially react with suspicion. It is our experience that, even under these circumstances, an assessor genuinely committed to collaboration and willing to explain this commitment will quickly develop a positive rapport with the client.

The results of static and psychometric assessments should be presented openly with the client being asked to collaborate in drawing conclusions from them. Further guidance on how to do this can be found in Miller and Rollnick's (1991) book. They recommended that the assessor present the information gleaned during evaluation in a motivational fashion. Assessment should be presented, Miller and Rollnick suggest, as "a way of finding out what problems (if any) need to be addressed and how best to begin" (p. 90). When a client shows awareness of his problems, the assessor should compliment him. If the client is not aware of his problems, assessment information can be presented as a way of helping the client identify how he ended up in his current situation (i.e. convicted of a sexual offence). This provides a starting point for the offender to determine the areas he would like to work on changing.

Offenders should be asked to assess the relevance of aspects of risk to reoffend. Once a report on the risk assessment is produced in draft form, the client should be asked to read this draft and comment on the views expressed. If he disagrees with any of the comments or conclusions he should be asked to explain why. If his comments appear accurate, the report should be modified accordingly. Each assessed risk factor should be carefully described, as the meaning may not be obvious to the client and some terms used routinely by assessors may be misleading or meaningless to a client (e.g. sexualized violence, entitlement thinking).

Collaborative assessors listen open-mindedly to the client's opinions and incorporate them wherever possible. Clients may know more about themselves than does the assessor, so they should be provided the opportunity to correct inaccurate factual information in the report. It is also important to listen to the client's view of risks. To our surprise, some clients did suggest that some factors presented greater risk while others were said to be less important than was initially thought.

Language should be used carefully. It is necessary to avoid pejorative or labelling terms such as "deviant", "dysfunctional" or "dangerous". Simply describing the behaviour avoids this; for example, describing problematic sexual fantasies as "fantasies about sexual activity with children" rather than "deviant sexual fantasies" reduces the possibility that the offender will see himself as "deviant" and therefore untreatable or certain to reoffend. Treatment goals should be described as "approach goals" (i.e. goals he can work towards) rather than simply describing deficits that put the client at risk. For example, a client might be told, "You would benefit from further opportunities to examine the experience of the victim during the offence", rather than simply saying, "You have outstanding empathy deficits."

These principles, when followed in a genuine manner, have in our experience revolutionized our relationships with our clients. One English prison team, convinced by the value of this approach, recently trained all treatment staff in the collaborative approach and committed itself to conducting all future risk assessments in a collaborative manner. They found that client dissatisfaction, as evidenced by complaints from lawyers acting for the offenders in that prison, very quickly diminished to almost zero. More importantly, the risk assessors and the treatment staff involved discovered a renewed sense of motivation about writing risk assessment reports, as well as more clearly seeing the connection between risk assessment and treatment.

CONCLUSIONS

A collaborative approach is a key feature of numerous well-established treatments for disorders that share similarities with sexual offender treatment and assessment. Despite recent steps forward in research and practice into the importance of therapeutic style in sexual offender treatment, the associated field of risk assessment has remained firmly within the medical model. We have attempted to highlight the advantages of taking a more collaborative approach in risk assessment, and provided clinical examples of our success in implementing this. The next step needs to involve a rigorous evaluation of the benefits of collaborative risk assessment.

REFERENCES

Beck, A.T. (1976). *Cognitive Therapy and the Emotional Disorders*. New York: International Universities Press.
Beck, A.T. & Freeman, A. (1990). *Cognitive Therapy of Personality Disorders*. New York: Guilford Press.
Beck, A.T., Rush, P.J., Shaw, B.F. & Emery, G. (1979). *Cognitive Therapy of Depression*. New York: Guilford Press.
Beck, J. (1995). *Cognitive Therapy: Basics and Beyond*. New York: Guilford Press.
Beech, A. & Fordham, A.S. (1997). Therapeutic climate of sexual offender treatment programs. *Sexual Abuse: A Journal of Research and Treatment*, **9**, 219–37.
Dimeff, L.A. & Marlatt, G.A. (1995). Relapse prevention. In R.K. Hester & W.R. Hiller (eds), *Handbook of Alcoholism Treatment Approaches*, 2nd edn (pp. 176–94). Boston: Allyn & Bacon.
Finkelhor, D. (1984). *Child Sexual Abuse: New Theory and Research*. New York, Free Press.
Hanson, R.K. & Harris, A.J.R. (2001). A structured approach to evaluating change among sexual offenders. *Sexual Abuse: A Journal of Research and Treatment*, **13**, 105–22.

Harris, A.J.R. & Hanson, R.K. (1999). Dynamic predictors of sex offender recidivism—new data from community supervision officers. In B.K. Schwartz (ed.), *The Sex Offender: Theoretical Advances, Treating Special Populations and Legal Developments*, vol. **III** (pp. 9.1–9.12). Kingston, NJ: Civic Research Institute.

HM Inspectorate of Prisons (2001). *Through the Prison Gate: A Joint Thematic Review by HM Inspectorate of Prisons and Probation*. London: HM Inspectorate of Prisons.

Laws, D.R. (ed.) (1989). *Relapse Prevention with Sex Offenders*. New York: Guilford Press.

Laws, D.R., Hudson, S.M. & Ward, T. (eds) (2000). *Remaking Relapse Prevention with Sex Offenders: A Sourcebook*. Thousand Oaks, CA: Sage Publication.

Linehan, M.M. (1993). *Cognitive Behavioral Treatment of Borderline Personality Disorder*. New York: Guilford Press.

Lord, A. & Willmot, P. (in press). The process of overcoming denial in sexual offenders. *Journal of Sexual Aggression*.

Mann, R.E. (2000). Managing resistance and rebellion in relapse prevention intervention. In D.R. Laws, S.M. Hudson & T. Ward (eds), *Remaking Relapse Prevention with Sex Offenders: A Sourcebook* (pp. 187–200). Thousand Oaks, CA: Sage Publications.

Mann, R.E. & Beech, A. (2002). Cognitive distortions, schemas and implicit theories. In T. Ward, D.R. Laws & S.M. Hudson (eds), *Sexual Deviance: Issues, Theories and Treatment* (pp. 135–53). Thousand Oaks, CA: Sage Publications.

Mann, R.E., Ginsburg, J. & Weekes, J. (2002). Motivational interviewing with offenders. In M. McMurran (ed.), *Motivating Offenders to Change: A Guide to Enhancing Engagement in Therapy*, (pp. 87–102). Chichester, England: John Wiley & Sons.

Mann, R.E. & Shingler, J. (1999, September). The role of schemas in sexual offending. Paper presented at the Conference of the National Association for the Treatment of Abusers, York, England.

Marlatt, G.A. & Gordon, J.R. (1985). *Relapse Prevention*. New York: Guilford Press.

Marshall, W.L. (1989). Intimacy, loneliness and sexual offenders. *Behaviour Research and Therapy*, **27**, 491–503.

Marshall, W.L., Anderson, D. & Fernandez, Y.M. (1999). *Cognitive Behavioural Treatment of Sexual Offenders*. Chichester, England: John Wiley & Sons.

Marshall, W.L., Serran, G.A., Fernandez, Y.M., Mulloy, R., Mann, R.E. & Thornton, D. (2003). Therapist characteristics in the treatment of sexual offenders: tentative data on their relationship with indices of behaviour change. *Journal of Sexual Aggression*, **9**, 25–30.

Marshall, W.L., Serran, G., Moulden, H., Mulloy, R., Fernandez, Y.M., Mann., R.E. & Thornton, D. (2002). Therapist features in sexual offender treatment: their reliable identification and influence on behaviour change. *Clinical Psychology and Psychotherapy*, **9**, 395–405.

Miller, W.R. & Rollnick, S. (1991). *Motivational Interviewing: Preparing People to Change Addictive Behaviour*, 2nd edn. New York: Guilford Press.

Pithers, W.D. (1997). Maintaining treatment integrity with sexual abusers. *Criminal Justice and Behavior*, **24**, 34–51.

Proulx, J., Tardif, M., Lamoureux, B. & Lussier, P. (2000). How does recidivism risk assessment predict survival? In D.R. Laws. S.M. Hudson & T. Ward (eds), *Remaking Relapse Prevention with Sex Offenders: A Sourcebook*. Thousand Oaks, CA: Sage Publications.

Salkovskis, P.M. (1996). *Frontiers of Cognitive Therapy*. New York: Oxford University Press.

Salter, A.C. (1988). *Treating Child Sex Offenders and Victims: A Practical Guide*. Newbury Park, CA: Sage Publications.

Smallbone, S.W. & Dadds, M.R. (2000). Attachment and coercive sexual behaviour. *Sexual Abuse: A Journal of Research and Treatment*, **12**, 3–15.

Starzyk, K.B. & Marshall, W.L. (2003). Childhood family and personological risk factors for sexual offending. *Aggression and Violent Behaviour*, **8**, 93–105.

Still, J., Faux, M. & Wilson, C. (2001). The Thames Valley Project Partners' Programme. *Thames Valley Probation Service and Lucy Faithfull Foundation*.

Thornton, D. (2002). Constructing and testing a framework for dynamic risk assessment. *Sexual Abuse: A Journal of Research and Practice*, **14**, 137–51.

Ward, T., McCormack, J. & Hudson, S.M. (1995). Sexual offenders' perceptions of their intimate relationships. *Sexual Abuse: A Journal of Research and Treatment*, **9**, 57–74.

Webster, S.D., Mann, R.E., Carter, A.J., Long, J., Milner, R.J., O'Brien, M.D., Wakeling, H.C. & Ray, H.L. (2004). *Inter-rater Reliability of Dynamic Risk Assessment with Sexual Offenders*. Submitted for publication.

Williams, L.M. & Finkelhor, D. (1990). The characteristics of incestuous fathers: a review of recent studies. In W.L. Marshall, D.R. Laws & H.E. Barbaree (eds), *Handbook of Sexual Abuse: Issues, Theories, and Treatment of the Offender* (pp. 231–55). New York: Plenum Press.

Young, J.E. (1990). *Cognitive Therapy for Personality Disorders: A Schema Focussed Approach* (rev.). Sarasota, FL. Professional Resource Press.

Chapter 17

WHEN ONE SIZE DOESN'T FIT ALL: THE REFORMULATION OF RELAPSE PREVENTION

D. Richard Laws[*] and Tony Ward[†]

[*] Pacific Psychological Assessment Corp., Victoria, British Columbia, Canada
[†] Victoria University, Wellington, New Zealand

In 1978 the senior author was encouraged by a clinical psychology intern named Janice Marques to have a look at an unpublished manuscript. It was entitled "Relapse prevention: A self-control program for the treatment of addictive behaviors" (Marlatt, 1980). At the time Marques was a doctoral student supervised by Alan Marlatt at the University of Washington and had been influenced by his thinking on self-regulation. While the program that Marlatt described was intended for use with alcoholics, Marques stated that she believed that the method he described, relapse prevention (RP), might also work with sexual offenders.

Five years later, Pithers, Marques, Gibat and Marlatt (1983) published a theoretical chapter entitled "Relapse prevention with sexual aggressors: A method for maintaining therapeutic gain and enhancing external supervision". This was the opening salvo in the introduction of RP to the sexual offender treatment field. This chapter was followed shortly by the publication of Marlatt and Gordon's (1985) influential book, *Relapse Prevention: Maintenance Strategies in the Treatment of Addictive Behaviors*. This was a general work intended for the substance abuse field. It was a densely academic work, weaving together theory, recommendations for clinical practice and some empirical data. This book lent RP an enormous cachet of academic and scientific credibility. Firmly entrenching the approach in the sexual offender field, in 1989 Laws published the edited volume, *Relapse Prevention with Sex Offenders*. Although Laws cautioned readers not to take any of the information in the book too seriously, it soon attained an almost cult status in the field, largely because it appeared to be highly programmatic and attempted to show the reader how to perform many of the tasks that seemed essential in the implementation of RP. Unfortunately, the uncritical acceptance of the Marlatt and Gordon (1985)

Sexual Offender Treatment: Controversial Issues. Edited by W.L. Marshall, Y.M. Fernandez, L.E. Marshall and G.A. Serran. © 2006 John Wiley & Sons, Ltd.

and Laws (1989) works resulted in the widespread implementation of a largely unproven treatment approach. Over the following 15 years, the RP approach proliferated, supported by program descriptions (e.g. Marques, Day, Nelson & Miner, 1989; Pithers, Martin & Cumming, 1989), journal articles (e.g. Pithers, 1991), and program manuals (e.g. Steen, 2000), all lacking empirical validation. From the mid-1980s to the mid-1990s, while treatment programs enthusiastically embraced this model, the fundamental tenets of RP successfully escaped empirical scrutiny.

The major attempt at empirical validation was the Sex Offender Evaluation and Treatment Project (SOTEP) in California (Marques *et al.*, 1989; Marques, Nelson, Alarcon & Day, 2000). Begun in 1985 and terminated in 1995, SOTEP has followed program completers, dropouts and nonparticipants ever since. In 1999 Marques reported that a treatment effect had not yet emerged. Marques *et al.* (2000) and Marques, Nelson, Wiederanders and Day (2002) continued to report this result and termed it "unanticipated". These are unfortunate results for the RP approach, particularly since the SOTEP has become so well known and is now imprinted upon the literature. Rice and Harris (2003, p. 433) described SOTEP as "the most well-designed and executed study the sex offender field has ever seen or is likely to see for some time..." Berliner (2002) has summarized what has become the prevailing view toward the classical model of relapse prevention:

> [I]t should not be overlooked that the most well designed and executed study, the California...study that used random assignment, that included volunteers and nonvolunteers, that implemented a state of the art intervention program, that had a follow-up treatment component, and that calculated recidivism in the most comprehensive way found no significant effects for treatment (pp. 196–7).

What does this tell us? In our view the lack of results from the SOTEP say very clearly that there must be something very wrong with this approach, so wrong that the most stringent experimental design has proven unable, over a period now exceeding ten years, to demonstrate a treatment effect.

Is SOTEP an isolated case? Schweitzer and Dwyer (2003) reported an outcome evaluation of a prison-based program in Australia. Like SOTEP it contained the typical cognitive-behavioral components including relapse prevention. Like SOTEP the evaluation was performed on three groups: completers, dropouts and nonparticipants. Like SOTEP no differences in recidivism were found among the groups over an average at-risk period of five years.

The balance of this chapter will be devoted to examining what we believe is wrong with the classical model of relapse prevention with sexual offenders. We will then offer a new approach that is more realistically descriptive of the risks presented by this clientele, and how those risks might be managed. But first, in order to determine its shortcomings, we must examine how RP developed.

RELAPSE PREVENTION WITH SEXUAL OFFENDERS

Marques, Day and Nelson (1992) have described the general RP model as applied to sexual offenders. Basically, the general goal was to help clients anticipate and cope with the problems encountered in a potential relapse. Behavioral, cognitive,

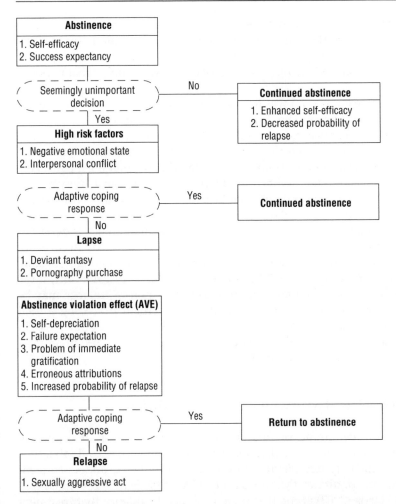

Figure 17.1 The cognitive-behavioral model of relapse in sex offenders. Reprinted with permission of the Centre for Applied Psychology – Forensic Section, University of Leicester, UK.

educational and skill training approaches were employed. The client learned to recognize and interrupt the chain leading to reoffense. There was a specific focus upon identifying and modifying the steps in this behavioral chain.

The basic model of sexual offender RP may be seen in Figure 17.1 (Centre for Applied Psychology, 2000 / 2001; Pithers, 1990, 1991). Although this model might be modified somewhat for any program or individual, the steps always remain approximately the same. It differs very little from the model originally proposed by Marlatt (1985, p. 38).

The original model of RP was intended as a post-treatment maintenance program (Marlatt & Gordon, 1985). In the sexual offender application it has become *both* the treatment program *and* the maintenance program. We find sexual offender RP implemented in two ways. It can simply be an element of an existing program (e.g.

Schweitzer & Dwyer, 2003), or it can become an integrating concept that unifies an entire program. The SOTEP in California is an example of the latter application. The model shown in Figure 17.1 is most often referred to as the cognitive-behavioral model of relapse. The figure is intended to describe only what happens post-treatment.

The model shown in Figure 17.1 was first described by Pithers *et al.* (1983) and has changed very little in 20 years. The downward course from abstinence to relapse is very similar to the schematic described by Marlatt (1985, p. 38) but has been modified to be applicable to sexual offending. For example, in the original substance abuse model, a lapse was defined as taking a single drink or smoking a marijuana cigarette. In the sexual offender modification a lapse is defined as an activity related to but short of a reoffense, such as deviant fantasizing or cruising for victims. Other than this, the models are very similar.

The classical model of relapse prevention applied to sexual offenders describes a downward course from a state of post-treatment abstinence through levels of increasing threat to an initial lapse and ultimately to a relapse involving a sexually aggressive act. In examining Figure 17.1 note that at several critical points, if the individual makes what is called an "adaptive coping response", relapse may be averted. This is true, says the model, up to the last moment preceding a total relapse. This is often called the "one size fits all" model because it assumes, as did the original Marlatt model, that all sexual offenders lapse and relapse in more or less the same manner. And therein lies the problem.

WEAKNESS OF THE SEXUAL OFFENDER RP MODEL

As we noted at the beginning of this chapter, the effectiveness of cognitive-behavioral treatment and, in particular, relapse prevention with sexual offenders, has not been convincingly demonstrated even when conducted under stringent experimental design conditions (Marques *et al.*, 2000, 2002; Schweitzer & Dwyer, 2003). Rice and Harris (2003) argue that there is no good evidence that treatment for sexual offenders works at all. In light of these observations we must examine some of the faults of the RP approach with sexual offenders.

The term "relapse prevention" has been employed in such a profligate fashion that it is often difficult to understand what is actually happening in treatment. The Pithers *et al.* (1989) and Marques *et al.* (1989) program statements were closely aligned with the original Marlatt model of RP. These were initially seen as the standards toward which other programs should aspire. However, as Laws (1995) has noted, many programs have organized activities under an umbrella called "relapse prevention", although many of them had nothing to do with an RP model. Marshall and Anderson (2000) examined the Marques and Pithers models and concluded that, while they were comprehensive, they may have contained too many components and placed unreasonable demands on their participants, convincing them that relapse was all but inevitable.

Thornton (1997) argued that the whole notion of a Marlattian or Marquesan RP model might not even be necessary. According to Thornton, the sexual offender model of RP contains three major problems. First, the constant focus on deviant behavior makes that behavior too visible and tempting. Second, RP was intended for motivated clients, and sexual offenders are typically poorly motivated to alter their behavior. Third, too much time is spent on identifying risk and talking about coping mechanisms while little or no time is spent on actually teaching coping skills. In Thornton's view, the main task of treatment should be the targeting of the essential dynamic risk factors involved in sexual offending and targeting interventions specific to them.

Hanson (2000) finds little in sexual offender RP that is actually new.

> [T]he fundamental principles are not new and ... many distinctive features of RP appear to have limited applicability to sexual offenders. The concepts drawn from traditional behavioural therapy, such as high risk situations and behavioural chains, have generally withstood scrutiny. It is not clear, however, that RP's more innovative concepts, such as the abstinence violation effect or the lapse / relapse distinction, accurately describe the problems faced by sex offenders ... [O]ffenders whose crime patterns do not match the assumptions of RP theory ... are unlikely to derive benefit from attempts to force their accounts into a standard RP mold. (Hanson, 2000, p. 36)

In short, one size does not fit all sexual offenders.

Laws, Hudson and Ward (2000) have noted that one of the main promises of RP was that it would exactly describe what offenders do when they are offending. It has not done this. The scope of the Marques–Pithers model has proven insufficiently broad to encompass the many varieties of sexual offending that are commonly observed:

> The issue of scope ... is a fundamental criticism of the model. For too long we have pretended, while knowing otherwise, that all offenders reflected one offense process or pathway. This must affect how well treatment needs were determined and met, which in turn may well have affected efficacy. (Laws *et al.*, 2000, p. 22)

Should we abandon this model completely? In our judgement we should not. We must acknowledge that the cognitive-behavioral model of relapse pictured in Figure 17.1 does not describe a generic cycle of lapse / relapse. As the 20th century ended, it was abundantly clear that a new model for preventing relapse in sexual offenders was badly needed. It is to this possible solution that we now turn.

THE SELF-REGULATION MODEL OF THE RELAPSE PROCESS

In our view, an adequate model of the relapse process needs to contain a number of offense or relapse pathways, preferably taking into account different types of goals (e.g. approach versus avoidance goals), diverse emotional states (both initial and ongoing), and different types of planning (see Ward & Hudson, 2000). It should explain how cognitive, affective and behavioral factors interact during the offense process. Furthermore, it should account for the dynamic nature of the offense process; that is, the fact that sexually abusive behavior unfolds over time in specific contexts. Finally, it needs to be able to account for the various phases, or milestones, of the offense process, at least as they are currently understood. This is because there is some empirical evidence for phenomena such as background factors, distal vulnerability factors, decisions that lead to high risk situations, the initial lapse, the sexual offense and the impact of the offense on subsequent offending (Ward & Hudson, 2000; Ward, Louden, Hudson & Marshall, 1995).

We have developed a model based on self-regulation and goal theory that meets these criteria for an adequate account of the relapse process (see Ward & Hudson, 2000). In essence, self-regulation consists of the internal and external processes that allow an individual to engage in goal-directed actions over time, and in different contexts (Baumeister & Heatherton, 1996). This includes goal selection, planning, action, monitoring, evaluation and the subsequent modification of behavior (if necessary) in order to accomplish one's goals in an optimal or satisfactory manner (Thompson, 1994).

Goals are key constructs in theories of self-regulation and function to guide the planning, implementation and evaluation of behavior, and essentially represent states that individuals seek to obtain (approach goals) or to avoid (avoidance goals). Avoidance goals are particularly difficult to achieve and are typically associated with negative or anxious emotional states and cognitive ruminations concerning the possibility of failure.

Three types of dysfunctional self-regulation have been identified in the literature (Baumeister & Heatherton, 1996; Carver & Scheier, 1981). First, individuals can fail to control their behavior or emotions, and subsequently behave in a disinhibited manner. This type of self-regulatory failure can be associated with either positive or negative emotions, depending on the actual goals involved. Second, despite possessing generally effective self-regulational skills, individuals may use ineffective strategies to achieve their goals resulting in a loss of control in a specific situation; that is, a misregulation pattern. In the third type of self-regulatory failure, the major problem resides in the choice of goals rather than a breakdown in the components of self-regulation. While the setting of goals and their subsequent planning and implementation by a preferential child molester may be perfectly adequate, the goals themselves could be extremely problematic. An instance of such a problematic goal is the desire to seek an intimate sexual relationship with a child.

We would like to note that the description of the self-regulation (SR) model in this chapter is relatively brief and we refer interested readers to our recent published work for a richer presentation of this approach (e.g. Ward & Hudson, 2000).

The SR model consists of nine different phases which may appear quite seamless to the individual concerned. An offender is able to exit the relapse process at any time by using appropriate coping strategies. In our model, there are four pathways, each characterized by a type of goal and self-regulation strategy or means of achieving the goals (avoidant-passive, avoidant-active, approach-automatic and approach-explicit). There are two relapse pathways associated with avoidance or inhibitory goals where the aim is to not sexually offend. In addition, there are two pathways associated with approach or acquisitional goals. Each of these relapse trajectories is characterized by the use of distinct strategies in relation to sexually offensive contact, and can be further divided into implicit and explicit subpathways. That is, one approach and one avoidant pathway is associated with

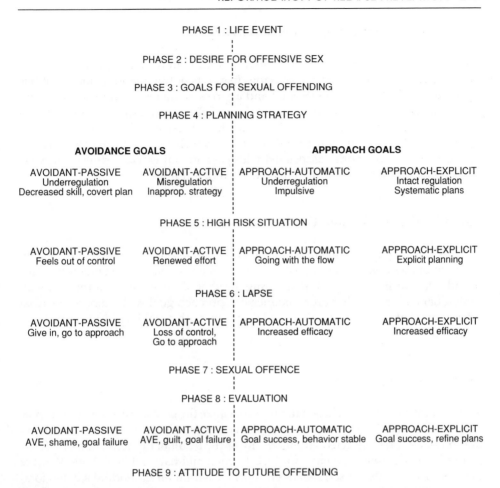

PHASE 1 : LIFE EVENT

PHASE 2 : DESIRE FOR OFFENSIVE SEX

PHASE 3 : GOALS FOR SEXUAL OFFENDING

PHASE 4 : PLANNING STRATEGY

AVOIDANCE GOALS   **APPROACH GOALS**

AVOIDANT-PASSIVE	AVOIDANT-ACTIVE	APPROACH-AUTOMATIC	APPROACH-EXPLICIT
Underregulation	Misregulation	Underregulation	Intact regulation
Decreased skill, covert plan	Inapprop. strategy	Impulsive	Systematic plans

PHASE 5 : HIGH RISK SITUATION

AVOIDANT-PASSIVE	AVOIDANT-ACTIVE	APPROACH-AUTOMATIC	APPROACH-EXPLICIT
Feels out of control	Renewed effort	Going with the flow	Explicit planning

PHASE 6 : LAPSE

AVOIDANT-PASSIVE	AVOIDANT-ACTIVE	APPROACH-AUTOMATIC	APPROACH-EXPLICIT
Give in, go to approach	Loss of control, Go to approach	Increased efficacy	Increased efficacy

PHASE 7 : SEXUAL OFFENCE

PHASE 8 : EVALUATION

AVOIDANT-PASSIVE	AVOIDANT-ACTIVE	APPROACH-AUTOMATIC	APPROACH-EXPLICIT
AVE, shame, goal failure	AVE, guilt, goal failure	Goal success, behavior stable	Goal success, refine plans

PHASE 9 : ATTITUDE TO FUTURE OFFENDING

Figure 17.2 A self-regulation model of the relapse process. Reprinted with permission of the Centre for Applied Psychology – Forensic Section, University of Leicester, UK.

relatively automatic or implicit psychological processes. Because the implicit pathways are characterized by disinhibition, they may be traversed more quickly than the explicit ones. Figure 17.2 illustrates our model.

Phase 1: Life Event

In this first phase some kind of life event occurs and is appraised by an individual who is attempting to remain "abstinent". That is, the individual evaluates the significance and meaning of these life events. The meaning of the event is established in light of the individual's pre-existing implicit theories, needs and abstract goals, and the interpersonal context in which the event occurs.

Phase 2: Desire for Deviant Sex or Activity

The life event and its subsequent evaluation results in the emergence of a desire for offensive sex or maladaptive activities (e.g. acts of humiliation), and emotions associated with these desires. Sexual and aggressive fantasies often co-exist with these desires and could function as mental simulations, increasing the possibility of abusive behavior occurring. These desires are hypothesized to be directly triggered by the person's associations to the event, and may well be outside of his awareness. The activation of memories associated with past offending may prime or increase the accessibility of core dysfunctional beliefs and attitudes.

Phase 3: Offense-Related Goals Established

The desire to engage in deviant sex or a maladaptive activity results in the establishment of an offense-related goal. An offender considers the acceptability of his maladaptive desire and what, if anything, he should do about it. At this point an individual endorses either an avoidance or approach goal with respect to sexual offending. That is, he decides that sexual activity with a child or adult is a good or bad thing.

Phase 4: Strategy Selected

At this point a strategy is chosen in order to realize the goal in question. It is important to stress that this may not be an explicit decision. Goals and their accompanying strategies can be selected automatically as the result of the activation of offense scripts; that is, action sequences for well-learned and habitual behaviors (Ward & Hudson, 2000). Offense scripts are entrenched within an individual's behavioral repertoire and unfold in an automatic and seamless way, typically reflecting years of offending and acquired expertise.

The *avoidant-passive* pathway is characterized by both the desire to avoid sexual offending and the failure to actively attempt to prevent this happening. It involves the inability to control sexually deviant intentions and is an underregulation or disinhibition pathway. Essentially, an offender lacks the skills to cope effectively with a stressor or problem.

The *avoidant-active* or misregulation pathway involves an active attempt to avoid sexual offending. It represents a direct attempt to control deviant thoughts, fantasies or affective states that threaten to lead to a loss of control. The major difference between this relapse route and the avoidant-passive one is that there is an explicit attempt to deal with the threat to restraint. The problem is that the selected strategies are not appropriate and, paradoxically, increase the probability of an offense occurring. That is, they backfire on the person concerned.

The third pathway, *approach-automatic*, involves following entrenched behavioral scripts designed to lead to a sexual offense. Such behavior is relatively impulsive and only planned in a fairly rudimentary way; it appears to occur "out of the blue" and unfolds in a relatively short period of time. It is essentially an underregulation or disinhibition pathway, but differs from the avoidant-passive route to relapse by virtue of its association with an approach goal and appetitive processes. In a sense, it represents a planned impulsiveness (Pithers, 1990).

Finally, the fourth pathway, *approach-explicit*, involves conscious, explicit planning and well-crafted strategies that result in a sexual offense. Thus, there is intact self-regulation but problematic goals as, for example, where there are inappropriate standards concerning sex with children or attitudes toward women. The notion of disinhibition does not apply to such individuals; they do not lose control and do not use sex to escape from or reduce powerful negative emotional states. Rather, the reverse might very well be true; these offenders may have the goal of maintaining or heightening positive emotions through the offending act.

Phase 5: High Risk Situation Entered

In the next stage, contact with the victim comes about as a consequence of the earlier implicit or explicit planning or counterproductive strategies. The individual is hypothesized to re-evaluate his situation at this point because of contact, or the opportunity for contact, with a potential victim. This represents an important event and the nature of this evaluation reflects the offender's initial goals. For those attempting to control or inhibit their behavior, it means failure, and for offenders whose goals are acquisitional ones, it signals the likelihood of success.

Phase 6: Lapse

The next phase in the model concerns the immediate precursors to the sexual offense, involving behaviors such as entering a child's bedroom. In relapse prevention terms, the offender has lapsed and is intending to engage in a sexual offense. We suggest that at this point individuals following the avoidant-passive pathway will replace their avoidance goals with an approach goal. This may be only temporary, and reflects the impact of disinhibition and regulation at a lower level of control. They are hypothesized to give up attempting to control their behavior and become preoccupied with the prospect of sexual gratification. Similarly, the avoidant-active individual will also judge the attempt to actively control his deviant sexual desires as a failure and, as a consequence, adopt an approach or acquisitional goal. Those offenders with approach goals will continue to strive towards goal satisfaction. Offenders whose offending is driven by automatic processes may exhibit aggressive behavior reflecting their impulsivity. Those individuals with explicit approach strategies should demonstrate careful planning and management of the situation and any potential obstacles.

Phase 7: Sexual Offense

At this point the sexual offense occurs. The style of offending (i.e. degree of violence, type of activity, relationship with victim) is hypothesized to reflect the specific features associated with the different pathways. It is important to note that chronically accessible goals and interpersonal themes will partly determine the manner in which offending is manifested and accomplished. For example, offenders with longstanding negative attitudes towards women are expected to relish the opportunity to express these feelings in their offending behavior. The undercontrolled or misregulated individual (left pathways) is likely to be more self-focused, presumably related to the fact that he has become disinhibited and intent on meeting his own needs. Because of the loss of control the sexual offense may be extremely intrusive, and associated with greater levels of violence.

Phase 8: Post-offense Evaluation

Following the sexual offense, an appraisal process is likely to occur because of the implications for individuals' goals. That is, offenders will ask themselves, "Was what happened a good or bad thing? Did I achieve what I set out to, and if not, why?" Offenders following the avoidant pathways are hypothesized to evaluate themselves negatively and feel guilt or shame (a classic abstinence violation effect— see Ward, Hudson & Marshall, 1994). This is because they failed to achieve the important goal of abstinence from further sexual offending. Offenders who have approach goals should experience positive affect due to the fact they have achieved their goals.

Phase 9: Attitude Towards Future Offending

The final stage of the model concerns the impact of sexual offending on future intentions and expectations. Those men whose goals are inhibitory may resolve to not offend in the future and attempt to reassert control or return to the use of misregulation strategies. However, it is possible that they could re-evaluate their goals and decide that they lack the ability to refrain from further sexual abuse and therefore continue offending. Alternatively, some individuals might be persuaded that sexual offending represents a positive option and change their goals to approach or acquisitory ones.

Individuals characterized by the approach-automatic offense route are likely to have the lower-level behavioral scripts associated with their sexual offending reinforced and strengthened because of their "success". Relatedly, those men following the approach-explicit pathway should continue to refine and develop their abuse-related strategies (i.e. "expertise"); they are expected to learn from their experiences and to adjust their *modus operandi* accordingly. Because of the successful achievement of their approach goals, men following the two acquisitional relapse routes are expected to continue pursuing their goals of sexually assaulting women or children and are unlikely to attempt future restraint.

The above model represents an advance over the classical RP approach because of its inclusion of diverse offense pathways and a theoretically richer account of the goals and strategies associated with the relapse process. It also provides a coherent conceptual basis for the self-management focus of cognitive-behavioral therapy. The motivational properties of goals means that therapists should assess the kind of goals individuals possess, and whether or not they are acquisitory or inhibitory. For example, preferential child offenders are more likely to have distorted or problematic goals, and attempt to establish sexual contact with a child, rather than try to control their behavior.

In addition, the treatment needs of offenders who are characterized by undercontrol or misregulation are strikingly different from those with intact self-regulation skills. For example, problems with impulse control, mood management and managing unexpected high risk situations are likely to be common in offenders generally characterized by self-regulatory deficiencies. However these issues are unlikely to be primary treatment targets for a classic pedophile with distorted beliefs about adult–child sexual contact; such individuals are hypothesized to possess good self-regulatory skills.

FUTURE DIRECTIONS

We would like to briefly describe two exciting developments concerning the SR model. The first refers to an emerging research literature explicitly designed to (independently) evaluate the construct validity and clinical utility of the model. The second involves the theoretical integration of the SR model with the good lives theory of offender rehabilitation.

Two recent studies have examined the empirical adequacy of the self-regulation model. Bickley and Beech (2002) considered the four pathways and their implications for intervention at the Lucy Faithfull Foundation's Wolvercote Clinic, a residential assessment and treatment facility for adult male child abusers in the UK. They found that the SR model could be reliably employed in the classification of an independent sample of 87 child abusers, with interrater agreement found in more than 80% of the sample. Furthermore, differences across the two group distinctions (avoidant / approach and active / passive) in both the psychometric and offense demographic data provided objective support for the validity of the framework. The results showed that in comparison to avoidant goal abusers, approach goal abusers had significantly higher levels of cognitive distortions regarding the appropriateness of sexual contact with children; higher levels of emotional congruence (identification) with children; and more distortions regarding the likely impact of their abuse on their victims.

Webster (in press) investigated the validity of the SR model with a UK sample of child molesters and rapists (n = 25) who had sexually recidivated after completing sexual offender treatment. An additional aim was to ascertain whether offense pathways remain stable pre-treatment and after a post-treatment sexual reoffense. Participants were administered an offense-specific semi-structured pathways interview, which assessed their affect and behavior related to their offending both pre-treatment and post-treatment. The interview consisted of questions for each of the nine phases of the SR model. Webster found that the overwhelming majority of the participants' offense characteristics could be coded into the nine phases of the model. He also found that the pathways tended to remain stable between pre- and post-treatment, indicating that treatment had no appreciable effect on this process.

Webster noted that the SR model was not used to identify treatment needs and therefore the lack of change was not surprising. An interesting finding was that the majority of offenders were classified as approach-explicit, a group typically not considered by the classical RP model with its focus on disinhibition and negative affect.

Ward and Stewart (2003) have recently argued that the treatment of sex offenders should amount to more than the management or reduction of risk factors. They have developed the good lives model which stipulates that treatment should focus on the promotion of goods in an offender's life (goods of relationship, autonomy, health, work, etc.) alongside the management of risk (i.e. relapse prevention). They propose that treatment plans for sexual offenders should be explicitly constructed in the form of a good lives conceptualization, that—taking into account their preferences, strengths, primary goods, and relevant environments—specifies exactly what competencies and resources are required to achieve these goods. In this model, risk factors are viewed as distortions in the internal and external conditions required to secure basic human goods rather than being viewed as relatively isolated, free-floating factors.

Conceptualizing RP (a risk management approach) within the framework of a strength-based, positive theory such as the good lives model, means that therapists will avoid the trap of primarily focusing on avoiding and reducing risk factors and think more broadly about the kinds of lives offenders may need to adopt in lieu of an offense lifestyle. In other words, by helping individuals acquire the internal and external conditions required to live more satisfying and socially acceptable lives, therapists automatically target risk factors. This is because risk factors are the skill deficits, maladaptive belief systems and social and relationship problems that obstruct or distort the pursuit of personal goods. For example, impulsivity means an individual will find it almost impossible to achieve the goods of autonomy, competency, community connectedness and relatedness. This is because his actions will inevitably undermine his attempts to achieve these valued outcomes; a lack of behavioral control could result in interpersonal violence, job loss or the failure of a cherished life plan.

CONCLUSIONS

In this chapter we have critically examined the classical RP model with respect to its ability to accommodate individual differences in offending style and subsequent treatment needs. In our view, its lack of scope and internal conceptual problems means that it does not have the resources to guide the treatment of sexual offenders. In place of this approach we outlined the SR model recently developed by Ward and Hudson. According to this model there are at least four relapse pathways, each associated with specific clusters of problems that require different interventions. Aside from its greater comprehensiveness this theory arguably provides a more coherent account of the relapse process. In the final section two recent empirical studies supporting the SR model were briefly described and an attempt to integrate it with a positive, strength-based treatment framework was discussed. These initiatives are important as they ensure theory underpinning practice is scrutinized and systematically evaluated. While theories and ideas matter and provide clinicians with roadmaps for their day-to-day encounters with offenders, a poor map can derail treatment efforts and even result in extremely negative outcomes. We owe it to the community, our colleagues and the offenders themselves to think more critically about the practical and theoretical components of treatment.

REFERENCES

Baumeister, R.F. & Heatherton, T.F. (1996). Self-regulation failure: an overview. *Psychological Inquiry*, **7**, 1–15.

Berliner, L. (2002). Commentary. *Sexual Abuse: A Journal of Research and Treatment*, **14**, 195–7.

Bickley, J. & Beech, A.R. (2002). An empirical investigation of the Ward and Hudson self-regulation model of the sexual offence process with child abusers. *Journal of Interpersonal Violence*, **17**, 371–93.

Carver, C.S. & Scheier, M.F. (1981). *Attention and Self-regulation: A Control Theory Approach to Human Behavior*. New York: Springer-Verlag.

Centre for Applied Psychology (2000 / 2001). *Module 1. Cognitive-behavioural Theory and Practice*. Leicester, UK: University of Leicester.

Hanson, R.K. (2000). What is so special about relapse prevention? In D.R. Laws, S.M. Hudson & T. Ward (eds), *Remaking Relapse Prevention with Sex Offenders: A Sourcebook* (pp. 27–38). Thousand Oaks, CA: Sage Publications.

Laws, D.R. (ed.) (1989). *Relapse Prevention with Sex Offenders*. New York: Guilford Press.

Laws, D.R. (1995). Central elements in relapse prevention procedures with sex offenders. *Psychology, Crime, and Law*, **2**, 41–53.

Laws, D.R., Hudson, S.M. & Ward, T. (2000). The original model of relapse prevention: promises unfulfilled. In D.R. Laws, S.M. Hudson & T. Ward (eds), *Remaking Relapse Prevention with Sex Offenders: A Sourcebook* (pp. 3–24). Thousand Oaks, CA: Sage Publications.

Marlatt, G.A. (1980). Relapse prevention: A self-control program for the treatment of addictive behaviors. Unpublished manuscript, University of Washington, Seattle.

Marlatt, G.A. (1985). Relapse prevention: theoretical rationale and overview of the model. In G.A. Marlatt & J.R. Gordon (eds), *Relapse Prevention* (pp. 3–70). New York: Guilford Press.

Marlatt, G.A. & Gordon, J.R. (eds) (1985) *Relapse Prevention: Maintenance Strategies in the Treatment of Addictive Behaviors*. New York: Guilford Press.

Marques, J.K., Day, D.M. & Nelson, C. (1992). Findings and recommendations from California's experimental treatment program. Unpublished manuscript, Sex Offender Treatment and Evaluation Project, Atascadero State Hospital, California.

Marques, J.K., Day, D.M., Nelson, C. & Miner, M.H. (1989). The Sex Offender Treatment and Evaluation Project: California's relapse prevention program. In D.R. Laws (ed.), *Relapse Prevention with Sex offenders* (pp. 247–67). New York: Guilford Press.

Marques, J.K., Nelson, C., Alarcon, J.-M. & Day, D.M. (2000). Preventing relapse in sex offenders : What we learned from SOTEP's experimental treatment program. In D.R. Laws, S.M. Hudson & T. Ward (eds), *Remaking Relapse Prevention with Sex Offenders: A Sourcebook* (pp. 321–40). Thousand Oaks, CA: Sage Publications.

Marques, J.K., Nelson, C., Wiederanders, M. & Day, D.M. (2002, October). Main effects and beyond: new findings from California's Sex Offender Treatment and Evaluation Project (SOTEP). Symposium presented at the meeting of the Association for the Treatment of Sexual Abusers, Montreal (abstract).

Marshall, W.L. & Anderson, D. (2000). Do relapse prevention components enhance treatment effectiveness? In D.R. Laws, S.M. Hudson & T. Ward (eds), *Remaking Relapse Prevention with Sex Offenders* (pp. 39–55). Thousand Oaks, CA: Sage Publications.

Pithers, W.D. (1990). Relapse prevention with sexual aggressors: a method for maintaining therapeutic gain and enhancing external supervision. In W.L. Marshall, D.R.

Laws & Barbaree, H.E. (eds), *Handbook of Sexual Assault* (pp. 343–61). New York: Plenum Publishing.

Pithers, W.D. (1991). Relapse prevention with sexual aggressors. *Forum on Corrections Research*, **3**, 20–3.

Pithers, W.D., Marques, J.K., Gibat, C.C. & Marlatt, G.A. (1983). Relapse prevention: a self-control model of treatment and maintenance of change for sexual aggressives. In J. Greer & I. Stuart (eds), *The Sexual Aggressor* (pp. 214–39). New York: Van Nostrand Reinhold.

Pithers, W.D., Martin, G.R. & Cumming, G.F. (1989). Vermont Treatment Program for Sexual Aggressors. In D.R. Laws (ed.), *Relapse Prevention with Sex Offenders* (pp. 292–310). New York: Guilford Press.

Rice, M.E. & Harris, G.T. (2003). The size and sign of treatment effects in sex offender therapy. In R.A. Prentky, M.C. Seto & A. Burgess (eds), *Understanding and Managing Sexually Coercive Behavior* (pp. 428–40). New York: Annals of the New York Academy of Sciences 989.

Schweitzer, R. & Dwyer, J. (2003). Sex crime recidivism: evaluation of a sexual offender treatment program. *Journal of Interpersonal Violence*, **18**, 1292–1310.

Steen, C. (2000). *Adult Relapse Prevention Workbook*. Brandon, VT: Safer Society Press.

Thompson, R.A. (1994). Emotional regulation: a theme in search of definition. In N.A. Fox (ed.), *The Development of Emotion Regulation: Biological and Behavioral Considerations* (pp. 25–52). Monographs of the Society for Research in Child Development, Vol. 59, Serial No. 240.

Thornton, D. (1997, October). Is relapse prevention really necessary? Paper presented at the 16th Annual Research and Treatment Conference of the Association for the Treatment of Sexual Abusers, Arlington, VA.

Ward, T. & Hudson, S.M. (2000). A self-regulation model of relapse prevention. In D.R. Laws, S.M. Hudson & T. Ward (eds), *Remaking Relapse Prevention with Sex Offenders: A Sourcebook* (pp. 79–101). Thousand Oaks, CA: Sage Publications.

Ward, T., Hudson, S.M. & Marshall, W.L. (1994). The abstinence violation effect in child molesters. *Behaviour Research and Therapy*, **32**, 431–7.

Ward, T., Louden, K., Hudson, S.M. & Marshall, W.L. (1995). A descriptive model of the offense chain for child molesters. *Journal of Interpersonal Violence*, **10**, 453–73.

Ward, T. & Stewart, C.A. (2003). The treatment of sex offenders: risk management and good lives. *Professional Psychology: Research and Practice*, **34**, 353–60.

Webster, S.D. (in press). Pathways to sexual offence recidivism following treatment: an examination of the Ward and Hudson self-regulation model of relapse. *Journal of Interpersonal Violence*.

Chapter 18

APPRAISING TREATMENT OUTCOME WITH SEXUAL OFFENDERS

William L. Marshall

Rockwood Psychological Services, Kingston, Ontario, Canada

Evaluating the effectiveness of sexual offender treatment is no simple task. Tracking the offenders after treatment is fraught with problems. In the first place different countries have tracking systems that vary considerably in their completeness. Canada, for example, has a national data base accessible to approved researchers. This national data base is fed by police and prosecuting attorneys who are required by law to enter all charges and convictions. Thus official recidivism rates in Canada can be accurately tracked. In the United States, on the other hand, while there is a national data base, some states do not participate and others vary in the degree of thoroughness with which they enter convictions. Some other countries have either no national data base or a similarly inadequate one. These discrepancies in the completeness of data bases make it difficult to know how adequate treatment evaluations are across different countries.

However, before we even get to problems of the adequacy of the data upon which treatment evaluations depend, there are serious problems in designing a study to evaluate sexual offender treatment. Some programs simply report the recidivism rates post-treatment without offering any comparative data on untreated offenders; clearly these reports do not provide acceptable grounds for inferring the effectiveness of treatment. Evaluations must provide data on a comparable group of untreated offenders if we are to determine the value of treatment. The question is: how is this untreated group to be formed? The following discussion will examine strategies that have been employed in such appraisals. There have been ongoing discussions for some years concerning both how treatment programs for sexual offenders should be evaluated and what the body of outcome evaluations tell us about effectiveness. These two issues are intimately related in that the stance taken regarding the standards for evaluating treatment determines which outcome studies will enter into consideration in an evaluation of the overall effectiveness of treatment.

Sexual Offender Treatment: Controversial Issues. Edited by W.L. Marshall, Y.M. Fernandez, L.E. Marshall and G.A. Serran.   © 2006 John Wiley & Sons, Ltd.

THE RCT DESIGN

Harris, Quinsey and Rice and their colleagues (Harris, Rice & Quinsey, 1998; Quinsey, Harris, Rice & Lalumière, 1993; Rice & Harris, 1997, 2003) as well as McConaghy (1998, 1999), have strongly recommended what is called the *randomized controlled trial* (RCT; Bangert-Drowns, Wells-Parker & Chevillard, 1997; Boruch, Synder & De Moya, 2000; Chambless & Hollon, 1998; Geddes & Harrison, 1997; Shadish & Ragsdale, 1996). Basically the RCT strategy applied to treatment evaluations requires that clients who are willing to participate be randomly assigned to either treatment or no-treatment. Clearly such a design permits strong inferences concerning the efficacy, or not, of the program under evaluation. The question of relevance, however, concerns the inferences drawn from RCT efficacy studies for the effectiveness of programs applied in clinical practice.

Generalization Issues Concerning RCT Designs

Rice and Harris (2003) follow the practice of researchers in psychotherapy in distinguishing between "efficacy" and "effectiveness" studies of treatment. They state their position as demanding "relatively high quality" research which they say is closer to efficacy evaluation (i.e. RCT studies). In the past they have demanded RCT designs as the only basis for inferring treatment efficacy *and* effectiveness (Quinsey et al. 1993). The clear implication from their published statements and conference presentations is that an RCT design is the best way (and perhaps the only way) to inform clinicians about the value of their treatment of sexual offenders. Efficacy is said to be demonstrated by studies in which methodological rigor takes precedence over considerations of clinical relevance; effectiveness, on the other hand, is shown by studies evaluating the clinical application of treatment (see Persons & Silberschatz [1998]) for a detailed consideration of the relevance of these two approaches for actual practice).

Rice and Harris (2003) note that most research evaluating sexual offender treatment has skipped efficacy studies and gone directly to the evaluation of effectiveness. They then indicate that such studies of effectiveness have not, but should have, used RCT designs. They insist that an RCT design is "the gold standard" and the only form of evaluation from which clear inferences can be made. Presumably anything less cannot provide confidence in the meaning of the results. As Rice and Harris (2003) and numerous other authors (Goldfried & Wolfe, 1996; Howard, Moras, Brill, Martinovich & Lutz, 1996; McGuire, 2002b; Persons, 1991; Seligman, 1995), have noted, RCT designs are the typical methodology used in efficacy studies. Unlike Rice and Harris, however, these other authors do not believe RCT designs can be applied to effectiveness research and still retain relevance for clinical practice. In fact these other authors declare that evidence from RCT-designed studies (whether of efficacy or effectiveness) essentially fails to inform clinicians or anyone else of the value of a particular treatment. Even Persons, who, in her joint paper with Silberschatz (Persons & Silberschatz, 1998), argues for the value of efficacy studies using RCT designs, points to factors "that make it difficult to export RCT-supported protocols from research to clinical settings" (p. 126). She notes in particular the need for flexibility in the clinical application of treatment, a point that is relevant to Andrews *et al.*'s (1990) *"principle of specific responsivity"*. This refers to the need to adjust treatment to each client's personal style including his learning style. In addition, several authors (Beech & Hamilton-Giachritsis, in press; Drapeau, in press; Marshall *et al.*, 2002, 2003) have shown that, in the treatment of sexual offenders, the therapist's style and the therapeutic alliance are significant predictors of the attainment of treatment targets (i.e. reduced denial/minimizations, the development of empathy and prosocial attitudes, the enhancement of intimacy and effective coping, reductions in deviance, identification of offence precursors and the generation of relapse prevention plans). It is difficult, if not impossible, to ensure flexibility and effective therapist style within the necessarily highly structured format required in RCT designs.

In all the discussions of efficacy versus effectiveness studies in the general therapeutic literature, the point is made repeatedly that RCT designs require detailed treatment manuals to be followed unswervingly, otherwise the value of RCT designs is lost. Precisely because RCT designs require strict adherence to detailed manuals (and have careful procedures to ensure the integrity of this adherence), they allow us to conclude with confidence that the treatment did or did not produce the hoped-for results (Chambless & Hollon, 1998; McFall, 1991; Persons, 1991; Seligman, 1995, 1996). This very feature, however, markedly limits the generalization of the results of RCT studies to clinical practice.

As Seligman (1995), a very reputable clinical scientist, points out, the very properties that make an RCT design scientifically exemplary make it "the wrong method for empirically validating psychotherapy as it is actually done, because it omits too many crucial elements of what is done in the field" (p. 966). In order to maximize internal validity (i.e. differences between groups are due only to differences in the treatment provided) RCT designs necessarily compromise external validity (i.e. relevance to clinical work). In particular, Seligman notes the deliberate elimination of flexibility on the part of the therapist and yet, as so many authors point out, flexibility, rather than strict adherence to a manual, is what is required in clinical practice (Goldfried & Wolfe, 1996; Howard *et al.*, 1996). As Silberschatz and his colleagues (Silberschatz & Curtis, 1993; Silberschatz, Fretter & Curtis, 1986) have shown, effective therapists tailor treatment to the needs of their clients. In addition, Goldfried and Wolfe (1996) point to the dangers of overmanualizing treatment which they say functions as "more of a straitjacket than a set of guidelines" (p. 1014), and they describe research demonstrating that therapists who stick closely to manuals compromise effectiveness. Also programs that lend themselves to detailed manualization (as in RCT designs) are not widely implemented in clinical practice (Parloff, 1979). RCT designs not only involve detailed manuals that must be inflexibly followed; they also set other rigid rules including defining the precise number of treatment sessions. In clinical practice, hopefully, clients are kept in treatment, or required to repeat treatment, until either the goals are achieved or it is concluded that extending treatment will produce no further gains. In all respects the essence of good treatment is the very flexibility that RCT designs preclude.

Given these considerations, it seems reasonable to propose that the application of RCT designs to the evaluation of sexual offender treatment is very likely to result in a demonstration of a lack of efficacy. The RCT-designed study of California's SOTEP study (Marques, 1999), as predicted, reported little or no effects for treatment, although it is fair to say that Marques (1999) has reanalyzed her data to reveal somewhat encouraging effects.

SUGGESTED IMPLICATIONS OF TREATMENT FAILURES

There have been suggestions reported in Canadian newspapers, as a result of the publicity surrounding the treatment failures reported by Quinsey, Khanna and Malcolm (1998) and Rice, Quinsey and Harris (1991), that treatment be abandoned and replaced by extended supervision and electronic monitoring. However, there is no evidence that extended and intense monitoring has an impact on recidivism. In fact, Gendreau and Goggin (1996) report no effect at all for electronic surveillance and intensive monitoring of general offenders. With offenders in general, McGuire (2002a) reports evidence indicating quite clearly that community service orders, probation orders and probation with extra requirements have no effect on recidivism rates. Although these data do not speak directly to the issue of extended monitoring they are relevant, and McGuire's overall conclusion that punitive measures are ineffective in reducing reoffending is persuasively supported by the literature. No doubt sexual offenders would construe extensive and intensive post-release monitoring (including electronic monitoring) to be punitive.

If unequivocal evidence derived from RCT-designed studies is the gold standard for determining effectiveness, how can monitoring be recommended in lieu of treatment when the evidence indicates these monitoring procedures are ineffective? More to the point, the two studies (Quinsey *et al.*, 1998; Rice *et al.*, 1991) on which the Rice, Harris and Quinsey team based their conclusions and recommendations did not rest upon RCT designs. Interestingly, Rice and Harris (2003) quite correctly point out, when considering the advocacy of "low standards", that one risk such advocacy involves is "that outsiders will perceive that weak inference is promoted in the evaluation of one's own clinical efforts while strong inference is demanded of the efforts of others" (p. 430).

Rice and Harris go to lengths to claim that the Quinsey *et al.* (1998) study is of sufficient methodological sophistication to justify inferences about effectiveness (or in this case, ineffectiveness). However, Quinsey *et al.* compared treated subjects with those who refused treatment and those who were deemed to not need treatment. Rice and Harris (2003) subsequently dismiss other studies using treatment refusers because they claim the evidence indicates that "those who refuse represent greater risk than those who volunteer". Of course using refusers in the Quinsey *et al.* study should, therefore, bias outcome in favour of treatment but the inclusion of clients who did not need treatment would bias against treatment and yet these subjects constituted the major proportion (67%) of the untreated comparison group in Quinsey *et al.*'s study. Rice and Harris conclude, "In our view, the most parsimonious interpretation of these analyses by Quinsey *et al.* . . . is that treatment did not reduce recidivism" (p. 431). Just how this interpretation is seen as parsimonious is not clear. Oddly enough a subsequent re-analysis of this same data (Looman, Abracen & Nicholaichuk, 2000), but using matched untreated sexual offenders (who neither were refusers nor were they judged to not need treatment) is dismissed on methodological grounds. Rice and Harris' primary objection to this study is that the matched no-treatment group was derived from a different location within Correctional Service of Canada prisons. The failure of Rice and Harris to provide grounds for why this might constitute a threat to the validity of the comparison is of concern. Canadian researchers are aware that the laws and sentencing rules are the same across Canada and that federal prisons house all offenders with sentences of two or more years. There is no apparent reason to suppose that groups of sexual offenders from different prisons across Canada would differ in ways that matching would not eliminate.

Rice and Harris (2003) identify six studies in a meta-analysis of treatment outcome studies by Hanson *et al.* (2002) that they consider "meet our criteria for minimally useful evaluation" (p. 436). Among these is the Rice *et al.* (1991) study that found no effect for treatment. The only justification they offer for including this nonrandomized study is provided in the following footnote: "Because dropping out and refusing treatment are risk factors, studies finding no effects of treatment, though not reporting outcomes for dropouts and refusers, do provide useful data about the *lack* of effectiveness of the treatment evaluated" (p. 432, italics in original). This justification cannot be countenanced without also allowing that similar, nonrandomized studies showing treatment effectiveness be given credence. The important points here concern whether dropouts are included among treated subjects (thereby artificially inflating recidivism and biasing against finding an effect), and whether refusers are included among the no-treatment comparison group (thereby inflating their rates of recidivism and biasing in favour of a treatment effect). Rice and Harris do not explain what they did with dropouts and refusers in their 1991 study and a careful read of that report (Rice *et al.*, 1991) fails to clarify this issue. Of perhaps greater relevance, Rice and Harris (2003) note that "In our opinion, few useful scientific data on effectiveness can come from studies contrasting treatment completers with sex offenders not offered treatment because such contrasts almost inevitably entail non-comparable groups" (2003, p. 432). Yet both the Rice *et al.* (1991) study and the Quinsey *et al.* (1998) study used, as comparisons, groups who were not offered treatment.

The facts of the matter are that Rice and Harris (2003), as they have in earlier reports (e.g. Quinsey *et al.*, 1993), set standards for others that they make no attempt to meet themselves. I have no argument with their claim that a randomized design maximizes confidence in the inferences drawn from the results, although I believe these inferences have little relevance for clinical practice. The point of concern is, can we reasonably expect an RCT design study to be enacted in the field of sexual offender treatment appraisal? In commenting on Marques' RCT study (Marques, 1999; Marques, Day, Nelson & West, 1994), which they describe as "the most well-designed and executed study the sex offender treatment field has ever seen", Rice and Harris (2003) add *"or is likely to see for some time"* (p. 433, italics added). No doubt Rice and Harris had in mind the practical constraints that typically limit the possibility of conducting an RCT design study.

PRACTICAL PROBLEMS WITH THE RCT DESIGN

There can be no doubt about the scientific status of the RCT procedures. If such an approach could be applied to the evaluation of the effectiveness (not just efficacy) of treatment then strong inferences could be made about the value of the treatment under examination. This scientific high ground, however, does not overcome the lack of practical relevance of RCT studies as already discussed. In its application to the evaluation of sexual offender treatment, however, the RCT presents both practical and ethical problems. These problems have been identified before and elaborated in greater detail than I have room for here. The interested reader is referred to Barbaree and Langton (in press), Marshall (1993) and Marshall and Pithers (1994).

In order to conduct an outcome study it is currently necessary (or should be) that the proposed research be approved by a committee whose job it is to determine that the project meets adequate scientific and ethical standards. Committees approving an RCT study typically demand that once the accepted follow-up period is complete, subjects allocated to the no-treatment condition be provided treatment, unless of course the treatment fails to produce results in which case an alternative effective treatment should be offered. In treatment evaluations of sexual offenders these requirements (i.e. delayed treatment or the later offer of an effective alternative treatment) typically cannot be met.

In order to clarify this let me use as an illustration projects designed to determine the effectiveness of treatment for anxiety disorders. Several aspects of these studies may be helpful in understanding some of the difficulties that the RCT model presents in the evaluation of sexual offender treatment. Researchers are able to routinely receive approval from research/ethics committees to use RCT strategies in evaluating treatment for various anxiety disorders because of four features of these disorders. First, when anxiety disordered patients agree to enter an evaluation, where they might initially receive no treatment, they are the only ones who continue to suffer until effective treatment is later offered. Their anxiety disorder primarily causes distress only to themselves so they are able to make an informed decision to participate. Second, the follow-up period necessary to determine the effectiveness of treatment for anxiety disorders is typically in the range of six to 12 months. Thus, although this must seem a long time to someone suffering from an anxiety disorder, it does, comparatively speaking, involve a relatively brief delay in providing treatment to those allocated to the no-treatment condition. Third, for anxiety disorders there exist various effective treatments so that if the intervention under study fails to reduce the participants' anxiety they could be offered an effective alternative. Finally, in anxiety studies it is possible to ensure, by closely monitoring the two groups (treatment and no-treatment) during the follow-up period, that no confounds occur that would essentially negate the scientific soundness of the evaluation.

Unfortunately in the evaluation of sexual offender treatment none of these four conditions, necessary to the integrity of the RCT model, can be met. When treatment is withheld from sexual offenders the only distress they may suffer is a delay in release from prison. Sexual offenders, unlike those with other Axis 1 disorders, do not typically suffer ongoing distress as a result of their problem behaviors; those who may suffer are their potential victims. Who then should give informed consent for sexual offenders to enter an RCT evaluation? If their potential victims as a group are among those who must give informed consent, I doubt their consent would be forthcoming after they were told of the risks posed to them.

In terms of a second feature of treatment evaluation (i.e. the length of follow-up required), the failure rates (i.e. recidivism rates) for sexual offenders extend for up to at least 25 years (Bonta & Hanson, 1994). More to the point, recidivism rates are too low prior to at least four years to allow any possibility of detecting differences between treated and untreated subjects (Barbaree, 1997). Thus untreated sexual offenders, or rather their victims, would be at risk of suffering for up to four or more years. At the end of a four-year follow-up study the untreated sexual offenders would be difficult if not impossible to locate in order to offer them treatment (the third feature of a proper evaluation), providing of course treatment proved to be effective. Thus the requirements demanded by ethical and scientific oversight committees cannot typically be met in evaluating sexual offender treatment, which should ensure that the project not be approved.

In addition, the necessarily long follow-up period would make it all but impossible to monitor the subjects carefully enough to minimize confounds. In fact in some circumstances confounds would necessarily arise. Incarcerated sexual offenders in some jurisdictions (e.g. Canadian federal prisons) are not considered eligible for parole if they do not satisfactorily complete treatment. This means that the untreated subjects in an RCT study would remain imprisoned for a longer period than the treated subjects thereby introducing a confound. No doubt this would also increase the likelihood that sexual offenders in such circumstances would not volunteer for an RCT evaluation project. Finally, it seems unlikely that most prison systems that have treatment programs for sexual offenders would allow researchers to deliberately withhold treatment from some in order to evaluate their programs. The potential public response to the commission of a heinous sexual crime by an offender for whom treatment was deliberately withheld is likely to constrain most prison systems from approving an RCT evaluation. It is true that some, but very few, systems have allowed (and in one case significantly funded) an RCT study of sexual offender treatment to be implemented, but to demand this model as the standard for all such evaluations seems unrealistic.

One final point on the RCT approach concerns the adequacy of such an approach to produce appropriate matching of the treated and untreated groups. Both Miner (1997) and Marques (1999), who were involved in California's comprehensive evaluation study, report that the randomization method they employed failed to produce matched treated and untreated groups. The degree to which groups do not match determines the confidence we can place in the findings of such a study. While Hanson *et al.* (2002) note that such differences should "wash out" once a sufficient number of random assignment studies become available, for any one study this problem of adequate matching remains a problem.

TREATMENT EFFECTS

How then can we go about evaluating the effectiveness of sexual offender treatment if we are to eschew the RCT design? Howard *et al.* (1996) discuss quasi-experimental designs and Seligman (1996) outlines several possible approaches that would increase the scientific rigor of such studies. Matching treated subjects with those from an available pool of untreated subjects is the most common suggestion. Hanson (2000; Hanson *et al.*, 2002) has suggested such a design for evaluating sexual offender treatment. Examples of what he calls "incidental" designs compare treated subjects with "offenders from the same jurisdiction before or after in the implementation . . . of a treatment program (or) offenders from parallel jurisdictions who receive (or not) services" (Hanson, 2000, p. 489).

Recognizing the fact that few randomization studies were available of treatment outcome with sexual offenders, Hanson *et al.* (2002) decided to accept into their meta-analysis both RCT reports and studies that employed "incidental" (or "convenience") designs, or what Barbaree and Langton (in press) describe as "quasi-experimental" designs. These incidental designs involved searching the records of the institution or clinic, where the treated subjects were from (or a parallel institution or clinic), for untreated sexual offenders whose offence histories and demographic features matched those in the treatment group. From such reports, it can then be demonstrated statistically that the untreated group matches the treated group, thereby reducing some of the most important potential confounds.

Despite some concerns about the methodologies of studies that have entered meta-analyses evaluating treatment for sexual offenders, the outcome from these meta-analytic reports does appear to offer encouraging signs that treatment with these offenders can be effective. Since sexual offenders are quite heterogeneous, particularly in terms of features relevant to treatment needs and amenability, and since the design of programs differs across centres, no reasonable person would expect all programs to be effective and certainly not equally effective. It is, therefore, not surprising that some of the studies entering Hanson *et al.*'s (2002) meta-analysis were ineffective in reducing recidivism rates. In particular, only one of the three RCT studies entering the meta-analysis demonstrated a significant benefit for treatment. On the other hand, the 17 studies employing incidental designs produced treatment benefits. This discrepancy between RCT and incidental designs in demonstrated treatment effectiveness might be expected given what I previously said about the constraints on the appropriate delivering of treatment demanded by RCT designs.

While it is proper to be reserved in our interpretation of the results of incidental designs (see comments by Berliner [2002], Letourneau [2004], and McConaghy [1998, 1999]), I will present results from recent meta-analyses as illustrative of the potential of sexual offender treatment. Let me point out that, in meta-analyses of treatment for mental health disorders and treatment for nonsex offenders, RCT studies are far from common. For example, in Dowden, Antonowicz and Andrews' (2003) meta-analysis of 40 studies of relapse prevention programs with offenders, only ten used RCT designs. In meta-analytic studies of the treatment of general mental health problems, the proportion using RCT designs is even lower (Lambert & Bergin, 1994). Furthermore, as we have seen there are practical constraints on implementing RCT designs in evaluating sexual offender treatment that are unlikely to disappear in the near future so we have to rely on what is available without overstating the findings. In fact, I will use the findings simply to make the point that criticisms of the magnitude of the effects of sexual offender treatment are misplaced. For example, Berliner (2002) notes in considering the results of the Hanson *et al.* (2002) report that "the effect sizes . . . are not large" (p. 196). In fact, as will be shown below, the effect sizes from sexual offender treatment are quite meaningful and compare favourably with treatment for various other problems. Although it would be better, of course, if our treatment eliminated future offending, we cannot expect it to do substantially better than treatment for other offenders or for medical or mental health problems. In this next section these comparisons will be seen to be favourable.

In order to compare the benefits derived from sexual offender treatment with the benefits generated by the treatment of other problems, it is necessary to convert all treatment effects to a common metric. Conversion to effect sizes achieves this goal. The most common methods of calculating effect sizes involve comparing the mean outcome (i.e. reductions in the problem behavior) of a treated group, with that of an untreated group with the comparison being adjusted for the variability in outcome. In the procedures recommended by Cohen (1969) and Hedges (1981, 1982), the difference between the two means is divided by (or standardized by) the estimate of the overall standard deviation. Various other methods essentially achieve the same thing (Rosenthal, 1994).

In his consideration of the meaning of effect sizes, Cohen (1962) indicated that effect sizes of 0.20 are to be considered small but meaningful, effect sizes of 0.50 are medium, and those at or above 0.80 are large. It should be noted that Cohen was not specifically discussing treatment effects but rather differences between groups in general psychological research. We would not expect treatment effects to approach the magnitude of effects resulting from laboratory-controlled studies in abnormal or social psychological studies so readers may wish to be somewhat more liberal than Cohen in their interpretation of the effect sizes reported in the tables below. This might be particularly appropriate in the case of fields such as sexual offender treatment where we are still learning the factors that control the behavior in question. Effect sizes of treatments for physical and mental disorders, as well as for the treatment of nonsex offenders and sexual offenders, have been presented by Marshall and McGuire (2003) and will be elaborated and extended here.

Effect Sizes for Medical and Mental Disorders

In the treatment of physical disorders there are numerous reports of treatment outcome where the effect sizes are quite low and yet these treatment approaches continue to be applied. The best illustration of this is the so-called "aspirin study" (Steering Committee of the Physicians' Health Study Research Group, 1988). Table 18.1 describes the aspirin study effect size as well as effect sizes for other medical problems.

The aspirin study involved a large-scale, randomized, double-blind study examining the effects on cardiovascular problems of a twice-daily dosage of 81 mg of aspirin. At some point during the study an appraisal was made finding the effect size reported in Table 18.1. At this point the study was stopped as it was claimed it would be unethical to continue to withhold this effective treatment from people who were at risk to die, despite the remarkably small effect size. A controlled study of the effects of propanolol was similarly terminated early by the US National Heart, Lung and Blood Institute because the results were deemed to be so impressive that it would have been wrong to withhold the drug from the placebo subjects. Again the effect size was very small (ES = 0.04). It is also important to note that some established medical treatments when carefully evaluated have been found

Table 18.1 Effect sizes for treatment of physical disorders

	Effect size
Aspirin for myocardial infarction (Steering Committee of the Physicians' Health Study Research Group, 1988)	0.03
Aortocoronary bypass surgery* (Lynn & Donovan, 1980)	0.15
Dipyridamole for angina pectoris* (Sacks et al., 1988)	0.12
Chemotherapy for breast cancer* (Early Breast Cancer Trialists' Collaborative Group, 1988)	0.08
Neuroleptics for dementia* (Schneider et al., 1990)	0.37
Memantine for Alzheimer's Disease (Reisberg et al., 2003)	0.32
AZT for AIDS (Barnes, 1986)	0.23

Note: *Meta-analytic studies. All others are single, large sample studies.

to be ineffective. After several years of using dosages of estrogen plus progestin to reduce the risk of coronary heart disease in post-menopausal women, a careful study revealed no benefits and even suggested the combination may increase the risk of coronary disease (Manson et al., 2003). I make these points not to cast doubts on the overall efficacy of medical approaches; I simply wish to note that scepticism is rarely expressed about the value of medicine in treating disorders whereas scepticism, and even cynicism, is rampant in the media about all psychological treatments particularly those involving sexual offenders.

Contrary to the perception of some media commentators, treatment of mental health problems is quite effective. Table 18.2 describes a somewhat random selection of meta-analytic studies of treatment outcome for various mental health disorders.

The reader will note that, in contrast to the effect sizes reported in Table 18.1 for physical disorders, treatment effects presented in Table 18.2 are almost all above Cohen's standard for large effect sizes (i.e. ≥ 0.80). Lambert and Bergin's (1994) comprehensive examination of the effectiveness of psychotherapy reveals that almost all studies since the early 1980s have reported effects for what Lambert and Bergin call "eclectic" approaches. Upon examination, however, the bulk of the effective studies are behavioral or cognitive-behavioral or have significant components derived from these approaches.

Effect Sizes for Criminal Populations

Table 18.3 describes the results of selected meta-analyses of outcome effects with nonsex offenders and sexual offenders.

Table 18.2 Effect sizes for treatment of mental health disorders

	Effect size
Depression (Quality Assurance Project, 1983)	0.65
Depression (Robinson *et al.*, 1990)	0.84
Agoraphobia (Mattick *et al.*, 1990)	1.62
Agoraphobia (Trull *et al.*, 1988)	2.10
Obsessive-Compulsive disorders (Quality Assurance Project, 1985)	1.34
Public speaking anxiety (Allen *et al.*, 1989)	0.51
Stuttering (Andrews *et al.*, 1980)	1.30
Bulimia (Laessle *et al.*, 1987)	1.14
Marital communication (Wampler, 1982)	0.43

Note: All reports are meta-analyses.

Table 18.3 Effect sizes for treatment of offenders

	Effect size
Nonsex Offenders	
Juvenile offenders	
Garrett (1985)	0.18
Dowden *et al.* (2003)	0.23
Gottschalk *et al.* (1987)	0.22
Adult offenders	
Mayer *et al.* (1986)	0.33
Lösel & Köferl (1989)	0.13
Whitehead & Lab (1989)	0.13
Lipsey (1992)	0.10
Dowden *et al.* (2003)	0.13
Adults and Juveniles	
Andrews *et al.* (1990)	0.10
Redondo *et al.* (1999)	0.15
McGuire (2002a)	0.29
Sexual Offenders	
Hall (1995)	0.24
Alexander (1999)	0.10
Gallagher *et al.* (1999)	
Overall	0.43
CBT/RP	0.47
Hanson *et al.* (2002)	
Overall	0.11
CBT/RP	0.28
Dowden *et al.* (2003)	
RP only	0.13

Note: All studies are meta-analyses.

Nonsex Offenders

As can be seen in Table 18.3 the range of effect sizes with nonsex offenders is $ES = 0.10$ to $ES = 0.33$. Effect sizes lower than $ES = 0.10$ have been reported in meta-analyses (see e.g. Andrews, Dowden & Gendreau, 2003), with some showing no effects (see Wasserman & Miller's [1999] review of juvenile programs and McGuire's [2002b] review of adult programs), and others producing negative effects (see Lipsey & Wilson's [1999] meta-analyses of juvenile programs).

Wasserman and Miller (1999) compared single-focus programs for juvenile offenders with more comprehensive programs and found that the former were typically ineffective (e.g. Bank, Marlowe, Reid, Patterson & Weinrott, 1991; Guerra & Slaby, 1990) while comprehensive approaches produced significant reductions in recidivism. Approaches with juveniles that targeted a range of issues (including interpersonal skills) and employed cognitive behavioural methods were the most effective (see Lipsey & Wilson, 1999).

Similarly with adult offenders those programs that were cognitive-behavioral/social-learning based, were found to be the most effective. For example, Izzo and Ross (1990) demonstrated that cognitive-behavioral (CBT) approaches generated reductions in recidivism that were 2.5 times greater than that produced by other programs. In Table 18.3, the meta-analyses of Mayer, Gensheimer, Davidson and Gottschalk (1986) include only CBT programs with the resulting effect size being the best in the Table ($ES = 0.33$).

Andrews *et al.* (1990) identified as effective only those programs that adhered to what they called the "principles of correctional intervention". The principles Andrews *et al.* adumbrated were: (1) *risk* (treatment should target those at greatest risk to reoffend); (2) *need* (treatment should be directed at empirically identified criminogenic needs); (3) *general responsivity* (treatment should use the most powerful social learning and cognitive behavioural strategies); and (4) *specific responsivity* (treatment should be adjusted to each client's specific personal and learning style and be responsive to mood fluctuations).

In an attempt to directly evaluate the utility of relapse prevention (RP) programs with offenders (both nonsex offenders and sexual offenders), Dowden *et al.* (2003) selected from their larger meta-analyses (Andrews *et al.*, 2003) only those that were identified by their authors as RP programs. Andrews *et al.* (2003) had previously shown that RP programs were associated with a larger effect size ($ES = 0.22$) than were non-RP programs ($ES = 0.07$). Dowden *et al.* identified 24 programs generating 40 tests of effectiveness. Of these tests, nine were derived from programs that did not specify the RP elements in their treatment and another 15 identified only one RP element. These programs were demonstrably less effective than those that specified two or more RP elements.

In a further set of analyses, Dowden *et al.* (2003) found that programs employing CBT/social learning strategies were very effective (eta $= 0.52$), as were those that targeted criminogenic needs (eta $= 0.52$), whereas those that adhered to the risk principle were least effective (eta $= 0.03$). Programs where these principles were relatively absent had no impact on recidivism. Concerning the elements of RP, Dowden *et al.* (2003) found that involving the offender's support group was associated with very significant reductions in recidivism (eta = 0.51) as was identifying offence precursors (eta = 0.40) and rehearsal within treatment of response to potential future risks (eta = 0.51). Interestingly, the provision of booster sessions had a negative impact (eta = −0.18).

Sexual Offenders

As I noted, Berliner (2002) pointed out that while the overall results from the Hanson *et al.* (2002) report are encouraging, the effect size is not large. It is not clear on what basis Berliner was making her evaluation since the effect size reported by Hanson *et al.* for programs that were CBT/RP in approach yielded an effect size (ES = 0.28) above Cohen's rather conservative estimate of an acceptable effect. Berliner suggests that the public demands zero failures. Actually this may not be true as Cullen, Cullen and Wozniak (1988) found that the public is not as severe in their expectations as is often alleged. In addition, the alternatives to treatment that have been evaluated with nonsex offenders (e.g. more severe punishment, longer sentences, intensive supervision, electronic monitoring, "boot camps") have been shown to be clearly ineffective at best and at worst to increase recidivism (Gendreau, Paparozzi, Little & Goddard, 1993) and, of course, the effect of current sentencing practices for sexual offenders is indexed in Hanson *et al.*'s study by the recidivism rates for the untreated group. So long as treatment reduces the number who would offend if treatment was not provided, then surely it is our task as knowledgeable professionals to do our best to accurately inform the public about the benefits of treatment and the lack of effects of alternative strategies. Rice and Harris (2003) quite rightly note that we should not unrealistically raise the public's expectations about the effects of treatment but that does not mean we should belittle the results we do obtain.

There have been criticisms of some of the meta-analyses presented in Table 18.3. Hall's (1995) report has been criticized by both Harris *et al.* (1998) and Hanson *et al.* (2002), as have Alexander's (1999) and the appraisal by Gallagher, Wilson, Hirschfield, Coggeshall and McKenzie (1999). However, Gallagher *et al.*'s study is the more technically sophisticated of the three and can be given more credence. These three reports are included to allow the readers to make up their own mind about the strength of the inferences they wish to draw. Clearly, however, reviewers (except, of course, Rice & Harris, 2003) have found less to be concerned about with Hanson *et al.* (2002) and meta-analytic appraisals by Andrews and his colleagues (in this case Dowden *et al.* 2003) are held in high regard in the field of criminal justice research.

The first point to note from Table 18.3 is that the effects for sexual offender treatment are greatest when programs utilize a CBT/RP approach. Hanson *et al.*, in particular, found a significant effect size for CBT/RP programs but no effect for all other programs. In their evaluation of RP programs for sexual offenders, Dowden *et al.* report an effect size that is approximately half that reported by Hanson *et al.* for CBT/RP programs in general. When we attempted to review studies reporting the effects of RP programs for sexual offenders (Marshall & Anderson, 1996, 2000) we discovered that the details provided, concerning the elements of RP involved, varied very considerably across programs. Dowden *et al.* found the same problem when examining programs for nonsexual offenders, and the reader will recall that those programs that were specific about their RP elements, and that had the most RP elements, were the ones that were most effective. Perhaps, if we removed from the Hanson *et al.* analysis of the CBT/RP programs those that did not specify their RP elements or had only one of less RP elements, the effects might be even greater.

On this point concerning the potential value of RP elements, it is worth remembering that Dowden *et al.*'s analyses also revealed that only some RP elements are associated with reduced recidivism; namely, identifying offence precursors, rehearsing responses to potential risks and training the offender's support group in tracking and monitoring his risk factors.

From a consideration of what has been reviewed in this chapter, I suggest that the type of program most likely to be effective with sexual offenders is one that: (a) is based on a social learning model that employs a cognitive behavioural approach with specified RP elements (particularly those mentioned above); and (b) targets appropriate criminogenic factors (i.e. those features of the offender that are known or thought to present risks and that are amenable to change). Harris and Hanson (1999), for example, have identified empirically established dynamic risk factors that should be the target of both interventions and post-release supervision. In addition, treatment should include Ward's (2002; Ward & Marshall, in press) well-argued claims about the value of enhancing the offender's attitudes and skills necessary to attain a "good life", and Haaven's (Haaven & Coleman, 2000; Haaven, Little & Petre-Niller, 1990) concept of the "new me". Treatment should also be delivered by an empathic, warm, rewarding and somewhat directive therapist (Marshall *et al.*, 2002) who is sufficiently flexible to adjust their own behavior to accommodate the specific responsivity issues relevant to each offender (Andrews *et al.*, 1990). I believe that this type of program will offer the best hope for the future of sexual offender treatment.

At present, however, we can with reasonable confidence claim that sexual offenders can be effectively treated. The benefit of such treatment is to reduce, but unfortunately not eliminate, the number of future victims, and the costs associated with treatment are more than offset by the subsequent reduction in future costs to prosecute, convict and incarcerate reoffenders (Marshall, 1992; Prentkey & Burgess, 1990).

REFERENCES

Alexander, M. (1999). Sexual offender treatment efficacy revisited. *Sexual Abuse: A Journal of Research and Treatment*, **11**, 101–16.

Allen, M., Hunter, J.E. & Donohue, W.A. (1989). Meta-analysis of self-report data on the effectiveness of public speaking anxiety treatment techniques. *Communication Education*, **38**, 54–76.

Andrews, D.A., Dowden, C. & Gendreau, P. (2003). Clinically relevant and psychologically informed approaches to reduce reoffending: a meta-analytic study of human service, risk, need, responsivity, and other concerns in justice contexts. Manuscript submitted for publication, Carleton University, Ottawa, Canada.

Andrews, D.A., Zinger, I., Hoge, R.D., Bonta, J., Gendreau, P. & Cullen, F.T. (1990). Does correctional treatment work? A clinically relevant and psychologically informed meta-analysis. *Criminology*, **28**, 369–404.

Andrews, G., Guitar, B. & Howie, P. (1980). Meta-analysis of the effects of stuttering treatment. *Journal of Speech and Hearing Disorders*, **45**, 287–307.

Bangert-Drowns, R.L., Wells-Parker, E. & Chevillard, I. (1997). Assessing the methodological quality of research in narrative reviews and meta-analyses. In K.J. Bryant, M. Windle & S.G. West (eds), *The Science of Prevention: Methodological Advances from Alcohol and Substance Abuse Research* (pp. 405–29). Washington, DC: American Psychological Association.

Bank, L., Marlowe, J.H., Reid, J.B., Patterson, G.R. & Weinrott, M.R. (1991). A comparative evaluation of parent-training interventions for families of chronic delinquents. *Journal of Abnormal Child Psychology*, **19**, 15–33.

Barbaree, H.E. (1997). Evaluating treatment efficacy with sexual offenders: the insensitivity of recidivism studies to treatment effects. *Sexual Abuse: A Journal of Research and Treatment*, **9**, 111–28.

Barbaree, H.E. & Langton, C.M. (in press). Deviant sexual behavior. In D.A. Wolfe & E.J. Mash (eds), *Behavioral and Emotional Disorders in Children and Adolescents: Nature, Assessment and Treatment*. New York: Guilford Press.

Barnes, D.M. (1986). Promising results halt trial of anti-AIDS drug. *Science*, **234**, 15–16.

Beech, A.R. & Hamilton-Giachritsis, C.E. (in press). Relationship between therapeutic climate and treatment outcome in group-based sexual offender treatment programs. *Sexual Abuse: A Journal of Research and Treatment*.

Berliner, L. (2002). Commentary. *Sexual Abuse: A Journal of Research and Treatment*, **14**, 195–7.

Bonta, J. & Hanson, R.K. (1994). Gauging the risk for violence: measurement, impact and strategies for change (User Report No. 1994–09). Ottawa: Ministry Secretariat, Solicitor General of Canada.

Boruch, R., Snyder, B. & DeMoya, D. (2000). The importance of randomized field trials. *Crime and Delinquency*, **46**, 156–80.

Chambless, D.L. & Hollon, S.D. (1998). Defining empirically supported therapies. *Journal of Consulting and Clinical Psychology*, **66**, 7–18.

Cohen, J. (1962). The statistical power of abnormal-social psychological research: a review. *Journal of Abnormal and Social Psychology*, **65**, 145–53.

Cohen, J. (1969). *Statistical Power Analysis for the Behavioral Sciences*. New York: Academic Press.

Cullen, F.T., Cullen, J.B. & Wozniak, J.F. (1988). Is rehabilitation dead? The myth of the punitive public. *Journal of Criminal Justice*, **16**, 303–17.

Dowden, C., Antonowicz, D. & Andrews, D.A. (2003). The effectiveness of relapse prevention with offenders: a meta-analysis. *International Journal of Offender Therapy and Comparative Criminology*, **47**, 516–28.

Drapeau, M. (in press). Research on the processes involved in treating sexual offenders. *Sexual Abuse: A Journal of Research and Treatment*.

Early Breast Cancer Trialists' Collaborative Group (1988). Effects of adjuvant tamoxifen and of cytotoxic therapy on mortality in early breast cancer. *New England Journal of Medicine*, **319**, 1681–92.

Gallagher, C.A., Wilson, D.B., Hirschfield, P., Coggeshall, M.B. & MacKenzie, D.L. (1999). A quantitative review of the effects of sexual offender treatment on sexual offending. *Corrections Management Quarterly*, **3**, 19–29.

Garrett, C.G. (1985). Effects of residential treatment on adjudicated delinquents: a meta-analysis. *Journal of Research in Crime and Delinquency*, **22**, 287–308.

Geddes, J.R. & Harrison, P.J. (1997). Closing the gap between research and practice. *British Journal of Psychiatry*, **171**, 220–25.

Gendreau, P. & Goggin, C. (1996). Principles of effective correctional programming. *Forum on Corrections Research*, **8**, 38–41.

Gendreau, P., Paparozzi, M., Little, T. & Goddard, M. (1993). Does "Punishing Smarter" work? An assessment of the new generation of alternative sanctions in probation. *Forum on Corrections Research*, **5**, 31–4.

Goldfried, M.R. & Wolfe, B. (1996). Psychotherapy practice and research: repairing a strained alliance. *American Psychologist*, **51**, 1007–16.

Gottschalk, R., Davidson, W.S., II, Mayer, J. & Gensheimer, R. (1987). Behavioral approaches with juvenile offenders: a meta-analysis of long-term treatment efficacy. In E.K. Morris & C.J. Braukmann (eds), *Behavioral Approaches to Crime and Delinquency: A Handbook of Application, Research, and Concepts* (pp. 399–422). New York: Plenum Press.

Guerra, N.G. & Slaby, R.G. (1990). Cognitive mediators of aggression in adolescent offenders: 2. Intervention. *Developmental Psychology*, **26**, 269–77.

Haaven, J.L. & Coleman, E.M. (2000). Treatment of the developmentally disabled sex offender. In D.R. Laws, S.M. Hudson & T. Ward (eds), *Remaking Relapse Prevention with Sex Offenders: A Sourcebook* (pp. 369–88). Thousand Oaks, CA: Sage Publications.

Haaven, J.L., Little, R. & Petre-Miller, D. (1990). *Treating Intellectually Disabled Sex Offenders: Model Residential Program*. Orwell, VT: Safer Society Press.

Hall, G.C.N. (1995). Sexual offender recidivism revisited: a meta-analysis of recent treatment studies. *Journal of Consulting and Clinical Psychology*, **63**, 802–9.

Hanson, R.K. (2000). Treatment outcome and evaluation problems (and solutions). In D.R. Laws, S.M. Hudson & T. Ward (eds), *Remaking Relapse Prevention with Sex Offenders: A Sourcebook* (pp. 485–99). Thousand Oaks, CA: Sage Publications.

Hanson, R.K., Gordon, A., Harris, A.J.R., Marques, J.K., Murphy, W.D., Quinsey, V.L. & Seto, M. (2002). First report of the Collaborative Outcome Data Project on the effectiveness of psychological treatment for sex offenders. *Sexual Abuse: A Journal of Research and Treatment*, **14**, 167–92.

Harris, A.J.R. & Hanson, R.K. (1999). Dynamic predictors of sex offender recidivism. New data from community supervision officers. In B.K. Schwartz (ed.), *The Sex Offender: Theoretical Advances, Treating Special Populations and Legal Developments*, vol. **III** (pp. 9.1–9.12). Kingston, NJ: Civic Research Institute.

Harris, G.T., Rice, M.E. & Quinsey, V.L. (1998). Appraisal and management of risk in sexual aggression: implications for criminal justice policy. *Psychology, Public Policy, and Law*, **4**, 73–115.

Hedges, L.V. (1981). Distribution theory for Glass's estimator of effect size and related estimators. *Journal of Education Statistics*, **6**, 107–28.

Hedges, L.V. (1982). Estimation of effect size from a series of independent experiments. *Psychological Bulletin*, **92**, 490–9.

Howard, K.I., Moras, K., Brill, P.L., Martinovich, Z. & Lutz, W. (1996). Evaluation of psychotherapy: efficacy, effectiveness, and patient progress. *American Psychologist*, **51**, 1059–64.

Izzo, R.L. & Ross, R.R. (1990). Meta-analysis of rehabilitation programs for juvenile delinquents. *Criminal Justice and Behavior*, **17**, 134–42.

Lambert, M.J. & Bergin, A.E. (1994). The effectiveness of psychotherapy. In A.E. Bergin & S.L. Garfield (eds), *Handbook of Psychotherapy and Behavior Change*, 4th edn (pp. 143–98). New York: John Wiley.

Laessle, R.G., Zoettle, C. & Pirke, K.M. (1989). Meta-analysis of treatment studies for bulimia. *International Journal of Eating Disorders*, **6**, 647–53.

Letourneau, E.J. (2004). A comment on the first report. *Sexual Abuse: A Journal of Research and Treatment*, **16**, 77–81.

Lipsey, M.W. (1992). Juvenile delinquency treatment: a meta-analytic inquiry into the variability of effects. In T. Cook, D. Cooper, H. Conday, H. Hartman, L.V. Hedges & R. Light (eds), *Meta-analysis for Explanation: A Cookbook* (pp. 83–127). New York: Russell Sage Foundation.

Lipsey, M.W. & Wilson, D.B. (1999). Effective intervention for serious juvenile offenders: a synthesis of research. In R. Loeber & D.P. Farrington (eds), *Serious and Violent Juvenile Offenders* (pp. 313–45). Thousand Oaks, CA: Sage Publications.

Looman, J., Abracen, J. & Nicholaichuk, T.P. (2000). Recidivism among treated sexual offenders and matched controls. *Journal of Interpersonal Violence*, **15**, 279–90.

Lösel, F. & Köferl, P. (1989). Evaluation research on correctional treatment in West Germany:

a meta-analysis. In H. Wegener, F. Lösel & J. Haisch (eds), *Criminal Behavior and the Justice System: Psychological Perspectives* (pp. 334–55). New York: Springer-Verlag.

Lynn, D.D. & Donovan, J.M. (1980). Medical versus surgical treatment of coronary artery disease. *Evaluation in Education*, **4**, 98–9.

Manson, J.E., Hsia, J., Johnson, K.C., Rossouw, J.E., Assaf, A.R., Lasser, N.L. *et al.* (2003). Estrogen plus progestin and the risk of coronary heart disease. *New England Journal of Medicine*, **349**, 523–34.

Marques, J.K. (1999). How to answer the question, "Does sex offender treatment work?" *Journal of Interpersonal Violence*, **14**, 437–51.

Marques, J.K., Day, D.M., Nelson, C. & West, M.A. (1994). Effects of cognitive-behavioral treatment on sex offenders' recidivism: preliminary results of a longitudinal study. *Criminal Justice and Behavior*, **21**, 28–54.

Marshall, W.L. (1992). The social value of treatment for sexual offenders. *Canadian Journal of Human Sexuality*, **1**, 109–14.

Marshall, W.L. 1993). The treatment of sex offenders: what does the outcome data tell us? A reply to Quinsey *et al.*, *Journal of Interpersonal Violence*, **8**, 524–30.

Marshall, W.L. & Anderson, D. (1996). An evaluation of the benefits of relapse prevention programs for sexual offenders. *Sexual Abuse: A Journal of Research and Treatment*, **8**, 209–21.

Marshall, W.L. & Anderson, D. (2000). Do relapse prevention components enhance treatment effectiveness? In D.R. Laws, S.M. Hudson & T. Ward (eds), *Remaking Relapse Prevention with Sex Offenders: A Sourcebook* (pp. 39–55). Thousand Oaks, CA: Sage Publications.

Marshall, W.L. & McGuire, J. (2003). Effect sizes in treatment of sexual offenders. *International Journal of Offender Therapy and Comparative Criminology*, **46**, 653–63.

Marshall, W.L. & Pithers, W.D. (1994). A reconsideration of treatment outcome with sex offenders. *Criminal Justice and Behavior*, **21**, 10–27.

Marshall, W.L., Serran, G.A., Fernandez, Y.M., Mulloy, R., Mann, R.E. & Thornton, D. (2003). Therapist characteristics in the treatment of sexual offenders: tentative data on their relationship with indices of behavior change. *Journal of Sexual Aggression*, **9**, 25–30.

Marshall, W.L., Serran, G., Moulden, H., Mulloy, R., Fernandez, Y.M., Mann, R.E. & Thornton, D. (2002). Therapist features in sexual offender treatment: their reliable identification and influence on behavior change. *Clinical Psychology and Psychotherapy*, **9**, 395–405.

Mattick, R.P., Andrews, G., Hadzi-Pavlovic, D. & Christensen, H. (1990). Treatment of panic and agoraphobia. *Journal of Nervous and Mental Disease*, **178**, 567–73.

Mayer, J.T., Gensheimer, L.K., Davidson, W.S. & Gottschalk, R. (1986). Social learning treatment within juvenile justice: a meta-analysis of impact in the natural environment. In S.A. Apter & A.P. Goldstein (eds), *Youth Violence: Programs and Prospects* (pp. 24–39). Elmsford, NJ: Pergamon.

McConaghy, N. (1998). Neglect of evidence that relapse prevention is ineffective in treatment of incarcerated sexual offenders. *Sexual Abuse: A Journal of Research and Treatment*, **10**, 159–62.

McConaghy, N. (1999). Methodological issues concerning evaluation of treatment for sexual offenders: randomization, treatment dropout, untreated controls, and within-treatment studies. *Sexual Abuse: A Journal of Research and Treatment*, **11**, 183–93.

McFall, R.M. (1991). Manifesto for a science of clinical psychology. *Clinical Psychologist*, **44**, 75–88.

McGuire, J. (2002a). Criminal sanctions versus psychologically based interventions with offenders: a comparative empirical analysis. *Psychology, Crime and Law*, **8**, 183–208.

McGuire, J. (2002b). Integrating findings from research reviews. In J. McGuire (ed.), *Offender Rehabilitation and Treatment: Effective Practice and Policies to Reduce Reoffending* (pp. 3–38). Chichester, UK: John Wiley.

Miner, M.H. (1997). How can we conduct treatment outcome research? *Sexual Abuse: A Journal of Research and Treatment*, **9**, 95–110.

Parloff, M.B. (1979). Can psychotherapy research guide the policymaker? A little knowledge may be a dangerous thing. *American Psychologist*, **34**, 296–306.

Persons, J.B. (1991). Psychotherapy outcome studies do not accurately represent current models of psychotherapy: a proposed remedy. *American Psychologist*, **46**, 99–106.

Persons, J.B. & Silberschatz, G. (1998). Are the results of randomized controlled trials useful to psychotherapists? *Journal of Consulting and Clinical Psychology*, **66**, 126–35.

Prentky, R.A. & Burgess, A.W. (1990). Rehabilitation of child molesters: a cost-benefit analysis. *American Journal of Orthopsychiatry*, **60**, 80–117.

Quality Assurance Project (1983). A treatment outline for depression disorders. *Australian and New Zealand Journal of Psychiatry*, **17**, 129–46.

Quality Assurance Project (1985). Treatment outlines for the management of obsessive-compulsive disorders. *Australian and New Zealand Journal of Psychiatry*, **19**, 240–53.

Quinsey, V.L., Harris, G.T., Rice, M.E. & Lalumière, M.L. (1993). Assessing treatment efficacy in outcome studies of sex offenders. *Journal of Interpersonal Violence*, **8**, 152–523.

Quinsey, V.L., Khanna, A. & Malcolm, P.B. (1998). A retrospective evaluation of the Regional Treatment Centre sex offender treatment program. *Journal of Interpersonal Violence*, **13**, 621–44.

Redondo, S., Sanchez-Meca, J. & Garrido, V. (1999). The influence of treatment programmes on the recidivism of juvenile and adult offenders: a European meta-analytic review. *Psychology, Crime, and Law*, **5**, 251–78.

Reisberg, B., Doody, R., Stöffler, A., Schmidt, F., Ferris, S. & Möbius, H.J. (2003). Alzheimer's Disease Cooperative Study Activities of Daily Living Inventory. *New England Journal of Medicine*, **348**, 1333–41.

Rice, M.E. & Harris, G.T. (1997). The treatment of adult offenders. In D.M. Stoff, J. Breiling & J.D. Maser (eds), *Handbook of Antisocial Behavior* (pp. 425–35). New York: John Wiley.

Rice, M.E. & Harris, G.T. (2003). The size and sign of treatment effects in sex offenders therapy. *Annals of the New York Academy of Sciences*, **989**, 428–40.

Rice, M.E., Quinsey, V.L. & Harris, G.T. (1991). Sexual recidivism among child molesters released from a maximum-security psychiatric institution. *Journal of Consulting and Clinical Psychology*, **59**, 381–6.

Robinson, L.A., Berman, J.S. & Neimeyer, R.A. (1990). Psychotherapy for the treatment of depression: a comprehensive review of controlled outcome research. *Psychological Bulletin*, **108**, 30–49.

Rosenthal, R. (1994). Parametric measures of effect size. In H. Cooper & L.V. Hedges (eds), *The Handbook of Research Synthesis* (pp. 231–44). New York: Russell Sage Foundation.

Sacks, H.S., Ancona-Berk, V.A., Berrier, J., Nagalingam, R. & Chalmers, T.C. (1988). Dipyridamole in the treatment of angina pectoris: a meta-analysis. *Clinical Pharmacologic Therapy*, **43**, 610–15.

Schneider, L.S., Pollock, V.E. & Lyness, S.A. (1990). A meta-analysis of controlled trials of neuroleptic treatment in dementia. *Journal of the American Geriatric Society*, **38**, 553–63.

Seligman, M.E.P. (1995). The effectiveness of psychotherapy: the Consumer Reports Study. *American Psychologist*, **50**, 965–74.

Seligman, M.E.P. (1996). Science as an ally of practice. *American Psychologist*, **51**, 1072–9.

Shadish, W.R. & Ragsdale, K. (1996). Random versus nonrandom assignment in controlled experiments: do you get the same answer? *Journal of Consulting and Clinical Psychology*, **64**, 1290–305.

Silberschatz, G. & Curtis, J.T. (1993). Measuring the therapist's impact on the patient's therapeutic progress. *Journal of Consulting and Clinical Psychology*, **61**, 403–11.

Silberschatz, G., Fretter, P.B. & Curtis, J.T. (1986). How do interpretations influence the process of psychotherapy? *Journal of Consulting and Clinical Psychology*, **54**, 646–52.

Steering Committee of the Physicians' Health Study Research Group (1988). Preliminary report: findings from the aspirin component of the ongoing Physicians' Health Study. *New England Journal of Medicine*, **318**, 262–4.

Trull, T.J., Nietzel, M.T. & Main, A. (1988). The use of meta-analysis to assess the clinical significance of behavior therapy for agoraphobia. *Behavior Therapy*, **19**, 527–38.

Wampler, K.S. (1982). Bringing the review of the literature into the age of quantification: meta-analysis as a strategy for integrating research findings in family studies. *Journal of Marriage and the Family*, **44**, 1009–23.

Ward, T. (2002). Good lives and the rehabilitation of offenders: promises and problems. *Aggression and Violent Behavior*, **7**, 513–28.

Ward, T. & Marshall, W.L. (in press). The role of good lives features in the etiology of sexual offending. *Journal of Sexual Aggression*.

Wasserman, G.A. & Miller, L.S. (1999). The prevention of serious and violent juvenile offending. In R. Loeber & D.P. Farrington (eds), *Serious and Violent Juvenile Offenders* (pp. 197–247). Thousand Oaks, CA: Sage Publications.

Whitehead, J.T. & Lab, S.P. (1989). A meta-analysis of juvenile correctional treatment. *Journal of Research in Crime and Delinquency*, **26**, 276–95.

CONCLUSIONS AND FUTURE DIRECTIONS

The history of any area of science demonstrates that the thorough exploration of a theory is a productive way to generate new knowledge (Ronan, 1982). However, such a history also demonstrates that ways of looking at phenomena typically become entrenched over time with an associated refusal on the part of most investigators to abandon what have been productive viewpoints even when contrary evidence has accumulated (Mahoney, 1976). The same has been evident in the history of therapeutic approaches to human problems (Eysenck, 1966). The intent of the present book is to challenge established notions in the area of sexual offender treatment and evaluation, and to suggest new ways of looking at current issues.

Empirical and theoretical formulations have offered valuable insights into our understanding of the motivation behind sexual offending as well as our approach to treatment. However, this same body of knowledge has expanded our understanding to the point where the directions for research and practice are not necessarily all being explored. The intention of our book was to explore possibilities that might otherwise be neglected.

This volume has provided unique views of a wide range of issues relevant to working with sexual offenders. The chapters present the most recent empirical evidence on these critical issues, but go a step further by challenging thinking in each area. In doing so, the authors of each chapter have pointed to issues that need further examination. In most cases these topics for future research represent novel suggestions or alternative conceptualizations of the issues.

What we hope is clear from this volume is that we are at a point where a reconceptualization of what we know and what we do in various areas of treatment and evaluation may drive the field forward. This is an exciting time for those working with sexual offenders. We have a sufficiently firm knowledge base that treading the same paths no longer seems to be the only way (although it remains a potentially fruitful way) to expand our understanding and improve our assessment and treatment of these troublesome clients. The strength of the present book, we hope, rests on the fact that our authors have suggested potential ways forward that may not be so readily apparent.

The goal of collaborating on these topics was to offer a critical view of some important areas in our field. By doing so, we hope to have opened up new ideas for theory, treatment and intervention. The main value of these chapters for further research is the attempt to guide our approach in new directions. By addressing areas of controversy and offering new insights into critical topics, more productive research might be undertaken and different approaches to treatment may be devised.

Risk assessment is a critical aspect of our field, yet there is much more work to be done to improve our current assessments. Doren's chapter (1) offers an appraisal of actuarial instruments which provide an essential basis for risk assessments but he points to the need to develop mechanisms incorporating other client-specific information that may emerge from clinically interacting with the client. When a client indicates that he feels driven to offend again then, no matter what actuarial estimates say, he should obviously be considered a serious risk. Doren offers suggestions on how to incorporate clinical issues into risk assessments. Hanson (Chapter 2) points out that more research into the area of dynamic risk is also needed. In particular, research needs to determine how changes in dynamic risks, as a result of treatment, can be incorporated into end-of-treatment estimates of risk. We suggest that researchers need to develop a way of estimating the likely degree of harm that might ensue should a particular offender recidivate. Laws (2003), for example, has drawn attention to the need to consider reductions in harm as a way of evaluating treatment effectiveness but this has not yet been taken up in the risk assessment literature. Some sexual sadists, on the basis of actuarial risk measures, would score in the lowest risk category because they have just one offence, no non-sexual criminal record and an otherwise prosocial lifestyle. However, if a sexual sadist does reoffend the harm he does would be expected to be significant.

The civil commitment programs (or Sexually Violent Predator Programs) that proliferated in the 1990s in the United States, and similar "Dangerous Offender" classifications in other jurisdictions, have presented serious, and at times very discouraging, situations that clinicians have to face (see Schlank's Chapter 4). The costs of these approaches, and the failure to have more than a handful of these offenders exit the systems built to house them, present serious problems. The application of diagnoses in sexual offender evaluations (these are required, for example, in civil commitment processes) appears to be beset with problems (see Marshall's Chapter 3). The reliability of these diagnoses appears problematic as does the interpretation of the diagnostic manual's criteria. Similarly sexual sadists present conceptual and treatment problems which have yet to be resolved. We cannot, however, begin to develop approaches to evaluate and treat these men until we are better able to accurately identify them and describe their characteristics. Proulx *et al.*'s Chapter 5 takes steps toward these goals.

The Internet has brought many blessings but unfortunately along with these blessings have come possibilities for harm. Cooper *et al.*'s Chapter 6 demonstrates the various routes by which problematic use of the Internet for sexual purposes can cause serious problems for some users and can lead some people to access child pornography. Cooper *et al.* indicate some of the compulsive-like features of men who use the Internet for these purposes.

Smallbone has taken a particular etiological model of sexual offending and introduced novel elements (Chapter 7). These novel elements suggest numerous possibilities for research particularly in terms of how attachment issues interact with sexual desires to produce deviance.

Although relapse prevention approaches have emphasized the value of training in specific coping skills, little or no research has been directed at this issue and the whole issue of coping styles has been relatively neglected. Serran and Marshall bring us up-to-date on developments on coping and extend this to incorporate the role of mood modulation and its influence on offending (Chapter 8). They offer research strategies for examining these issues. Another rather neglected issue concerns the shame or guilt sexual offenders experience. Proeve and Howells take us through what is currently known and point to the needed research that will give us a more solid foundation to deal with shame and guilt in treatment (Chapter 9).

The amenability of psychopathic sexual offenders, many of whom end up in Sexually Violent Predator or Dangerous Offenders programs, has been an issue that has generated heated debate. The chapter by Barbaree and his colleagues (11) demonstrates one of the essential features of good science; that is, the ability to change their views in response to new evidence. They progressively refined their research projects and demonstrated that their original findings were in error. Psychopaths, they showed, are not made worse by treatment. The question now is "Can their tendency to reoffend be reduced by treatment?" If we decide psychopaths are untreatable and exclude them from therapy programs we will never learn how to change their behaviors. Ogden Lindsley, one of Skinner's students, spent some time in the 1950s working with people housed in institutions for those who were at that time unfortunately called "mentally retarded". Lindsley boldly, and correctly, declared that it was not these unfortunate souls who were retarded but rather it was our scientific understanding about how to help them function more effectively that was retarded. His work helped to radicalize the way our services dealt with these people. This is a lesson, or perhaps a motto, we might keep in mind when we consider what can, or cannot be done, with psychopathic and other problematic sexual offenders (e.g., sexual sadists).

Innovations continue to occur with respect to interventions, but as experience shows us, uncritically accepting any model (e.g. the early relapse prevention model) may hinder progress. Therefore, we must continually challenge ourselves to improve our intervention programs. Responding to our clients in a more positive and compassionate way should help (see the chapter by Fernandez [13]). Working more cooperatively with our clients (see Shingler and Mann's Chapter 16) should enhance their engagement and lead to more positive outcomes. As Ward and Fisher point out, defining goals that help clients lead more productive lives (the good lives model) should not only enhance the effectiveness of our treatment programs in terms of reducing offending, it should also allow our clients to become more productive, and therefore more valuable, members of society.

The innovative preparatory program described by Marshall and Moulden has produced exciting results and makes sense in terms of what is known about motivating clients (Chapter 14). We look forward to seeing similar programs implemented in other jurisdictions. The emphasis on reviving behavioral ways of construing treatment advanced by Fernandez and her colleagues (Chapter 15) might seem like a march back to the past. However, the way in which they formulate behavioral notions is quite consistent with current practice but stresses the most effective way to conduct the behavioral aspects of treatment.

Consistent with these various ideas about how to implement treatment, Laws and Ward point to the necessity for flexibility in treatment delivery so that the responsivity needs of each client are met (Chapter 17). They make the point that unless our programs meet the need for flexibility we will ignore unique individual needs of each client, and put them all through a "one size fits all" approach. Identifying these unique needs and adapting treatment accordingly should contribute to increasing the effectiveness and human value of our programs.

Finally, as Marshall notes (Chapter 18), we need to develop strategies for conducting treatment outcome studies that are accessible to all who provide treatment. Setting standards for treatment evaluations that essentially exclude the majority of treatment providers from examining the benefits of their programs results in the loss of a tremendous amount of information. We need to have good quality research but not at the expense of losing potentially valuable data.

We hope that readers have enjoyed this book and gained at least some new ways of viewing things. We look forward to developments over the next few years which we believe will be exciting and will lead to an even great reduction in the harm our clients cause to innocent people.

REFERENCES

Eysenck, H.J. (1996). *The Effects of Psychotherapy*. New York: International Science Press.
Laws, D.R. (2003). Harm reduction and sexual offending: is an intraparadigmatic shift possible? In T.Ward, S.M. Hudson & D.R. Laws (eds), *Sexual Deviance: Issues and Controversies* (pp. 280–96). Thousand Oaks: CA: Sage Publications.
Mahoney, M.J. (1976). *Scientist as Subject: The Psychological Imperative*. Cambridge, MA: Ballinger.
Ronan, C.A. (1982). *Science: Its History and Development among the World's Cultures*. New York: Facts on File Publications.

INDEX